THE WORLD OF MR CASAUBON

The World of Mr Casaubon takes as its point of departure a fictional character – Mr Casaubon in George Eliot's classic novel, *Middlemarch*. The author of an unfinished 'Key to All Mythologies', Casaubon has become an icon of obscurantism, irrelevance and futility. Crossing conventional disciplinary boundaries, Colin Kidd excavates Casaubon's hinterland, and illuminates the fierce ideological war which raged over the use of pagan myths to defend Christianity from the existential threat posed by radical Enlightenment criticism. Notwithstanding Eliot's portrayal of Casaubon, Anglican mythographers were far from unworldly, and actively rebutted the radical freethinking associated with the Enlightenment and French Revolution. Orientalism was a major theatre in this ideological conflict, and mythography also played an indirect but influential role in framing the new science of anthropology. *The World of Mr Casaubon* is rich in interdisciplinary twists and ironies, and paints a vivid picture of the intellectual world of eighteenth- and nineteenth-century Britain.

COLIN KIDD is Wardlaw Professor at the University of St Andrews and a Fifty-Pound Fellow of All Souls College, Oxford. He is a Fellow of the British Academy and the Royal Society of Edinburgh. He is a regular contributor to the *London Review of Books* and to the *Guardian*, and has lectured in all parts of the British Isles, in France and in the United States.

IDEAS IN CONTEXT

Edited by David Armitage, Richard Bourke, Jennifer Pitts
and John Robertson

The books in this series will discuss the emergence of intellectual traditions and of related new disciplines. The procedures, aims and vocabularies that were generated will be set in the context of the alternatives available within the contemporary frameworks of ideas and institutions. Through detailed studies of the evolution of such traditions, and their modification by different audiences, it is hoped that a new picture will form of the development of ideas in their concrete contexts. By this means, artificial distinctions between the history of philosophy, of the various sciences, of society and politics, and of literature may be seen to dissolve.

The series is published with the support of the Exxon Foundation.

A list of books in the series will be found at the end of the volume.

THE WORLD OF MR CASAUBON

Britain's Wars of Mythography, 1700–1870

COLIN KIDD
University of St Andrews

CAMBRIDGE
UNIVERSITY PRESS

University Printing House, Cambridge CB2 8BS, United Kingdom

One Liberty Plaza, 20th Floor, New York, NY 10006, USA
477 Williamstown Road, Port Melbourne, VIC 3207, Australia
4843/24, 2nd Floor, Ansari Road, Daryaganj, Delhi – 110002, India
79 Anson Road, #06-04/06, Singapore 079906

Cambridge University Press is part of the University of Cambridge.

It furthers the University's mission by disseminating knowledge in the pursuit of education, learning, and research at the highest international levels of excellence.

www.cambridge.org
Information on this title: www.cambridge.org/9781107027718
DOI: 10.1017/9781139226646

© Colin Kidd 2016

This publication is in copyright. Subject to statutory exception and to the provisions of relevant collective licensing agreements, no reproduction of any part may take place without the written permission of Cambridge University Press.

First published 2016

Printed in the United Kingdom by Clays, St Ives plc

A catalogue record for this publication is available from the British Library.

ISBN 978-1-107-02771-8 Hardback

Cambridge University Press has no responsibility for the persistence or accuracy of URLs for external or third-party Internet Web sites referred to in this publication and does not guarantee that any content on such Web sites is, or will remain, accurate or appropriate.

Contents

Acknowledgements		*page* vi
1	Prologue: Casaubon's Dubious Bequest	1
2	The Key to All Mythologies	29
3	The Legacies of the Ancients in Enlightenment Mythography	79
4	The Obsessions of Jacob Bryant: Arkite Idolatry and the Quest for Troy	111
5	The Dispute of the Orient: Anglo-French Rivalries in an Age of Revolution	131
6	Fish-gods, Floods and Serpent-worship: From Apologetics to Anthropology	176
7	Epilogue: The Keys to All Mythology in 1872	200
Index		227

Acknowledgements

This book was begun in Glasgow; the bulk of the research was done during an interval at Queen's University Belfast; and the typescript was completed at St Andrews. The project was supported throughout by All Souls College, Oxford, where Rosemary Hill was a fellow venturer into the thickets of eighteenth- and nineteenth-century antiquarianism. Nigel Leask inspired one of the central ideas for the book, and it also owes much to a long friendship with Scott Mandelbrote. John Hudson, Stuart Jones, Brian Young, Jacqueline Rose and Lucy Kidd read the draft typescript, made several penetrating suggestions and have saved me from several howlers. I am grateful to Keith Thomas, George Woudhuysen, Harvey Shoolman and Thomas Munck for passing on various references, and I learnt a great deal from the Cambridge Victorian Studies Group, where an early version of the book was summarised over a sandwich lunch to an audience of historians and classicists in January 2011. I am grateful to David Armitage and Richard Fisher who commissioned this book for Ideas in Context; and to Andy Eccles for technical advice. I also owe huge debts of a more general nature to David Hayton, Gerry Carruthers and Adam Sisman.

CHAPTER I

Prologue: Casaubon's Dubious Bequest

> My mind is something like the ghost of an ancient, wandering about the world and trying mentally to construct it as it used to be. (*Middlemarch*, ch. 2)
>
> George E was not quite 'goddess' – or was 'goddess' with a flaw. (F. W. Maitland to Henry Jackson, 25 February 1904, in C. H. S. Fifoot [ed.], *The Letters of Frederic William Maitland* [Selden Society, 1965], p. 296)

Unusually, perhaps, this work of history takes as its point of departure a fictional character: Mr Casaubon, the bookish and unworldly clergyman who plays a central role in the plot of George Eliot's novel *Middlemarch* (1871–2). Postmodern playfulness, however, stops here. What follows is anchored in the realm of eighteenth- and nineteenth-century intellectual life, and tries to describe the contours and content of the once-lively genre of religious apologetics to which the Reverend Edward Casaubon aspired to contribute. The title of Casaubon's unfinished manuscript is 'The Key to All Mythologies', which is also used as shorthand here for the field in which Casaubon operates. It is very important to stress at the outset that the primary emphasis of this book does not fall upon the various influences which directly shaped Eliot's portrayal of Casaubon and his activities as a mythographer – or, as often as not, his sluggish and misdirected inactivity. Rather this study anatomises Casaubon's hobby horse. It attempts to recover the discipline and strategies of the 'science' of mythography – not only what can be traced to Eliot's known reading or assumed reasonably to be part of her wider general knowledge (dauntingly extensive as these were),[1] but also what lay far beyond. Eliot's sources, inspiration and literary art are, naturally enough, integral to the story, but they do not constitute this book's marrow.

---

[1] See, in the context of *Middlemarch*, J. C. Pratt and V. A. Neufeldt (eds.), *George Eliot's Middlemarch notebooks* (Berkeley and Los Angeles, 1979), esp. 'Appendix: a check list of George Eliot's reading Jan. 1868 to Dec. 1871', pp. 279–88; A. Fleishman, *George Eliot's intellectual life* (Cambridge, 2010), pp. 164–5.

The desire to find an original of Mr Casaubon has turned into one of the more enjoyable, if recherché, snark-hunts in modern literary scholarship.[2] Such was the range of Eliot's reading, and such the fertility of her imagination, that Mr Casaubon lives in fiction as himself, not as a mere cipher for a scholar of whom Eliot had made the acquaintance in real life – that is, as Mary Ann or Marian Evans, for whom 'George Eliot' was a pseudonym – or on the page. Although the study which follows comprehends a good number of learned antiquarians, who will sometimes be painted in Casaubonish colours, our primary object is to reconstruct the vanished world of the old mythographers, a group which sought in mythology a set of unlikely answers to some of the most pressing problems of both the age of Enlightenment and the crisis of faith. Might the earliest secrets of humankind's history be found in the mythologies of pagan peoples? Might pagan mythology provide corroboration from an unexpected quarter for the threatened truths of Christianity? From the eighteenth century these questions informed ideological struggles between defenders of the Church and its radical infidel critics, and would leave an imprint on the new nineteenth-century sciences of philology and anthropology. Much more was at stake, it transpires, in the quest for a 'key to all mythologies' than Eliot, who was aware of these debates, reveals to the readers of *Middlemarch*.

Our real subject matter is these lost wars of eighteenth- and nineteenth-century mythography, which are alluded to – fleetingly and obliquely – in *Middlemarch*. Posterity is peripherally aware of these conflicts, but largely by way of Mr Casaubon's sad, at best semi-scholarly, failure; which means that nineteenth-century mythography stands representative of abject antiquarian pointlessness. To be fair, there is considerable truth in this received idea. Mr Casaubon was not on a high road to major intellectual breakthroughs. Nevertheless, the vast hinterland behind the mythographical debates mentioned in *Middlemarch* is a more significant and variegated terrain than Eliot – a freethinking convert from Christianity – lets on. Ironically, indeed, as we shall see, the backstory of Casaubonish mythography diverges dramatically from the sterile, unworldly disengagement of which Mr Casaubon has for so long been an emblem.

---

[2] See e.g. J. Sparrow, *Mark Pattison and the idea of a university* (Cambridge, 1967), ch. 1; R. Ellmann, 'Dorothea's husbands', *Times Literary Supplement* (16 February 1973); A. D. Nuttall, *Dead from the waist down: scholars and scholarship in literature and the popular imagination* (New Haven, 2003), pp. 72–83; H. S. Jones, *Intellect and character in Victorian England: Mark Pattison and the invention of the don* (Cambridge, 2007), pp. 81–4; R. Ashton, 'Lunch with the Rector: George Eliot and Mark Pattison revisited', *Times Literary Supplement* (31 January 2014).

Prologue: Casaubon's Dubious Bequest

Mr Casaubon has, of course, become a byword for erudite futility.[3] Within the plot of *Middlemarch*, which is set around 1830–2, the Reverend Edward Casaubon, who is tucked away for much of the novel in the study of his obscure rectory in the village of Lowick somewhere in the Midlands, is engaged on his fruitless scholarly enterprise, 'The Key to All Mythologies'. In this quixotic work of syncretism Mr Casaubon hopes to find an intellectual system for reconciling the diverse richness of the world's pagan beliefs and legends with an aboriginal Old Testament religion of which all forms of heathenism are in their different ways corruptions. Mr Casaubon's unfinished, perhaps unfinishable, *magnum opus* turns out to be something of an albatross for the enervated antiquarian. Not only is Casaubon's task over-ambitious and misconceived, but he is also out of touch with recent paradigm-shifting developments in German mythography and Biblical criticism which render his work old-fashioned and an anachronism in its own time.

It transpires that Mr Casaubon's life-enhancing young cousin, the cosmopolitan Will Ladislaw, is aware of these new advances in early nineteenth-century German intellectual life, notwithstanding his own disdain for the drudgery of a scholar's existence. Ladislaw communicates to Casaubon's much younger wife, Dorothea, this sense of the old clergyman's absurdly distant remoteness from the cutting edge of contemporary scholarship. Ladislaw announces that '"the Germans have taken the lead in historical inquiries, and they laugh at results which are got by groping about in the woods with a pocket-compass while they have made good roads. When I was with Mr Casaubon I saw that he deafened himself in that direction."'[4] As a consequence, Dorothea, who had married Casaubon as a willing amanuensis of the towering genius she mistakenly identifies in the begetter of 'The Key to All Mythologies', becomes yet further disillusioned with her husband's multifarious pettinesses.

Oddly, for such a nonentity, Mr Casaubon possesses an iconic status well beyond the pages of a book; indeed, *Middlemarch* itself enjoys a reputation and remains beloved as something more than a mere novel.[5] Casaubon's name is synonymous with arid pedantry and mindless antiquarianism: he is a kind of patron saint of empty underachievement. Eliot calls him 'a lifeless embalmment of knowledge'.[6] Casaubon represents

---

[3] Cf. Nuttall, *Dead from the waist down*.
[4] George Eliot, *Middlemarch* (1871–2: Harmondsworth, 1965), ch. 21, p. 240. (In footnote references to *Middlemarch*, I give page numbers from the Penguin edition, but also chapter references for those readers with other editions.)
[5] See e.g. K. Chase (ed.), *Middlemarch in the 21st century* (Oxford, 2006).
[6] Eliot, *Middlemarch*, ch. 20, p. 229.

lethargy, futility, and – as a dark, wrinkled 'bat of erudition'[7] – that all-too-familiar deformity found in scholars, the cowardly retreat from engagement with the full-bloodedness of life in the round. To identify with Casaubon is to align oneself with a certain kind of bloodless perversity, to reject life. For instance, Ferdinand Mount, the conservative man of letters, presents himself in his memoirs as something of a dry stick, an Englishman of a certain class and generation, who finds irrepressible vitality something which a person should really have tried harder to repress. 'I always take against the heroine who is on the side of Life', Mount confesses, 'which is a side I am not at all sure about … In *Middlemarch* I long for Mr Casaubon to discover the key to all mythologies so he can say snubs to the ghastly Dorothea. As for Lady Chatterley, when we finally get hold of a copy, my sympathies are entirely with Sir Clifford.'[8]

The Casaubon figure tends to feature in literature as a figure of absurd presumption. Matthew Kneale's novel *English Passengers* (2000) features the deluded quest in the late 1850s of a Casaubonish clergyman, the Reverend Geoffrey Wilson, who believes he has located the whereabouts of the Garden of Eden in Tasmania. Wilson rides a clerical hobby horse akin to the 'key to all mythologies', in this case a theory of 'divine refrigeration' at odds with the atheistic implications of nineteenth-century geology.[9] Even where the homage to the figure of Casaubon is less obviously subversive, the end result captures something of Casaubon's leadenness. Casaubon is the name of the central character in Umberto Eco's novel *Foucault's Pendulum* (1988), a modern grail quest whose object is the deciphering of the arcane mysteries which enshroud humanity and its history, but which, not unlike Mr Casaubon's unfinished 'Key to All Mythologies', sags somewhat as a narrative under the weight of its author's and its protagonists' precocious erudition.[10]

Mr Casaubon looms particularly large within the field of intellectual history, for he embodies hypertrophied erudition; a condition about which academics, particularly in the humanities, are prone to feel embarrassed, anxious and defensive. Casaubon has become a pathetic symbol of the frustrated scholar thwarted in his studies by the sheer superabundance of sources and commentaries, who ends his unfulfilled career buried under an avalanche of books about books about books.[11] Casaubon stands

---

[7] *Ibid.*, ch. 21, p. 237.
[8] Ferdinand Mount, *Cold cream* (2008: London pbk, 2009), p. 88.
[9] Matthew Kneale, *English passengers* (2000: Harmondsworth, 2001), pp. xx, 19–23.
[10] U. Eco, *Foucault's pendulum* (1988: transl. London, 1989).
[11] For this perennial predicament of scholarly life, see A. Blair, *Too much to know: managing scholarly information before the modern age* (New Haven, 2010).

representative of what might be called pejoratively the higher stamp-collecting,[12] the exponent of a scholarship that occupies itself with learned shallows but is utterly lacking in depth. Casaubon's is a life in scholarship exclusively devoted, it seems, to shreds and trifles, to marginalia and footnotes.

This was certainly the intention of Eliot, who describes Casaubon – 'that faded scholar' – as a mere husk of learning. But Eliot's low estimation of her own fictional creation has been taken, understandably, as a determining yardstick for evaluating the significance of mythography as a whole. Were other mythographers quite as puny and insignificant as Eliot's iconic fictional character? We need to remember that Eliot had axes of her own to grind; that she was engaged in serious combat with Christianity, and unwilling to accord too much heft and weight to a character who stood proxy for the stifling orthodoxy she repudiated. Moreover, the novel – however accurate an intended representation of the state of affairs in society – must accommodate the story-telling imperative, or it will fail. In other words, Eliot's well-known depiction of early nineteenth-century mythography is not the last word on the subject; far from it. But *The World of Mr Casaubon* is much more a labour of love than it is a dominie's perverted attempt to mark *Middlemarch* down as a piece of flawed intellectual history. Lest there be any misunderstanding, the intention here is not to upbraid Eliot – a presumptuous notion – but to wallow in irony. This is because the wider world of Mr Casaubon turns out to be very different in certain critical respects from the particular story of Mr Casaubon set out in *Middlemarch*.

The aim of this book is to use actual mythographers and mythographical strategies mentioned in *Middlemarch* as a foundation for reconstructing the ideological environments of eighteenth- and nineteenth-century mythological debate. In *Middlemarch* Eliot mentions – or alludes indirectly to – several of the most significant antiquaries, theologians and orientalists of eighteenth- and early nineteenth-century England, as well as their mythographical hobby horses. The itinerary of each of this book's main chapters will start from particular passages in *Middlemarch* which refer to real eighteenth-century and early nineteenth-century scholars, such as William Warburton (1698–1779), Conyers Middleton (1683–1750), Jacob Bryant (1715–1804), Robert Lowth (1710–87) and George Stanley Faber (1773–1854), or their preoccupations, such as the interpretation of

---

[12] Cf. G. Beer, *Darwin's plots: evolutionary narrative in Darwin, George Eliot and nineteenth-century fiction* (1983: 3rd edn, Cambridge, 2009), p. 163.

the Cabiri (pre-Hellenic gods who were the object of an ancient mystery cult) or the identification of fish-deities, and will then broaden out to examine the debates in which these figures found themselves. The epilogue will present a smorgasbord of the existing mythographical theories extant in 1872 at the time *Middlemarch* was published.

As late as 1830, the period in which *Middlemarch* is set, the world of mythographical scholarship was still dominated by figures from the eighteenth century. In chapter 29 of *Middlemarch* it is announced that Casaubon would publish 'a new Parergon' – that is, a supplementary work – 'a small monograph on some lately-traced indications concerning the Egyptian mysteries whereby certain assertions of Warburton's could be corrected'.[13] Warburton was the author of the most debated work of eighteenth-century mythography – arguably the most debated text in eighteenth-century English letters – *The Divine Legation of Moses* (1738–41). Perhaps the second most significant contribution to eighteenth-century British mythography was Bryant's *A New System or Analysis of Ancient Mythology* (1774–6), which surfaces in chapter 22 of *Middlemarch*, when Ladislaw asks: '"Do you not see that it is no use now to be crawling a little way after the men of the last century – men like Bryant – and correcting their mistakes? – living in a lumber room and furnishing up broken-legged theories about Chus and Mizraim?"'[14] In the course of the same chapter of *Middlemarch*, Ladislaw finds himself 'in agreement with Mr Casaubon as to the unsound opinions of Middleton concerning the relations of Judaism and Catholicism'.[15] Middleton was a cunning, semi-closeted mid-eighteenth-century freethinker who explored continuities between Roman paganism and Roman Catholicism, while hinting that Christianity more generally was a heathen inheritance.

Other identifications are less straightforward. In chapter 37 Casaubon asks Dorothea, '"I shall be obliged, since you are up, if you will read me a few pages of Lowth."'[16] But which Lowth? Perhaps this is a reference to William Lowth (1660–1732), who in his *Directions for the Profitable Reading of Scripture* advanced a mythographical defence of the authority of Genesis, noting that 'the heathens' had 'an obscure tradition' of the creation, fall and deluge, but one whose wide diffusion 'doth sufficiently attest the truth of the scripture records'. Lowth reckoned that the 'oldest monuments of the heathen story, and all their ancient theology is derived from

---

[13] Eliot, *Middlemarch*, ch. 29, p. 315.
[14] *Ibid.*, ch. 22, p. 254.
[15] *Ibid.*, ch. 22, p. 244.
[16] *Ibid.*, ch. 37, p. 409.

the scriptures, though disguised with fables for the confirming their own superstitions and idolatries'.[17] However, it seems more likely that this is a reference to the Hebraist Robert Lowth, Professor of Poetry at Oxford and later Bishop of London, who entered the lists against Warburton. Other references suggest particular mythographers without naming them explicitly. A description of Casaubon 'lost among small closets and winding stairs, and in an agitated dimness about the Cabeiri',[18] alludes to the work of the Christian mythographer George Faber, author of *A Dissertation on the Mysteries of the Cabiri* (1803). We also hear that Dorothea 'had listened with fervid patience to a recitation of possible arguments to be brought against Mr Casaubon's entirely new view of the Philistine god Dagon and other fish-deities'.[19] Here the reference is less particular, for several mythographers debated the significance of fish deities, a fact further acknowledged, perhaps, in the fictional antagonists of Casaubon that Eliot invents: Messrs Pike, Tench and Carp, who are mentioned in chapter 29 of *Middlemarch*.[20]

As the eighteenth-century legacy of polemical mythography looms large for Mr Casaubon, so it provides one of the three main contexts for *The World of Mr Casaubon*. Broadly speaking, the book will attempt to recover the arguments of three different eras: first, the eighteenth-century golden age of apologetic mythography; second, the age of Revolution and Reform down to the early 1830s, the period in which the novel is immediately set, when mythography remained an urgent calling for Anglican scholars who wished to conserve Christian truth against the poisons of Enlightenment deism, scepticism and atheism; and third, the years between the 1830s and the novel's publication in 1871–2, during which Eliot's own views of mythography were formed.

The study of pagan mythologies – however abstruse the field of mythography now seems, or indeed seemed to Eliot – constituted a vitally important terrain of political and religious debate throughout the eighteenth and nineteenth centuries. Many religious apologists argued that 'their' myths were merely corrupted versions of 'our' truth; that, by a marvellous providential irony, interpreted correctly the mythologies of non-Christian peoples served to validate the historic truth of the Old Testament. But mirages of this sort did not only delude the orthodox, notwithstanding what Eliot suggests. Critics of scripture had their own delusively unitary solutions,

---

[17] William Lowth, *Directions for the profitable reading of the Holy Scriptures* (3rd edn, London, 1726), pp. 43, 150.
[18] Eliot, *Middlemarch*, ch. 20, p. 229.
[19] *Ibid.*, ch. 20, p. 228.
[20] *Ibid.*, ch. 29, pp. 314–15.

their own particular 'keys to all mythology', grounded in all-encompassing hypotheses about an aboriginal natural religion, or, later, in philological and anthropological theories of primal belief.

Mythography was far from being a distinctive ecclesiastical category of rural idiocy or the mere cabbage-patch of village Casaubons. Of course, college sets at Oxford and Cambridge and rural parsonages were, as Eliot suggests, the principal habitats of the mythographer. Nevertheless, such was the prestige of classical learning in the upper reaches of society that several aristocrats and gentlemen were drawn into mythographical researches and debates, including a future Prime Minister, Lord Aberdeen (1784–1860).[21] Indeed, as we shall see, for another Prime Minister, William Gladstone (1809–98), the relationship of Homeric lore to sacred history was as central a preoccupation as balancing the books at the Treasury or pacifying Ireland.[22] Similarly, at the other end of the social hierarchy, radical artisans engaged in mythographical enquiries as a means of undermining the authority of the established church and state. The French Revolution was accompanied by its own radical mythography which used pagan legends not to support but to interrogate Christian scripture. Mythographical debates resounded at every level of society, and internationally too, not least between Britons (Anglicans especially) and French infidels, as well as with the Deistic enemy within. Notwithstanding Eliot's condescension towards Casaubon, mythographical argument – as she knew – was not confined to a backwater.

Before we investigate the practice of mythography, it is worth devoting some space to the provenance of Mr Casaubon, for this subject is not only capable of shedding light on the field of mythography, but is also rich in ironies and unexpected connections. Most obviously, Mr Casaubon's surname calls to mind the celebrated early modern scholars Isaac Casaubon (1559–1614) – the flower of Protestant humanist erudition – and his son Meric Casaubon (1599–1671), also a significant scholar in his day. Isaac Casaubon was noteworthy even in a golden age of classical erudition; he was the contemporary, for example, of the brilliant critic and chronologer Joseph Justus Scaliger (1540–1609).[23] Casaubon – like Scaliger – came of French Huguenot stock, and spent most of his adult life in France, at

---

[21] Aberdeen was educated at St John's College, Cambridge, a seat of mythographical learning, and was later a companion of the mythographer Sir William Drummond of Logiealmond (for whom see below chs. 3 and 5).

[22] D. Bebbington, *The mind of Gladstone: religion, Homer and politics* (Oxford, 2004), pp. 142–215.

[23] A. Grafton, *Joseph Scaliger* (2 vols., Oxford, 1983–93).

Montpellier and later Paris. However, after the assassination of the French king, Henri IV, in 1610 he prudently accepted the invitation of Richard Bancroft, the Archbishop of Canterbury, to come to London, and to the agreeably learned atmosphere presided over by the prodigiously erudite James VI and I. Here Casaubon spent the last years of his life attempting to complete his enormous humanistic labours and engaging in ecclesiastical polemic with the papacy and its champions. Although Casaubon never completed his major project on Polybius, he did – unlike Mr Casaubon – produce versions of Strabo, Suetonius, Aristotle, the *Deipnosophistae* of Athenaeus, and in 1592 a remarkably erudite edition of the extant *Characters* of Theophrastus.[24]

If Mr Casaubon's pet project was to use pagan mythology in defence of Christian truth, it is ironic in this light that the most significant scholarly achievement of his namesake Isaac Casaubon was to undermine the status of ancient pagan sources which had appeared to predict the coming of Christ. Isaac Casaubon had been invited to London in large part because it was hoped he might answer the massive bombardment of the biggest cannon in Catholic polemical scholarship, Cardinal Baronius's *Annales ecclesiastici* (1588–1607). In the course of his answer to Baronius, *De rebus sacris et ecclesiasticis exercitationes xvi* (1614), Casaubon challenged the claim of Baronius that the divine will had been known in pagan circles long before the coming of Christ ('longe ante Christi adventum').[25] He patiently deconstructed the casual reliance of Baronius on the assertions of the patristic writer Lactantius that the coming of Christ had been foreshadowed in certain pagan works, including the writings of the fabled Egyptian priest Hermes Trismegistus and the oracles of the ancient prophetesses, the Sibyls.[26] Casaubon used his skills as a textual critic to demonstrate that the Hermetic writings recycled Platonic and Christian materials, contained knowledge and allusions to matters which long postdated the supposed era of Trismegistus and were composed in a Greek style which was far less consonant with archaic forms than with diction and idioms used by Greeks of a later era ('qua posteriores Graeci sunt usi').[27] Nor was there any mention

---

[24] *Theophrasti Characteres ethici* (Leiden, 1592); A. Grafton and J. Weinberg, *'I have always loved the holy tongue': Isaac Casaubon, the Jews and a forgotten chapter in renaissance scholarship* (Cambridge, MA, 2011), pp. 4–5, 15–17.
[25] Isaac Casaubon, *De rebus sacris et ecclesiasticis exercitationes xvi* (London, 1614), p. 71.
[26] Casaubon, *De rebus sacris*, pp. 70–87; F. Yates, *Giordano Bruno and the Hermetic tradition* (1964: London and New York, 1999), pp. 398–403; A. Grafton, 'Protestant versus prophet: Isaac Casaubon on Hermes Trismegistus', *Journal of the Warburg and Courtauld Institute*, vol. 46 (1983), pp. 78–93.
[27] Casaubon, *De rebus sacris*, p. 86.

of Hermes Trismegistus or the Sibyls throughout the early canon of pagan authors ('nullum penitus extat vestigium').[28] In other words, the writings of Hermes Trismegistus were an early Christian – or Christian–Platonist – forgery purporting to belong to an earlier period.[29]

If we turn our attention back to Eliot's Mr Casaubon, we are struck here by an additional irony: the name we now associate with deluded apologetic futility was borrowed not from a backwoods bigot or dunce, but from a scholar of genius who had exposed as a fraud the patristic claim that ancient pagan authorities had been bearers of primeval proto-Christian truth. In a bizarre reversal of our expectations, Isaac Casaubon – who was, we discover, far from Casaubonish – had successfully demolished an ancient forerunner of the 'key to all mythologies'.

Nevertheless, Isaac's son, Meric Casaubon, also a distinguished scholar, was himself implicated in mythography and the Christian appropriation of pagan idolatry. In 1624 a puritan treatise entitled *The Originall of Idolatries* was mistakenly ascribed to Isaac Casaubon. Out of filial piety, Meric published a defence of his father, *Vindicatio patris, adversus impostores qui librum ineptum et impium, De origine idolatriae etc nuper sub Isaaci Casuboni nomine publicarunt* (1624), explaining that the work was not Isaac's but had been foisted upon him. Meric had his own interests in pagan religion and its relationship to the Judaeo-Christian tradition. Indeed, in the 1640s Meric would write a manuscript treatise – now lost – in Latin on the origin of idolatry. However, it is possible to reconstruct from other writings, as Richard Serjeantson has shown, some of Meric's beliefs about ancient heathendom. That world was not, for instance, utterly benighted or bereft of authentic spiritual insight. Meric Casaubon seems to have been persuaded by the thesis – influential among early modern scholars – that classical pagans had inherited from primeval antiquity, or from the Jews directly, some lineaments of the primeval religion of Noah and the divine promises to mankind; in particular, Meric took the view, also widely held, that Virgil's fourth Eclogue had foreshadowed with prophetic accuracy the coming of Christ.[30]

---

[28] *Ibid.*, p. 73.
[29] *Ibid.*, pp. 77–9.
[30] R. Serjeantson, 'Introduction', Serjeantson (ed.), *Generall learning: a seventeenth-century treatise on the formation of the general scholar by Meric Casaubon* (Cambridge, 1999), pp. 5, 48, 50; P. Milward, *Religious controversies of the Jacobean age* (London, 1978), pp. 214–15; A. Milton, *Catholic and reformed: the Roman and Protestant churches in English Protestant thought 1600–1640* (Cambridge, 1995), p. 92.

Prologue: Casaubon's Dubious Bequest

The Casaubon connection within Eliot's oeuvre is not limited to *Middlemarch*. Eliot had made use of Isaac Casaubon's edition of Theophrastus,[31] and, under its inspiration, composed an allusive late work of her own, entitled *Impressions of Theophrastus Such* (1879), which touched on themes of learning and research. Indeed, *Theophrastus Such* has many Casaubonish echoes, not least in a sketch devoted to the scholar Proteus Merman. Just as Eliot populates *Middlemarch* with a shoal of fishy-sounding scholars – Pike, Tench and Carp – who provide a backdrop of allies and antagonists for Mr Casaubon, so in *Theophrastus Such* Merman interacts with an international cast of scholars who have marine associations, this time of a cetacean type: his opponent Grampus, the American academic Professor Whale, the Frenchmen M. Cachalot and M. Porpesse, and the Germans Butzkopf and Dugong. Merman is depicted as a Casaubonish obsessive who believes he has made a theoretical discovery in the field of antiquities akin to the key to all mythologies: 'a new idea seized him with regard to the possible connection of certain symbolic monuments common to widely scattered races'. He, Merman, and not the leading authority in the field, Grampus, has 'the right clue' which will yield up the hitherto invisible tissue which will connect 'the comparative history of the ancient civilizations'. However, his wife, Julia, does not immediately grasp the import of her husband's discovery, which provokes Proteus into an expostulation which recapitulates the situation of Dorothea Brooke and Mr Casaubon in *Middlemarch*: ' "Why, if a woman will not try to understand her husband's ideas, or at least to believe that they are of more value than she can understand – if she is to join anybody who happens to be against him, and suppose he is a fool because others contradict him – there is an end of our happiness." ' Unfortunately, Grampus holds the field against his younger antagonist, and Merman's thesis becomes a byword for 'speculative aberration'. The experience produces a sad Casaubonish deformation of Merman's character: 'The gall of his adversaries' ink had been sucked into his system and ran in his blood. He was still in the prime of life, but his mind was aged by that eager monotonous construction which comes of feverish excitement on a single topic.' Yet by a cruel irony, over time – and after Merman himself has begun to refine his 'former guesses in a new light' – 'the main idea' underpinning 'his too rash theorizing' is 'adopted by Grampus and received with general respect'; in other words, Merman's key to all mythologies is ultimately – but silently – appropriated

---

[31] G. S. Haight, 'Poor Mr Casaubon', in C. de Ryals *et al.* (eds.), *Nineteenth-century literary perspectives: essays in honor of Lionel Stevenson* (Durham, NC, 1974), pp. 255–70, at p. 264.

by his rival. Eliot is toying with her readers, from her playful invention of a learned German journal 'the *Selten-erscheinende Monat-schrift* [the Seldom-appearing-monthly journal] or Hayrick for the insertion of split hairs' to the quiet insertion of leitmotif-words from *Middlemarch*, for example, 'key' and 'labyrinth', rich in Casaubonish associations; she mentions Merman's critics who sought 'the best key to his argumentation' and Butzkopf's work, *Die Bedeutung des Aegyptischen Labyrinthe*s (The Significance of the Egyptian Labyrinth).[32]

The character of Mr Casaubon is further indebted to Walter Scott's rich and curious gallery of antiquarian absurdity. Scott was a lifelong favourite of Eliot's,[33] and in the Waverley Novels he sketched – with considerable affection as well as gentle mockery – a parade of erudite obsessives, unworldly literati and deluded semi-scholars: Baron Bradwardine, the forgetful Jacobite Latinist in *Waverley* itself,[34] Jonathan Oldbuck and his antagonists in *The Antiquary*,[35] Bartolemus Saddletree, the uneducated tradesman and would-be Romano-canonical jurist in *Heart of Midlothian*,[36] and *The Pirate's* Triptolemus Yellowley, an agrarian improver attentive more to the georgics of Roman antiquity than to the chill realities of cultivation in the barren northern isles.[37] Nor should we forget an earlier mythographer in British literature, Mr Ramsbottom, the 'zodiacal mythologist' in Thomas Love Peacock's philosophical tale *Crotchet Castle* (1831), who maps Hindu deities onto their classical counterparts.[38]

Seth Lerer has drawn attention to the influence on the antiquarian underbelly of *Middlemarch* of a once influential but now largely forgotten body of reflections on matters of – broadly speaking – literary, philosophical and philological interest, entitled *Guesses at Truth*, first published in 1827.[39] This began as a commonplace book, compiled by the brothers Julius Charles Hare (1795–1855) – a fellow of Trinity College, Cambridge, Archdeacon of Lewes and eventually Regius Professor of Divinity at Cambridge – and Augustus William Hare (1792–1834), like his brother a clergyman with learned interests. A further set appeared in 1848, and

---

[32] George Eliot, *Impressions of Theophrastus Such* (2nd edn, Edinburgh and London, 1879), pp. 37–52.
[33] R. Ashton, *George Eliot: a life* (1996: London, 2013), pp. 28, 54, 313.
[34] Walter Scott, *Waverley* (1814: London, 1969), ch. 6, p. 92.
[35] Walter Scott, *The antiquary* (1816: Edinburgh, 1993), chs. 4, 6, pp. 28–33, 51–4.
[36] Walter Scott, *The heart of Midlothian* (1818: New York, 1948), ch. 5, pp. 43–9.
[37] Walter Scott, *The pirate* (1822: Lerwick, 1996), ch. 4, p. 32.
[38] Thomas Love Peacock, *Crotchet Castle* (pubd with *Nightmare Abbey*) (Harmondsworth, 1969), p. 128. See M. Butler, 'Myth and mythmaking in the Shelley circle', *English Literary History*, vol. 49 (1982), pp. 50–72.
[39] S. Lerer, '*Middlemarch* and Julius Charles Hare', *Neophilologus*, vol. 87 (2003), pp. 653–64.

Prologue: Casaubon's Dubious Bequest 13

both series together were reprinted in 1866 and again in 1871, on the eve of *Middlemarch*. There are distinct anticipations of the strange, shadowy world of Mr Casaubon, not least in its passages on idolatry, on the 'confused, tangled mass' of ancient mythology, on the study of error and delusion, and on the relationship of fragmentary knowledge to a grand unity. More particularly, the Homeric scholar J. H. Voss (1751–1826) is described in Casaubon-like terms as having an imagination akin to a 'kitchen-garden', and poetry is presented as 'the key to the hieroglyphics of nature'. Not that either of the Hares is a prototype for Casaubon, for they were – unlike Casaubon – attuned to the new idioms of Germanic scholarship which were superseding the old mythographies.[40]

There are, moreover, several anticipations of the Reverend Edward Casaubon in Eliot's own writings, including the invention, in a letter of 1846 to Charles Bray, of a Professor Bücherwurm of Modering University (Professor Bookworm of Musty University), author of a lengthy treatise on the digamma (the archaic Greek letter w, which slipped out of the classical Greek alphabet).[41] The clerics in her first ensemble of short fictional pieces, *Scenes of Clerical Life* (1857–8), embody premonitions of Casaubon's failings, anguish and stunted personal development. Just as Casaubon is depicted as a scholar sadly out of his depth, indeed a man of limited talents quite unfitted to the task of discovering a key to all mythologies, so in *Scenes of Clerical Life* the Reverend Amos Barton provides an earlier attempt to depict not only clerical dullness but also the lack of an inner compass by which a mediocre intelligence, having assessed its own seaworthiness, might navigate a less ambitious course through life. Although Barton 'had gone through the Eleusinian mysteries of a university education', he was no master of the Biblical tongues of Greek and Hebrew, or even of 'English orthography and syntax'. He is portrayed as 'palpably and unmistakably commonplace', indeed, 'the quintessential extract of mediocrity'. Yet, notwithstanding his lack of real learning or of any innate cunning which might compensate for its absence, the deluded Barton thinks he possesses 'the wisdom of the serpent'. Moreover, exposure to the world of ecclesiastical debate prompts Barton to 'feel that he had opinions a little too far-sighted and profound to be crudely and suddenly communicated to ordinary minds'.[42]

---

[40] Julius and Augustus Hare, *Guesses at truth* (1827: new edn, London, 1871), esp. pp. 296, 322–4, 435–6.
[41] Ashton, *Eliot*, pp. 57–8.
[42] Eliot, *Scenes of clerical life* (Oxford, 2009), pp. 19, 26, 36, 40.

Eliot's *Romola* (1862–3), a novel set in Renaissance Florence during the 1490s, has at its core scholarship – and the congealing of genuine scholarship into mere pedantry. The novel is set in the distant aftermath of the fall of Constantinople to the Turks in 1453, in consequence of which exiled Greek scholars made their way – with their manuscript treasures – to Italy, where they extended the achievements of the Renaissance by reviving classical Greek alongside classical Latinity. Moreover, the advent of printing is drastically reshaping the world of communications and scholarship, and the novel's Casaubonish figure, the blind scholar Bardo de' Bardi, expresses concern about 'these mechanical printers who threaten to make learning a base and vulgar thing'. Greek and print play the same roles as German mythography in the nineteenth-century England of *Middlemarch*, transformative influences which reshape the scholarly landscape. However, in *Romola*, the blind Bardo feels himself less incapacitated than one of his heroes, Petrarch, who had the 'inward blindness' that Greek was a 'dead letter to him'. Bardo's own blindness is, of course, metaphorical as well as physical, for, as he confesses to his daughter Romola, 'even when I could see, it was with the great dead that I lived; while the living often seemed to me mere spectres – shadows dispossessed of true feeling and intelligence'. Romola, Bardo's willing slave and amanuensis, is the novel's Dorothea figure, who leads a 'young but wintry life' with only 'memories of far-off light, love, and beauty, that lay embedded in dark mines of books', for the Bardi household foreshadows in certain ways life in the vicarage at Lowick. Furthermore, Bardo too is described, in terms which eerily foreshadow the Casaubon of *Middlemarch* a decade later, as 'a man with a deep-veined hand cramped by much copying of manuscripts, who ate sparing dinners, and who wore threadbare clothes … who sat among his books and his marble fragments of the past'. Nor should we forget Bardo's unfinished *magnum opus*, 'that great work in which I had desired to gather, as into a firm web, all the threads that my research had laboriously disentangled, and which would have been the vintage of my life was cut off by the failure of my sight and my want of a fitting coadjutor' – for, naturally, Romola, as a mere woman, however blessed with scholarly ability to be her father's actual amanuensis, was unfitted to be his scholarly collaborator.[43]

There were also vivid and precise real-life anticipations of Casaubon and his hobby horse. 'I have just swallowed without much mastication', Eliot wrote in a letter to Maria Lewis in November 1839, '*The Doctrine of the Deluge* by the Revd V. Harcourt … After tracing the image of the Ark and

---

[43] George Eliot, *Romola* (1862–3: London, 1996), pp. 47, 50–2, 59.

Mount Ararat through the faded tapestries that line the temple of mythological history, until one is ready to fancy one sees the first in a linen chest and the last in Van Dyke's frills ... the author deduces from the doctrine of the deluge that of baptismal regeneration, and I humbly opine supports or rather shakes a weak position by weak arguments.'[44] Here in outline was Casaubon's 'key to all mythologies'. The obsessive stalking of mythological figures and episodes as disguised characters and happenings from the Old Testament was a phenomenon which Eliot had encountered thirty years before she began work on *Middlemarch*. Leveson Vernon Harcourt (1788–1860) thought, for example, that the Argonauts had 'remembered the Ark in the name which they gave their ship'. Such identifications were mere cogs in Harcourt's larger project: a defence of the historicity of the Biblical Flood, in which the facts of mythography would supplement those of natural science, and in particular a catastrophist account of geological change. Harcourt thought that as well as trying to find support for Genesis in geology, he would seek for 'evidences impressed not upon the surface of the earth, but upon the memory of its inhabitants, and derived from their traditions, their superstitions, their monuments, and their usages', believing that 'the doctrine which it inculcated, was kept alive obscurely, in various parts of the world', from the mythology of the exotic Aztecs to that of the ancient Greeks. The tradition of the Flood even promised 'a key to explain much that occurred in the Trojan war'.[45]

Most discussion of *Middlemarch* in the context of intellectual history has, of course, focused on the question of how far the Oxford scholar Mark Pattison was – or was not – a prototype for Casaubon. This introductory chapter has charted a very different course, setting Eliot's Mr Casaubon in the context of his hobby horse, mythographical scholarship and debate. However, something deserves to be said about the Pattison question, for it brings into focus the subtle scholarly jokes which pepper Eliot's oeuvre and which are in themselves clues to her own sense of the intellectual history with which she engaged.

At first sight it looks as if the Casaubon marriage in *Middlemarch* was an intellectual in-joke based upon the unhappy marriage of Mark Pattison (1813–84), the erudite Rector of Lincoln College, Oxford, with a young woman twenty-seven years his junior, Emily Francis Strong (1840–1904).[46]

---

[44] George Eliot to Maria Lewis, 22 November 1839, in G. S. Haight (ed.), *George Eliot Letters* (9 vols., New Haven and London, 1954–78), vol. I, p. 34.
[45] Vernon Harcourt, *The doctrine of the deluge* (2 vols., London, 1838), vol. I, pp. 9, 388; vol. II, p. 195.
[46] Cf. K. Israel, *Names and stories: Emilia Dilke and Victorian culture* (Oxford, 2002).

Pattison was, moreover, fascinated by the figure of Isaac Casaubon. Although Pattison did not publish his book on Isaac Casaubon until 1875, he had written a long piece on him in the *Quarterly Review* in 1853.[47] After Pattison's death Francis married the debonair man of the world Sir Charles Dilke (1843–1911). The pattern seems obvious, but the chronology is wrong. In several important respects, it seems as if the link between *Middlemarch* and the Pattisons is less a banal matter of art imitating life than the wonderfully uncanny phenomenon of life imitating art. Only in 1875 – some time after the composition and publication of *Middlemarch* – were the tensions in the Pattison marriage fully revealed, though the close friendship of Eliot and Francis Pattison dates from the period when Eliot was composing the novel. Nevertheless, the most authoritative commentators on this problem agree that the Pattisons did not provide 'direct models' for the marriage of Mr Casaubon and Dorothea, though it is possible that an affectionate allusion might have 'backfired'.[48]

Furthermore, Pattison – though a donnish curmudgeon – was not altogether a Casaubonish figure;[49] in certain respects and by a reverse irony, his immersion in modern German scholarship made him a kind of anti-Casaubon, and, like Will Ladislaw, he was all too well aware of the developments in German critical theology which threatened to make a mockery of Mr Casaubon's pet hobby horse.[50] Pattison had also authored a lengthy article on the major developments in Homeric criticism by Friedrich August Wolf (1759–1824), a piece which Eliot had read.[51] Moreover, as D. B. Nimmo has observed, George Eliot had met 'her fair share of real life crypto-Casaubons', including R. H. Brabant and the comparative mythologist R. W. Mackay, well before she became familiar with the Pattisons.[52]

Yet the thread, gossamer-slight as it is, which binds Pattison and Mr Casaubon proves surprisingly hard to break. Eerily, Pattison's diary of his reading for 1841 – presumably a private document which Eliot never saw – is very suggestive of his own interest in finding a key for the decoding of mythology: 'The right clew [clue] for those who aim at tracing the

---

[47] 'Diary of Casaubon', *Quarterly Review*, vol. 93 (September 1853), pp. 462–500.
[48] Ashton, 'Lunch with the Rector'; Jones, *Intellect and character*, pp. 72–84.
[49] However, for an alternative view focusing on Pattison's own unitarist approach to intellectual history, see P. Thonemann, 'Wall of ice', *London Review of Books* (7 February 2008).
[50] Mark Pattison, 'Present state of theology in Germany', *Westminster Review* (April 1857), pp. 327–63.
[51] Mark Pattison, 'Wolf', *North British Review*, vol. 42 (1865), pp. 245–99; Haight (ed.), *Letters*, vol. V, p. 124.
[52] D. B. Nimmo, 'Mark Pattison, Edward Casaubon, Isaac Casaubon, and George Eliot', *Proceedings of the Leeds Philosophical and Literary Society: Literary and Historical section*, vol. 17, part iv (1979), pp. 79–100, at p. 79.

common elements in the varying web of popular mythology is not to consider nations as having borrowed from one another, but as having each retained a modification of the belief of the parent stock.'[53]

Pattison went on in this section of his diary to identify the 'uniform principle' by which 'all mythology [had] been governed'. Primitive man had been unable to 'discover the true grounds and vindication of human freedom'; therefore in his ignorance he had come to conceive of the universe fatalistically as 'a battlefield of endless strife' between good and evil powers. Though not the all-too-easily-assumed prototype of Mr Casaubon, Pattison did indeed have his own reductive key to all mythologies – the notion that 'popular mythology [was] wholly founded upon fatality by the doctrine of conflicting powers'.[54]

By a further stroke of irony, Pattison, who possessed a critical eye for Casaubonish absurdity, had himself published on the search for a key to mythology, in his lengthy article on the French mythographer Pierre Daniel Huet (1630–1721), Bishop of Avranches, in the *Quarterly Review* (1855). Here Pattison gently – and, to be fair, sympathetically – poked fun at Huet's own key to all mythologies, his attempt in the *Demonstratio evangelica* (1679)[55] to unmask pagan mythology as a set of distorted memories of the ancient Hebrews, Moses in particular: 'The more original and characteristic part of the book is the fanciful tracing of pagan personages and ceremonies to Hebrew sources. He liberally reduces to myths the sages of antiquity, most of whom he finds to be only fancy-portraits, copied from Moses – imaginations pursued to such a length as to be rejected at once even at a period in which the derivation of the heathen religions from the Jewish was an accepted belief.'[56] The quest for a key to all mythologies was something which no one who immersed him- or herself in the erudition of the early modern era could fail to miss, and which was, as we shall see, still energetically pursued well into the nineteenth century.

Nimmo has argued that Pattison chose subjects in which he could see reflections of himself, and makes a convincing case that a complex set of influences, including Pattison's narcissistic interest in Isaac Casaubon, shaped the figure of Edward Casaubon. Indeed, given Eliot's own early

---

[53] Mark Pattison, 'Diary 1838–44', *Bodleian Library Pattison MS 6*, f. 101 r.
[54] *Ibid.*, f. 101 r.
[55] Pierre-Daniel Huet, *Demonstratio evangelica* (Paris, 1679), esp. propositio iv, pp. 56–131.
[56] Mark Pattison, 'Peter Daniel Huet', *Quarterly Review*, vol. 97 (September 1855), pp. 291–335, at p. 313. For Huet, see A. Monod, *De Pascal à Chateaubriand: les défenseurs français du christianisme de 1670 à 1802* (Paris, 1916), pp. 83–90, esp. pp. 87–8 on Huet's identification of Moses as the key to all mythologies; A. Shelford, *Transforming the republic of letters: Pierre-Daniel Huet and European intellectual life 1650–1720* (Rochester, NY, 2007).

confusions – both religious and sexual – and her slowly dawning awareness of her own intellectual vocation, Nimmo wonders whether Edward Casaubon also contains something of Eliot herself, as well as Pattison and Isaac Casaubon.[57] In a letter to Harriet Beecher Stowe in October 1872, Eliot confessed that 'the Casaubon-tints are not quite foreign to my own mental complexion'.[58] Pattison's intellectual biography of Isaac Casaubon – which appeared three years *after* the publication of *Middlemarch* – places him in the category of those scholars 'crushed under the burden of their own accumulations'. Isaac Casaubon, in Pattison's view, 'must be reckoned among those who hoarded more than he could ever use'.[59] Once again, ironically, the depiction of the non-fictional Casaubon seems to be imitating Eliot's portrayal of his fictional namesake.

Notwithstanding the lack of any straightforward correspondence between the Rector of Lincoln's marriage and that of Mr Casaubon, Pattison did provide considerable grist to the mill of late Victorian lady novelists. He was the obvious prototype for Professor Forth in *Belinda* (1883), where Rhoda Broughton (1840–1920) describes the cold, bitter and unhappy marriage between the young and spirited Belinda Churchill and James Forth, the elderly Professor of Etruscan at the University of Oxbridge. 'Old, sickly and peevish', with his 'pinched pedant face', 'arid smile' and 'stiff donnish voice', Forth is a 'chilly' and decidedly unattractive figure. Not only is he 'fastidious' and tight-fisted, with a narrow range of sympathies and a 'good many dislikes', but his 'soul', according to his wife, is 'occupied by mean parsimonies'. Given his obsessions with his scholarship – his 'cheval de bataille' is the digamma – and his frail health, Forth has no regard for his wife except as an overworked and unpaid amanuensis for his new project on the fragments of Menander.[60] But how much of this is Pattison, and how much Pattison through the distorting lens of *Middlemarch*? By the 1880s it is hard to discriminate echoes of the real-life Pattison–Strong marriage from intertextual allusions to the by now iconic fictional marriage of Dorothea and Mr Casaubon.

Indeed, the anthropologist and man of letters, Andrew Lang (1844–1912), saw the comic potential of this higher hearsay. What was no more than unverified academic tittle-tattle had now been given a literary imprimatur – not once, but twice. In his *Old Friends: Essays in Literary Parody*,

---

[57] Nimmo, 'Pattison', pp. 89–96.
[58] Haight (ed.), *Letters*, vol. V, p. 322.
[59] Mark Pattison, *Isaac Casaubon 1559–1614* (London, 1875), p. 476.
[60] Rhoda Broughton, *Belinda* (1883: London, 1887), pp. 12, 22, 54, 132, 161, 183, 189, 218, 225, 238, 255, 260, 288–9, 405–6, 460, 467.

a work ironically enough dedicated to Broughton, Lang confected a hyper-fiction out of the well-established fictions of Eliot and Broughton, with a hilarious set of intermarital (and intertextual) letters between the protagonists in the unhappy donnish marriages of *Middlemarch* and *Belinda*. These are premised on the excuse that the Casaubons happened to visit Oxford during Forth's occupancy of the chair of Etruscan. Not only do Dorothea and Belinda correspond, with other suitors, including Will Ladislaw, lurking ominously in the background, but so too do Professor Forth and Mr Casaubon. Lang, whose own intellectual hobby horses were – as we shall see in later chapters – themselves mythographical, took particular delight in the Forth–Casaubon exchange. The two fictional scholars discuss, for example, the significance of the mysterious ancient deities the Cabiri, whose name, Casaubon contends, comes from the Latin root 'cavus', meaning hollow, but whose ultimate sense derives – as ever, it seems, in the realm of Casaubonish speculation – from 'the Ark of Noah, which, of course, before the entrance of every living thing, according to his kind, must have been the largest artificial hollow or empty space known to our Adamite ancestors'. By extension, the very expression 'Cave-men', by the later nineteenth century, of course, a familiar term of art in a secularised prehistoric archaeology, is redeemed for old-fashioned Casaubonish mythography as a crucial piece of evidence which serves rather to 'perpetuate the memory of Arkite circumstances'.[61] By a further coincidence, life imitating art imitating life, Lang was himself later in his career to become a harsh critic of those who claimed to find a unitary key to all mythologies of the sort sought after by Mr Casaubon. Yet Lang's targets were not only old-fashioned Christian mythographers of the Casaubon stamp, but also the new-fangled Aryan philologists, with whom Lang had long tangled in combat, and even his own allies among the ranks of anthropologists. By the 1890s, of course, James Frazer's *Golden Bough* was a blatant example of mythographical over-reach. To the mature mythographer, 'resolutions of myths into this or that original source – solar, nocturnal, vegetable or what not' were 'often very perilous', for often myths tended to be 'extremely composite', and being drawn from several sources it was often 'difficult', if not 'impossible', so Lang argued, to identify 'the real fountain-head'.[62]

---

[61] Andrew Lang, *Old friends: essays in literary parody* (1890: London, 1892 edn), pp. 108–17, esp. pp. 110–11.
[62] Andrew Lang, *Modern mythology* (London, 1897), p. xxii.

Pattison also contributed something to the character of the desiccated Oxford tutor, Edward Langham, in Mrs Humphry Ward's novel, *Robert Elsmere* (1888). Langham, whose mind was 'a storehouse of thought and fact', found it impossible to be 'spontaneous' with his students. In a short time Langham's initial 'dream' of the scholar's life faded, his lectures becoming 'gradually mere dry, ingenious skeletons, without life or feeling', while his literary ambitions shrivelled too: 'he became a translator, a contributor to dictionaries, a microscopic student of texts, not in the interest of anything beyond, but simply as a kind of mental stone-breaking'. In the course of the novel – and perhaps in allusion to the Pattison–Strong relationship – Elsmere's bright and vivacious sister-in-law Rose kindles some romantic feelings in the middle-aged bachelor, who ultimately recoils from love and life and returns to his accustomed state of farouche and nihilistic 'paralysis': 'in the end, the spectre self, a cold and bloodless conqueror, slipped back into the soul which remorse and terror, love and pity, a last impulse of hope, a last stirring of manhood, had been alike powerless to save'.[63] Critics and historians have also suggested that there is something of Pattison in yet another of the characters in *Robert Elsmere* – the sneeringly sophisticated ultra-rationalist squire, Roger Wendover, who seduces the Anglican cleric Elsmere from a literal belief in the historic miracles – and hence divinity – of Christ. Intellectually speaking, Pattison is, after all, much closer to the critics of the old apologetic mythographers than he is to Casaubon himself.[64]

It is, perhaps, an understandable mistake to go a-questing after Mr Casaubon alone. But in certain respects Casaubon functions, as it were, as an anti-Ladislaw, a foolish old Anglican foil for the daring new insights of the Higher Criticism, which were represented in *Middlemarch* by way of Casaubon's cosmopolitan and vital young cousin, Will Ladislaw. Arguably, Ladislaw was a representative of Eliot herself, embodying the insights she gained in her fraught disengagement from evangelical Christianity. The Hennell connection – her friendship with the freethinking post-Unitarians Sara Hennell (1812–99) and Cara Bray (née Hennell, 1814–1905) and exposure to the work of their brother Charles (1809–50) – played a decisive role in Eliot's intellectual formation. Charles Hennell's *An Inquiry concerning the origin of Christianity* (1838) – first read, it seems, between November 1841 and January 1842, the point when Eliot broke with Christianity,[65] and to

---

[63] Mrs Humphry Ward, *Robert Elsmere* (1888: Oxford, 1987), pp. 56, 434.
[64] Jones, *Intellect and character*, p. 133.
[65] Ashton, *Eliot*, p. 36.

which she returned in 1847 and again when it reappeared in 1870[66] – helped set Eliot on the intellectual road to what might be called 'the world of Will Ladislaw', the realm of the Higher Criticism. In his *Inquiry* Hennell demonstrated – in a sober, naturalistic way devoid of any need to invoke supernatural intervention – how the tale of the Resurrection had most probably arisen in the midst of the tensions which accompanied Christ's crucifixion. While the crucifixion was corroborated by reliable pagan sources, the resurrection lacked a similar historical foundation, being a tissue of 'confusion, contradiction and chasms'. How, then, had the story arisen? At the heart of Hennell's cautious historical reconstruction was the figure of Joseph of Arimathea, a man whose undoubted generosity of spirit was tempered with an understandable measure of self-serving prudence and practicality. While Joseph of Arimathea had managed to obtain an 'honourable burial' for Jesus' body, Joseph's garden soon became 'the centre of attention' for the late teacher's followers, and he was worried that 'any tumult would be laid to his charge' and that he himself would be the next victim of the authorities. Therefore, Joseph decided to 'extricate himself' from his predicament by finding a way of encouraging Jesus' following to 'return immediately to their own country, Galilee'. First, he had the body 'secretly removed from the tomb, or from that part of it where the women had seen it laid', and had then 'stationed an agent in the tomb, who informed the first visitants that Jesus was not there, but risen, and gone into Galilee, whither they were to follow him'. Although the disciples had not at first believed this story, nevertheless when they saw the empty tomb they concluded that their departed master had received 'proof of the Divine approbation' and they wondered whether he would 'before ascending into heaven, make himself visible to his faithful followers'. Soon, stories of just this sort of apparition began to surface, and, Hennell reckoned, the Bible preserved those tales of the resurrected Christ's appearance 'such as were current from forty to sixty years after the death of Jesus'. Hennell's history was one of ironies and unintended consequences, of how 'Joseph of Armithea succeeded in diverting the attention of the disciples from himself' and in preventing one kind of tumult, but only fostered another, for 'the excitement, which he probably expected would die away on their return to Galilee, continued, and took a somewhat new form'. The eventual rise of Christianity was, however, a more protracted process, Hennell believed. Gentiles had, at first, little appetite for the cult of 'a crucified Jew', but there were affinities of approach between Essene Judaism and gentile Platonism, and it was the Platonist philosophers, with their taste for

---

[66] N. Henry, *The life of George Eliot* (Malden, MA and Oxford, 2012), p. 48.

allegory and symbolism, who had contrived to formulate a theology – with a strong appeal for the Greek and Roman world – out of the materials of 'reformed Judaism'. For Hennell what remained of Jesus Christ himself out of the rumours of the resurrection and the elegant symbolical contrivances of the Platonisers was simply a moral code. Interestingly, Hennell hinted at a psychological key to unlocking the pretensions of religion and mythology: 'in the circumstances attending the death of Jesus', he noted, 'we are forced to see a striking instance of the tendency of the mind to invest ordinary events with a higher beauty and interest than unimpassioned observation alone could discover'.[67]

What *did* Will Ladislaw know – and, more to the point, *when* could he have known it? Which of the pioneering works of nineteenth-century German mythographical scholarship were in the public domain by the time in which *Middlemarch* was set around 1830–2? It is tempting[68] to turn to Eliot's own translations from German, notably her daring translation of D. F. Strauss's *Life of Jesus, critically examined* (1846), as well as her version of Ludwig Feuerbach's *Das Wesen des Christenthums* (1841) (*Essence of Christianity* [1854]).[69] Nevertheless, for our purposes these leads turn out to be reddish herrings. Strauss's *Das Leben Jesu, kritisch bearbeitet* was only published in 1835, and Feuerbach's *Das Wesen des Christenthums* in 1841. Strauss famously inverted the arguments of Christian mythography, explaining the supposed supernatural dimension in the life of Jesus as the product of mythologising; Jesus was a mythical personage. Feuerbach went further, reinterpreting all religion in sociological terms as a projection of human needs. It is, of course, possible that Eliot did indeed have Strauss (1808–74) and Feuerbach (1804–72) in mind when Ladislaw alludes to the new approaches of the Germans on mythological questions, as critics have not unreasonably supposed; that she allowed herself a measure of literary licence in blurring not the immediate English foreground of the novel, but its less obtrusive general context. After all, her hero Walter Scott had proved adept at performing manoeuvres of just this sort in his historical fiction. An over-scrupulousness about historical accuracy was an unwelcome impediment to narrative flow. Clearly, in *Middlemarch* Eliot wanted to present an English Midlands town during the run-up to the Great Reform Act of 1832, but it was permissible, perhaps, to be less precise about

---

[67] Charles Hennell, *An inquiry concerning the origin of Christianity* (London, 1838), pp. 35–7, 47, 56–61, 153, 359–62.
[68] P. C. Hodgson, *Theology in the fiction of George Eliot* (London, 2001), p. 6, also warns against the further temptation to identify Eliot as a disciple of either Strauss or Feuerbach.
[69] Cf. Nuttall, *Dead from the waist down*, pp. 51–2.

the novel's off-stage German hinterland. On the other hand, Eliot hardly favoured imprecision of this kind. Casaubon cannot be fairly convicted of ignorance of scholarship in German that was yet to be published. It seems more likely, then, that Ladislaw was drawing attention to the Creuzerstreit of the 1810s and 1820s.[70]

Georg Friedrich Creuzer (1771–1858) published his *Symbolik und Mythologie der alten Völker* in four volumes between 1810 and 1812. Ancient Greek culture was indebted to earlier oriental cultures. India, indeed, was the scene of a primitive monotheism from which polytheism – ultimately – derived. Indian priests had migrated to Greece, bringing with them a monotheistic religion, whose truths they expressed in symbols which encapsulated particular capacities of the Deity. However, these symbols were further adapted to the needs of the Greek population and had degenerated into narrative tales. Thus myth had evolved out of symbolic representation, and in a similarly unpremeditated fashion the supposed promulgation of monotheism accidentally gave rise to the errors of polytheism.[71] Creuzer combined naturalistic accounts of the origins of mythology with a keen awareness of human spiritual needs and a diffusionist thesis about how mythology had spread from the Orient by way of a priestly caste. Notwithstanding the originality of Creuzer's work, some of its strategies – diffusionism, the relationship of oriental and classical paganism, an obsession with the Cabiri, the degeneration of allegory, the two-fold division between an inner mystery doctrine known to initiates by way of symbols (*Symbolik*) and an outer superstition for the vulgar – had (as we shall see in later chapters) obvious enough precedents in the realm of eighteenth-century English mythography. Indeed, Mr Casaubon's ignorance of German mythography needs to be carefully parsed. Either Casaubon was ignorant of the paradigm-shattering-though-yet-to-be-published work of Strauss and Feuerbach, or he was ignorant of the insights of Creuzer, which hardly shattered the paradigms operating in eighteenth- and early nineteenth-century British mythography. Moreover, although Creuzer's work was not translated wholesale into English, it started to become accessible via the French translation of Joseph-Daniel Guigniat (1794–1876), as *Religions de l'antiquité considerées*

---

[70] G. S. Williamson, *The longing for myth in Germany: religion and aesthetic culture from romanticism to Nietzsche* (Chicago, 2004), pp. 121–50; S. Marchand, *German orientalism in the age of empire* (Cambridge, 2009), pp. 66–71; J. H. Blok, 'Quests for a scientific mythology: F. Creuzer and K. O. Müller on history and myth', *History and Theory*, vol. 33 (1994), pp. 26–52.

[71] Williamson, *Longing*, pp. 127–9; B. Feldman and R. D. Richardson, *The rise of modern mythology 1680–1830* (Bloomington, IN, 1972), pp. 387–8.

principalement dans leurs formes symboliques et mythologiques (10 vols., 1825–51).[72]

Creuzer's work provoked a massive outpouring of bilious scholarship. The invective of German Protestant scholars was oddly misdirected, for Creuzer, though accused of advancing a Catholic interpretation of ancient mythology, was himself a Protestant. Creuzer's most significant opponent, among a legion of adversaries, was Karl Otfried Müller (1797–1840), who rejected the universalist interpretation of myth advanced by Creuzer and instead emphasised the role of particular, local circumstances in shaping distinctive mythologies. For Müller, mythologies were *sui generis*, the product of conditions in each particular tribal culture (*Stammeskultur*), while for Creuzer mythological diversity was more apparent than real. In a major departure from the grandiose universalism of traditional mythography, Müller confined himself to the immediate national, ethnic and cultural contexts in which mythology developed. He set out the principles of his nationalist approach to mythology in *Prolegomena zu einer wissenschaftlichen Mythologie* (1825). Here Müller rejected outright the cross-cultural correspondences among myths which were the bread and butter of traditional mythographers. He exploded the assumption, for example, that certain symbols – the serpent, for example – always corresponded to a certain idea.[73] This was not the case. Rather, Müller insisted, Greek myths were particular to ancient Greek culture, not – as Creuzer had argued – imports from the east. Each corpus of national legends needed to be explored on its own terms, with sensitivity to the particularities of culture and place. There was in reality, Müller argued, no myth without its roots in a particular locality ('gibt es eigentlich … keinen Mythus ohne Lokal').[74] Ultimately, Müller, unlike Creuzer, did not subscribe to a unitary key to all mythologies.

The conflict of Müller and Creuzer reminds us that there was no single school of German mythography; what Casaubon was missing was a full-throated debate. Indeed, Creuzer was not a lone voice in German mythography. Joseph Görres (1776–1848), author of the *Mythengeschichte der asiatischen Welt* (1810) posited 'Brahmaismus' as the Ur-religion.[75] Of course,

---

[72] M. K. Louis, 'Gods and mysteries: the revival of paganism and the remaking of mythography through the nineteenth century', *Victorian Studies*, vol. 47 (2005), pp. 329–61, at p. 336; D. Figueira, *Aryans, Jews, Brahmins* (Albany, NY, 2002), pp. 31–2.
[73] K. O. Müller, *Introduction to a scientific system of mythology* (transl. John Leitch, London, 1844), p. 219.
[74] Quoted in A. Momigliano, 'K. O. Müller's *Prolegomena zu einer wissenschaftlichen Mythologie* and the meaning of myth', *Annali della Scuola Normale Superiore di Pisa*, vol. 13 (1983), pp. 673–89, at p. 678.
[75] Figueira, *Aryans*, pp. 32–3.

Prologue: Casaubon's Dubious Bequest   25

there were deeper tides at play in German critical scholarship. Some of this was available to anglophone scholars via the familiar international medium of neo-Latin scholarship. In particular, the fertility of early nineteenth-century German mythography can be traced back to the Homeric scholarship of Wolf, whose *Prolegomena ad Homerum* (1795) – which Eliot read as part of her encyclopaedic preparation for *Middlemarch*[76] – explained the *Iliad* and *Odyssey* as compilations cemented together from the primeval hymns of an original Homer, whose work had been orally transmitted by generations of rhapsodes and eventually captured in writing – and interpolated and emended – in the multiple recensions of scholiasts.[77] Wolf's patient deconstruction of a single-author reading of the Homeric texts galvanised German philology and the related study of mythography.[78] Moreover, one of the most comprehensive assaults on Creuzerian ideas was a neo-Latin work, *Aglaophamus, sive de theologiae mysticae Graecorum causis* (1829), by Christian August Lobeck (1781–1860), professor of rhetoric and ancient literature at Königsberg. Lobeck questioned some of Creuzer's central contentions about ancient Greek religion, including its oriental provenance and the supposed distinction between esoteric mystery cults and wider patterns of belief.[79] Mr Casaubon was not so completely cut off from contemporary German scholarship as Ladislaw suggests.[80]

Eliot was, of course, well-versed in German mythography and keenly aware of the Creuzerstreit.[81] Indeed, in her article 'Silly novels by lady novelists', she explicitly invoked Creuzer when denouncing novels with preposterously polymathic heroines, paragons whose Christian ideals were underpinned by first-hand contact with ancient languages: 'Greek and Hebrew are mere play to a heroine. Sanskrit is no more than abc to her ... She is a polking polyglot, a Creuzer in a crinoline.'[82] Moreover, Eliot's review of Robert Mackay's *The progress of the intellect, as exemplified in the religious development of the Greeks and Hebrews* (1850) uncannily

---

[76] Pratt and Neufeldt (eds.), 'Appendix', *Middlemarch notebooks*, p. 288.
[77] There is a fine modern edition of F. A. Wolf, *Prolegomena to Homer, 1795* (ed. and transl. A. Grafton, G. Most and J. Zetzel, Princeton, 1985). See also A. Grafton, 'Prolegomena to Friedrich August Wolf', *Journal of the Warburg and Courtauld Institutes*, vol. 44 (1981), pp. 101–29; J. Turner, *Philology: the forgotten origins of the modern humanities* (Princeton, 2014), pp. 118–19, 173.
[78] See L. Baltazar, 'The critique of Anglican biblical scholarship in George Eliot's *Middlemarch*', *Literature and Theology*, vol. 15 (2001), pp. 40–60, at p. 46.
[79] S. C. Humphreys, 'Ancient theologies and modern times', *Kernos*, vol. 25 (2012), pp. 149–61.
[80] Haight, 'Poor Mr Casaubon', p. 262.
[81] Pratt and Neufeldt (eds.), *Middlemarch notebooks*, p. xlvii; A. Fleishman, *George Eliot's reading: a chronological list*, supplement to no. 54–5, *George Eliot-George Henry Lewes Studies* (2008), pp. 13, 44, 47–8, 52, 55.
[82] Eliot, 'Silly novels by lady novelists', *Westminster Review* (October 1856), pp. 442–61, at p. 445.

foreshadowed the matter of Casaubon and Ladislaw. Just as her creature, Mr Casaubon, would be depicted as out of touch with German thought, so in her review of 1851 she saw Mackay's book as a vital corrective for English scholarship, which had been 'slow to use or to emulate the immense labours of Germany in the departments of mythology and biblical criticism'. She noted Mackay's intellectual debts to Creuzer, and celebrated the 'introduction of a truly philosophic spirit into the study of mythology – an introduction for which we are chiefly indebted to the Germans'.[83]

Mackay's work was a major step forward, a book which firmly separated mythological enquiry from the apologetic agenda of Christian mythography. All religion, argued Mackay, partook of mediation, that is an attempt to repair a supposed breach between humankind and the divine. This estrangement was evident even in the simplest form of nature-worship, where deity needed to be propitiated in order that the natural cycle of life and fertility be renewed in the wake of seasonal decay: 'The notion of a dying god, so frequent in oriental legend, was the natural inference from a literal interpretation of nature worship; since nature, which in the vicissitudes of the seasons seems to undergo a dissolution, was to the earliest religionists the express image of the Deity.' Nature presented to primitive man a paradoxical scene of topsy-turvy divine displeasure and continued divine favour, of seasonal death and recurrent fertility. How was early man to 'dispose of the death of the nature-god without prejudice to his immortality'? Not only were virgin births and miraculous conceptions recurring features of the world's mythologies, it turned out that neither were probationary suffering and 'sanguinary propitiation' peculiar to, or indeed logically intrinsic to, Christian theology. Atonement, spiritual reunion with deity and the restoration of a golden age were the grand themes of all religion, but rooted ultimately in concerns about the renewed fruitfulness of the natural world, in particular the wintery anxiety that 'sterility continues until sacrificial reparation is made'. If it is the sophistication of Mackay's anticipations of Frazer's *Golden Bough* (1890) which now strikes the reader so forcefully, it remains still the case that Mackay was a reductive decoder of mythology, keen to shoehorn it into a narrow-fitting scheme of interpretation, and no less a proponent of a unitary key to all mythologies than Casaubon himself. Mackay identified mythology as a phase in the intellectual development of humanity, a stage consequent upon the early emergence of emblems and symbols as comprehensible physical

---

[83] *Westminster Review* (January 1851), pp. 353–68, at pp. 354, 359–60.

substitutes for the abstract conceptions towards which primitive people were slowly and blindly groping. According to Mackay, mythology was a kind of intermediate 'narrative symbolism', which arose when 'figurative imagery' outgrew the function of 'mere illustration' and came to assume 'the character of a belief'. While Mackay challenged the findings of the Christian mythographers who detected in the apparent similarity of the world's legends an orthodox key to all mythologies, he replaced it not with an open-minded scepticism, but with his own mythographical scheme; critical and subversive, to be sure, but still a key to all mythologies. The mythologies of the world were composed of similar kinds of symbolic ingredients – flood legends featuring doves and fish-men, light as a metaphor for deity – not because all religions bar one were copies of an Ur-religion, but because all mythologies and religions bore the marks of a common humanity and common mental processes. 'The history of religion', Mackay contended, was 'that of the human mind; the conception formed of deity being always in exact relation to its moral and intellectual attainments'. Mythology was 'no gratuitous fiction or wanton invention, but had its necessary basis in nature'.[84]

Eliot recognised that 'any attempt extensively to trace consistent allegory in the myths must fail', and that Mackay had not 'escaped the influence of the allegorizing mania'.[85] There are suggestions here – no more than that, perhaps – that Eliot recognised, for all her new-won convictions as a convert from the follies of old-style religion, the snares attendant on any kind of mythological decoding; that the 'key to all mythologies' was not simply the folly of the orthodox.

Of course, there is no point trying to mount a salvage operation to retrieve the reputation of a fictional clergyman. Notwithstanding the caveats that have been advanced about Mr Casaubon's supposed insignificance, he has become a notorious emblem of pedantry, of 'intellectual pettiness', of self-indulgent dawdling over an 'endlessly deferred masterwork' and of irrelevance, given that work's 'deadly title'.[86] However, the historian of mythography needs to sift the general from the particular, to discriminate between the personal attributes of a specific fictional character and the wider ideological significance of the mythographer. What were the

---

[84] Robert Mackay, *The progress of the intellect, as exemplified in the religious development of the Greeks and Hebrews* (2 vols., London, 1850), vol. I, pp. 11, 65–7, 77, 88–94, 110, 115, 127; vol. II, pp. 4, 7, 41, 52, 260, 348–9, 398–9, 460.
[85] *Westminster Review* (January 1851), p. 362.
[86] R. Mead, *My life in Middlemarch* (New York, 2014), pp. 3, 163.

primary arguments of mythography? And what were the genres in which mythographers operated? More to the point, what exactly did Eliot mean – or indeed, if they themselves used the expression, what did the Christian mythographers she debunks mean – by the memorable conceit of a 'key to all mythologies'?

CHAPTER 2

The Key to All Mythologies

[H]e had undertaken to show (what indeed had been attempted before, but not with that thoroughness, justice of comparison, and effectiveness of arrangement at which Mr Casaubon aimed) that all the mythical systems or erratic mythical fragments in the world were corruptions of a tradition originally revealed. (*Middlemarch*, ch. 3)

The 'Key to All Mythologies' has become a byword for the mind-numbingly recondite and is typically thought of as a scene of arid and misguided pedantry. Readers of *Middlemarch* also gain a sense of the windy and unfocused emptiness of Casaubon's project, its seemingly unrealisable immensity bringing into relief the mythographer's pettiness. Casaubon did, of course, pay attention to detail – an excessive antiquarian attention to trifles indeed; but the logic of his bloated project led him to superimpose a universal pattern on immensely varied elements, regardless of their context or provenance. Mr Casaubon, readers soon divine, had bitten off more than he could chew.

Casaubon seems in that respect like one of the other central characters in *Middlemarch*, Dr Tertius Lydgate, who is engaged on a medical quest to unravel the scientific secrets of the most basic building block of life,[1] what he calls 'primitive tissue'.[2] The supposed parallel here is obvious, for Lydgate, whose vainglorious dreams and ambitions exceed his grasp, is, under the influence of the French anatomist Marie-François Xavier Bichat (1771–1802),[3] attempting to discover what might be called a key to all biology. Indeed, Lydgate, like Casaubon who desperately tries to reduce all myths to a common cipher, has a totalising and reductive approach to knowledge and is keen to unravel 'the homogeneous origin of all the

---

[1] G. Beer, *Darwin's plots: evolutionary narrative in Darwin, George Eliot and nineteenth-century fiction* (1983: 3rd edn, Cambridge, 2009), p. 154.
[2] George Eliot, *Middlemarch* (1871–2: Harmondsworth, 1965), ch. 15, pp. 177–8.
[3] E. Haigh, 'Xavier Bichat and the medical theory of the eighteenth century', *Medical History*, supplement no. 4 (London, 1984).

tissues'.⁴ Yet in both cases there are more generous ways of assessing each man's pretensions to learning, though Eliot, it seems, only grants such indulgence to Lydgate (who, to be fair, was also inspired – unlike the quietly misanthropic Casaubon – by philanthropic intentions to improve the lot of his fellow humans). As Eliot and her readers knew, Lydgate was onto something, and the knowing reader appreciates that despite being a young man in a hurry Lydgate was an unsung pioneer in the development of cell theory by Matthias Schleiden (1804–81) and Theodor Schwann (1810–82).⁵ The road, which for Lydgate proved to be a cul-de-sac, turned out to be a throughway. Sympathetic understanding of this sort is not extended to Casaubon or to his enterprise.

Casaubon is gloriously individual as a character, but his mythography comes off-the-peg. Casaubon's hunt for a key to all mythologies was not a bespoke delusion peculiar to a lone eccentric manufactured out of whole cloth by Eliot from the resources of her imagination. Rather Casaubon was a familiar figure, in part based on the type of the antiquary, but also more precisely on the ranks of practising mythographers. Of course, Eliot correctly parsed the impossibility of Casaubon's deluded enterprise – something that would be recognised today by academic theologians as much as by secular intellectuals – however, she failed to mention its vitality, relevance and ideological purchase. While Eliot is surely right to condemn the inadequacies of Casaubon's brand of apologetic mythography, it was not so peripheral or detached from current controversy as she appears to suggest. Assuredly Casaubon was a charlatan of sorts, and a torpid and inert pedant to boot; nevertheless, Mr Casaubon and his kind mattered. Christian mythographers were involved in an intense struggle for the mind of European civilisation. Potentially Casaubon's work would serve as a piece of advanced artillery for wreaking havoc on the polemics and satires of Christendom's deistic enemies. Notwithstanding the otherwise perceptive insinuation that the 'key to all mythologies' was quixotic, as a lively anti-deistic genre it was neither obscure nor in short supply.

There is a sly costiveness to Eliot's treatment of mythography. She deliberately obscures from her readers the polemical battlefield to which Mr Casaubon's *magnum opus* is intended to contribute.⁶ The key to all mythologies was not – as it appears in *Middlemarch* – the recondite hobby of an otherworldly and reclusive monomaniac who rarely ventured from

---

⁴ Eliot, *Middlemarch*, ch. 45, p. 495.
⁵ A. Fleishman, *George Eliot's intellectual life* (Cambridge, 2010), pp. 167–8.
⁶ Yet she knew the deconstructive works of the likes of Dupuis: J. C. Pratt, and V. A. Neufeldt (eds.), *George Eliot's Middlemarch notebooks* (Berkeley and Los Angeles, 1979), pp. 51–2.

his burrow. Mr Casaubon stood at the end of a distinguished lineage of accommodationist scholarship which since the beginnings of Christianity had tried to reconcile the Christian message with the civilisations of Greece and Rome. The relationship of Christian truth to the undeniable achievement of pagan high culture presented a vexing problem. Was any issue more pressing for the western intellectual tradition than the disentangling of Christian truth from the insights – and errors – of refined classical heathendom?

At the core of mythographical scholarship was the notion that myths did not yield their true meaning to those who read them literally. The most obvious insight into this phenomenon came from the straightforward way in which many Roman deities patently had their exact Greek equivalents. Jupiter was Zeus, Mercury was Hermes, Neptune was Poseidon, and so on. Were there, perhaps, other examples of congruence between belief systems? Might the world of heathen idolatry – when properly interpreted – reveal other patterns of correspondence, not only between paganisms, but also between Judaeo-Christianity and paganism? Decodings of this sort were at the core of early modern and nineteenth-century mythographical analysis.[7]

This related in turn to another problem with which Christian theologians had long wrestled, most intensely since the sixteenth-century expansion of Europe and the discovery of heathen high civilisations in Asia and the Americas. Where did other religions come from? Was each religion *sui generis*, or did every religion map – at least in some small measure – onto the first religion, the religion of Noah?[8] If all the world's peoples sprang

---

[7] See e.g. F. Manuel, *The eighteenth century confronts the gods* (1959: New York, 1967); B. Feldman and R. D. Richardson, *The rise of modern mythology 1680–1830* (Bloomington, IN, 1972); G. J. Toomer, *John Selden* (2 vols., Oxford, 2009), vol. I, pp. 211–56; J. Assmann, *Moses the Egyptian* (Cambridge, MA, 1997); G. Stroumsa, 'John Spencer and the roots of idolatry', *History of Religions*, vol. 41 (2001), pp. 1–23; J. Sheehan, 'Sacred and profane: idolatry, antiquarianism and polemics of distinction in the seventeenth century', *Past and Present*, no. 192 (2006), pp. 35–66; R. Serjeantson, 'David Hume's natural history of religion (1757) and the end of modern Eusebianism', in S. Mortimer and J. Robertson (eds.), *The intellectual consequences of religious heterodoxy 1600–1750* (Leiden, 2012), pp. 267–95; D. Stolzenberg, *Egyptian Oedipus: Athanasius Kircher and the secrets of antiquity* (Chicago, 2013). See also the encyclopaedic apparatus, exploring pagan religion and links with the science of chronology, in Robert Mankin's edition of Edward Gibbon, *Essai sur l'étude de la littérature* (Oxford, 2010), pp. 30–9, 68–73, 292–326.

[8] See e.g. A. Grafton, *New worlds, ancient texts* (Cambridge, MA, 1992); A. Pagden, *The fall of natural man* (1982: Cambridge, 1986 edn), esp. pp. 198–209; Manuel, *Eighteenth century*; P. J. Marshall and G. Williams, *The great map of mankind* (London, 1982); D. A. Pailin, *Attitudes to other religions: comparative religion in seventeenth- and eighteenth-century Britain* (Manchester, 1984); P. J. Marshall (ed.), *The British discovery of Hinduism* (Cambridge, 1970); C. Kidd, *British identities before nationalism* (Cambridge, 1999), pp. 9–72; G. Stroumsa, *A new science: the discovery of religion in the age of reason* (Cambridge, MA, 2010); U. App, *The birth of orientalism* (Philadelphia, PA, 2010); J.-P. Rubiés, 'From antiquarianism to philosophical history: India, China, and the world history of religion in

from a common origin in the family of Noah which had survived the global deluge, then might not all the world's religions bear some trace – however faint or distorted – of the original religion of Noah and his family's knowledge of the antediluvian past, including the Fall and then the Flood itself? For instance, Patrick Delany (1685/6–1768), the Dean of Down in the Anglican Church of Ireland, who gathered testimonies from many cultures to the truth of the Flood, noted, happily, that 'some imperfect memory of Noah and his ark, seems to subsist even among the Hottentots. They say, their first parents came into their country through a window; that the name of the man was Noh'.[9]

Notwithstanding the originality displayed by many mythographers in matters of detail, certain familiar formulae tended to recur in the decoding of pagan myths.[10] It is important to note at the outset that the defenders and subverters of Christianity tended to use the same repertoire of methods when making sense of mythology, often with a twist or inversion to suit a particular purpose. The foundational approach within orthodox Christian mythography was to assume that most myths were in essence memories, however distorted, of the patriarchal era in Genesis. Every pagan flood myth was an allusion to Noah's Flood, every myth featuring a snake (or dragon) or apple a memory of the Fall. One major variant of this kind of interpretation was Euhemerism, a strategy devised in pagan antiquity by Euhemerus of Messina, by which heathen gods were revealed in their true colours as deified heroes or kings or generals.[11] Christian Euhemerists, such as Edward Stillingfleet (1635–99), the future Bishop of Worcester, in his *Origines sacrae* (1662), used the method to unmask pagan deities as corrupted memories of historical personages from the patriarchal era of Old Testament history.[12] Supposedly heathen gods turned out on closer inspection, Christian Euhemerists contended, to be pagan depictions of, say, Noah or his sons Ham, Shem and Japhet. Thus, by a cunning twist, a style of deconstructive pagan mythography might be applied to pagan religion to yield a most surprising and ironic result: that heathen mythology

---

European thought (1600–1770)', in P. Miller (ed.), *Antiquarianism and intellectual life in Europe and China 1500–1800* (Ann Arbor, 2012), pp. 313–67.

[9] Patrick Delany, *Revelation examined with candour* (3rd edn, 2 vols., London, 1735), vol. I, p. 255.

[10] For Eliot's grasp of the strategies of early modern mythographers, see Pratt and Neufeldt (eds.), *Middlemarch notebooks*, pp. 48–52.

[11] Manuel, *Eighteenth century*, pp. 103–5.

[12] Edward Stillingfleet, *Origines sacrae* (London, 1662), pp. 593–8; S. Hutton, 'Edward Stillingfleet, Henry More and the decline of Moses Atticus: a note on seventeenth-century apologetics', in R. Kroll, R. Ashcraft and P. Zagorin (eds.), *Philosophy, science and religion in England 1640–1700* (Cambridge, 1992), pp. 68–84.

provided compelling corroboration for the historic truth of Old Testament history. Not all of heathen mythology was claimed to be derived from Genesis. Some of it, argued the antiquary Francis Wise (1695–1767), was also drawn from profane history, especially, he contended, from the deeds of Noah's later descendants in India.[13]

Diffusionism provided the dominant theory in Christian mythography. It rested on the notion that religion – true religion, that is – was a unique cosmic phenomenon, not a category which encompassed plural forms. Therefore by extension it was assumed that religions or myths did not spring up independently in several places, but that on the whole mythologies were copied from one culture to another. However, diffusionism was not a strategy open only to the orthodox; two could play at this game. While Christian mythographers contended that Babylonians and Hindus, say, borrowed their myths ultimately from the patriarchal religion of the Old Testament, sceptics and deists – operating in the same idiom – argued the exact reverse. Freethinkers claimed that the supposed histories set out in the Old Testament were but appropriations from Babylonians and Hindus (whose own religions, while older than Judaeo-Christianity, were, of course, also false).

How was something as luxuriant and outlandish as pagan polytheism to be reconciled with monotheistic orthodoxy? The insight that polytheistic mythologies resulted from the personification of the various powers and attributes of a monotheistic deity is one now most closely associated with the philological work of Friedrich Max-Müller in the nineteenth century. Max-Müller argued that religion was ultimately 'a disease of language', by which he meant that verb forms, inflection and – by extension – metaphor encouraged the manufacture of deities.[14] This perception was foreshadowed – though not in exactly the same terms – by a few of the shrewder mythographers of the late seventeenth and eighteenth centuries. The Cambridge Platonist Ralph Cudworth (1617–88), for instance, in his encyclopaedic *True Intellectual System of the Universe* (1678), exposed polytheism as but the wispiest veil of 'polyonomy', that is, the tendency to multiply the names and attributes of a single Creator-God into a range of apparent deities.[15] The ancients, it transpired, were not true polytheists, at least by Cudworth's strict definition, for they did not believe in 'unmade

---

[13] [Francis Wise], *The history and chronology of the fabulous ages considered particularly with regard to the two ancient deities Bacchus and Hercules* (Oxford, 1764), esp. pp. vi, 4–5, 9–10, 61, 81, 101–9.
[14] Friedrich Max-Müller, *Lectures on the science of language* (2nd ser., London, 1864), p. 425; Max-Müller, *Chips from a German workshop* (4 vols., London, 1867–75), vol. I, p. 358.
[15] A. Grafton, 'Sleuths and Analysts', *Times Literary Supplement* (8 August 1986), p. 867.

self-existent deities'. Rather the pagan pantheon – such as it was – involved the personification of a range of attributes of the Creator as well as features of the natural world, which were but aspects of His creation. Most heathen gods and goddesses turned out to be – literally – nominal: 'nothing but several names and notions of one supreme deity, according to its different manifestations, gifts and effects in the world, personated'. The ancient pagans, in Cudworth's interpretation, had been disinclined to have 'all their devotion towards the deity ... huddled up in one general and confused acknowledgement of a supreme invisible being', but preferred that 'all the several manifestations of the deity in the world, considered singly and apart by themselves, should be made so many distinct objects of their devout veneration'.[16]

Some mythographers perceived the layering in ancient fables. Simple monotheism had first of all given rise to multiple emblems which represented particular aspects of the deity's omnipotence; then emblems had in turn been transformed into mythological personages. The mythographer had to work from the topmost strata downwards, peering beneath the characters of ancient fables to uncover first the emblem or symbol which each character represented, and then ultimately the particular divine attribute which the emblem encapsulated. Indeed, sceptical critics of religion took the process a stage further and used this strategy to undermine – potentially – all personification in theology, including the monotheistic. The early nineteenth-century freethinker Robert Taylor (1784–1844) toyed with the notion of religion as a disease of language: 'The taking of the name of a thing in any unknown language for the name of a person, would naturally render these personifications infinite; and cause the natural history of things without life to be related or understood as if they had been real adventures of actually existing personages.' Thus not only animals, vegetables and 'inanimate substances' but even the 'abstractions' of men's 'thoughts' were, Taylor suggested, endowed with 'actions and sufferings, sentiments and affections'.[17] As we shall see, the arguments and strategies of Christian mythographers needed only the slightest tweak to become potent weapons in the hands of biblical Christianity's freethinking adversaries.

Rarely did Christian mythographers crudely reduce pagan myths to simple, exclusive reflections of events or personages in the book of

---

[16] Ralph Cudworth, *The true intellectual system of the universe* (London, 1678), pp. 225, 228–9.
[17] Robert Taylor, *The diegesis; being a discovery of the origin, evidences, and early history of Christianity* (London, 1829), p. 174.

Genesis. More typically, they advanced double- or multiple-pronged theses in which pagan mythologies were seen as hybrids – portions of distorted Judaeo-Christian memory combined with some kind of mythological representation of nature. For instance, astronomical theories abounded. Many mythographers read pagan myths as solar or zodiacal allegories. The most influential strain of mythographical orthodoxy in late eighteenth- and early nineteenth-century England was the helio-arkite theory of Jacob Bryant – a prototype of Mr Casaubon – who reduced pagan myths to compound structures derived both from memories of Noah's Flood and from worship of the sun.[18] Another common trope rested upon the identification of heathen religions as the worship of what were politely called the generative powers of nature. Put more crudely, this involved a priapic interpretation of mythology. Were most pagan myths ultimately allegories of the sexual act?[19] Needless to say, such strategies could be turned by clever freethinkers against their orthodox begetters. Some freethinkers, especially from the late eighteenth century onwards, began to explore the question of whether Christianity itself might take its rise from an allegory of this sort.[20] Arguments devised with reference to pagan religions in order to expose their origins in fiction could just as easily be applied to Christianity itself.

Protestant critics of 'pagano-popery' argued that Roman Catholicism was more Roman than Christian; infected with the *genius loci* of pre-Christian Rome, Roman Catholicism had at first, perhaps, unconsciously inherited – or, more probably, under the sway of a wily priesthood, had consciously borrowed, and certainly perpetuated – the deities and rites of ancient Roman paganism. The eternal city and its heathen legends remained central to the culture of supposedly – but only nominally – Catholic Rome. However, Protestant complacency about this exposure of Romish pretensions was misplaced. For from the second quarter of the eighteenth century onwards, a new strain of subversive freethinking argument began to wear away at the rock of heathendom on which Protestant Christianity too appeared to rest. If Roman Catholicism was to all intents and purposes a repackaging of Roman mythology – with a gallery of saints standing in for a polytheistic pantheon of deities – was there not a danger that, however reformed it might claim to be, Protestantism too bore the taint of paganism?

---

[18] See below, ch. 4.
[19] Cf. J. Godwin, *The theosophical enlightenment* (Albany, NY, 1994), pp. 1–24.
[20] Richard Payne Knight, *An account of the remains of the worship of Priapus* (London, 1786); Knight, *An inquiry into the symbolical language of ancient art and mythology* (London, 1818).

One plausible answer to this sort of question, of course, was to differentiate between the inner truth of a religion and its accidental outer trappings. Indeed, mythographers spent a great deal of energy exploring the differences between the inner kernel of ancient religions and their outer husks. This distinction tends to be known as the 'double doctrine': the hypothesis that the ancient polytheistic outer claddings of pagan religions often concealed inner esoteric religions of much greater philosophical sophistication, possibly even monotheisms or the relics of earlier monotheisms. A central battlefield of mythographical debate during the early modern era concerned this question of how one drew the line between outer fable and inner philosophy, between the patent nonsense of ancient mythologies and the striking philosophical achievements of the cultures which appeared to succour them. Surely intellectually credible figures such as Plato and Cicero did not fall for the rubbish vaunted by the societies in which they lived? This opened a further chink into the cultures of classical antiquity. Might some of the esoteric mystery cults of classical civilisation have harboured monotheistic truths which ran counter to the official outer religions of ancient paganism? Might ancient paganisms have sustained core elements – or perhaps only the faintest glimpses – of patriarchal Judaeo-Christian truth? The double doctrine certainly complicated the early modern picture of classical paganism and created opportunities for Christian interpretations of ancient polytheism.

One particular body of mythography addressed the relationship between Homeric mythology and the Bible. To what extent, Christian mythographers wondered, were patriarchal Christian truths embedded in the works of Homer? This aspect of the Homeric question was a live issue in the second half of the seventeenth and early eighteenth centuries, in works such as Zachary Bogan's *Homerus Hebraizon* (1658), James Duport's *Homeri Gnomologia* (1660) and *Homeros Hebraios* (1704) by the Dutch scholar Gerard Croese;[21] and it still occupied the attentions of Britain's Prime Minister, William Gladstone, in the second half of the nineteenth century.[22]

Despite the reductive associations of the term 'key to all mythologies', mythographers tended in fact to combine some of these basic strategies, rather than confining themselves to rigidly unitarist theories of how myths had originated. Mythography – whatever its faults, illusions and delusions – was a sophisticated branch of intellectual life, rich in hybrids. The Anglican

---

[21] K. Simosuuri, *Homer's original genius* (Cambridge, 1979), pp. 146–52.
[22] D. Bebbington, *The mind of Gladstone: religion, Homer, and politics* (Oxford, 2004).

cleric Arthur Young (1693–1759), for instance, stressed that idolatry arose 'insensibly and by degrees', both through identification of the planets as mediators between humans and a supreme deity and the deification of dead kings and leaders, most prominent among them Ham, the son of Noah. Indeed, a multiplicity of deities in the teeming pantheons of supposed polytheists turned out on closer inspection to be versions of Ham. The idolatrous worship of statues only came later, but the ebbing of paganism was similarly gradual, and Young could not resist a few jibes at the idolatrous residues still manifest in the Church of Rome.[23] In a similar vein to Young's, Faber emphasised pagan deifications of Noah (this in itself a combination of patriarchal inheritance and Euhemerism), but noted how this had existed in combination with a kind of astral mythologising; hence the seemingly oxymoronic 'solar fish-god'.[24] Hybrid strategies were also found in the ranks of freethinking mythographers; Richard Payne Knight (1750–1824) interwove an interpretation focusing on the priapic origins of pagan mythology with the recognition of pagan continuities in Roman Catholicism.[25]

Moreover, there was considerable cross-pollination within mythography between different confessions and national traditions. British mythographers commonly referred to leading Catholic mythographers, such as Huet, or to the French Huguenot scholar, Samuel Bochart (1599–1667), for whom Noah was the prototype for heathen legend.[26] Indeed, distinctive sub-genres of Christian mythography flourished in different confessions and contexts. None was more vivid than Figurism, which emerged within the French Jesuit mission in China. The leading Figurists – such as Joachim Bouvet (1656–1730), Jean-François Foucquet (1665–1741) and Joseph-Henri-Marie de Prémare (1666–1736) – contended that the supposed founding deity of ancient China, Fo Hi (Fu Xi) was identical with Zoroaster and Hermes Trismegistus, his identity ultimately revealed as the Old Testament patriarch, Enoch. Moreover, in the ancient classics of Chinese literature, most notably the *I ching*, the Figurists detected foreshadowings of the coming of Christ.[27] Notwithstanding the sympathetic

---

[23] Arthur Young, *An historical dissertation on idolatrous corruptions in religion* (2 vols., London, 1734), vol. I, pp. 25, 28, 31–2, 39, 72–4, 79–80, 85–90, 97, 107, 116, 120, 124.
[24] George Stanley Faber, *A dissertation on the mysteries of the Cabiri* (2 vols., Oxford, 1803).
[25] Knight, *Account of the remains*.
[26] Samuel Bochart, *Geographiae sacrae pars prior Phaleg seu de dispersione gentium* (Caen, 1646), esp. lib. I, cap i, pp. 1–11.
[27] A. H. Rowbotham, 'The Jesuit Figurists and eighteenth-century religious thought', *Journal of the History of Ideas*, vol. 17 (1956), pp. 471–85; D. E. Mungello, *Curious land: Jesuit accommodation and the origins of sinology* (1985: Honolulu, 1989), pp. 307–28; I. Landry-Deron, *La preuve par la Chine* (Paris, 2002), p. 18; N. Standaert (ed.), *Handbook of Christianity in China vol. I* (Leiden, 2001), pp.

depth of the Figurists' immersion in Chinese culture, mythography was at bottom about 'us' rather than 'them'. Christian mythography at its most misguidedly brilliant was a matter of finding oneself in the other.

The ramparts of Christian orthodoxy were adorned by some curious crenellations. Pagan mythology turned out to be a widely authenticated and seemingly impregnable vindication of the early portions of the Book of Genesis. How strange and unlikely this seems to us; quite apart from any lack of commitment we might have to Christianity as doctrine, this seems – even within the logic of Christianity itself – to be a revolt against reason. Many early modern theologians would have agreed on this last point. It seemed only common sense to them too that heathendom was a gross inversion of Christianity, defined as the polar opposite of Christian truth. However, for others the relationship between Christianity and paganism was one rather of adulteration. Naturally, the pure message of Christian truth had been overlaid by misunderstandings, fantastical accretions and other unwanted excrescences, but beneath these there lurked something true. To the polemical mythographer heathen mythology and idolatry were not the opposites of Christian truth; rather they were its corruptions, however curdled and mouldy, which had over time solidified – sometimes in bizarre indigestible clumps of legend – out of the milk of patriarchal Christianity. An able mythographer, however, was able to separate the curds and whey of pagan corruption and the patriarchal religion.

By the age of Mr Casaubon in the first third of the nineteenth century, Anglican apologetics had become seriously committed – not wholly, but quite substantially – to the cause of mythographical evidences. Providence, it seemed, achieved its ends by way of the most sublime paradox: heathen error, unbeknown to its deluded votaries, ultimately disclosed Christian truth. Beneath the illusion of mythological heterogeneity there lurked a singular history. Properly deciphered, every one of the world's pagan mythologies bore unexpectedly impartial witness to the historical veracity of the first ten chapters of Genesis, the common past of all humankind, heathen as well as Judaeo-Christian. Encounters with new religions, new civilisations, and even with the most primitive fringes of the inhabited world did nothing to disprove this thesis, and instead provided ever more exotic confirmations of the truth of Genesis. How had this come about?

668–76; J. Spence, *The question of Hu* (1988: New York, 1989), pp. 14–15; F. Perkins, *Leibniz and China* (Cambridge, 2004), pp. 9–10.

In the first instance, we must examine the reason why mythography had come to assume a probative function within the theology of evidences. In the realm of Christian apologetics there were, basically, two types of evidence which confirmed the truths of Christianity. First, there was internal evidence, which lay in the perfection of scripture as well as its overall harmony and doctrinal coherence. In *A View of the Internal Evidence of the Christian Religion* (1776) Soame Jenyns (1704–87) argued that Christianity, unlike the general run of the world's religions, was no mere 'human imposture', but bore 'clear marks of supernatural interposition'. In particular, the penetrating moral insights and ethical coherence of Christianity – by comparison with pagan religions – provided compelling evidence of its 'divine origin'. Moreover, how did a religion which lacked any political support manage to conquer the known world under the leadership of a carpenter's son followed by 'twelve of the meanest and most illiterate mechanics'? Without the providential sponsorship of supernatural power, this task would have been an impossibility. The internal evidences, Jenyns contended, demonstrated that Christianity was an authentically supernatural religion.[28] Needless to say this seemed a tad subjective, even by comparison with the manifest flaws of other religions. Greater objectivity seemed to be offered by external evidences, whereby the claims of Christianity were measured against some external standard. Miracles and prophecies offered external criteria for the assessment of Christian truth. The suspension of the laws of nature or accurate predictions of later happenings bolstered Christianity's claims to supernatural authority. During the Enlightenment external evidences had been exposed to considerable critical fire, not least from Hume's devastating deconstruction of the evidential authority for miracles.[29] 'Enlightened' critics of scripture were no longer convinced by either the internal or external evidences. The internal and external evidences still dominated the field of apologetics, but in the wake of Hume's scepticism seemed wobbly. As a result, an alternative apologetic tactic came to assume a more significant role in polemical divinity. This involved the invocation of a third category of evidences, often called 'collateral evidences'. Here Christianity received independent corroboration from outside the faith – from the testimonies, surprisingly enough, of heathendom. Casaubon's 'key to all mythologies' concerned Christian evidences of this third kind. Bryant, whose career

---

[28] Soame Jenyns, *A view of the internal evidence of the Christian religion* (4th edn, London, 1776), esp. pp. 2, 7, 36, 101–6, 110.

[29] David Hume, *An enquiry concerning human understanding* (1748: Indianapolis, 1993), section x, pp. 72–90.

provided one of the principal models for Casaubon's quest, claimed that attacks on scripture made 'it necessary to accumulate these additional proofs' from heathen cultures for the authority of the Bible.[30] Arguably the search for collateral evidences was the principal motivation behind the intellectual career of Sir William Jones (1746–94), now best remembered for his discovery of the Indo-European language group. According to Jones's friend, Sir John Shore, later Lord Teignmouth (1751–1834), Jones's 'researches had corroborated the multiplied evidence of revelation'.[31]

Under the will of the Reverend John Hulse (1708–90), the Hulsean Lectures at Cambridge were endowed to combat atheism and deism, not only by demonstrating the evidences for Christianity found in prophecies and miracles but also by advancing 'any other proper and useful arguments, whether the same be direct or collateral proofs of the Christian religion'.[32] Collateral proofs featured occasionally in the Bampton Lectures at Oxford, which were first delivered in 1780 and whose purposes included the confirmation and establishment of the Christian faith and the confutation of heretics. The mythographical deployment of collateral proofs was most apparent in Faber's Bampton lectures of 1801, entitled *Horae Mosaicae*, in John Carwithen's 1809 lectures *A view of the Brahminical Religion*, and as late as 1859 in George Rawlinson's *Historical Evidences of the Truth of the Scripture Records*.

Christian apologists had long used pagan testimony to buttress their claims for the divinity of Christ and the historicity of the New Testament. Thomas Dawson, the vicar of New Windsor, invoked the authority of the second-century pagan writer, Phlegon of Tralles, whose annals covering the long history of the Olympiads mentioned an eclipse at the time of Christ's passion. This portentous darkening of the sky had occurred around the fourth year of the two hundred and second Olympiad, in the eighteenth year of the reign of Tiberius. Remarkably, by comparing Chinese and classical chronologies, it appeared that the eclipse was further confirmed in the Chinese annals. Evidence which came from an adversary, Dawson argued, enjoyed a particularly high level of credibility. It was for this reason, he explained, 'that the Fathers in the early times of Christianity, took an

---

[30] Jacob Bryant, *A new system, or, an analysis of ancient mythology* (2nd edn, 3 vols., London, 1775–6), vol. II, p. 534.
[31] Sir John Shore, 'A discourse delivered at a meeting of the Asiatic Society in Calcutta, on the 22nd May 1794', in William Jones (ed.), *Eleven discourses* (Calcutta, 1875), p. viii.
[32] *Abstract of the Rev. John Hulse's will, dated the 21st of July 1777* (Cambridge?, 1790?), p. 7. See e.g. Richard Chenevix Trench, *Christ the desire of all nations, or the unconscious prophecies of heathendom: being the Hulsean Lectures for the year MDCCCXLVI* (Cambridge, 1846).

especial care to corroborate the doctrines of their religion, by the evidence which they alleged out of the most eminent heathen writers'.[33] Various scholars amassed evidences from pagan authorities which appeared to provide independent witness to the historical truth of the New Testament. The Christian story gained added force from the testimony of adversaries; not only were historians such as Tacitus and Suetonius of the utmost reliability, whatever biases they possessed were obviously not pro-Christian. Such was the rationale of Gregory Sharpe (1713–71), a Fellow of the Royal Society, who in 1755 produced *An argument in defence of Christianity, taken from the concessions of the most antient adversaries, Jews and pagans, philosophers and historians*. In the ranks of Dissent, the English Presbyterian minister Nathaniel Lardner (1684–1768) gathered *A large collection of ancient Jewish and heathen testimonies to the truth of the Christian religion* in four volumes between 1764 and 1767.

However, it was not just the gospel which could be corroborated from pagan evidence. The Old Testament too, and even the earliest parts of the Pentateuch might, it transpired, receive an unlikely – and because unlikely all the more robust – vindication from pagan sources. But, whereas for the New Testament this was a straightforward matter of correlating statements in pagan historians such as Suetonius and Tacitus with the gospel, as a means of providing independent non-Christian verification of the existence of Christ, for the Old Testament, and the earliest parts of the Pentateuch in particular, the methods deployed were much more oblique and decidedly ingenious.

Hearing secret harmonies between patriarchal Christianity and heathenism constituted the special gift of the Christian mythographer. What was conventionally derided as the barbaric din of pagan mythology might, it seemed, be reinterpreted more sensitively by scholars attuned to the distorting processes by which the sublime music of patriarchal truth had been transformed into the empty noise of heathen legend. Was paganism absolutely devoid of Judaeo-Christian intimations, or had God allowed Himself, by one means or another, the odd nod and wink to the gentile nations?

Mythography enabled Christian apologists to harvest the windfall fruits of paganism. Heathen idolatry, it seemed, provided a window onto the religious transformations of primeval antiquity, and, by extension, established a verifying link between pagan evidence and the truths of the

---

[33] Thomas Dawson, *An appeal to the genuine records and testimonies of heathen and Jewish writers; in defence of Christianity* (London, 1733), part I, pp. 13, 17–21, 43–4.

Pentateuch. Sometimes, indeed, mythology offered a supplement to other kinds of proof, such as those drawn from the natural sciences, as in Vernon Harcourt's *Doctrine of the Deluge*, which Eliot mocked so mercilessly.[34] The point here was corroboration. Pagan mythology bolstered other kinds of evidence, including, most obviously, geological catastrophism. Alexander Lindsay, the 25th Earl of Crawford (1812–80), argued that geological evidences for an historic deluge were 'corroborated in the strongest manner by the traditions of all nations'. On this point, the flood legends of many peoples, from the Greeks, Romans, Persians, Hindus and Chinese to the Mexicans and Sandwich Islanders, were so 'very closely approximate to the Mosaic account'.[35]

Although Hume's assault on miracles had challenged – in some eyes undermined – a central category of external evidence, collateral evidences offered an unexpected means of conserving the claims for supernatural interposition in the history of the world. For instance, the Reverend William Adams invoked collateral proofs in his rebuttal of Hume's critique of miracles, noting that the events of the Pentateuch, however miraculous, were 'corroborated by the strongest concurring testimony', not least the 'memory of a general flood' which 'seems to have been preserved for some ages among almost all nations'.[36] The Reverend Joseph Townsend of Pewsey in Wiltshire reckoned that a special authority inhered in evidence vindicating sacred history which came from 'profane authors, who could have no inclination to mislead our judgment'.[37]

In his very influential *Elements of Christian Theology* (1799), which had gone through twelve editions by 1818, George Pretyman (later Pretyman Tomline) (1750–1827), the Bishop of Lincoln, was spoilt for choice in his selection of collateral proofs for the authenticity of the Pentateuch. In so many respects did 'the most ancient histories and earliest traditions very remarkably coincide with the Pentateuch' that he found it 'easy to bring forward nearly demonstrative evidence to prove the positive agreement of antiquity with the narrative of the sacred historian'. Creation stories, accounts of a 'golden age, when man had open intercourse with heaven', the necessity of sacrifice, the existence of an evil spirit ill-disposed to humanity, a 'general deluge', and even the hope of 'universal happiness' which might be 'restored, through the intercession of a mediator' – all these components of Egyptian, Phoenician, Greek, Roman and now also,

---

[34] Vernon Harcourt, *The doctrine of the deluge* (2 vols., London, 1838).
[35] Alexander Lindsay, *A letter to a friend on the evidences and theory of Christianity* (London, 1841), p. 36.
[36] William Adams, *An essay on Mr Hume's Essay on Miracles* (London, 1752), pp. 115–16.
[37] Joseph Townsend, *The character of Moses established for veracity as an historian* (2 vols., Bath, 1813–15), vol. I, p. 18.

it seemed from recent discoveries, Hindu mythology, provided 'singularly striking' corroboration of the historic truth of the Old Testament. Often, of course, these 'facts' of Mosaic history were 'mixed with fable', 'wrapped up' in pagan 'mysteries' and 'disguised' by 'fanciful conceits', yet they might be 'evidently discerned', Pretyman asserted, lurking behind the bizarre accretions of legend.[38]

The key to all mythology depended on the notion that Scripture had a hinterland. Beyond the text of the Bible itself and the sacred history of God's chosen people lay the question of what had happened to the descendants of Ham and Japhet, not forgetting, of course, the non-Israelite descendants of Shem. In this realm of para-theology there was another set of stories to be told about how the Ur-Judaic peoples of patriarchal times had become the pagan gentiles of antiquity, or more precisely about the ways in which the religion of Noah had degenerated into various polytheistic pantheons, sets of absurd fables and collections of bizarre and unseemly legends. Scholars attempted to wrestle with the knotty chronological problems involved in reconciling scripture history with the histories of these other pagan peoples in a genre known as the 'connection'. Within the Anglican world this genre was established by Humphrey Prideaux (1648–1724), the Dean of Norwich, who between 1716 and 1718 published *The Old and New Testament connected in the history of the Jews and neighbouring nations*, which went through numerous editions in the eighteenth century, and was still being republished in 1851. However, other scholars pursued such 'connections' *avant la lettre*. Richard Cumberland sought 'synchronisms' between ancient pagan legends and the chronology of sacred history.[39] Isaac Newton too, in *The Chronology of Ancient Kingdoms amended* (1728), attempted to calibrate the events of sacred and profane antiquity. As Prideaux's 'connection' only began in 747 BC, the Reverend Samuel Shuckford (1693/4–1754) produced a prequel, *The sacred and profane history of the world connected, from the creation* (1728–37).[40] The genre continued to flourish into the nineteenth century. Other contributions included the *Chronological Antiquities* (1752) of John Jackson (1686–1763) and the various works of the astronomer-cum-mythographer George Costard (1710–82).[41] In 1816 Robert Gray (1762–1834), the future Bishop

---

[38] George Pretyman, *Elements of Christian theology* (1799: 3rd edn, 2 vols., London, 1800), vol. I, pp. 37, 42–4, 47–8.
[39] Richard Cumberland, *Sanchoniatho's Phoenician History* (London, 1720), p. 301.
[40] For Shuckford, see R. J. Arnold, 'Learned lumber: the unlikely survival of sacred history in the eighteenth century', *English Historical Review*, vol. 125 (2010), pp. 1139–72.
[41] See e.g. George Costard, *A further account of the rise and progress of astronomy amongst the antients* (Oxford, 1748); Costard, *The uses of astronomy in history and chronology* (London, 1764); Costard, *The history of astronomy* (London, 1767).

of Bristol, produced *The connection between the sacred writings and the literature of Jewish and heathen authors, particularly that of the classical ages, illustrated, principally with a view to evidence in confirmation of the truth of revealed religion.* Gray, indeed, provided a compelling theological justification for the study of the classics, against carping zealots who questioned why young men should be so much exposed to the erroneous values of profane antiquity. Pagan writings, he insisted, offered an 'independent and collateral report' confirming the truths of sacred history, not least by way of 'the gradually perverted representations' which heathen records 'give of revealed doctrines and institutions'. Of course, Gray conceded, there was also a great deal of falsehood, fantasy and nonsense in pagan literature, but when 'searching the mines of antiquity, we must be satisfied with a few remnants of sacred ore recovered from amidst the dross'. The very fact that these 'subsidiary proofs' of Christian truth were found 'casually scattered' in the works of writers 'who had no interest to confirm the sacred accounts' meant that – however small a portion of pagan mythology – they enjoyed even greater apologetic authority.[42] The 'connection' genre was not exclusive to England. In Scotland, the Episcopalian Bishop of Glasgow and Galloway, Michael Russell (1781–1848), compiled *A connection of sacred and profane history: from the death of Joshua* (3 vols., London, 1827–37). Dr David Davidson in his *Connexion of Sacred and Profane History* (1842) brought into focus the affinity between the 'connexion' genre and the mythographical corroboration of scripture, asking 'who has examined idol and image worship, in all its forms, and not perceived that it carried strong marks of its original derivation from the religious worship of the patriarchs? Every false religion is a perverted imitation of the true.'[43]

Scholars sought, too, some kind of stable footing in the treacherous but dimly lit terrain at history's dawn. What evidence was there which might offer non-biblical corroboration for the truths set out in the early chapters of the book of Genesis? Obviously, the Greek and Latin classics were too far removed – both geographically and chronologically – from the scene of the action at Eden, the land of Nod, Ararat, Babel and the plain of Shinaar, to provide cogent support for Judaeo-Christian claims. Were there, perhaps, any other sources nearer to hand which might furnish external proof of the primeval events of sacred history? There was, it transpired, not much to go on, but a few fragmentary sources nonetheless, in which a great amount

---

[42] Robert Gray, *The connection between the sacred writings and the literature of Jewish and heathen authors, particularly that of the classical ages, illustrated, principally with a view to evidence in confirmation of the truth of the revealed religion* (2nd edn, 2 vols., London, 1819), vol. I, pp. 1, 3, 5, 34.

[43] David Davidson, *Connexion of sacred and profane history* (Edinburgh, 1842), p. 11.

of apologetic effort was invested. Although obscure now even to experts, several ancient fragments – sometimes fragments of fragments (or possibly 'works' foisted on non-existent authors by later 'editors' and 'translators') – became canonised as an authoritative body of evidence on the dimmest dawn of sacred history. This canon of authorities – Sanchoniathon, Manetho and Berosus – makes an appearance in Oliver Goldsmith's novel *The Vicar of Wakefield* (1766),[44] but has otherwise slipped out of modern notice. However, things were otherwise in the eighteenth and nineteenth centuries. Sanchoniathon, an ancient Phoenician author, was a much-cited figure in early modern apologetic literature. Parts of Sanchoniathon's work on the creation and mythological history had been translated into Greek by the similarly obscure Philo of Byblos, fragments of which were in turn preserved in the work of the Christian author Eusebius.[45] A similar fanfare accompanied the name of Berosus, a Babylonian priest, quoted by Abydenus, whose account of ancient Mesopotamia discussed the creation of the world, the prediluvian world and the coming of a great flood. Indeed, Berosus seemed to provide compelling heathen confirmation of Noah under the character of Xisuthrus. In chapter 8 of *Middlemarch*, Dorothea's uncle and guardian, Mr Brooke – a philistine huntin'-shootin'-fishin' type, but with a surprising fund of overheard learning – alludes to Berosus and the Sumerian flood myth: 'I know no harm of Casaubon. I don't care about his Xisuthrus and Fee-fo-fum and the rest; but then he doesn't care about my fishing tackle.'[46] Fee-fo-fum is probably an allusion to the Chinese deity Fo, also believed to be, like Xisuthrus, a distorted memory of Noah. Berosus's text also included a reference to Oannes – a creature half-fish, half-man – who was also read by his early modern interpreters as an emblem of Noah. Manetho was an Egyptian writer, purportedly a member of the priestly hierarchy, whose work, excerpted in Josephus and other later authors, listed the earliest dynasties of the kings of Egypt and other ancient events.

Freethinkers were unconvinced by these dubiously preserved sources. Viscount Bolingbroke (1678–1751), in his *Letters on the study and use of history*, contended that little reliance should be placed on profane sources which survived extant only in patristic writings. What reliance could be placed on materials which were 'conveyed to posterity' and 'digested' according to the theological 'system' which their editors, translators and

---

[44] Oliver Goldsmith, *The vicar of Wakefield* (1766: New York, 2007), p. 65.
[45] H. W. Attridge and R. A. Oden (eds.), *Philo of Byblos: the Phoenician history* (Washington, DC, 1981).
[46] Eliot, *Middlemarch*, ch. 8, p. 95.

collators were committed to sustaining? Here, surely, mythology and history proper parted company? Yet as late as the 1830s, Sharon Turner (1768–1847), in his *Sacred History of the World*, reckoned Berosus's history of the flood 'impressive testimony to the reality of the catastrophe, and of its moral causes'.[47] Indeed, Sanchoniathon, Berosus and Manetho provided a continuous backbone of source material for apologetic mythographers between the early eighteenth century and the publication of *Middlemarch*. In 1720 Squier Payne, the son-in-law and domestic chaplain of Richard Cumberland (1632–1718), the Bishop of Peterborough, published his late father-in-law's translation of *Sanchoniatho's Phoenician History*. The commentary and apparatus made it clear that Cumberland had seen himself as engaged in clearing ancient history of the errors superimposed on scripture history by the pretensions of Phoenician idolatry. A century later, in 1828, Isaac Preston Cory (1802–42), a Fellow of Caius College, Cambridge, whose apologetic project remained similar in outline to that of Cumberland, published *The ancient fragments; containing what remains of the writings of Sanchoniatho, Berossus, Abydenus, Megasthenes and Manetho* (London, 1828).

The highest form of the collateral evidences lay in what we might now call, after Eliot, 'the key to all mythologies', an attempt to systematise the jumble of the world's mythologies as vindications of Biblical truth, which flourished from the late eighteenth century. Once one had identified within paganism a core of Creation myths, myths of golden ages and falls, serpent myths, flood myths and so forth, the resemblances to the book of Genesis were obvious and overwhelming. By the early nineteenth century, heathen mythology occupied – at the very least – an important niche in English Protestant apologetic. The current state of advanced apologetics ran as follows: that heathenism was a riddle whose solution, through the cunning of providence, had been conveniently bequeathed to modern-day Christians in order that they might apply modern learning and scholarship to see off the scepticism and infidelity of the radical Enlightenment.

It was no longer the case that a pagan proof of Christian truth was *ipso facto* an absurdity. For sophisticated Casaubonish mythographers, Truth lay concealed in error; for their more conventionally-minded opponents within the Church, heathen error should never be elevated to the level even of quasi-truth, and it was a gross delusion to scavenge for vindications of Christianity in the rubbish of idolatry. Of course, if the tradition of Jewish–Christian revelation was unique, then other intimations of the

---

[47] Bolingbroke, *Letters on the study and use of history* (London, 1752), p. 8; Sharon Turner, *The sacred history of the world* (3 vols., London, 1832–9), vol. II, pp. 312–13.

numinous and divine were frauds of one sort or another. But the very fact that God had revealed Himself at different times and in different ways to Jews as well as Christians opened up the possibility – no more than that, perhaps – that other peoples might have been vouchsafed something of the divine truth.

Nor is the key to all mythologies quite as nonsensical as readers of *Middlemarch* might initially imagine. Today we are familiar with the ways in which the various deities of the Greek and Roman pantheons map onto one another. Just as the Greek gods had their counterparts in the Roman pantheon, so apologetic mythographers of the eighteenth and nineteenth centuries related pagan deities in a very similar way to what they believed to be the original *historical* characters they represented in the book of Genesis. Were there not in ancient paganisms, suggested Cumberland, 'a variety of names belonging to the same person'?[48] Might the Greek gods be revealed as derivations from other ancient polytheistic systems, whether from Egypt, say, or Babylon? Might there be, in fact, some ultimate Ur-source for the seemingly interchangeable deities of the polytheisms of antiquity? Might there be indeed a single cipher, or key, to all the world's mythologies? One tantalising possibility mapped ancient polytheistic deities onto Old Testament originals. Noah and his sons, it was argued, provided the models for all the polytheisms of the ancient Near East and Mediterranean, thus disproving the divinity of these spurious pantheons and by extension proving the historicity of the narrative set out in Genesis. The Reverend John Mead Ray (1754–1837), an Independent dissenting minister in Sudbury, thought that he could identify Noah's son Ham in Zeus, Japhet in Poseidon (or sometimes in the Titan Iapet), Canaan in Mercury, Nimrod in Bacchus, Cain's wife in Vesta, Tubal-Cain in Vulcan, and Adam and Eve in the Egyptian deities Osiris and Isis. On the other hand, the Roman deity Saturn was, Ray believed, a composite, drawn variously from primeval memories of Adam, Noah and Abraham.[49]

After all, interest in the collateral evidences was not confined to Anglicans. The Congregationalist theologian George Redford (1785–1860) contended that the 'ethnical traditions' of the world's heathens – Phoenicians, Persians, Mesopotamians, Greeks, Romans, Hindus, Chinese, Mexicans, Peruvians, North Americans, Tahitians – together provided 'presumptive truth' of the Deluge. Across the globe one encountered stories of

---

[48] Cumberland, *Sanchoniatho's Phoenician History*, p. 291.
[49] John Mead Ray, *Synopsis, or a comprehensive view of philosophical, political and theological systems, from the creation to the present time* (London?, 1792?), pp. 34, 147; [Ray], *An interpretation of the scriptures in the ancient Eastern manner* (London, 1797), pp. 86–7, 92–3.

a great flood which had destroyed a pre-existing race, apart from a select few preserved on 'some floating vessel'. Of course, the 'leading facts' were 'sometimes obscured by fabulous and absurd additions, or mythological fancies', yet they still included 'the grand catastrophe, together with the means stated by Moses, for the preservation of the human race from total extinction'. Ultimately, argued Redford, the teeming – or merely seeming – diversity of the world's mythologies scarcely disguised an underlying unity drawn from the earliest portions of Genesis: 'They all embody but one story.'[50]

According to Daniel Dewar (1788–1867), a Scots Presbyterian divine and Principal of Marischal College, Aberdeen, most pagan accounts of the Creation followed the Genesis pattern of a creation from chaos. More strikingly, while the division of time into days, months and years was obviously based on astronomical observation, from where did so many cultures derive the practice of dividing time into weeks of seven days, a practice which was otherwise 'perfectly arbitrary'? Distorted memories of the Fall were universal, the most obvious including the tale of Pandora and myths of a former golden age of innocence. The Garden of Eden gave rise not only to legends such as the tale of the garden of the Hesperides, but also to the widespread pagan practice of consecrating groves. 'Expiatory sacrifice' was also to be found universally, from the South Seas to the polytheisms of Greco-Roman antiquity. The translation of the patriarch Enoch into heaven was mirrored throughout the pagan world in the deification of heroes. Needless to say, the Flood featured in 'the traditionary testimony of almost all nations'. There were even heathen traditions of primeval human longevity which parroted Genesis. Cumulatively, and with such unerring precision in small – and seemingly arbitrary – details, the mythology of widely separated peoples 'confirms and demonstrates the authenticity of scripture'. The rich vein of 'absurdities' obvious in pagan religion had never 'totally' erased – only partially obscured – the ultimate provenance of all profane mythology.[51]

Nor should we imagine that the literature of evidences was an obscure byway only inhabited by enervated Casaubons. The contested terrain of Christian evidences would provide the central theme of one of the bestselling novels of the late nineteenth century, Mrs Humphry Ward's *Robert Elsmere* (1888). The novel's eponymous protagonist, a parish clergyman in

---

[50] George Redford, *Holy scripture verified* (London, 1837), pp. 112–13.
[51] Daniel Dewar, *Divine revelation; its evidences, external, internal and collateral* (2nd edn, London, 1854), pp. 234–45.

Surrey, loses his faith when exposed to the destructive arguments of the local squire, Roger Wendover, a hypnotic figure Gibbonian in his cosmopolitan background, sophistication and erudition, but whose taste for irony has a tendency to manifest itself in a brutal sarcasm. Wendover's *magnum opus* – 'a History of Evidence, or rather, more strictly, a History of Testimony' – he conceives as an antidote to apologetic. The 'history of human witness in the world, systematically carried through' (put more crudely, the study of witness to the miraculous), the squire perceives, constitutes a phase in an evolutionary history of ideas. The plot turns on the question of whether Christianity – as it is seen through the eyes of Elsmere – is supported by solid historical evidences or is itself a kind of mythology, the unreliable 'witness' of an 'incompetent, half-trained, pre-scientific' age of miracles. In the course of the novel Elsmere's former Oxford tutor, Langham, defines 'mythology' as 'ideas, or experiences personified', and suggests that these constitute 'the subject-matter of all theologies'. After a great deal of heart-searching as well as a difficult estrangement from his evangelical wife, who thinks the gospels worthless if they are not historically true, Elsmere abandons the supernatural 'fairy-tale' Christianity of the risen 'Man-God' and feels morally obliged to resign his social position as rector of a parish. Nevertheless, he holds fast to his deep-seated theism and to the achievements of Jesus as a moral teacher. Elsmere is, in fact, repelled by the anti-Christian satire and Painite raillery he finds among working-class radicals in London, and attempts to found a *demythologised* religion of Jesus, which he calls the New Brotherhood of Christ.[52] The question of evidences, it seems, remained a live one decades after the fictional Casaubon's supposed redundancy. Indeed, *Robert Elsmere* provoked a lengthy pained review from Britain's most prominent Christian intellectual, Gladstone, who thought that as a dramatic conflict of ideas the novel was wildly unbalanced and did not present the evidences for Christianity in a fair-minded way.[53]

The fascination of eighteenth- and nineteenth-century Christian theologians with the potential meanings and coded significance of paganism was far from novel or freakish, but derived from the central tension in the origins of European civilisation: how to reconcile the spiritual claims of Christianity with the bounteous and unmissable fruits of pagan culture.

---

[52] Mrs Humphry Ward, *Robert Elsmere* (1888: Oxford, 1987), pp. 68, 84, 181, 194–5, 261, 272, 274, 304, 307, 311–16, 332, 394–5, 457–8, 475–80, 550.
[53] W. E. Gladstone, 'Robert Elsmere and the battle of belief', *Nineteenth century* (May 1888), pp. 766–88; P. Waller, *Writers, readers and reputations: literary life in Britain 1870–1918* (Oxford, 2006), p. 1036; J. Sutherland, *Mrs Humphry Ward* (Oxford, 1990), pp. 127–8.

Paganism, as even the most devout Christian thinkers recognised, could not simply be consigned to oblivion. It needed to be accommodated. Indeed, this curious and seemingly eccentric entanglement had been part of the warp and woof of the Christian philosophical tradition from the very outset. In the first centuries of Christianity its intellectual leaders – themselves as often as not converted pagans, who wished to convert more of their former co-religionists to the new religion – had probed potential linkages between classical paganism and Christian truth. Syncretism – the aspiration to amalgamate different religions – was a common feature of primitive Christianity. Justin (c.100–c.165) perceived a convergence between Judaeo-Christian sacred history and the supposedly (but perhaps not altogether) profane heritage of heathen peoples in the coming of Christ. Surely divine truth was not exclusively confined to a single tradition? Were there perhaps intimations of Christ's coming and of the millennium in the Sibylline oracles and other pagan prophecies?[54] Other patristic writers tried to fuse Christian insights with pagan philosophy, particularly Platonic wisdom. Accommodation was both a proselytising tactic and, for some, a necessary groundwork for a philosophical theology. Origen (c.186–c.254), in particular, could scarcely conceive of a Christian theology which did not have its foundations in classical philosophy and ethics. Sometimes accommodation grew out of defensiveness. After all, early Christian apologists needed to answer pagan criticisms. Unsurprisingly, they drew at times on the dominant matter of their pagan surroundings in the ways they shaped and presented the new religion. The shadowy Egyptian Hermes Trismegistus was pressed into service as a pre-Christian witness to Christian truth, as was the poet Virgil. Plato too was retrospectively Christianised. Patristic writers plundered the oracular books of pagan theology in search of 'Christian proof texts'.[55] This trend reached its high point in the early fourth century in the works of Lactantius (c.240–c.320) who explored numerous connections between the Sibylline oracles and Christian truth, and also discerned cryptic versions of Christian truth semi-obscured in other pagan texts.[56] Indeed, Lactantius quoted the Sibyls more often than he quoted the Old Testament.[57] This strain of accommodation also received public reinforcement from the first Christian Emperor, Constantine, for whose

---

[54] H. Chadwick, *The early Church* (Harmondsworth, 1967), p. 78.
[55] R. Lane Fox, *Pagans and Christians* (1986: London, 1988), pp. 190, 415, 515–16, 520–1.
[56] Lactantius, *Divine institutes* (ed. and transl. A. Bowen and P. Garnsey, Liverpool, 2003), esp. pp. 65–72, 151–7, 427–37.
[57] B. D. Ehrman, *Forgery and counter-forgery: the use of literary deceit in early Christian polemics* (Oxford and New York, 2013), p. 515.

son Lactantius served as imperial court tutor. In a celebrated oration of 325 Constantine yoked both the Sibylline oracles and Virgil's fourth Eclogue to the Christian tradition.[58]

Various aspects of this patristic bequest were reinvigorated during the Renaissance. Had the civilised, law-bound peoples of pagan antiquity been abandoned totally to the squalor of utter falsehood and irreligion? Had they not acquired some knowledge of the truth? Otherwise, was it not rather embarrassing that Christianity was the religion of a less sophisticated people of Palestine? Surely, Christian Platonists reckoned, there was a scintilla, or more, of patriarchal truth in Greco-Roman civilisation? Was Homer a kind of minor prophet, who had preserved in his great poems aspects of the ancient patriarchal truth?[59] Was Plato a proto-Christian philosopher?[60] Had the Roman Sibyls – a line of female prophetesses supposedly descended from the wives of Noah and his sons – been entrusted, providentially, with the task of bringing the light of Truth, or a flickering illumination of a portion thereof, to the pagan gentiles?[61] Had the coming of Christ been vouchsafed to the ancient Romans centuries before His birth? Was Virgil too a kind of prophet manqué?[62] The evidences of the *prisca theologia*, the Sibylline verses and Virgil's remarkable Fourth Eclogue remained an important sub-strand of Christian apologetic throughout the early modern period and well into the nineteenth century.[63]

Here, of course, Isaac Casaubon himself represented a sceptical position that looked askance at naïve deployment of accommodationist ploys. Casaubon distanced himself from the seventeenth-century tendency to idolise the primitive Church Fathers precisely because patristic works casually made use of forgeries, whether of the Sibylline oracles or the supposed writings of Hermes Trismegistus.[64] Yet, notwithstanding Casaubon's cogent debunking of the authority and age of the Hermetic and Sibylline writings, in the latter case affirming their deconstruction by Johannes Opsopoeus (1556–96),[65] there were many theologians who

---

[58] Lane Fox, *Pagans and Christians*, pp. 605, 640–61, 680–1.
[59] Stroumsa, *New science*, pp. 49–57.
[60] Cf. J. Israel, *Enlightenment contested* (Oxford, 2006), p. 475.
[61] A. Grafton, *Forgers and critics* (London, 1990), pp. 73, 94–5.
[62] A. Grafton and J. Weinberg, '*I have always loved the holy tongue*': *Isaac Casaubon, the Jews and a forgotten chapter in renaissance scholarship* (Cambridge, MA, 2011), p. 35.
[63] Cf. D. P. Walker, *The ancient theology: studies in Christian Platonism from the fifteenth to the eighteenth century* (London, 1972); A. Ossa-Richardson, *The devil's tabernacle: the pagan oracles in early modern thought* (Princeton, 2013).
[64] J.-L. Quantin, *The Church of England and Christian Antiquity: the construction of a confessional identity in the seventeenth century* (Oxford, 2009), p. 147.
[65] A. Grafton, 'Higher criticism ancient and modern: the lamentable deaths of Hermes and the Sibyls', in A. Dionisotti, A. Grafton and J. Kraye (eds.), *The uses of Greek and Latin* (London, 1988), pp. 155–70, esp. pp. 168–9.

queried Casaubon's findings or their full implication, not least by suggesting that one might discriminate between authentic and inauthentic portions of the *prisca theologia*. As Frances Yates noted, many seventeenth-century theologians 'clung obstinately to the old obsessions', and even among Protestants there was a determination to salvage something from the wreckage.[66] The Laudian scholar Peter Heylin (1559–1662) noticed that 'Casaubon and some other of our great philologers' reckoned the Sibylline oracles to be mere '*piae fraudes*', deliberately forged 'to win credit for the faith of Christ', yet Heylin found it impossible to believe that the primitive church fathers would 'borrow help from falsehood to evict a truth'.[67]

On the other side, the French Huguenot scholar David Blondel (1599–1655) launched a direct attack on what he believed to be the Sibylline frauds in *Des sybilles célébrées* (1649), which was soon translated into English as *A Treatise of the Sibyls* (1661). Blondel believed that the Fathers, especially Justin Martyr, Clemens of Alexandria and Lactantius, had been duped by what seemed most probably a mid-second-century forgery. In particular, Blondel quashed the absurd notion that the first Sibyl had been one of Noah's daughters-in-law. Nor, Blondel argued, had Virgil been of the requisite standing to have gained access to whatever older Sibylline verses had been preserved in Rome. This issue was not a mere antiquarian sideshow remote from the main themes of Christian theology, for Blondel contended that the major errors of purgatory and prayers for the dead took their rise from the Sibylline forgeries.[68] However, Blondel's attempt to debunk the Sibylline tradition met an immediate response from John Twysden (1607–88), who reviewed the entire early modern canon of anti-Sibylline scholarship.[69]

Ralph Cudworth steered a judicious *via media* between the 'two extremes' of interpretation in his assessment of the standing of the Sibylline prophecies. To be sure, there was 'much counterfeit and suppositious stuff, in this Sibylline farrago', not least the 'pious and religious frauds' of well-meaning forgers among the early Christians. On the other hand, it was a mistake to assume that the entire corpus of Sibylline prophecies was 'a mere cheat and figment'. In particular, the Cumean Sibyl's prediction in

---

[66] F. Yates, *Giordano Bruno and the Hermetic tradition* (1964: London and New York, 1999), pp. 398, 431.
[67] Peter Heylin, *Cosmographie book iv* (London, 1652), p. 15.
[68] David Blondel, *A treatise concerning the Sibyls* (transl. J. Davies, London, 1661), see esp. pp. 3–6, 10–11, 34–9, 61, 97, 115, 132, 151–4.
[69] John Twysden, *A disquisition touching the Sibyls* (London, 1662).

Virgil's Fourth Eclogue, Cudworth felt, seemed to be an accurate foretelling of the coming of Christ.[70]

Argument on the question persisted, even in comparatively enlightened circles. The medic Sir John Floyer (1649–1734) claimed that the Sibylline oracles encapsulated 'the old antediluvian religion, and all the moral precepts communicated to Japhet's family'. As such the oracles provided 'clear proof' of the Christian religion.[71] The ecclesiastical historian Laurence Echard (c.1670–1730) argued that providence had paved the way for the Messiah in the pagan world, while critics questioned the authority of Hermes Trismegistus and the Sibyls, 'yet they were never fully disproved, their arguments being rather presumptions than proofs' (though some had indeed been forged by Platonist Christians in Alexandria).[72] Although the Reverend Robert Turner of Colchester detected 'many evident marks of forgery' in the extant Sibylline writings, he was more circumspect about the entire body of oracles, and reluctant to issue a general condemnation of the evidence that providence had prepared the pagan world – including the eastern magi – for the coming of Christ.[73] The English theologian and mathematician William Whiston (1667–1752) conceded that there were clearly some forgeries within the body of Sibylline oracles, but – equally – he insisted there was also a genuine core of authentic materials whose authenticity was surely confirmed 'by the light they give to a vast number of ancient traditions, notions and expectations, not to be derived but from them'. Whiston was excited by the persuasive apologetic potential of the Sibylline prophecies. The 'force of this evidence', he claimed, derived from the fact that ancient heathens had accepted these oracles notwithstanding the fact that the message of the Sibyls was otherwise 'very ungrateful to the pagans, and directly contrary to their inclinations, superstitions and practices' and thus – *prima facie* – 'not likely to find encouragement among them'. Yet the fact that pagans had nonetheless championed an oracular tradition which ran against the grain of their own religion proved the very robustness of this unexpected strain of evidence for the truth of sacred history. From the unlikeliest of sources lurking at the very heart of ancient paganism, contended Whiston, antiquaries were able to discern 'a new and very great confirmation' of Christian truth.[74] Over the next century and

---

[70] Cudworth, *True intellectual system*, pp. 281–4.
[71] John Floyer, *The Sibylline oracles* (London, 1713), 'Dedication', A2r–A3v.
[72] Laurence Echard, *A general ecclesiastical history* (2nd edn, 2 vols., London, 1710), vol. I, p. 35; vol. II, p. 461.
[73] Robert Turner, *The calumnies upon the primitive Christians accounted for* (London, 1727), pp. 201, 206, 209–10, 219–23.
[74] William Whiston, *A vindication of the Sibylline oracles* (London, 1715), pp. 36, 45, 48, 70–1, 84.

a half this insight would become the seemingly perverse hallmark of an apologetics of corroborative evidences: that confirmations of sacred truth drawn from the unholiest of wells, from the stagnant depths of pagan iniquity, were for that very reason of impeccable quality. Pagans could hardly be accused of forging testimonies in the cause of Christianity. That being the case, any indirect evidence for Christian truth which might seep out unawares from the writings of ancient pagans was all the more trustworthy because obviously not intended to support the case of their religious adversaries. Contrariness of this sort was nevertheless slow to gain acceptance.

Surveying the controversy over the Sibylline oracles, the nonconformist Biblical scholar Matthew Henry (1662–1714) noted that it had generally been Roman Catholic writers such as Baronius who had championed the authenticity of the Sibylline tradition, though some Protestants had also argued for the divine inspiration of the Sibyls. Nevertheless, the more conventionally Protestant line was that the Sibylline oracles constituted a pious – perhaps well-meaning – fraud, forged by early Christian writers.[75] For example, the Anglican historian John Jortin (1698–1770) reckoned that the oracles were 'from first to last, and without any one exception, mere impostures'.[76] Edward Chandler (1668?–1750), the Bishop of Lichfield and future Bishop of Durham, placed the pious fraud at an earlier stage, coming to the conclusion that the Sibylline oracles had been fabricated by the Jews.[77] Notwithstanding the question of their begetters, it seemed implausible, Henry warned, that the Sibyls seemed to 'speak so much more particularly and plainly concerning our Saviour and the future state than any of the prophets of the Old Testament do'. Henry found it difficult to 'conceive that heathen women' – the Sibyls – 'and those acted by demons, should speak more clearly and fully of the Messiah than those Holy Men did, who we are sure were moved by the Holy Ghost; or that the gentiles should be entrusted with larger and earlier discoveries of the great salvation, than that people of whom as concerning the flesh Christ was to come'.[78] It was counter-intuitive, and just plain wrong, to put more trust in pagans than in Christians; that was surely to put one's apologetic eggs in the wrong religious basket.

---

[75] Matthew Henry, 'Preface' (dated 1712), *An exposition of the prophetical books of the Old Testament* (London, 1721), p. iii.
[76] John Jortin, *Remarks on ecclesiastical history* (5 vols., London, 1751–75), vol. I, p. 284.
[77] Edward Chandler, *A vindication of the defence of Christianity from the prophecies of the Old Testament* (2 vols., London, 1728), vol. II, pp. 472–502.
[78] Henry, 'Preface', *Exposition*, p. iii.

Robert Lowth, the renowned Hebrew scholar and future Bishop of London, wandered in a fug of embarrassed perplexity when contemplating the vision set out in Virgil's Fourth Eclogue. It seemed all too wonderful, an uncannily accurate prophecy; and yet how, this scrupulous eighteenth-century scholar wondered, was it to be explained? Lowth certainly did not reject the Sibylline tradition, but feared to venture beyond vague and anodyne articulations of amazement which left plenty of scope to perform a future about-turn if circumstances demanded.[79] These cautious remarks earned Lowth some condescending praise from Edward Gibbon in a footnote to a section of the *Decline and Fall* which discussed the Sibylline and Virgilian 'proofs': 'In the examination of the fourth eclogue, the respectable Bishop of London has displayed learning, taste, ingenuity, and a temperate enthusiasm, which exalts the fancy without degrading his judgment.'[80]

The Sibylline prophecies would remain a potent apologetic tool into the nineteenth century. Samuel Horsley (1733–1806), the High Church Bishop of St Asaph,[81] contended that by way of the supposed Sibylline prophecies the Romans had preserved evidence from the patriarchal era of the future coming of a Messiah. Thus there had been a universal 'expectation' among the pagan Romans in the years leading up to Christ's birth – evidenced, of course, in the work of Virgil – that a 'great personage' was to 'arise in some part of the East for the general advantage of mankind'. Not that the prophecies were quite what the Romans advertised them to be. The Romans had inherited written records of ancient promises made by God to the patriarchs of the Old Testament, but had lost sight of their pedigree, though not their message and importance. Notwithstanding the pagan corruptions which followed the ancient dispersal of humankind and the inevitable distancing of the lines of Japhet and Ham especially from the chosen people of Israel, the divine promises were 'preserved' and 'carefully laid up under the care of the priests', becoming 'a part of the treasure of the heathen temples'. Nevertheless, their true provenance was forgotten and another foisted upon these sacred records. The Sibyls were 'fabulous personages, to whom the ignorant heathens ascribed the most ancient of their sacred books, when the true origin of them was forgotten'. Nor were the Romans alone among pagan peoples in preserving specific prophecies

---

[79] Robert Lowth, *De sacra poesi Hebraeorum* (Oxford, 1775), pp. 289–93; see also the translation, Lowth, *Lectures on the sacred poetry of the Hebrews* (2 vols., London, 1787), vol. II, pp. 103–20.
[80] Edward Gibbon, *The history of the decline and fall of the Roman Empire* (ed. D. Womersley, 3 vols.), vol. I, p. 744.
[81] F. C. Mather, *High Church prophet: Samuel Horsley (1733–1806) and the Caroline tradition in the later Georgian Church* (Oxford, 1992).

of the coming of Christ. Among the Persians, a similar set of patriarchal promises was attributed to the ancient magus Hystaspes, who had collated them, but was, of course, not their true author.[82] More conventionally, the Scottish theologian Sir Henry Moncrieff Wellwood (1809–83) reckoned that the Sibylline verses were forgeries of the first three centuries AD 'intended, very absurdly, to furnish, an argument for Christianity, from pretended pagan divinations'.[83]

Too often we straightforwardly assume that Christian theologians have universally despised pagan idolatry as a farrago of wickedness. However, at certain times there was no such consensus. For several cohorts of theologians, heathen myths were not diabolic *fictions* so much as unhappy distortions of primeval *fact*. Strange as it may seem, some sophisticated Christian theologians believed – up to a point – in the truth of Greek mythology; that is, in the underlying grounds of veracity on top of which baroque confabulations of the most preposterous kind had arisen. The rubbish of ancient heathendom was not entirely dross; properly filtered it yielded what was for the Christian apologist the purest form of gold – unimpeachable (precisely because it was heathen) witness to the truth of the Old Testament. Put another way, idolatry – in some quarters at least – was much less an outright abomination than a very revealing perversion, one which might yield up vital testimony of the historical truth which underlay the earliest portions of Genesis.

Within the discipline of mythography, there was a subtle blurring of the cartoonish primary-coloured opposition of Christian truth and idolatrous un-truth. For some accommodationists, paganism constituted a shaded zone of partially remembered truth. The most daring of mythographers perceived that heathenism might provide a forge for the production of apologetic weaponry with which to smite deistic scoffers.

Considered in the light of the grand narratives we inherit of Reformation and Enlightenment, idolatry is a loaded term freighted with negative associations. Yet, as we shall see, quite contrary to our received assumptions, idolatry came to enjoy an ironic purchase on Protestant apologetic in England by the late Enlightenment. Although for many Christians paganism loomed obvious as the antithesis of Christianity, for some ingenious commentators heathen mythology represented rather the putrefaction of

---

[82] Samuel Horsley, 'A dissertation on the prophecies of the Messiah dispersed among the heathen', in Horsley, *Sermons* (2 vols., London, 1829), vol. II, pp. 263, 274, 314, 317–18.

[83] Henry Moncrieff Wellwood, *Discourses on the evidence of the Jewish and Christian revelations* (Edinburgh, 1815), p. 503.

primeval sacred history. The diffusionist logic of sacred history planted the possibility that heathens were heirs in some degree, however vestigial, of the truths known to Noah and his descendants. Never was a grey area so rich in intriguing possibilities.

John Bossy has argued that in the wake of the Reformation the Ten Commandments came to assume a dominant position in early modern moral theology, with the corollary that idolatry or the worship of false gods – the subject of the first commandment (and the second too) – loomed larger in importance than hitherto as 'the primary offence of Christians'.[84] Alexandra Walsham concurs with this broad reading of early modern religious culture, describing it as 'a climate ever sensitive to the perils of idolatry'.[85] Protestants of the sixteenth and seventeenth century were on guard against subtle satanic 'impersonation' of God, the imperceptible means by which the Devil won adherents away from the worship of the true God and in its stead inculcated 'false doctrine'.[86]

Not everyone took such a bleakly monolithic view of idolatry. In his capacious and quasi-encyclopaedic *Anatomy of Melancholy* Robert Burton (1577–1640) explored the various forms of religious error and superstition which belonged to the broad category of idolatry. For a start, he noted, idolatry encompassed both the worship of false gods and the false worship of the true God. Idolatry, therefore, was to be found both among nominal Christians as well as among openly pagan peoples. Indeed, Burton sensed that Roman Catholicism was really at bottom a heathen legacy of Roman superstition, for just 'as those old Romans had several distinct gods for divers offices, persons, places', so the modern Roman Catholics had their saints; the names had changed, but the modern Romans had succumbed to the same delusion. Notwithstanding his subtle and discriminating tour of the world's idolatries, Burton was nonetheless convinced that these perversions of true religion – whether outside Christendom or an abomination lurking within – were the work of the devil and utterly without any redeeming features.[87]

Yet God's chosen people – the ancient Israelites – had themselves been guilty of worshipping the golden calf. The case of Jewish idolatry significantly tempered seventeenth-century Protestant understandings of idol

[84] J. Bossy, 'Moral arithmetic: seven sins into ten commandments', in E. Leites (ed.), *Conscience and casuistry in early modern Europe* (Cambridge, 1988), pp. 216, 229.
[85] A. Walsham, 'Angels and idols in England's long Reformation', in P. Marshall and A. Walsham (eds.), *Angels in the early modern world* (Cambridge, 2006), p. 134.
[86] N. Johnstone, *The Devil and demonism in early modern England* (Cambridge, 2006), pp. 43–4.
[87] Robert Burton, *The anatomy of melancholy* (New York, 2001 edn), vol. III, pp. 320–42.

worship.⁸⁸ Indeed, according to Thomas Tenison (1636–1715), a future Archbishop of Canterbury, idolatry came in several shapes and forms, whether fixated on animals or statues, or issuing from the 'blasphemous arrogance' of rulers, or arising from within, from mistaken ideas about Deity, including 'negative idolatry', essentially a diminished concept of God and his powers. Tenison's account of idolatry encompassed a range of ancient hybrids, which he was reluctant to condemn too vehemently. How was the critic of idolatry to parse the Egyptian worship of Moses as Apis? What was idolatry in this case, reckoned Tenison, but 'veneration overmuch strained'? Nor was Tenison inclined to berate too harshly the obvious pagan idolatry of ancient Rome; 'the acknowledgment of one supreme deity was not wholly banished from all parts of the pagan world', and the *monotheistic* worship of Jupiter, for example, had flourished alongside the cults of minor demons.⁸⁹

Read carefully the legacy of the patristic era suggested a similarly nuanced approach to pagan religion. No work had been more explicit in its condemnation of ancient heathendom than St Augustine's *City of God*, which emphasised the depravity and gross immorality of pagan rites and ceremonies. Yet, while the rhetoric of anti-pagan denunciation was a loud booming presence in the *City of God*, Augustine did also consider – admittedly as a minor theme – intimations and anticipations of Christian truth, such as the Sibylline prophecies.⁹⁰

As the focus of Protestant polemic shifted at the very close of the seventeenth century from the threat of Rome to the threat of deism, so heathendom came to assume a different form, and to suggest alternative apologetic possibilities. Prideaux contended that heathenism had not arisen, as deists alleged, by 'imposture'. The deistic implication, of course, was that all religions, the Judaeo-Christian included, were products of imposture, the political contrivances of cunning leaders such as Moses and other self-appointed Machiavellian prophets, to gull, delude and rule. In response, Prideaux cleverly used pagan idolatry as a shield against deistic attack. Heathen polytheisms emerged, he claimed, 'by corruptions insensibly growing on from that religion which was first true'. Heathenism was a gradual and ironic by-product of the very core truths of the patriarchal religion bequeathed by Noah. So entranced were primeval peoples by the promise of a redeemer, that in their eagerness 'they began

---

⁸⁸ Sheehan, 'Sacred and profane', esp. pp. 38–46.
⁸⁹ Thomas Tenison, *Of idolatry* (London, 1678), esp. pp. 14–15, 18–19, 23, 29–30, 33, 52, 61–2, 133.
⁹⁰ Augustine, *City of God* (transl. H. Bettenson, London, 1972), esp. pp. 51–3, 86–7, 330–7, 788–91.

to determine themselves to such mediators as their own imaginations led them to fancy', whether 'angels' or 'men deceased'. A corrupted version of a Christ-figure, a falsely imagined redeemer, was, it transpired, 'the fundamental principle' at the root of every single heathen religion. Moreover, all the polytheistic idolatries of the heathen world 'still held to their notion of one supreme God, and reckoned all the others to be no more than God's mediators under him'. Paganism, far from being the despicable antithesis of Christianity, was for Prideaux but a distorted simulacrum of the truth.[91]

Mythography had a crucial part to play in the defence of Christianity against deistic condescension. Thomas Halyburton (1674–1712), the Professor of Divinity at St Andrews, argued that deists were mistaken when they ascribed the ethical insights of ancient pagan philosophy to 'the light of nature'; rather there was such a 'plain resemblance' to Christianity in pagan opinions about the origin of the world and a great deluge as 'could not be casual'.[92] The nonconformist educator Philip Doddridge (1702–51) reckoned that the 'agreement there is between many facts recorded in the Old Testament, and the testimony of many heathen historians of considerable note, is a further evidence in favour of its credibility'. Doddridge thought it was the state of innocence in Eden and then the Fall 'to which it is probable we are to refer what so many writers say of the golden age; nor is it an improbable conjecture, that the worship of serpents, which has prevailed among so many heathen nations, may have some reference to the form, in which Moses tells us the tempter appeared to the first human pair'.[93]

While many learned Christians did indeed relegate idolatry to a cesspit of error, others perceived how it might be utilised as an outer bulwark of Christian truth, not least in the age of Enlightenment when Christian orthodoxy confronted opponents and weaponry of a sophistication never encountered since the waning of classical paganism. After all, its critics acknowledged that idolatry could take more than one form. It encompassed, for example, the deification of mere matter and the empty worship of stone or wooden images as well as the cults of false gods. Far from idolatry being at worst an unmitigated evil, at best an empty folly signifying nothing, an ingenious and influential school of Christian mythography

---

[91] Humphrey Prideaux, 'A letter to the Deists', *The true nature of imposture* (8th edn, London, 1723), pp. 227–32.
[92] Thomas Halyburton, *Natural religion insufficient* (Edinburgh, 1714), ch. xvi, pp. 41, 44 (second pagination).
[93] Philip Doddridge, *A course of lectures on the principal subjects in pneumatology, ethics and divinity* (London, 1763), pp. 293, 296.

recognised the worship of the pagan gods as a confused – but ultimately decodable – memory of the most ancient days of patriarchal history set out in the first ten chapters of the book of Genesis.

Apologetic mythographers blurred the stark distinction which had traditionally been drawn between the verities of the Christian faith and heathen falsehood. In their hands mythography functioned as a kind of chemistry for extracting nuggets of Christian truth from the ore of pagan untruth. William Knox (1732–1810), a self-described 'Layman of the Church of England', contended that God had not abandoned the gentiles to utter darkness and ignorance. While the principal evidences for Christianity – prophecy and miracles – had been confined to God's chosen people of Israel and to the Christian Church, the pagan peoples had also been under God's special care, receiving 'sufficient information' to construct religious systems which, while defective and erroneous in certain regards, had nonetheless embodied a kernel of vital truths handed down from the common traditions of humankind in the patriarchal era before the Flood. These core truths included belief in a presiding supreme being, a belief which Knox contended was universal. Polytheism – a 'secondary worship' – had arisen not only from the commemoration of ancestors, but also directly from a distorted memory of God's own interventions in the earliest periods of human history. Minor deities in the pagan pantheons were but exaggerated versions of God's 'original personified communications to Adam and Noah'. Angels, in other words, provided the matter for heathen idolatry. The religion of Noah formed the skeleton for most of the world's heathen religions, from classical Greece and Rome to India, Persia, China, Africa and the Americas. The Devil, Knox stressed, was not the father of idolatry; arguably, God Himself was its parent.[94]

No apologist did more to rehabilitate pagan idolatry from ill-informed Christian scorn and denigration than Horsley, who championed ancient heathendom for its guardianship – sometimes, admittedly, unwitting – of the primeval truths vouchsafed to the patriarchs of Genesis. When the descendants of Noah had gradually dispersed across the earth in the earliest post-Diluvian eras they had taken with them the ancient patriarchal religion revealed to their great ancestor, but had inevitably come to lose touch over time both with their far-flung extended kindred and with the whole truth and finer points of their religion. However, these 'defections' from the true religion were slow and 'partial'. There was, according to Horsley, no sudden

---

[94] [William Knox], *Considerations on the universality and uniformity of the theocracy* (London, 1796), esp. pp. 23–4, 52–3, 62–77, 81–2, 84, 114, 150.

wholesale abandonment of Noachic truth for heathen idolatry. Instead, during a lengthy 'intermediate period', core truths survived but were progressively compromised by additions, omissions and distortions. Far from an early heathen world characterised by 'total apostasy' from the true God, Horsley conjectured the 'slow' emergence of an 'idolatry of the older and milder sort, which retaining the worship of the true God and acknowledging his providence, added a superstitious adoration of certain inferior spirits'. According to Horsley, 'paganism in this milder form was rather to be called a corrupt than a false religion; just as at this day the religion of the Church of Rome is more properly corrupt than false'. The analogy with Roman Catholicism was precise and exact: the pagan 'Gentiles were nothing less than the corrupt branch of the old patriarchal church, the church of Noah and of Shem; and the family of Abraham were nothing more than the reformed part of it'. To be fair, conceded Horsley, a more 'malignant' idolatry came later in the gradual descent of patriarchal religion into the abyss of outright heathenism. But it had been a very long process, in the course of which the symbols of the true religion only very gradually lost their significance, becoming 'first inconsistent, then obscure, absurd and unintelligible', and only eventually 'lascivious and obscene'. The heathens – even 'in the ages of their worst idolatry' – had preserved 'explicit prophecies of Christ' which, while unsure quite why they did so, they had held in 'religious veneration'. Contrary to the stock caricature of heathendom, ancient pagans had 'enjoyed the light of revelation in a very considerable degree'.[95]

But how much 'light'? The seventeenth-century mythographer Theophilus Gale (1628–78) reckoned that while the ancient pagan Greeks had inherited from their neighbours to the east 'some fragments and broken traditions of the first origin of things', he nevertheless took the view that the pagans had enjoyed 'only a purblind light', what he termed 'a night-day knowledge of divine things'.[96] While for us and for some early modern theologians it seems only commonsensical that heathendom was a gross inversion of Christianity, defined as the polar opposite of Christian truth, for others the relationship between Christianity and paganism was a twilit one of gradual darkening falling short of black obliteration. The nineteenth-century mythographer Matthew Bridges contended that 'vestiges' of the 'precious' promise of deliverance from evil were 'never entirely erased even from the darkest corners of pagan mythology'.[97]

[95] Horsley, 'Dissertation on the prophecies', pp. 273–5, 278–80, 282, 285–8.
[96] Theophilus Gale, *The Court of the Gentiles*, part III (London, 1677), pp. 3–4.
[97] Matthew Bridges, *The testimony of profane antiquity to the account given by Moses of Paradise and the Fall of Man* (London, 1825), p. 160.

For sophisticated Casaubonish mythographers, Truth lay concealed in error; for their more conventionally-minded opponents within the Church, heathen error should never be elevated to the level even of quasi-truth, and it was a gross delusion to scavenge for vindications of Christianity in the rubbish of idolatry. John Conybeare (1692–1755), the future Bishop of Bristol, took what might be regarded now as the stereotypical view, namely that heathens were totally ignorant of religious truth.[98] Throughout the eighteenth century there remained plenty of commentators within the Church of England who regarded paganism with the utmost suspicion. At best it was the misguided worship of inanimate idols, at worst the work of the Devil and a crucial element in his plan to mislead humankind. In a sermon entitled 'On the Folly of Heathenism', preached at an episcopal visitation to Bury St Edmunds in 1753, Roger Kedington (1711/12–60) warned that the pagan world had contained little of value; the ancient heathens had worshipped 'the sun, moon, and stars, and even brute animals, plants and images of wood and stone, which their own hands had made, and even gave divine honours to the vilest affections and lusts. And all this abundantly shows the fatal progress of error, and into what wild conceits men naturally deviate, when once they forsake the worship of the one true God and by the deception of the Devil become vain'.[99] Similarly, Jenyns based his argument for the internal evidences on the very contrast between the moral coherence of Christianity and the 'universal darkness' of paganism, whose acolytes were 'immersed in the grossest idolatry, which had little or no connection with morality', engaged in 'impious, obscene and ridiculous ceremonies', and enveloped in 'one common cloud of ignorance and superstition'.[100]

Even in the golden age of collateral apologetics – the late eighteenth and early nineteenth centuries – some prominent works on the Christian evidences skirted or rejected outright the glimmerings pagans might have had of the sacred through a glass darkly. The mathematician and theologian Olinthus Gregory (1774–1841), for example, argued that the wholesale deification in which the ancients had indulged – of stars, rulers, even human characteristics – had led to unsavoury consequences. By deifying some of the less attractive aspects of the human personality, ancient pagans had come to indulge in the 'worship of evil beings', which in turn brought 'licentiousness and impurity into worship'. As far as Gregory was

---

[98] John Conybeare, *A defence of reveal'd religion* (London, 1732), pp. 418–19.
[99] Roger Kedington, *On the folly of heathenism and insufficiency of reason in religious enquiries* (Cambridge, 1753), p. 13.
[100] Jenyns, *View of the internal evidence*, pp. 42–3, 47.

concerned, the Greeks and Romans had been 'in a state of gross darkness and ignorance with respect to the knowledge of God'.[101]

There was no consensus on the notion that paganism was to be read – ultimately – as a kind of encoded Christianity. After all, the very idea was counter-intuitive, and, in many quarters at least, did little to dislodge firmly entrenched beliefs about the nature of heathen mythology. Even Faber, the doyen of collateral apologetics, acknowledged that corroborative proofs drawn from heathendom could be stretched too far, that 'to resolve every pagan tradition into some corresponding scriptural event' was 'the height of folly and credulity'; yet he contended that 'to deny all resemblance and all connexion between sacred and profane antiquity' was just as 'nearly allied to a blind and indiscriminate scepticism'.[102]

The very success – or apparent success – of this new strain of corroborative evidences worried commentators who feared that paganism was exactly what it had always hitherto seemed to be: no more than a set of anti-Christian errors. Not all of the critics of the Casaubonish project were avant-garde Ladislaws. Some of the most outspoken antagonists of the 'key to all mythologies' as a genre were Christian apologists of a more conventional and traditionalist stripe anxious that far too much reliance was being placed on heathen beliefs. Surely, these orthodox critics thought, the mythical beliefs of pagans constituted a decidedly swampy set of foundations upon which to build a fortress of Christian impregnability?

Some Christian theologians were convinced that this sort of enterprise was a quixotic pursuit of a non-existent grail; at best, perhaps, the quest had a genuine purpose, but the route was dotted with dangerous quicksands. Contemplating the eighteenth-century fixation on the mythographical connexion, the orientalist John Richardson (1740/1–95) wondered, 'how much learning has been most zealously misplaced, to injure the sacred writings, by improper references and illustrations?'[103] 'Zeal sometimes has in its results the same effect as infidelity', bemoaned the orientalist Edward Moor (1771–1848) in 1810, 'and one cannot help lamenting, that a superstructure requiring so little support should be encumbered by awkward buttresses, so ill applied, that they would, if it were possible, diminish the stability of the building that they were intended to uphold'. Such, Moor suggested, were the numerous attempts to identify Christ and Krishna, to

---

[101] Olinthus Gregory, *Letters to a friend, on the evidences, doctrines and duties of the Christian religion* (4th edn, 2 vols., London, 1822), vol. I, pp. 30, 33–4.
[102] George Stanley Faber, *Horae Mosaicae* (2 vols., Oxford, 1801), vol. I, p. 187.
[103] John Richardson, *A dissertation on the languages, literature, and manners of Eastern nations* (Oxford, 1778 edn), p. 301.

trace the story of Abraham and Sarah in that of Brahma and Saraswati, and to align the Christian Trinity and the 'monstrous triad of the Hindus'.[104] A year later the Methodist Biblical scholar Adam Clarke (1760/2–1832) reflected along the same lines, as we shall see below in chapter 6, that this sort of ill-conceived corroborative project was as likely to lower the credit of the Christian faith as to bolster belief.

Might mythographical arguments blow up in one's face, some wondered, rather than exploding the case of the Deists? Edward Nares (1762–1841), the rector of Biddenden and a former Fellow of Merton, was far from blind to the potential deployment of mythographical evidence, but he perceived the drawbacks too, and in the course of his Bampton Lectures wondered if it was perhaps ultimately counter-productive to invest too much effort in this area: 'Instead then of searching for resemblances in the pagan mythologies, which the infidel is too apt to turn against us, as supposing all to be equally mythological, let us for ever insist upon the notorious and marked differences between them.'[105]

Striking variations in emphasis and strategy emerged within the literature of Christian evidences, and not all apologists concurred on the value of collateral evidence from pagan mythology. Even in the heyday of collateral apologetics there was considerable distrust of supposed pagan corroboration for Genesis. Although Archdeacon William Paley (1743–1805) – the leading Anglican apologist of the late eighteenth century – welcomed profane testimony to the truths of the New Testament, being the unimpeachable 'concession of adversaries', he was reluctant to 'make Christianity answerable with its life, for the circumstantial truth of every separate passage of the Old Testament', and declined to defend the credibility of the Old Testament as history.[106] When the eminent Scots Presbyterian polymath Thomas Chalmers (1780–1847) turned to the question of evidences he assigned a purely negative role to paganism. After all, the historical fact that 'the first Christians of the Gentile world' had 'turned from dumb idols' and 'the absurdities of paganism' to worship the true God was in itself a powerful form of external evidence. Unsurprisingly, in the light of this argument Chalmers had little time for collateral proofs derived from heathendom, which was a degrading and debased scene of 'wretched delusions'. Chalmers perceived, moreover, that the 'historical evidence for the New Testament' was of necessity the core citadel of Christian belief. While

---

[104] Edward Moor, *The Hindu pantheon* (London, 1810), p. 200.
[105] Edward Nares, *A view of the evidences of Christianity at the close of the pretended age of reason* (Oxford, 1805), p. 252.
[106] William Paley, *A view of the evidences of Christianity* (11th edn, 2 vols., London, 1805), vol. I, p. 40; vol. II, pp. 291, 295.

the historicity of the gospel story must needs be impregnable, Chalmers was more relaxed in his apologetics about just how the terrain of Mosaic antiquity might be demarcated and defended.[107] It seems that it was the champions of a full-blown system of apologetics which emphasised the need to defend Old and New Testament alike who were most drawn to the possibilities profane mythologies offered for the vindication of the historical truth found in the Pentateuch. Beilby Porteous (1731–1809), the Bishop of London and another very popular exponent of the theology of evidences, actually used the 'deplorable ignorance' of the ancient heathens with regard to religion as evidence for the necessity of revelation and hence of the truth of Christianity. Using this apologetic strategy Porteous depicted paganism as an idolatrous wasteland utterly destitute of religious truth, not – as the literature of collateral evidences would have it – as a quarry of latent truths to be mined: heathens had worshipped 'dead men and women, birds and beasts, insects and reptiles … together with an infinite number of idols, the work of their own hands, from various materials, gold, silver, wood and stone'. Yet, on the other hand, Porteous did invoke the authority of 'several pagan authors of the highest antiquity and the best credit' as circumstantial confirmation of the historic truth of the Old Testament Flood.[108]

Some apologists charted a middle course between exploiting the apparent collateral evidences and dismissing them as a snare to the unwary. Daniel Guildford Wait (1789–1850) of St John's College, Cambridge, spotted the danger of seeking 'a correspondence between things, which really have no relation to each other'. He reasoned that sometimes 'coincidences' between the Old Testament and pagan mythology could be explained quite simply in terms of actual heathen exposure to the Jewish scriptures in the melting-pot of ancient Egypt or at some other point of contact among the adjacent cultures of the Middle East. Nevertheless, in other cases this line of interpretation would not suffice, he felt, and then it seemed more likely that the pagan peoples inherited from their distant ancestors 'perverted traditions' of the patriarchal era. In several instances, traditions 'common' to the people of the pre-dispersion era had been 'transmitted to their successors, and which in lapse of time became perverted, and formed into unwieldy systems'.[109] In these instances, it was the job of the mythographer

---

[107] Thomas Chalmers, *The evidence and authority of the Christian revelation* (1814: 6th edn, Edinburgh, 1818), pp. 195, 203–5, 279.
[108] Beilby Porteous, *A summary of the principal evidences for the truth and divine origin of the Christian revelation* (9th edn, London, 1805), pp. 6–7, 36.
[109] Daniel Guildford Wait, *An inquiry into the religious knowledge which the heathen philosophers derived from the Jewish scriptures* (Cambridge, 1813), pp. vi–vii, 69–70, 80.

to recover the scriptural key to the lost sacred histories concealed beneath the delusive systems of heathen mythology. Wait's particular obsession was with the recovery of the Trinity as a patriarchal truth revealed to humankind in its infancy and as such extant – if only in 'rude traces' at some points – in the world's pagan religions. Indeed, pagan mythology revealed not only triadic elements but also corrective monist elements, which seemed to indicate that the heathens acquired from their patriarchal forebears the unpredictable truth of a trinity-in-unity. 'We may discern', Wait noted, 'among the most enlightened philosophers of antiquity, whether grecian or oriental, the belief of a trias and a monas, which must have been derived either from some traditionary knowledge of the Hebrew scriptures, or from legends handed down from the era of the dispersion of mankind.' Unitarians might cavil at the provenance of the Trinity, but 'its general adoption by every known nation of antiquity yields no small collateral testimony to the elucidation we receive of it in the books of the New Testament'.[110]

This kind of ambivalence also reigned in missionary work and its offshoot in ethnographic enquiry among the world's primitive peoples. Such peoples, while backward and superstitious, were not necessarily totally unacquainted with the primeval truths of patriarchal tradition. The Reverend George Turner of the London Missionary Society conceded that the mythological folklore of Samoa was in most respects 'a heap of rubbish' which abounded in 'obscenities and absurdities', but just occasionally the listener to oral tales would 'pause in deep interest, as we recognise some fragment, or corroboration, of scripture history'.[111]

Some apologists deliberately eschewed mythographical evidence, and instead highlighted the differences between the simplicity of Christian history and the awkward incoherence of pagan mythology as an argument for the truth of Christianity. Richard Michell (1805–77), vice-president of Magdalen Hall, in his Bampton lecture for 1849, contended that 'the records of all other religions, the mythologies of classical heathenism, and the fantastic legends of the remote East ... notoriously exhibit a mass of disorderliness and confusion, strangely contrasting with the simplicity and consistency of the Christian records'.[112] Similarly, in *The Leading Christian*

---

[110] Daniel Guildford Wait, *A critical examination of some scriptural texts which maintain the doctrine of a trinity in unity* (London, 1819), pp. vi, 3–4, 20.

[111] George Turner, *Nineteen years in Polynesia: missionary life, travels and researches in the islands of the Pacific* (London, 1861), p. 244.

[112] Richard Michell, *The nature and comparative value of the Christian evidences considered generally* (Oxford, 1849), p. 137.

Evidences (1870) the Scots Presbyterian theologian Gilbert Wardlaw (1798–1873) took the line that the narratives of the Old Testament 'stand in marked contrast with the numerous fables of eastern or classical mythology, by the plain simplicity and matter-of-fact character of the narratives'.[113]

The most pointed attack on collateral mythological evidences came from the Reverend F. W. Farrar (1831–1903) – later Archdeacon of Westminster Abbey, then Dean of Canterbury – in a paper entitled 'Traditions, real and fictitious', which he delivered to the Ethnological Society of London on 23 February 1864. Farrar regarded 'the evidence of traditions' as 'most questionable', and felt that 'an importance wholly exaggerated has been attached to them'. Some mythological traditions were utterly spurious, and others, he believed, had an ironic provenance, 'being directly borrowed from the narrative which they are quoted to illustrate'. Indeed, Farrar identified five different classes of mythographical evidence, namely 'independent natural beliefs, wholly unconnected with the Bible', 'similar allegoric representations of common catastrophes' (floods, most obviously), 'vague and grotesque legends forced into an unreal resemblance with Biblical narratives', 'mere echoes and plagiarisms' of scripture, and, finally, 'absolute fictions and inventions', concocted by native peoples as imitations of Bible stories they had heard and hoped to foist on credulous white Europeans, whether scholars or missionary-apologists. In the first category of natural beliefs whose origin was independent of scripture, Farrar placed the rainbow as 'a promise of hope', 'the sacredness of the dove' and the idea of a lost 'golden age', an 'innocent paradisiacal childhood of humanity'. There was no need to invoke the influence of sacred history to account for such 'occasional minute resemblances in tradition or allegory'. Would it not be surprising, he wondered, 'if the human mind, being subjected everywhere to the same laws, working on the same materials, liable to the same influences, and aiming at the same results, should not have thought the same thought twice and independently, or endeavoured to convey the same *prima facie* conclusions by the same allegorical machinery'. In Farrar's second category he noticed that, of course, many of the world's mythologies were full of stories of floods, but only '*partial*' floods, while in much of Africa and Australia there were no legends of great deluges. Such materials were insufficient to prove the sacred historicity of Noah's flood. In his third class of traditions, there were many 'vague and often absurd stories' which had been 'forced into unreal resemblance with the biblical narrative'.

---

[113] Gilbert Wardlaw, *The leading Christian evidences and the principles on which to estimate them* (Edinburgh, 1870), p. 209.

The fourth category of tradition largely concerned stories which had been adopted into the histories of the neighbouring pagan nations of the Hebrews and then recycled, but interpreted within collateral apologetics as if independent corroborative testimony of the most ancient era of sacred history. On the other hand, Farrar's fifth class of suspicious mythological traditions were more recent, episodes of flagrant duplicity where native peoples had deceived Christian investigators with their own 'wilful' concoctions of 'sham legend', deliberately construed to sate, or perhaps even whet, the appetites of the white man. Farrar recounted particular examples of such fraud, including the unfortunate gulling of Sir William Jones's orientalist collaborator, Colonel Francis Wilford (1761–1822), by a pandit in India who composed what appeared to be an ancient Indian tradition of the Deluge, and the later scepticism of David Livingstone's father-in-law, the Congregationalist missionary Robert Moffat (1795–1883), when confronted with a supposedly indigenous African tale 'which coincided with the Bible in the most trifling details', so much so that 'the legend aroused his caution by the suspicious accuracy of its resemblance'. It transpired in this latter incident that the African had picked up the story from his own encounter with a missionary elsewhere in Africa. Farrar reckoned that most collateral evidences drawn from heathen mythologies did not amount to authentic corroborations of sacred history, despite the 'most undue prominence ... given to the arguments derived from the supposed unity of national traditions'. When exposed to tests for their genuineness and antiquity, most mythographical evidences 'evaporated'.[114]

Sometimes apologetic practice complicated, and indeed confounded, suspicions about the dangerous reliance on pagan proofs. Robert Mushet (1811–71), for one, declared an outspoken preference for a traditional scheme of evidences:

> The proofs of the Christian religion are various: 1. The prophetic proof; 2. The historical; and 3. The intrinsic proof, or proof derived from the divine perfection, sublimity, and harmony of all its parts. Some theologians, not satisfied with such ample demonstration, have marred the beauty and simplicity of those proofs, by descending to the low arena of bandying words and doctrines with pagan and heathen mythologists.

Mushet's great bugbear was the 'delusion' that the mystery of the Trinity could be found in the philosophy of Plato. This 'fallacy' was most apparent in the encyclopedic and still influential *True Intellectual System of the*

---

[114] F. W. Farrar, 'Traditions, real and fictitious', *Transactions of the Ethnological Society of London*, vol. 3 (1865), pp. 298–307.

Universe of Cudworth, who had believed Plato 'as orthodox a Trinitarian as himself'. Yet while Mushet declared his strenuous opposition to mythographical proofs, in practice he recognised that it was treacherously difficult to draw a line of 'demarcation' between revealed religion properly understood and the natural religion attained 'through the means of common sense and sound reason' by 'the philosophic pagan'. The rational Christian should 'rejoice when he can discover a few straggling broken rays of hallowed light emerging from the gloom and twilight in which the mind of man was steeped before Christ appeared'. Moreover, for all his apparent discomfort with collateral evidences, Mushet happily set out in some detail the transition of the pure monotheistic religion of the patriarchs – by way of 'the undue veneration of mankind' for the heroes associated with the Flood – into corrupt, polytheistic, semi-piscine idolatries, including the worship of Vishnu and Oannes. The pagan pantheon comprised 'compound divinities' based upon an elision of 'the symbol and that which it represented', blended together with sun-worship and the cult of 'deified mortals'. For all Mushet's misgivings, his works constitute a vigorous exposition of the branch of collateral evidences which he seemingly disparaged.[115]

Collateral apologetics lacked any defining litmus test which distinguished between reliable evidences and mere whimsy. Orthodoxy did not prescribe any direction to, or limits upon, the question of how, and how far, a Christian mythographer might interpret heathen legend. There was no consistency within the theology of evidences regarding the strategic significance of pagan mythology, as the freethinking Taylor found when he reviewed this genre of apologetic:

> [W]e see that Christian divines, according to their cue or drift, either endeavour to conceal or else boast of the resemblance between Christian and pagan mythology. At one time, or with one set of Christian-evidence writers, the very idea of naming Christ and Hercules together is held as the most frightening impiety; heaven and hell are not further asunder; with another set, equally orthodox, but driving at a different tact of argument, it is Satan himself who hath blinded our eyes, to prevent the light of truth shining upon us, if we cannot see that Hercules and Jesus are one and the same identical personage; that the labours of the one were the miracles of the other.[116]

[115] Robert Mushet, *The trinities of the ancients; or, the mythology of the first ages* (London, 1837), pp. v, 19–20, 24, 28, 33, 42, 66, 68–9, 80, 221; [Mushet], *The book of symbols* (London, 1844), pp. vii, xiii–xiv, 284, 310, 495.
[116] Taylor, *Diegesis*, pp. 155–6.

Taylor also noted the argument that 'the pagan religion, like the Jewish dispensation, was typical'; in other words, similarities between pagan deities and Christ were interpreted as 'types' or 'forerunners' of Christ. Indeed, Taylor set up his own misleadingly named Christian Evidence Society precisely in order to debunk the genre of collateral evidences by turning it on its head,[117] claiming that the recent deistic deconstruction of both pagan and Christian mythologies by French writers such as Dupuis[118] had rendered the 'now antiquated school of Christian-evidence writers' a tired and toothless anachronism.[119]

Yet as late as the 1860s Casaubonish apologetics was still a vigorous and far-from-discredited element in Anglican churchmanship. With a jaunty confidence in the continuing power of corroborative evidences, the Reverend Thomas Millington described his book, *The testimony of the heathen to the truths of Holy Writ* (1863), as 'a commentary *e profanis* on the Holy Scriptures'. After all, he perceived, 'parallelism' abounded between the primeval sacred history of the earliest part of Genesis and the mythological stories of the pagans. Such abundance was itself a kind of evidence of the divine dispensation. Of course, Millington recognised the objections that existed to a reliance on pagan error as a guide to Christian truth. Why should Christian theologians place so much emphasis on the fables of idolatrous polytheists? For a start, reckoned Millington, monotheism – if only one looked carefully enough – was omnipresent in the world's religions, even the superficially polytheistic: 'All nations, however ignorant, however corrupt and darkened in their natural hearts, believed and confessed the existence of a great and benevolent God, the Creator and Ruler of the universe.' There was also a highly potent corroboration of Christian truth which lurked in the very distortions of heathen religion and mythology. Millington championed the study of pagan history, myth and philosophy, for in it, he believed, one could 'discern the reflected light of divine revelation'. True, the 'facts' were 'greatly disguised, and the doctrine much obscured' by various heathen 'fallacies', but 'as the shadow, though distorted, bears still an unequivocal resemblance to the object which it represents, so these traditions afford sure testimony to the realities which they so feebly and imperfectly reflect'. Of course, he conceded, it might 'be objected that the Word of God has no need of such assistance from without', but equally it was reasonable to suppose that such 'relics of antiquity

---

[117] 'Manifesto of the Christian Evidence Society, established November 12 1824', in Robert Taylor, *Syntagma of the evidences of the Christian religion. Being a vindication of the manifesto of the Christian Evidence Society* (London, 1828).
[118] See below, ch. 5.
[119] Taylor, *Diegesis*, p. 175.

have been preserved through so many ages by the special providence of Him who ordereth all things according to His will'. 'All truth is God's', insisted Millington, 'He made the lesser light as well as the greater.'[120]

Generally, champions of collateral evidences sought traces of an original patriarchal monotheism in pagan mythologies, as well as vestigial memories of the Fall and the Flood. This, apologists reckoned, was as much of the Christian (or, more properly, proto-Christian) dispensation as the gentiles would have known prior to the dispersal of peoples on the plain of Shinaar described in chapter 11 of Genesis. Pagan peoples would have been exposed, it seemed, to knowledge of the great calamities of primitive mankind and to the basic tenets of the religion of Noah, but not to some of the essential truths of Christianity – such as the coming of a Redeemer or the Trinitarian nature of the godhead – which were only revealed at a later stage within the gradually unfolding process described in the prophetic books of the Old Testament and in the New Testament itself. Thus, there was little point, it seemed to many proponents of collateral evidences, in searching out anticipations of Christ or Trinitarian patterns in the mythologies of the heathens. Given the limited revelation to the patriarchs and earliest post-Diluvian peoples, it was most unlikely that either the Redeemer or the Trinity would provide the key to all mythologies. For many Christian mythographers such a key would have been a delusion, for it was founded on an anachronism: ancient heathen peoples could not have known these truths in the era of the Tower of Babel before their separation from that branch of the lineage of Noah's son Shem to whom, in time, a fuller body of truths would be vouchsafed.

Nevertheless, on this matter there was no consensus within the theology of evidences. In particular, the Hutchinsonian school of apologetics[121] (dominated by high Anglican clerics, but also including some evangelical supporters, dissenting adherents and the Scots Presbyterian lawyer and politician, Duncan Forbes of Culloden)[122] took a very different line on the contents of heathen mythology.[123] In some respects the followers of John

---

[120] Thomas Millington, *The testimony of the heathen to the truths of Holy Writ* (London, 1863), pp. vi, viii–ix, xi.

[121] For an overview of the changing character of Hutchinsonianism, see D. Gurses, 'Academic Hutchinsonians and their quest for relevance, 1734–1790', *History of European Ideas*, vol. 31 (2005), pp. 408–27.

[122] P. Nockles, *The Oxford movement in context: Anglican high churchmanship 1760–1857* (Cambridge, 1994), pp. 193, 258; C. D. A. Leighton, 'Hutchinsonianism: a counter-Enlightenment reform movement', *Journal of Religious History*, vol. 23 (1999), pp. 168–84, at p. 171.

[123] For the mythographical dimension of Hutchinsonianism, see A. J. Kuhn, 'English deism and the development of romantic mythological syncretism', *Publications of the Modern Language Association of America*, vol. 71 (1956), pp. 1094–116, at p. 1114.

Hutchinson (1674–1737), the author of *Moses's Principia*, shared some of the methods of standard apologetic and were driven by some of the same imperatives as other theologians who deployed collateral evidences. Their primary enemies were, of course, the deists, and the Hutchinsonians took delight, like many of their fellow Christians, that when deists raked up 'every scrap of heathen evidence' they merely weakened their own case, for 'these gentile witnesses, when cross-examined ... bear witness against themselves, and become evidence for the Bible; and even much better evidence than that which the friends of revelation have mostly relied on, namely, the rabbinical writings, and constructions of the apostate Jews'.[124] Nevertheless, the Hutchinsonians were also engaged in their own domestic battles within the bounds of religious orthodoxy. These internal skirmishes depended ultimately on what seemed arcane matters of textual exegesis. Hutchinsonians contended that the core truths of Christianity had been revealed from the earliest period and were known through the perfect medium of divine communication, the pure Hebrew language of the Pentateuch. As a result, Hutchinsonians assumed strong views on what now seem very technical matters of Biblical scholarship and ancient philology. They championed the Hebrew Bible at the expense of the Greek Septuagint, which they deemed to be corrupt precisely because of the language in which it was expressed. According to Hutchinson, 'Greek words ... could not answer the meaning of the Hebrew', for the latter was 'founded upon, and is a copy of the ideas or images of things, and their actions'.[125] Hutchinsonians also campaigned for pure Hebrew texts purged of vowel points. Hebrew vowel points, or niqqud, had only been added to the consonantal Hebrew alphabet in the ninth and tenth centuries AD by rabbinic scholars known as the Masoretes. Hutchinsonians claimed that this accretion distorted the meaning of the divinely inspired text of the Old Testament. According to Forbes of Culloden (1685–1747), vowel points 'darken the sense of the scriptures'.[126] The three revelations – to the antediluvian patriarchs, to the Israelites and then to Christians – were identical; what had obscured this identity were the vowel points added to the text of the Hebrew Bible.[127] Beyond these concerns with language

---

[124] [Robert Spearman], *Letters to a friend, concerning the Septuagint translation, and the heathen mythology* (Edinburgh, 1759), p. 6.
[125] [John Hutchinson], *A new account of the confusion of tongues* (London, 1731), pp. 216, 229.
[126] [Duncan Forbes of Culloden], *A letter to a bishop, concerning some important discoveries in philosophy and theology* (1732: 3rd edn, London, 1735), p. 11.
[127] G. White, 'Hutchinsonianism in eighteenth-century Scotland', *Records of the Scottish Church History Society*, vol. 21 (1982), pp. 157–69, at pp. 160–1.

and the text of scripture, Hutchinsonian theology possessed other distinctive features, most especially an anti-Newtonian physics. Hutchinsonians believed that the truths of nature were revealed to man, not, as Newtonian science claimed, by way of experiment and observation of God's book of nature, but through the exegesis of God's divine word set out in the unpointed Hebrew of the Pentateuch.

The Hutchinsonians were also actively engaged in advancing their own particular interpretation of Christian mythography. The unpointed Hebrew of the Pentateuch, they contended, had also revealed the doctrine of the Trinity and the coming of the Redeemer, facts which had been transmitted, notwithstanding the corruption of religion which had occurred at Babel, to the pagan world. Indeed, the divine truth of the Trinity was reflected in the tripartite structuring of the universe into the three core elemental forces of fire, light and air. God had inserted the message of the Trinity into the warp and woof of his own creation. Hutchinsonians also placed a great deal of emphasis on a particular Hebrew term for the deity – Elohim, or Elahim[128] – which they claimed captured the plurality of beings present in the godhead. According to Hutchinson, Elohim meant a 'Trinity of persons in the essence'.[129] If the later Hebrews of the nation of Israel had forgotten the aboriginal Trinitarian and Christian truths of the patriarchal tradition, then traces of that truth – albeit despiritualised[130] – could still be discerned, Hutchinsonians contended, in the polytheism of the ancient heathen world.[131] Ironically, Hutchinsonians appeared to argue, the truths of Christianity were more fully apparent in pagan idolatry than in the strict monotheism of Old Testament Judaism. Forbes of Culloden noted of the term 'Elohim' that 'at whatever time the Jews thought fit to translate the word singular, it is certain the heathens retained it in the plural sense; and the Jews, when translating that word applied to the heathen gods, render it plural'.[132] Redemption was another feature of heathen legend as decoded by the Hutchinsonians. Robert Spearman (1703–61) argued that 'the pagan mythology, when traced up to its original, is a traditional detail of the actions, sufferings and offices of the great Redeemer, couched under the veil of fables'. This explained the riddle of why the magi had come to bring

---

[128] D. Gurses, 'The Hutchinsonian defence of Old Testament Trinitarian Christianity: the controversy over Elahim, 1735–1773', *History of European Ideas*, vol. 29 (2003), pp. 393–409.
[129] [Hutchinson], *Confusion of tongues*, p. 10.
[130] C. B. Wilde, 'Hutchinsonianism, natural philosophy and religious controversy in eighteenth-century Britain', *History of Science*, vol. 18 (1980), pp. 1–24, at p. 5.
[131] Leighton, 'Hutchinsonianism', p. 180.
[132] [Forbes of Culloden], *Letter to a bishop*, p. 53.

precious gifts to Christ at his birth in Bethlehem: 'how could they know, and come to worship a person of whom they had not heard; and how could they hear without a preacher?' However, Spearman argued, 'from the first promise made to Adam', the elements of the Christian promise had been revealed to mankind, whether 'in type or hieroglyphics', and Christ-like figures had been anticipated in the mythologies of the heathens, in the forms, for example, of Anubis, Mercury, Apollo and Hercules. By the same token, according to Spearman, the Egyptian sphinx, a compound of man and lion, was an emblem of the Trinity and the incarnation of God in human form.[133] Similarly, according to John Parkhurst (1728–97) in a work of Hutchinsonian polemic disguised – if only slightly – as a Hebrew dictionary, *An Hebrew and English Lexicon, without points* (1762), which was in its seventh edition by 1813, the labours of Hercules were 'emblematic memorials of what the real son of God and Saviour of the world was to do and suffer for our sakes'.[134] Furthermore, Hutchinsonian mythographers also found in pagan rites and beliefs themes of purification and of covenanted relationships between mankind and heaven.[135] The Hutchinsonians took pagan mythology very seriously indeed, and were insistent that 'part of the heathen mythology' was ultimately of 'divine origination'.[136] Hutchinson showed how pagan idolatry had arisen through the corruption of the emblematic Trinity of fire, light and air into the direct worship of the elements themselves.[137] Indeed, Hutchinson, Forbes noted, had found himself 'out of humour with those, who fancy the ancients such idiots as to have worshipped brutes, reptiles, insects or any inanimate things'.[138] Pagan religion was founded upon emblems behind whose allegories lay Christian truths.

Unsurprisingly, the wider Hutchinsonian network of late eighteenth-century Anglican high churchmanship produced a remarkably incisive and concise case for the ironic, unexpected utility of paganism: *Considerations on the Religious Worship of the Heathens as bearing unanswerable testimony to the principles of Christianity* (1799) by the Reverend William Jones of Nayland (1726–1800). Though Jones is usually associated with the parish of Nayland in Suffolk, where he resided from 1777, he was born at Lowick

---

[133] [Spearman], *Letters to a friend*, pp. 65, 69–71, 79, 124, 151.
[134] John Parkhurst, *An Hebrew and English lexicon, without points* (7th edn, London, 1813), p. 520.
[135] [Forbes of Culloden], *Letter to a bishop*, pp. 61–2; Alexander Catcott senior, *The supreme and inferiour Elahim* (London, 1736).
[136] [Spearman], *Letters to a friend*, p. 127.
[137] [John Hutchinson], *The nature and attributes of the Trinity of the Gentiles* (London, 1731).
[138] [Forbes of Culloden], *Letter to a bishop*, p. 26.

in Northamptonshire. Lowick, it so happens, was also the name of Mr Casaubon's home in *Middlemarch*, and whether or not Eliot was dropping a small clue here for the connoisseurs of biographical trivia, Jones's *Considerations* constituted a kind of apologia for Casaubonish research into the mythographical evidences. Jones contended that 'the false religion of the heathens was borrowed from the true religion of revelation, and is a witness to its authority'. Of course, as Bryant and others had noticed, there were myths of an ancient flood – such as Ovid's story of Deucalion – and the subsequent renovation of humanity. But there were many other inexplicable associations between paganism and Christianity. 'Turn it about on every side', heathenism, proclaimed Jones, 'gives neverfailing testimony to an original revelation'. All the essential ingredients of Christianity as a body of rites and beliefs – priesthood, sacrifice, atonement, purification, prayer, miracles, and communications between man and God – were to be found in paganism. The resemblance was so close in so many unpredictable particulars, as made 'the one a proof of the other'. The late seventeenth-century English orientalist John Spencer (1630–93) had come close to this with his argument that the Israelites had borrowed from the Egyptians, only he had got the line of influence the wrong way round. Rather pagan religion was a 'plagiary' of Christianity. There was 'scarcely a sign or a wonder recorded in the Bible, but we find something of the same sort in the history which the heathens give of themselves'. Natural religion, for a start, could never provide a convincing explanation for so many of the features of pagan worship; only tradition – a tradition inherited from the Hebrews – could do that. After all, the very ceremonies of paganism rested on something akin to a Christian logic. The sacrificial rites of heathens were 'an absurdity' without any underlying concept of sin: 'To suppose sacrifice is to suppose sin: and the heathen practice bears universal testimony to it.' Indeed, Jones insisted, the corroborating evidence of paganism provided a devastating weapon to use against sceptics and deists, for it answered 'a purpose contrary to its intention and nature; it will confirm what it was intended to confound'. The heathen evidences were so compelling, Jones perceived, precisely because they 'make the false prove the true'.[139]

Hutchinsonian perspectives survived into nineteenth-century mythography, that is into the era of Mr Casaubon himself. Cory's *Mythological*

---

[139] William Jones, *Considerations on the religious worship of the heathens as bearing unanswerable testimony to the principles of Christianity* (London, 1799), pp. 2–3, 6, 14–17, 20, 22–3. For Spencer, see J. Assmann, *Moses the Egyptian* (Cambridge, MA, 1997), pp. 55–79.

inquiry into the recondite theology of the heathens (1837) aligned itself with Hutchinsonian conclusions – if not methods. The 'heathen system', Cory argued, 'universally recognised a triad of divine persons', yet these, while being 'distinct' as persons, were 'not exactly separate gods'. New evidence from Hindu mythology – Brahma–Shiva–Vishnu – provided spectacular confirmation of this striking pagan phenomenon. This was decidedly peculiar: 'How comes it that a doctrine so singular, and so utterly at variance with all the conceptions of uninstructed reason, as that of a Trinity in Unity, should have been from the beginning, the fundamental religious tenet of every nation upon earth?' The Trinity had clearly been part of the 'primary revelation' and 'one of the original and fundamental tenets of the patriarchal church'.[140]

In this chapter I have used Casaubon's grandiose title 'The Key to All Mythologies' as a kind of shorthand for apologetic mythography. Yet similar terms of art surface in the world of mythography throughout the eighteenth and nineteenth centuries. This observation is not intended to detract from Eliot's genius or imaginative fertility, but the 'key to all mythologies' was, it transpires, an expression on the very tip of the tongue.

In his *Tetradymus* (1720) the freethinker John Toland reckoned the double doctrine – or 'the double philosophy', as he called it – 'the true key, for opening the Egyptian and Pythagorean mysteries'.[141] Thomas Blackwell, the Aberdonian mythographer and Homeric scholar, came very close to using a phrase of this sort in a work published in 1748. Blackwell referred to a 'grand key' in 'the general plan of mythology'. However, this was only by way of warning that there was no single key to all mythologies. Mythology, Blackwell perceived, was 'a vast and various compound; a labyrinth through whose windings no one thread can conduct us'. No single 'system' would explain this teeming variety, 'however ingenious' the method devised.[142] Costard, an Oxford antiquary and scientist who specialised in the history of astronomy, tried to account for Egyptian legends as allegories based on astronomical observations and the changing of the seasons. As far as the stories of Isis and Osiris were concerned, Costard concluded that 'the true key to this mythology' was 'the rising of the Nile'.[143] Elsewhere in his oeuvre Costard claimed that he had 'accounted for the names of the five

---

[140] Isaac Preston Cory, *Mythological inquiry into the recondite theology of the heathens* (London, 1837), pp. 73–5, 78, 85 fn, 87–8.
[141] John Toland, *Tetradymus* (London, 1720), p. 85.
[142] Thomas Blackwell, *Letters concerning mythology* (London, 1748), pp. 232–3, 409.
[143] Costard, *Further account*, pp. 150–1.

planets; and in so doing have, I think, given the key to the ancient mythology, or to speak more truly, the theology of the heathen world'.[144]

Robert Spearman, the Hutchinsonian, thought that the mythology of the eastern nations appeared obscure 'from the want of the right key to decipher it'. However, Spearman's Hutchinsonian solution – reading the expectation of a redeemer into ancient pagan legends – promised to clear up any bewilderment: 'this key will decipher the pagan mythology in an easier manner than has yet been done, and clear up that learned confusion that has overspread the writings of such as have endeavoured to account for the origin and progress of idolatry'.[145] Faber reckoned the story of the Noachic Flood 'to be the only key, that can unlock the hidden meaning of the mysterious polytheism of the ancients'.[146]

Sampson Arnold Mackey, an early nineteenth-century deconstructionist, claimed that the mythological astronomy of the ancients was 'the key of Urania', Urania being in mythology the muse of astronomy.[147] Similarly, another radical debunker of traditional religion, the freethinker Richard Carlile, invoked the 'universality and truth' of 'pagan mythology' when 'revealed by the key of all the other mysteries', adding the need for the 'key of science' to be 'applied to unlock the words of the mystery'.[148] John Williams (1792–1858), the Archdeacon of Cardigan and Rector of Edinburgh Academy, claimed in *Homerus* (1842), which traced the legacy of the ancient religion of the patriarchs – hitherto 'utterly disguised' – in the Homeric epics, that the concept of *até* (fate) 'will furnish us with the key which, rightly used, will open to us new apartments in the magnificent structure of that great poem'.[149] As late as 1869 the Reverend William Galloway of St Mark's Regent's Park made sport with the figure of the 'key' which would unlock the relationship of Egyptology to Old Testament sacred history in the course of an attack on the extended chronology subversive of Biblical orthodoxy advanced by the Prussian Egyptologist Karl Richard Lepsius (1810–84).[150]

---

[144] George Costard, *Two dissertations, I. Containing an enquiry into the meaning of the word Kesitah … II. On the signification of the word Hermes* (Oxford, 1750), p. 46.
[145] [Spearman], *Letters to a friend*, pp. 65, 71–2.
[146] Faber, *Cabiri*, vol. I, p. 17.
[147] Sampson Arnold Mackey, *The mythological astronomy of the ancients* (2 vols., Norwich, 1822–3), vol. II, p. 23.
[148] Richard Carlile, *An abstract, embodying the evidences, of the lectures delivered by Mr Carlile, at Brighton and elsewhere, in the year 1836, to prove that the Bible is not a book of historical record, but an important mythological volume* (London, 1837), pp. 4, 9.
[149] John Williams, *Homerus* (London, 1842), pp. vi, 109.
[150] William Brown Galloway, *Egypt's record of time* (London, 1869), pp. 7–8.

The 'key to all mythologies' was not only on the tip of British tongues. It also made its way into the writings of the French philosophes who debunked traditional Christian orthodoxies in the field of mythography. While the allegorical basis of ancient legends enjoyed some currency among mythographers, Charles-François Dupuis argued that the originality of his own scheme of mythographical exegesis lay in his perception that the heavenly motions, including the rising and setting of stars and the passage of the sun across different constellations, provided the astronomical key ('la clef astronomique') to the seemingly absurd happenings of ancient mythology.[151] Similarly, Constantin Volney described how the original zodiacal allegories which underlay mythology had gradually degenerated into mere vulgar superstitions; eventually this subsidence reached the point where the sages in ancient societies, who had, unlike the common people, once possessed the cipher by which such allegories might be decoded, lost the key which had given them access to the esoteric meanings behind popular myths ('perdirent la clef des énigmes et de la doctrine secrète').[152]

The metaphor of the key meant different things to different mythographers — sometimes a means of reducing the world's lush religious biodiversity to a simple orthodox formula, occasionally a deistic method for unmasking Christianity as itself a kind of mythology, and at other moments pointing towards a more sophisticated process for examining the relationship of mythology and metaphor. As we shall see, mythography contained many mansions.

---

[151] C.-F. Dupuis, *Mémoire sur l'origine des constellations, et sur l'explication de la fable, par le moyen de l'astronomie* (Paris, 1781), p. 77: 'On a dit souvent que les prétendues absurdités de la théologie et de la mythologie des anciens n'étoient que des allégories; mais personne n'a employé la clef astronomique, et la théorie des levers et des couchers d'étoiles, et le passage du soleil dans les différentes constellations pour expliquer … les fables de l'antiquité.'

[152] C.-F. Volney, *Recherches nouvelles sur l'histoire ancienne* (2 vols., Paris, 1814), vol. I, p. 288.

CHAPTER 3

The Legacies of the Ancients in Enlightenment Mythography

> [H]e found himself in agreement with Mr Casaubon as to the unsound opinions of Middleton concerning the relations of Judaism and Catholicism. (*Middlemarch*, ch. 22)
>
> [T]here was to be a new Parergon, a small monograph on some lately-traced indications concerning the Egyptian mysteries whereby certain assertions of Warburton's could be corrected. (*Middlemarch*, ch. 29)

The city of Rome plays a significant part in the plot of *Middlemarch*. That Rome was the scene of the Casaubons' doomed honeymoon was not simply an occasion to indicate the failure of Mr Casaubon's libido to rise to his romantic surroundings; it also served to remind some of Eliot's more cerebral readers of the position Rome had occupied in the literature of mythography. An allusion of this sort might now seem too recondite for a general audience. However, the central allegation of pagano-popery (that Roman Catholicism derived in its essentials from classical paganism) was once a familiar trope of popular anti-Catholicism in early modern England, notwithstanding its more specialised function as a tool of mythographical speculation. Indeed, the claim that there had existed a sinister and depraved continuity between ancient pagan Rome and historic Roman Catholicism would remain a vivid element in Protestant polemic well into the middle of the nineteenth century.

Moreover, the supposed continuity between pagan and Christian Rome had also inspired a subtle and insinuating subversion in the hands of two of the most controversial figures of the English Enlightenment: Conyers Middleton[1] – to whom Eliot explicitly refers in *Middlemarch* – and Edward Gibbon, whose shade lurks in the recesses of the novel's Roman section. Both Middleton and Gibbon seemed to extend the similarity

---

[1] See H. Trevor-Roper, 'From deism to history: Conyers Middleton', in Trevor-Roper, *History and the enlightenment* (ed. J. Robertson, New Haven, 2010), pp. 71–119; B. W. Young, 'Conyers Middleton: the historical consequences of heterodoxy', in S. Mortimer and J. Robertson (eds.), *The intellectual consequences of religious heterodoxy 1600–1750* (Leiden, 2012), pp. 235–65.

between paganism and popery into a more general conflation of paganism and Christianity, Protestantism included. Was Christianity, they seemed to suggest, basically a reworking of a heathen original?

British culture during the eighteenth and nineteenth centuries was, of course, immersed in the classics. In spite of their pagan associations, ancient Greece and Rome occupied a central place in English life. Future Anglican clergymen learnt as much – probably more – at school and university about the language, literature and history of the ancient Greeks and Romans as they did about the Hebrews from whom the scriptures derived. Rarely did this tension between classical paganism and the Judaeo-Christian tradition become so overt or threatening as to suggest an impasse. On the whole, the classical and the biblical belonged in separate compartments. At points where the reliance of a supposedly Christian culture upon the educational foundations of profane heathendom seemed likely to produce difficulty, means of accommodation and reconciliation were found to retrieve the situation. However, Middleton and Gibbon were suavely subversive exceptions to the general rule. Their version of Enlightenment threatened to turn the untroubled relationship of Christianity and classical antiquity inside out: the two were, it transpired, all too easily – all too suspiciously – reconciled, for Christianity, they appeared to insinuate, was little more than an updated form of paganism masquerading as something distinct.

The vexed matter of Rome, to which Eliot quietly alludes, brings into focus a cluster of loosely connected issues. In the first place, what was the place of mythography in the British Enlightenment? When other sciences and bodies of learning were being refurbished to meet higher standards of proof and plausibility, was mythography – exceptionally – allowed to languish unimproved? And, if not, does that suggest that the eighteenth-century forerunners of Mr Casaubon propounded enlightened forms of mythography whose sophistication and ingenuity are not so easily captured in the pint-pot of Eliot's caricature? Were Middleton and Gibbon, perhaps, merely the most controversial outliers in a century of mythographical innovation and development? Indeed, does David Hume's *Natural History of Religion* (1757) also belong to an emerging body of critical mythography?

Eighteenth-century Britain exhibited a rich and variegated spectrum of enlightened mythographical activity, from Isaac Newton – heterodox in his Christology, though otherwise orthodox – to figures whose penetration and acuteness were guided, ultimately, by orthodox concerns, such as the Oxford astronomer George Costard and the Aberdonian classicist

Thomas Blackwell, but whose insights prefigured in some aspects the scientific mythology of the mid-nineteenth century. William Warburton – the doyen of the 'double doctrine' (a popular outer religion which conceals an inner esoteric cult known only to its initiates) and another noted mythographer mentioned by Eliot in *Middlemarch* – provoked the most extensive and prolix pamphlet debate of eighteenth-century England with his multi-volume masterpiece, *The Divine Legation of Moses* (1738–41). The Warburton affair – a prolonged debate waged via the pulpit and printing press that ran ultimately for several decades – reminds us of the neglected centrality of mythography in the English Enlightenment. Rival parties of Warburtonians and anti-Warburtonians soon emerged to struggle over the contested terrain of ancient pagan mythology, and Warburton himself was elevated to a bishopric. Moreover, Warburton himself entered the lists against the philosophy of Hume, who had positioned himself beyond the pale of conventional mythography, and had indeed overturned its core assumptions.[2]

The presiding genius of the early English Enlightenment, Isaac Newton, immersed himself in the study of mythography. His manuscripts abound in mythographical speculation, and in this particular avenue of scholarship he maintained some fairly conventional positions. Newton argued that the sons of Noah – and in particular the pagan progeny of Ham – had been divinised as the deities of heathen polytheisms: Noah as Saturn, Ham as Jupiter, Chus as Mars, and so on. If Newton's contribution to a narrowly-defined mythography was unoriginal, there was nevertheless considerable spillage between his pedestrian investigations of pagan polytheism and his revolutionary attempt to recalibrate the history of the world's civilisations, *The chronology of ancient kingdoms amended* (1728), which appeared, to much controversy, the year after his death. Newton's science of chronology was a project which – in retrospect at least – seems to blur the distinction between mythology and history. The pivotal element in Newton's revised chronological scheme was his revised date for the expedition of Jason and the Argonauts, an event which had become fixed in customary accounts of chronology *c*.1450–1500 BC. Newton located it 500 years later at 939 BC. By the same token, the Trojan War also occupied a central place in Newton's chronological scheme, relocated to 904 BC. If Newton's treatment of the Argonautic expedition and the Trojan war as historical events diminish

---

[2] A. W. Evans, *Warburton and the Warburtonians: a study in some eighteenth-century controversies* (London, 1932); B. W. Young, *Religion and enlightenment in eighteenth-century England* (Oxford, 1998), pp. 167–212.

the giant of science, this interpretative line was at least internally consistent, for Newton believed that mythological tales derived ultimately from the matter of history. Moreover, in spite of Newton's curious treatment of the Argonautic expedition, his science of chronology was bold and imaginative. As Jed Buchwald and Mordechai Feingold have shown, Newton's attempt to develop a coherent system of synchronisation among the civilisations of the ancient world rested not only on astronomy – in particular the calculation of the positions in the skies of antiquity of equinoxes and solstices – but also upon a kind of conjectural history of the origins of civilisation from the Flood, including a careful demographic investigation of the scale and plausible rate of population increase necessary to sustain the emergence of great cities and eventually the empires which they controlled. Here Newton was both cautious and sceptical of the cavalier assumptions about post-Diluvian demographic growth which prevailed in the field of primeval history.[3]

Blackwell, an eminent classicist and the Principal of Marischal College, Aberdeen, is best known today for his major contribution to the Homeric Question. In his *Enquiry into the Life and Writings of Homer* (1735), Blackwell broke with earlier assumptions about Homer's divinely inspired genius to situate the poet instead in a vividly realised and tangible historical context: an archaic society in which barbarism and an emerging 'classical' refinement coexisted. The richness of Homeric epic, Blackwell suggested, was owing to the interplay of the various social and cultural factors he parsed so precisely. Genius, it transpired, arose from a complex concatenation of secondary causes.[4]

Notwithstanding the penetration of the *Enquiry*, Blackwell's main contribution to contemporary mythographical debate came in *Letters Concerning Mythology* (1748). Of the nineteen letters (or chapters) in the volume, another anonymous author wrote the first half dozen or so, but Blackwell composed parts of the seventh and eighth letters, and all the letters thereafter. Blackwell's *Letters* recapitulated the cultural approach adumbrated in the *Enquiry*. In particular, Blackwell recognised that mythology played an integral part in the primeval civilising process. Mythology's original function, as Blackwell understood it, was to instil a belief in 'an invisible power or powers' above mankind, who would distribute rewards

---

[3] Isaac Newton, *The chronology of ancient kingdoms amended* (London, 1728); F. Manuel, *Isaac Newton historian* (Cambridge, MA 1963); J. Z. Buchwald and M. Feingold, *Newton and the origin of civilization* (Princeton, 2013).
[4] Thomas Blackwell, *Enquiry into the life and writings of Homer* (London, 1735); K. Simonsuuri, *Homer's original genius: eighteenth-century notions of the early Greek epic* (Cambridge, 1979), pp. 99–107.

to the just and punish the unjust. In this way, he contended, mythology was 'fitted to serve that noble end of civilizing nations'. However, this Ur-mythology – a systematic body of tales, including creation stories of the gods and the natural world, as well as moral fables, many of which were conveyed and reinforced by signs and symbols and by metaphor ('an allegory in embryo') – became corrupted by subsequent interpolations. Most notably, what had 'spoilt' mythology was the addition of historical episodes and tales of real human personages, which inevitably complicated and indeed undermined the ultimate educational thrust of the original core of myth. They 'threw' the original mythology 'off its hinge; and from explaining nature and instructing men, made it a rhapsody of inexplicable wonders'. There was, in other words, no single rhyme or reason to the miscellaneous pot-pourri of 'unmeaning fable' the modern world had inherited from the ancient world. Such corruptions reminded Blackwell of the ways in which the message of Christianity had been similarly adulterated in Roman Catholicism. There was the same 'confusion', rooted in popular credulity and the susceptibility to 'take representations for things, as we see happen daily in Popish countries'. Mythology, too, lost sight of the original allegory which had underpinned it and became a morass of meaninglessness. It became a mere superstition when the credulous vulgar reduced it to the literal meaning of the stories within which moral fables had been wrapped. The outer wrapping was misunderstood as the stuff of myth itself. Mythology was a hybrid, put together not only by ancient priests and poets but also by the crass uncomprehending stupidity of ordinary people. Cultural borrowing was an additional cause of the perplexing descent into nonsense. This was because mythological confusion arose – naturally enough – from basic misunderstandings of words and idioms as one ancient mythology was borrowed by another. Given that mythology had become a compound of different elements – some concerning the universe, some rooted in moral teachings, some stories about deified men, some mere mistranslations of one ancient mythology into the language of another ancient people – it defied a single all-encompassing explanation. Mythology, rather, was 'a road full of mazes, and frequented by phantoms, that promise to direct, and then deceive you'.[5]

George Costard, although an orthodox champion of sacred history, was a dedicated astronomer and, in the field of mythography, a pluralist sceptical of unitary explanations. He recognised that there was no single solution to the complexities of pagan mythology. The study of mythography

---

[5] Thomas Blackwell, *Letters concerning mythology* (London, 1748), pp. 70, 93, 171, 176–8, 182, 233, 235.

rather demanded painstaking consideration of individual details and of their gradual accumulation into mythological systems: 'The want of lights, sufficient to instruct us in an age when each mythology came into use, hath been the cause of almost infinite confusion. That all this mass of fable and history did not grow up to its full size all at once, hath, I think, been made already pretty plain.'[6]

Mythology developed, Costard contended, 'by a natural ambiguity, and very easy metaphor'. He showed how dense polytheistic mythologies had emerged in ancient Greece from its contacts with Egyptian and Babylonian cultures. Fanciful notions about gods, their emblems, responsibilities and deeds took rise from 'a similarity of names, many times not easily distinguished by the ear'. The mispronunciation of the eastern names of gods, combined with random mistakes of orthography in translating terms from one language into another and accidental resemblances between words, created fertile miasmas of ambiguity out of which mythologies rich in seeming – but mistaken – particularity emerged. Verbal slippages multiplied the attributes of deity and also led to a proliferation of symbols for gods. This explained in good measure why mythology was 'very wild, and frequently inconsistent'. It was a nonsense born of a sort of malapropism and confounded homonym, and not only from that. Costard not only took account of the 'fancies, arising from such ambiguities', but also perceived that supposition had its own self-propelling dynamic, for 'fancy usually begets fancy'. Superstition, Costard concluded, is 'endless, and still productive of new fancies'.[7]

Eliot had read the canonical works of both Middleton and Warburton,[8] each of whom was associated in the eighteenth century with a major grammatical feature of the language of mythography: in Middleton's case the detection of a pagano-popish continuum which conjoined heathen and Catholic Rome, and in Warburton's the distinction between the colourful outer husks of pagan religions – visible to the people at large – and esoteric inner doctrines, of greater philosophical cogency, known only to initiates. Pagano-popery and the double doctrine were ubiquitous in

---

[6] George Costard, *A further account of the rise and progress of astronomy amongst the antients* (Oxford, 1748), p. 148.
[7] Costard, *Further account*, pp. 97, 99, 110, 117, 135, 146, 150; Costard, *A letter to Martin Folkes, Esq.* (London, 1746), pp. 49–50; Costard, *Two dissertations, I. Containing an enquiry into the meaning of the word Kesitah … II. On the signification of the word Hermes* (Oxford, 1750), pp. 43–6.
[8] A. Fleishman, *George Eliot's reading: a chronological list*, supplement to no. 54–5, *George Eliot–George Henry Lewes Studies* (2008), pp. 14, 41.

eighteenth-century philosophy and mythography. Often they surfaced in close proximity, and there was a logical connection between them.

Eighteenth-century commentators – including antiquaries and mythographers – were fascinated by what might be called the inner life of classical political thought: the exotic world of pagan belief to which it was conjoined. Officeholding in ancient Rome was, after all, a far from secular business, and included both temporal magistracies and a quasi-political priesthood open to a lay elite. Augury – predicting future events from the flight of birds – was as much a civic concern as the more prosaic fiscal issues of the quaestorship. This was a realm, moreover, which Eliot herself knew from her knowledge of Plutarch and from Cicero's explorations of Roman religion.[9]

Pagan beliefs, the due observance of cultic rites and the duties of religious officeholding constituted an important – though now underappreciated – strand in eighteenth-century readings of ancient history. Eighteenth-century historians of Rome stressed the importance of the religious institutions established by Numa Pompilius as an institutional foundation for Roman greatness.[10] Moreover, Epicureanism – a non-providentialist philosophy which undermined the traditional religion of ancient Rome – was also identified as a significant factor in weakening the republican virtue of the citizenry.[11]

Eighteenth-century commentators were as transfixed on the inner beliefs which sustained ancient polities as on their institutional machinery. Indeed, where did one draw the line in pagan societies between the sacred and the profane dimensions of government? It was an axiom of political thought that all polities required belief in some superintending divinity and the promise (or threat) of rewards and punishments in the afterlife to maintain order. This was why the argument of the Huguenot ironist Pierre Bayle (1647–1706), that a society of atheists was no impossibility,[12] caused such a furore in the late seventeenth century. Hence, even in discussions of ancient pagan polities, scholars paid due attention to the necessary religious institutions without which society could not function. The Oxford historian Basil Kennett (1674–1715) began his discussion of Roman religious institutions with the unexceptionable statement that religion was

---

[9] *Ibid.*, pp. 18, 40, 53, 55.
[10] Laurence Echard, *The Roman history* (10th edn, London, 1734), pp. 21–2; Nathaniel Hooke, *The Roman history* (4 vols., London, 1738–71), vol. I, pp. 51–9; Oliver Goldsmith, *The Roman history* (2 vols., London, 1769), vol. I, pp. 23–4.
[11] Edward Wortley Montagu, *Reflections on the rise and fall of the ancient republicks* (London, 1759), pp. 23, 225–6, 270, 293–8, 301–10; Adam Ferguson, *The history of the progress and termination of the Roman republic* (3 vols., London, 1783), vol. I, p. 10; vol. II, pp. 112–15.
[12] Pierre Bayle, *Pensées diverses sur la comète* (1682: 2 vols., Paris, 1984), esp. vol. II, pp. 5–159.

'absolutely necessary for the establishment of civil government', which he termed 'a truth … far from being denied by any sort of persons'.[13] Historians of Rome focused not on the emptiness of pagan religion, but on the differing effects of Stoicism and Epicureanism on ancient manners.

Scholars were particularly indebted to the insights of the ancient polymath Marcus Terentius Varro (116 BC–27 BC), in particular his fragment on ancient theology preserved in Augustine's *City of God*. In this passage, Varro established a tripartite scheme for the analysis of ancient pagan religion.[14] Varro distinguished the fabulous mythology devised by poets from both the natural theology studied by philosophers and the civil theology deployed by politicians. The first comprised the fictitious matter of ancient mythology, the second an explanation of the physical world and its metaphysical underpinnings, and the third the practical appropriation of a theological façade by lawgivers and statesmen. Varro's attention seemed to dwell not so much on the truth or falsehood of ancient beliefs and practices, but on their various functions and overall utility.[15]

If Varro's message about classical religion was riddled with ambiguity, so too were the most influential classical authorities on ancient paganism. Plutarch had been a priest of the oracle of Apollo at Delphi as well as a prominent philosopher and historian, but one whose works were critical of superstition.[16] Decidedly slippery too was the legacy of Marcus Tullius Cicero (106 BC–43 BC) – often known as Tully in the eighteenth century – who was celebrated in Augustan Britain as a kind of honorary Whig.[17] Cicero had punctiliously observed the religious duties incumbent upon the offices he had held, but he seemed in his philosophical writings detached from paganism as a system of belief. The character of Cotta in Cicero's dialogue *De natura deorum* captures something of the author's ambivalence. Cotta, the representative of Academic scepticism in the dialogue, is also holder of the civic office of *pontifex*, a post which carried responsibility for the administration of religious rites. Speaking *ex officio* as *pontifex*, Cotta offers his view that public religious worship ought to be reverently observed, but adds that he would like to be persuaded that the gods do indeed exist, for he confesses that sometimes he is perplexed as to whether they exist at all.[18] Evidence of this sort, that among the ancients

---

[13] Basil Kennett, *Romae antiquae notitia* (London, 1696), p. 61.
[14] G. Stroumsa, *A new science: the discovery of religion in the age of reason* (Cambridge, MA, 2010), p. 44.
[15] Augustine, *City of God* (transl. H. Bettenson, London, 1972), pp. 234–43.
[16] Plutarch, *Moralia vol. V* (transl. F. C. Babbitt, Cambridge, MA, 1936).
[17] R. Browning, *The political and constitutional ideas of the court Whigs* (Baton Rouge, 1982).
[18] Cicero, *Nature of the gods* (transl. H. McGregor, Harmondsworth, 1972), p. 94.

scepticism in matters of religion had not been incompatible with religious office, contributed to the eighteenth-century fascination with the double doctrine and the capacity of the ancient philosophers to compartmentalise their beliefs.[19] The double doctrine of the ancients would tantalise both the orthodox – Warburtonians especially – and freethinkers. In 53 BC Cicero himself had been appointed to the civic office of *augur*, with responsibilities for the interpretation of portents and omens. Nevertheless, it is clear from his writings that he was far from convinced that augury served any useful purpose. Indeed, at more than one point in his corpus Cicero cited – approvingly – Cato's jest about whether any soothsayer (knowing his very profession was founded on hokum) could meet a fellow soothsayer without bursting out laughing.[20] However, Cicero's position was not so easily reduced to a crude denial of religion, except as a cynical instrument of due order and social decorum. For Cicero clearly distinguished between 'superstitio' – unfounded beliefs about the nature of the gods – and 'religio', which meant in part at least a civic observance of a community's traditional rites.[21]

Orthodox and freethinking readers of Cicero's ambiguous oeuvre took away from it strikingly divergent messages.[22] Was his *De divinatione* a defence or a critique of augury? With which character in *De natura deorum* did Cicero most closely identify? The deist Anthony Collins (1676–1729), in his *Discourse of free-thinking*, took issue with the complacently establishmentarian Cicero portrayed by orthodox churchmen. They tended, Collins argued, to misquote Cicero at every turn, and to misrepresent a versatile philosopher as a paragon of conformity. Nothing, he argued, could be further from the truth. According to Collins, Cicero's *De divinatione* 'destroyed the whole revealed religion of the Greeks and Romans, by showing the imposture of all their miracles, and weakness of all the other reasons on which it was pretended to be founded'. Plutarch too, though 'a heathen priest', had 'preserved his understanding free'. Plutarch had maintained his distance from his 'craft', eschewed superstition and satirised 'the public forms of devotion'. The ancient mythographer Varro also supplied matter for Collins's arguments, to the effect that 'there were many things

---

[19] J. Champion, *The pillars of priestcraft shaken: the Church of England and its enemies 1660–1730* (Cambridge, 1992), pp. 170–95.
[20] Cicero, *Nature of the gods*, p. 98; Cicero, 'On divination', in Cicero, *De senectute, de amicitia, de divinatio* (transl. W. A. Falconer, Cambridge, MA, 1923), pp. 428–9.
[21] Cicero, 'On divination', pp. 536–7.
[22] For the appeal of Cicero to deists, see G. Gawlick, 'Cicero and the Enlightenment', *Studies on Voltaire and the Eighteenth Century*, vol. 25 (1963), pp. 657–82, at p. 660.

false in religion, which it was not convenient for the vulgar to know; and again, some things which, though false, yet it was expedient they should be believed by them'. Augustine had recognised here, Collins noted, Varro's discovery of 'the whole secret of statesmen and politicians'. In other words, the flexible utility of mythological fables – and the rites and priesthoods which reinforced them – lay at the core of classical political thought.[23]

Collins's views did not go unchallenged. Britain's most eminent classical scholar, Richard Bentley (1662–1742), responded with the argument that it was Collins himself who had misrepresented Plutarch and Cicero; indeed, Varro and Cato the Elder too. Cicero reappeared in Bentley's pamphlet as a staunch believer in providence and the immortality of the soul, indeed an ancient avatar of Anglicanism *avant la lettre*. Bentley claimed, somewhat disingenuously, that it was Balba the Stoic, rather than Cotta the Academic–sceptic, who functioned as Cicero's mouthpiece in *De natura deorum*. Nor had Plutarch, a priest of Apollo, been a freethinker. He had, after all, written an attack on the atheistic Epicurean Colotes. Cato, moreover, had not been a critic of indigenous Roman practices; Bentley insisted that Cato's mockery of soothsaying was pointed at non-Roman importations he considered to be subversive of the homegrown rites of the earliest city-state. Cato's complaints were, in other words, xenophobic, not a sign of irreligion on his part.[24]

The Irish-born freethinker John Toland (1670–1722) made the ancient double doctrine – or 'double philosophy', as he called it – the subject of an essay, 'Clidophorus, or of the Exoteric and Esoteric Philosophy'. It was, after all, as Toland insisted, the 'key' which opened the mystery religions of the Egyptians and Pythagoreans. Toland argued that most ancient polities were 'built upon fraud'; that is, the noble lies associated with their founders and lawgivers, such as the encounter of Numa Pompilius and the nymph Egeria, provided the crucial ideological underpinnings of the state. The ancients had lied for the public good, on the grounds that the common people needed to be 'managed by guile, and to be deluded by agreeable fables into obedience to their governors'. Such fictions were not only instruments of civil policy; in city after city, priests had also used such tales to build their own power-base. Eventually, pagan priesthoods had managed to enforce stifling orthodoxies on the laity, to drive out the open-minded quest for truth with the religious fictions which supported their

---

[23] [Anthony Collins], *A discourse of free-thinking* (London, 1713), pp. 104–9.
[24] [Richard Bentley], *Remarks upon a late discourse of free-thinking. In a letter to N.N. Part the second* (6th edn, Cambridge, 1725), pp. 51–82.

own hold on power. Temporal magistracies had allowed this to happen, 'partly through superstition proceeding from their ignorance; and partly through policy, to grasp at more power'. In these ways, falsehood had triumphed over truth, indeed had become rigid orthodoxy, the questioning of which brought harsh penalties. As a result ancient philosophers had developed 'occult ways of speaking and writing' as a way of getting around such prohibitions:

> [C]onstrained by this holy tyranny to make use of a two-fold doctrine, the one popular, accommodated to the prejudices of the vulgar, and to the received customs or religions; the other philosophical, conformable to the nature of things, and consequently to truth, which with doors fast shut and under all other precautions, they communicated only to friends of known probity, prudence and capacity.

This dark 'veil of divine allegories' was a necessary prudential safeguard for philosophy in ancient polities. The oppressions of priestcraft were the norm, and so too was a covert philosophy by way of response. Toland found nothing atypical in the double philosophy of Greco-Roman antiquity; rather, the 'double manner of teaching' had been common among the 'oriental nations' as well as the Druids of ancient Britain and Gaul. Indeed, Toland used the ubiquity of the 'double philosophy' as a sly argument against the *consensus gentium*, that plank of Christian apologetic which equated universality with truth. The fact, Toland alleged, that 'this distinction of exoteric and esoteric doctrines' was 'the establishment of all nations' only went to show 'that universality is no infallible mark of truth'. Such allegories, moreover, generated misunderstandings; emblems degenerated into supposed persons, becoming 'objects of reverence and false worship'. Hence, unsurprisingly, Toland endorsed Plato's suppression of Homer; that is, the argument of Plato in the *Republic* that the Greek myths were ultimately corrosive of the social fabric. Plato's view, in Toland's words, was that ordinary people 'will never think that to be a vice or imperfection in themselves which is a virtue or perfection in the divinity'. Hence the Platonic view that knowledge of the various 'rapes, adulteries, slaughters, lies, thefts' of the Olympian gods constituted a social nuisance. Of course, if ancient states were founded on lies, then might Christianity, which emerged from that milieu, follow the same basic pattern, a system of imposture and deceit whose supposed truths were upheld in the cause of civil policy and the avaricious self-interest of entrenched priesthoods?[25]

---

[25] John Toland, 'Clidophorus, or of the exoteric and esoteric philosophy', in Toland, *Tetradymus* (London, 1720), pp. 64–6, 72, 80, 85–6, 94.

Over the course of the eighteenth century, the distinction of the double doctrine between an inner and outer religion came to displace the three-pronged system of fabulous, natural and civil theologies inherited from Varro. Not that the double doctrine was a novelty. The idea of a twofold philosophy had been, as Peter Harrison has argued, a foundational element in the western canon, and had surfaced in antiquity both in pagan and patristic literatures.[26] Nevertheless, it became a commonplace in eighteenth-century treatments of paganism. In effect, proponents of the double doctrine grouped together the fantastical and the political forms of ancient religion as complementary expressions of its vulgar outer cladding. Furthermore, from the late seventeenth century commentators tended to add the ploys of scheming and self-interested pagan priesthoods to the uses of religion advanced by ancient statesmen. Indeed, there was but a wafer-thin difference between Varro's concept of a political theology and the concept of an outer doctrine devised for public consumption.

The hackneyed notion of an outer doctrine surfaced more than once in Middleton's major laudatory biography of Cicero, a controversial work which rested, in some degree it seemed, on quicksands of forgery.[27] Middleton argued that in Cicero's day there was 'not a man of liberal education, who did not consider [religion] as an engine of state, or political system; contrived for the uses of government and to keep the people in order'. While an undoubted bulwark of Roman republican government, its religious institutions, Middleton perceived, were 'considered all the while by men of sense, as merely political, and of human invention'. Cicero was no different; 'a mind enlightened by ... noble principles ... could not possibly harbour a thought of the truth or divinity of so absurd a worship'. Yet Middleton's Cicero was a decided opponent of Epicureanism, and stood somewhere between stoicism and scepticism in his outlook.[28]

The double doctrine was a central feature in the interpretation of ancient politics advanced by the Tory freethinker Viscount Bolingbroke. Ancient legislators, argued Bolingbroke, had 'imposed revelations they knew to be false' as 'a proper expedient to enforce obedience to a political regimen'. Nevertheless, philosophical refinements among an elite quietly dissatisfied

---

[26] P. Harrison, *Religion and the religions in the English Enlightenment* (Cambridge, 1990), pp. 85–6.
[27] J. Levine, 'Et tu Brute? History and forgery in eighteenth-century England', in R. Myers and M. Harris (eds.), *Fakes and frauds: varieties of deception in print and manuscript* (Winchester, 1989), pp. 71–97.
[28] Conyers Middleton, *The history of the life of Marcus Tullius Cicero* (2nd edn, 3 vols., London, 1741), vol. III, pp. 344–7.

with the gruel of mere fable and its limited nutrition led to the emergence of 'the useful distinction between an outward and inward doctrine ... one for the vulgar and one for the initiated'. Among the vulgar, Bolingbroke noted, 'allegory passed for a literal relation of facts', while among the devotees of the secret doctrine, the public religion or mythology was regarded as mere 'fraud or folly'. Nevertheless, replacing the double doctrine and its outworks of 'philosophical lying' with something more transparent had not been a viable option. Bolingbroke contended that 'a system of philosophy, which had not contained a system of theology, as well as of politics, would have been held in no esteem among the ancients'.[29]

Cicero's religious ambivalence, moreover, continued to provide a compelling example of the way in which public and private doctrines might be compartmentalised. Thomas Stona (1727/8–92), a staunch opponent of freethinking, parsed Cicero as an easygoing establishmentarian conformist, though one 'far from being superstitiously attached to popular religion' and possessed, moreover, of deep monotheistic principles: 'Tully thought it incumbent upon every prudent man to conform to the established religion of his country, and so he always acted agreeable to that opinion, but his religion was of a much more exalted nature, being founded in the belief of a supreme being, the creator and preserver of the universe.'[30]

Ancient paganism was disputed terrain in the wars between orthodoxy and freethinking, and Cicero – strange as it might seem – was almost as strategically significant as the Fathers of the early church.

It is hard to fix the point at which the idea of pagano-popery became an established feature of English Protestant polemic. Such ideas had been in circulation from before the Reformation, and remained in circulation inside as well as outside the Catholic Church. The humanist historian Polydore Vergil (c.1470–1555), who was Henry VII's court historiographer, had conceded the existence of pagan survivals in the Catholic Church, though warranted as part of a strategy to win converts from the old heathenism. Moreover, some Catholics – such as Guillaume du Choul (c.1496–1560) and the Abbé Michel de Marolles (1600–81)[31] – admitted that skeletons of this sort did indeed lurk in the Roman closet. Nevertheless, it became

---

[29] Bolingbroke, *Philosophical works* (5 vols., London, 1754), vol. I, pp. 307–8, 310, 329; vol. II, pp. 109, 139.
[30] [Thomas Stona], *Remarks upon the natural history of religion by Mr Hume. With dialogues on heathen idolatry and the Christian religion* (London, 1758), pp. 85, 87.
[31] Conyers Middleton, *A letter from Rome* (5th edn, London, 1742), pp. cviii–cix; M. T. Hodgen, *Early anthropology in the sixteenth and seventeenth centuries* (Philadelphia, 1964), p. 327.

a more decisively Protestant trope. In 1606 Oliver Ormerod (d. 1626), the rector of Hunterspill in Somerset, published *The picture of a papist ... whereunto is annexed a certain treatise, intitled Pagano-papismus; wherein is proved that Papisme is flat Paganisme*.

Isaac Casaubon himself argued that the early Christians had called the sacraments 'mysteries' in deference to existing pagan nomenclature.[32] In addition, the identification of Popery with paganism also provided the central matter of *The Originall of Idolatries: or, the Birth of Heresies* (1624), a puritan work misattributed to Casaubon, though, arguably, an extension of his insight. The pseudo-Casaubon argued that the Christian church in Rome had compromised with the hardy and enduring rites of the civic religion established in Rome by one of its first pre-republican kings, Numa Pompilius. In its institutions and ceremonies, Roman Catholicism exhibited its pedigree in a virtually ineradicable 'Pompilian religion'. The Papacy owed something both to the position of Pontifex Maximus and to the heathen cult of the great father Jupiter. Similarly, the Mass was traced back to Roman practices of sacrifice, and transubstantiation was found lurking at 'the very bottom of this idolatrous labyrinth'.[33]

The Reverend Joshua Stopford (1635/6–75), the rector of All Saints in York, published *Pagano-Papismus: or an exact parallel between Rome-Pagan, and Rome-Christian, in their doctrines and ceremonies* (1675). Interestingly, Stopford also floated a version of the double doctrine alongside his ideas of pagano-popery, arguing that the ancients had kept the common people in ignorance of the sacred mysteries.[34]

In *Les conformitez des cérémonies modernes avec les anciennes* (1667) Pierre Mussard (1627–86), the Huguenot minister at the French church in Threadneedle Street, traced a whole range of disturbing parallels between pagan offices, rituals and beliefs and those of modern Catholicism. Mussard described in detail the umbilical linkage by which ancient heathen religion had nourished Roman Christianity. The Christian saints resembled the many inferior divinities of pagan mythology, the patron saints of places, crafts and the cure of illnesses reflecting the tutelary deities of classical paganism. Such similarities extended to priestly offices in the

---

[32] 'Sciendum vero est, primos Christianos, cum sacramenta vocarunt mysteria, teletas, mystagogiam, aut similibus nominibus, transtulisse ea vocabula ex iis paganorum sacris', Isaac Casaubon, *De rebus sacris exercitationes xvi* (London, 1614), p. 544.

[33] *The originall of idolatries: or, the birth of heresies* (transl. Abraham Darcie, London, 1624), esp. pp. 37–8, 40, 44, 50, 73, 83.

[34] Joshua Stopford, 'Epistle to the Reader', *Pagano-Papismus: or an exact parallel between Rome-Pagan and Rome-Christian, in their doctrines and ceremonies* (London, 1675).

historic religions of Rome. If one didn't know better, Mussard speculated, one might easily conflate descriptions of the heathen *pontifex maximus* and the papacy: 'ne jugeroit-on pas qu'il a eu dessein de décrier le Pape, tant ce portrait lui ressemble?' Worse still, the Mass seemed to be derived from the heathen rites of Isis. Alas, the common people fell easy prey to the deceptions of Romano-pagan priestcraft, happily drinking up the poison of its superstitious doctrines because presented in the golden cup of Christianity: 'ils boivent avec plaisir le poison des superstitions payennes, parce qu'il est présenté dans une coupe d'or couverte du nom chrestien'.[35] An English translation of Mussard's work, by James Dupré, would appear in 1732 under the title *Roma antiqua et recens*.

In *The Court of the Gentiles* (1677), Theophilus Gale described Roman Catholic theology as 'an imitation of pagan demon-doctrines'. 'Antichrist's canonised saints' he considered as 'parallel to the pagan demons', with canonisation, indeed, a variation on the heathen practice of deifying rulers. The concept of purgatory was but a 'temporary Tartary', based upon heathen ideas of the infernal regions of the underworld. Indeed, Gale contended that 'the whole body and spirit of Antichristianism had its conception and formation in the womb of pagan philosophy'. In particular, the Platonic school of Alexandria had helped to marry Christian themes to established pagan forms and categories.[36]

Michael Geddes (1650?–1713), the Scots-born Anglican cleric and chancellor of Salisbury, maintained that 'the door by which images did first creep into the Christian Church, was an unwarrantable compliance with the heathens'. Similarly, the saints of the Roman Catholic Church and their festivals seemed to parallel ancient pagan deities and their commemoration. 'If only', Geddes reckoned, 'we had but a full heathen Roman calendar, to collate with the present Roman martyrology, a great many ... would be found in them both, on the same days of the month.' It struck Geddes that the accommodationist tactics of the modern Jesuits in China were prefigured in the practices of early Catholicism. In addition, he attributed the pretensions of the Roman see to a supremacy over other bishops to the assumption that the heathen authority of the Pontifex Maximus 'had naturally devolved' upon the papacy.[37]

---

[35] [Pierre Mussard], *Les conformitez des cérémonies modernes avec les anciennes* (Leiden, 1667), pp. 16, 83, 165, 178–83, 299.
[36] Theophilus Gale, *The court of the Gentiles. Part III* (London, 1677), pp. 180, 219, 235, 238.
[37] Michael Geddes, *Miscellaneous tracts* (3 vols., London, 1702–14), 'A discovery of some gross mistakes in the Roman martyrology', vol. II, pp. 197, 201; 'A tract proving the adoration of images ... [etc] ... To be doctrines and practices not known in the Spanish church, in the beginning of the eighth century', vol. III, p. 3; 'An essay on the Canons of the Council of Sardica', vol. III, pp. 1–2.

Richard Cumberland, whose edition of the Phoenician Sanchoniathon proved an enduring contribution to British mythography, imagined the process by which pagan idolatry had gradually become interwoven with primitive Christianity:

> First were religious assemblies at the tombs, or memories of martyrs, where were commemorations of their virtues, joined with prayers directed only to the true God. Afterwards came in extravagant panegyrics, then canonization of saints, and invocation of them as intercessors with God, at length prayers were made to them, without any mention that they should intercede.[38]

In this way Catholicism – which partook of 'the heathen corruption, both in many idolatrous practices, and in lessening the authority of the scriptures'[39] – had degenerated into a kind of polytheism.

Originally, the notion of pagano-popery provided a method of deconstructing Roman Catholic pretensions, which was closely allied to Protestant polemic. True Protestantism meant a religion totally cleansed of the accretions of paganism. However, in the eighteenth century, it proved to be a versatile and flexible instrument for interrogating a range of wider Christian claims. The stakes in this area were raised by the gifted, low-key ironist Conyers Middleton in his *Letter from Rome*. According to Middleton, Catholicism consisted of 'mere copies ... of the originals of heathenism', contending that 'by a change only of name', supposedly Christian Romans 'found means to retain the thing; and by substituting their saints in the place of the old demigods, have set up idols of their own, instead of their forefathers'.[40]

Following, perhaps, in the footsteps of Geddes, for Middleton had a capacity to absorb the insights of others with barely a hint of attribution, he was able to explain how this state of affairs had come about. After all, Middleton perceived that the Jesuits of his own day in China made 'concessions' of a similar sort to appease their notional converts, and 'where pure Christianity will not go down, never scruple to compound the matter between Jesus and Confucius'. Such indeed were the very origins of Roman Christianity itself.[41]

While Middleton's *Letter from Rome* conventionally enough set out a whole range of practices and beliefs in which he detected the 'similitude of the Popish and pagan religion', it demonstratively raised – and

---

[38] Richard Cumberland, *Sanchoniatho's Phoenician History* (London, 1720), p. 253.
[39] *Ibid.*, p. 90.
[40] Middleton, *Letter from Rome*, pp. 152, 159.
[41] *Ibid.*, p. 223.

complacently evaded – broader questions concerning the relationship of Christianity as a whole to the world of heathendom. Middleton's ostensible message proclaimed that the 'Popish Church stands now adorned with all the furniture of their old paganism'. But Middleton seemed to be edging towards the unspoken question whether Protestant denominations might, for all their boasted anti-Roman reforms, turn out on closer examination to be similarly furnished. If the real bequest of antiquity to modern Catholicism was 'an uninterrupted succession from the priests of old, to the priests of new Rome', where did this leave the Church of England with its own claim to uphold patristic tradition and an apostolic succession of bishops? If Roman Catholic priestcraft was 'but the copy of an old cheat of the same kind', was Protestantism itself infected with the virus of pagan priestcraft? Middleton appeared to direct his readers towards worrying problems of this sort, but then – somewhat abruptly and very suspiciously, as it seemed to some perceptive critics – left such questions dangling.[42]

With Middleton's quietly subversive *Letter from Rome*, pagano-popery had acquired an additional dimension in English mythographical discourse. It functioned now both as a crucial trope of anti-Catholic rhetoric and as a discreet extra-Protestant roadmap for rational and enlightened critics of what might be called Christian folklore. However, Middleton – the falsest of false friends – had so cunningly camouflaged his tracks that it was not immediately apparent to many of his readers where he was leading them: to a secure Protestant citadel whose Christianity was at last purged of noxious heathen influences, or to a quicksand where there was no solid ground upon which an uncorrupted philosophically pure Christianity might be based?

Some readers perceived the dangerous tendency of Middleton's parallels. A playful Roman Catholic author, Simon Berington (1680–1755), used his pamphlet *A Popish pagan the fiction of a Protestant Heathen* (1743), which purported to be a translation from the Dutch of a conversation between a Dutch Deist and a 'doctor of heathen mythology', to paint the eponymous 'Protestant Heathen' or 'Doctor of Heathen Mythology' (Middleton, in other words) as less orthodox than the Dutch Deist, the latter character presumably a contemporary byword for heterodoxy.

However, the reception of Middleton's work was often all too straightforward, and some anti-Popish commentators took his strictures on pagano-popish continuities at face value, without any awareness of the ways in which Middletonian insights might be turned against – indeed, to

---

[42] *Ibid.*, pp. xxxvii, 131, 133, 209.

perceptive readers, had *already* been turned against – the traditions of the Church of England. A seemingly oblivious Thomas Seward (1747–1809), the rector of Eyam in Derbyshire and father of the poet Anna Seward, advertised his own conventionally orthodox pamphlet, *The conformity between Popery and Paganism* (1746), as a 'sequel' to Middleton's work. Seward simply lamented how some of the early Christians had 'accommodated themselves to the customs of the heathens to facilitate their conversion'. The household shrines of the pagan Romans – their *lares et penates* – had been, 'as it were, christened, but the superstition and idolatry were exactly the same'.[43]

Much closer to the substance of Middleton was the strict monotheism of Bolingbroke, a deist who perceived a clear continuum between pagan and Christian theologies. While 'the unity of God' was the 'primitive belief of mankind', this 'natural theology' had, Bolingbroke argued, become progressively corrupted into 'artificial' theologies – first into ditheism, such as the dualism found among the Zoroastrians, then to tritheism, and eventually to a more densely populated polytheism. These false theologies spawned crude mythologies, and – eventually – a system of Platonic metaphysics of emanations and spiritual entities, which functioned as a subtly disguised refinement of polytheism. Historically, there was nothing sinister about how this process of corruption had occurred. How was the existence of good to be reconciled with the existence of evil without the hypothesis of an evil twin deity? Running the whole universe was a big job for one god; surely 'governing the world required the ministration of a multitude of inferior beings'? However, amidst all this corruption the truth of monotheism had never entirely died. Indeed, it was preserved among the ancients in their mystery cults, by which pagans had 'learned to join a sort of mitigated polytheism with monotheism'. In other words, ancient paganism was a kind of hybrid, combining polytheism with monotheism. But, alas, so too was Christianity, which was similarly composed of 'jarring elements'. It too incorporated the tritheism of the Trinity, a pantheon of saints, and – less obtrusively – a Platonic metaphysics fundamentally indebted to polytheism which had shaped the enduring contours of Christian theology. Of course, Popery and the office of the pontiff were flagrantly pagan, but Christianity as a whole was not much closer to theistic truth than the paganism which it had – notionally – displaced. According to Bolingbroke, the entire history of theology ran without interruption, from pagan antiquity to the Christian present, as a single mixed thread

[43] Thomas Seward, *The conformity between Popery and Paganism* (London, 1746), p. 61.

in which two fibres – the polytheistic and the unitarian – were inextricably woven together: 'all the superstitious opinions of ancient nations have come down to us, intermingled with some scraps of good sense and of true theism'.[44]

Notwithstanding these subversive extensions of the genre found in the works of Middleton and Bolingbroke, pagano-popery as a vehicle of anti-Catholic polemic remained a commonplace feature of religious discourse. The work of Thomas Walker, a stoutly traditionalist Scots Presbyterian clergyman in Ayrshire, is suggestive of how widespread the rhetoric of pagano-popery was by the late eighteenth century. Walker took the view that 'it was the religion of the ancient heathens which the Church of Rome adopted, instead of the simplicity of the gospel. By degrees, the whole system of heathenism was incorporated with a nominal Christianity. Their idolatrous polytheism was truly and effectually restored.' Although the 'names indeed of their inferior deities were changed', the Roman Catholic church retained 'the same rites and ceremonies' and 'the same times and seasons of worship'.[45] In Ireland, too, the ideas of pagano-popery were part of the currency of Protestant polemic, as in Andrew Meagher's *The popish mass celebrated by heathen priests, for the living and the dead, for some ages before the birth of Christ* (Limerick, 1771).

Some scholars felt that the very idea of pagano-popery, though accurate up to a point, was too crudely reductive; for was not paganism itself – as the collateral evidences showed – a version of patriarchal truth? Robert Spearman, the Hutchinsonian mythographer, challenged the assumptions behind the charge that Christianity had developed as an accommodationist fusion with paganism. Quite the reverse, for the Hutchinsonians believed that there was a kernel of patriarchal Christian truth within paganism itself: 'Christianity was not instituted in compliance with paganism, but that paganism was nothing else but the great truths of Christianity split and debased into a legend of fables.'[46]

In his *History of the Corruptions of Christianity* (1782), the Unitarian Joseph Priestley (1733–1804) described – in terms which owed a great deal to Middleton – how the primitive Christian Church had succumbed to idolatry. Christianity was moulded by the surrounding pagan environment.

---

[44] Bolingbroke, *Philosophical works*, vol. II, esp. pp. 1–2, 6, 10–15, 18–20, 26–34, 41, 76–9, 112, 165–6, 179–80, 234–5; vol. III, pp. 2–3, 32, 107, 202; vol. IV, pp. 173, 191.
[45] [Thomas Walker], *A vindication of the discipline and constitution of the Church of Scotland* (Edinburgh, 1774), p. 356.
[46] [Robert Spearman], *Letters to a friend, concerning the Septuagint translation, and the heathen mythology* (Edinburgh, 1759), p. 151.

While the ostensible object of worship had changed, early Christians had maintained several of the forms of pagan religion.[47] Nevertheless, a massive gulf of tone and register stood between the sly and indirect subversion of Middleton – whose real target was not immediately apparent – and the troubled sincerity of Priestley. Notwithstanding an open acknowledgement of his debt to Middleton, Priestley proved a staunch opponent of Gibbon. Yet Gibbon's ironic feints as well as the very substance of his remarks on the making of Christianity also drew, in good measure, on the approach of Middleton.

Pagano-popery was not simply an instrument of sceptical deconstruction. It remained part of the vocabulary of contemporary Protestantism. A 'striking resemblance between the idolatry of the Papists and pagans' formed an integral component of the complex theological system of the Dissenting minister and controversialist Hugh Farmer (1714/15–87). Notwithstanding the force of revelation, according to Farmer, Catholicism could not prevent 'the supposed natural propensity to the worship of dead men'. Heathen converts to Christianity had 'retained strong prejudices in favour of many of the principles in which they had been educated'. In particular, the worship of the dead in Christian countries was 'a remnant of the pagan idolatry'. Acknowledging the influence of Middleton– seemingly misunderstood as a specimen of un-ironic Protestant analysis – Farmer traced the ways in which pagan 'demon-worship', as well as the oracles and miracle cures associated with it, lived on in extravagant and outlandish Catholic saint cults: 'The sepulchres of saints and martyrs have been converted by Christians into churches, just as the heathen sepulchres were into temples.'[48] Farmer's naïve invocation of Middleton's insights on pagano-popish continuities formed part of a wider intra-Christian debate about the nature and character of demons, in which his main antagonist was another Dissenting minister, the Independent John Fell (1735–97).[49]

Indeed, the debate between Farmer and Fell demonstrates that paganism was not simply a matter of idle antiquarian diversion. Even in the later eighteenth century it still mattered enormously to Christians. Who – or what – exactly were the pagan gods? Were they real, but inferior, deities – fallen angels or demons perhaps? Or were they rather deified men,

---

[47] Joseph Priestley, *A history of the corruptions of Christianity* (2 vols., Birmingham, 1782).
[48] Hugh Farmer, *The general prevalence of the worship of human spirits, in the antient heathen nations, asserted and proved* (London, 1783), pp. 468, 471, 473, 476–8.
[49] John Fell, *The idolatry of Greece and Rome distinguished from that of other heathen nations: in a letter to the Reverend Hugh Farmer* (London, 1785).

as the Euhemerists alleged? To what extent was the universe populated with divinities? More troubling was the apparent presence of demons in the New Testament. When Christ drove out demons and evil spirits from the possessed, was he miraculously curing people afflicted with mental illnesses of one sort or another, whether melancholy, madness or epilepsy, or was He exorcising real malevolent spiritual entities?[50]

Farmer propounded 'the nullity of all the heathen gods'.[51] The drama of life on earth did not run in unpredictable fits and starts according to the whims of subordinate *dei ex machina*. The 'heathen gods', which came in two classes, being either the inanimate elements of the natural realm personified or posthumously deified humans, were 'absolutely incapable of interposing at all in human affairs'. Rather Farmer insisted that the universe operated according to natural chains of causation under the superintendence of God, who was 'the only sovereign of the world'. Indeed, Farmer believed that Christians needed to pay particular attention to paganism, for at every significant transitional stage in the providential unfolding and development of the Judaeo-Christian tradition, God had ushered in new dispensations precisely in order to combat the threat of heathen idolatry. The leitmotif of sacred history was, Farmer insisted, 'the cure of idolatry'. The function of Moses as a lawgiver was to introduce measures which would eradicate idolatrous practices among the Israelites, in particular the worship of the dead. This practice, which 'necessarily implied a belief of the immortality of the soul', had sprung up in Phoenicia and Egypt, and had come to infect even the Israelites themselves. Under the Mosaic dispensation, the Israelites were informed that death was not a blessing, but a punishment, and that God would redeem humankind from the power of death at a future period. Between the eras of Moses and Jesus, pagan idolatry had undergone considerable philosophical development. Pagans had come to abandon the belief in a future state and to adopt the mortalist fallacy that the soul of man perishes with the body. In response to this new threat from pagan idolatry, God had sent Christ to earth to promote the doctrine of eternal life. Farmer insisted upon the providential interplay between heathen threats and reactive Judaeo-Christian dispensations, without which the contours of sacred history were blurred and difficult to discern. Knowledge of paganism was essential too in appreciating the primitive Church Fathers, whose works were 'unintelligible', he argued,

---

[50] Hugh Farmer, *An essay on the demoniacs of the New Testament* (London, 1775); John Fell, *Daemoniacs: an enquiry into the heathen and scripture doctrine of daemoniacs* (London, 1779).

[51] Hugh Farmer, *Letters to the Rev. Dr Worthington, in answer to his late publication intitled, an impartial enquiry into the case of the gospel demoniacks* (London, 1778), p. 222.

without a keen understanding of their immersion in, and dialogue with, 'the schools of the heathen philosophers'.[52]

Farmer attempted to repackage a rational Protestant Christianity shorn of its more fantastical folkloric accretions, in order to meet the criticisms of the Enlightenment. This was because, as Farmer believed, 'the objections of infidelity are not founded upon genuine Christianity, but upon gross misrepresentations of it by Christians'. In particular, 'the common explication of the scripture demoniacs' had given rise to 'numberless superstitions; particularly to those shameless impostures, the possessions and exorcisms of the Roman church'. By the 'dispossession of demons', Farmer insisted, Christ meant nothing more than 'the cure of a disease'.[53] Fell, on the other hand, firmly believed in the reality of demons. No Devil, no providence. Fell contended that the implications of Farmer's naturalistic attempt to explain away pagan and other demons undermined some of the essential but latent underpinnings of Christian doctrine, for 'on this scheme, it was God alone who introduced sin and death'. Was evil, then, an intrinsic part of God's creation? Fell worried that 'those things which the holy scriptures call the overthrow of Satan's kingdom', Farmer 'represents as nothing more than particular exertions of God's power in counteracting the effects of his own agency'. There was a need for a demon in the machine, otherwise Christianity as a moral system threatened to disintegrate under its own internal contradictions. Fell argued that Farmer's logic made God Himself the author of the Fall of Man, indeed of evil in the world, which must be wrong.[54]

Not only was it a common trope of the Protestant – and post-Protestant – Enlightenment that Catholicism was indebted to the dark gods of pre-Christian Rome, but a new and still more horrifying anxiety surfaced in the later eighteenth century – that behind the allegories of pagan polytheism and Roman hagiography obscenity lurked. In 1781 Sir William Hamilton (1731–1803), the British Ambassador to Naples, an antiquary and connoisseur of classical erotica now best known for his cuckolding by Admiral Horatio Nelson (1758–1805), composed a learned letter to the President of the Royal Society in which he traced pagan continuities in the bizarre fertility and nature cults which flourished – unacknowledged as such – in the folk-Catholicism of southern Italy. Priapus, the god of male fertility and generation, was now worshipped (obliviously it seemed)

---

[52] Farmer, *General prevalence*, pp. iii–xliii.
[53] Farmer, *Essay on demoniacs*, pp. 392, 394, 399–400.
[54] Fell, *Daemoniacs*, pp. 215, 402, 411.

under the nominal cult of St Cosmo, while the supposed 'Great Toe of the saint' – of which wax *ex-voti* were on sale to unsuspecting worshippers – seemed all too obviously to Hamilton to be quite another part of an altogether different demi-god's anatomy, now blindly mistaken for something less scandalous to Christian sensibilities. Given his antiquarian interests, Hamilton was intrigued rather than appalled that 'devotion is still paid to Priapus, the obscene divinity of the Ancients (though under another denomination)'. As a scholar – not least one of 'curious' tastes – Hamilton was excited that his study of Italian festivals and rites offered 'a fresh proof of the similitude of the Popish and pagan religion, so well observed by Dr Middleton'.[55]

During the Revolution era pagano-popery provided the basis for Tom Paine's notorious exposure of Christianity as 'an amphibious fraud' in *The Age of Reason* (1794). Paine's debt to Middleton was obvious. His central argument was that Christianity was a mere heap of fables largely 'sprung out of the tail of the heathen mythology', though with some grounding in Jewish traditions too. As a religion Christianity was the confection of what Paine called 'Christian mythologists', who had drawn on pagan precedents and examples in their handiwork. These 'Christian mythologists' had divinised Jesus the *man*, reduced the unmanageable proliferation of pagan deities to a more modest tritheistic trinity, converted the cult of Diana of Ephesus into the idol Mary, and transformed deified heroes into canonised saints. Whereas the pagans had gods for everything, the 'Christian mythologists' conjured up saints to meet the same human needs; indeed, 'the Church became as crowded with the one, as the pantheon had been with the other; and Rome was the place of both'. What did Christianity really amount to, wondered Paine, but 'the idolatry of the ancient mythologists, accommodated to the purposes of power and revenue'. The names of the deities changed, but priestcraft and its forms continued pretty much unaltered between pagan antiquity and the early Church.[56]

It should be apparent by now that Gibbon's debt in the most celebrated passage of his *Memoirs* (1796) was not only a particular one to the sceptical Middleton, but more generally to a long lineage of Protestant polemic: 'It was at Rome, on the fifteenth of October 1764, as I sat musing amidst the ruins of the Capitol, while the barefooted friars were singing vespers in the Temple of Jupiter that the idea of writing the decline and fall of the city

---

[55] 'Letter from Hamilton Dec. 30, 1781', in Richard Payne Knight, *An account of the remains of the worship of Priapus* (London, 1786), pp. 3–4, 7–8.
[56] Thomas Paine, 'The age of reason part I' (1794), in *Theological works of Thomas Paine* (London, 1819), pp. 6–11.

first started to my mind.'[57] This pagano-popish citadel was the Rome too of Eliot and her deluded Protestant mythographer.

In terms of the number of active combatants and the sheer volume of print involved, the biggest intellectual controversy in eighteenth-century England – of any sort – was the mythographical war between the Warburtonians and the anti-Warburtonians.[58] Warburton's *Divine Legation* was a response to the deist argument that the lack of any mention of a future state of heaven and hell in the Old Testament Jewish religion was a sign of its imperfection, a proof that it could not be of divine origin.[59] On the contrary, argued Warburton, this strange absence was itself compelling evidence of the divine provenance of the Jewish dispensation. Warburton's point of departure was the universal recognition of ancient legislators that belief in a doctrine of future rewards and punishments was an essential precondition of civil society. The only state not to promote this useful belief in its religion was ancient Israel. The unique absence of this vital prop of governance Warburton attributed to God's direct intervention in the temporal supervision of ancient Israel. The 'Jewish republic', Warburton pronounced, had been a literal theocracy. Ancient Israelite government diverged spectacularly from any known polity 'before or since'. In the 'Jewish republic' the rewards and punishments 'promised by heaven' were exclusively 'temporal' and confined to the here and now on earth. Instead of the promise of a heavenly reward after death, Israelites were assured long life, peace and plenty in their own terrestrial lifetimes. Warburton could not detect in the Israelite system 'any intelligible hint of the rewards and punishments of another life'. Certainly, Moses would have known of the conventional requirement in ancient government for a doctrine of future rewards and punishments, for he was well-versed, from his years in Egypt, with arts of legislation. Nor, Warburton argued ingeniously, would Moses, the lawgiver of ancient Israel, have omitted such a doctrine simply because he did not believe it himself. Warburton cited numerous examples of just such a double doctrine in the ancient world, whereby it was evident 'that the not believing a doctrine so useful to society was esteemed no reason for the legislator not to propagate it'.[60]

---

[57] Edward Gibbon, *Memoirs of my life* (Harmondsworth, 1984), p. 16.
[58] Evans, *Warburton*.
[59] J. Assmann, *Moses the Egyptian* (Cambridge, MA, 1997), p. 96.
[60] William Warburton, *The divine legation of Moses* (2 vols., London, 1738–41), vol. I, pp. 410; vol. II, part ii, pp. 358, 446–7.

En route to his striking conclusions, Warburton provided an encyclopaedic – if flawed, misinformed and idiosyncratic – survey of ancient pagan religions. Central to Warburton's account of classical paganism was his contention that it had consisted of two main elements. The outer layer was a colourful wrapping which was promoted in order to peddle polytheistic mythology to the gullible masses; the inner core took the form of mystery cults in which initiates acquired secrets. However, there were two kinds of secret. The lesser mysteries, which were in fact generally accessible to the common people, cleverly disseminated the necessary political theology which underpinned all government, the doctrine of a future state of rewards and punishments. The greater mysteries, which were more exclusive, went on to unmask polytheism as a mere delusion resting on the euhemeristic deification of dead rulers and heroes.[61] There were other elements of pretence in pagan policy. The founders and lawgivers of ancient polities had pretended that the laws and constitutions they proposed carried the force of divine sanction, indeed had been communicated personally to them by supernatural beings – Apollo to Lycurgus of Sparta, Egeria to Numa Pompilius, Ceres to Triptolemus the lawgiver of Athens. Endowing laws and institutions with a spurious aura of divinity was an essential element, Warburton believed, in the ancient art of government.[62]

Warburton's *Divine Legation* set out a sophisticated answer to one of the central questions in classical mythography – namely, did the ancients believe their own myths? How were commentators to account for the tension between the sophistication – philosophical, scientific and technological – of Greco-Roman civilisation and the patent nonsense which abounded in classical mythology? Surely the ancients did not believe that their mythologies embodied literal truth? On the other hand, what were the religious beliefs of the ancients if not the corpus of tales these societies told about the gods of Olympus?

Warburton was assailed on several fronts. Hutchinsonians like Julius Bate (1710–71) argued, characteristically, that the ancient Hebrews did indeed possess a doctrine of future rewards and punishments,[63] just as Hutchinsonians insisted Trinitarian doctrines could be discerned in what others perceived as a rigidly unitarian Judaism. Moreover other anti-Warburtonians questioned whether Warburton's assessment of Israelite religion was undermined by the Book of Job. After all, Job's tale of

---

[61] *Ibid.*, vol. I, pp. 133–49.
[62] *Ibid.*, vol. I, pp. 102–3, 150.
[63] Julius Bate, *An essay toward explaining the third chapter of Genesis* (London, 1741); Bate, *Remarks upon Mr Warburton's Remarks* (London, 1745).

calamities sat uneasily with Warburton's arguments about the role of temporal providence in a theocracy. Job 21:7 – 'Wherefore do the wicked live, become old, yea, are mighty in power?' – seemed to bemoan a state of affairs where the unjust prospered in this life, and in direct contradiction of Warburton's argument about a just equality of temporal rewards under the Mosaic dispensation. The exegesis of Job constituted a vital theatre in the war of the Warburtonians and the anti-Warburtonians. Warburton himself ingeniously argued that the Book of Job was an allegory and should not be read literally, which conserved his overall arguments but was a sidestep too far for a host of Biblical scholars, including Richard Grey (1696–1771), Charles Peters (1690–1774) and Thomas Sherlock (1677–1761).[64]

The double doctrine was another major point of contention. John Tillard agreed that the double doctrine had been a central feature of ancient culture. However, he disagreed with Warburton about the kind of doubleness that this phenomenon embodied. The ancient double doctrine had not entailed hypocrisy and deceit, but resembled rather two sides of the same coin. Ancient philosophers had believed in a future state in 'a spiritual, refined and rational sense, while they sometimes countenanced the people in their gross, vulgar and corporeal notions of it'. The double doctrine was, in other words, a matter of presentation. Fables, metaphors, similes and partial allusions were all part of the strategy by which philosophical elites wooed and cajoled the hoi polloi. The manner was two-fold, not the matter. Thus Tillard rejected Warburton's interpretation, 'that the philosophers preached the doctrine of a future state to the people, while themselves believed the direct contrary'. No real contradiction was involved in the double doctrine. Instead, Tillard claimed, 'the external doctrine related to the same things as the internal, and was used only out of necessity as the times required'.[65] Warburton, however, remained unconvinced by Tillard's distinction, which he dismissed as the mere 'ghost of a departed quibble'.[66]

In certain theatres of the Warburtonian controversy, the confrontations were decidedly personal, and none was more strangely involved than the relationship of Warburton and Middleton, former friends and *supposed* allies, now enemies. Warburton had a habit of attracting and keeping enemies, while Middleton – with his insinuating but cryptic heterodoxy and lack of scruples – was a reliable comrade only in the eye of an insensitive

---

[64] J. Lamb, 'The Job controversy, Sterne and the question of allegory', in H. Bloom (ed.), *The eighteenth-century English novel* (New York, 2004), esp. pp. 221–2.

[65] [John Tillard], *Future rewards and punishments believed by the ancients; particularly the philosophers* (London, 1740), pp. 5, 19–21, 26.

[66] Warburton, 'Appendix', *Divine legation* (2nd edn), vol. II, part ii, p. 14.

beholder. In correspondence, later published by one of Warburton's defenders, Middleton challenged Warburton's view that the double doctrine involved Cicero in duplicity and inconsistency. Middleton identified Cicero's relaxed probabilistic scepticism as the 'clue' of consistency to lead the perplexed critic through the 'labyrinth of contradictions' which Warburton saw in Cicero's writings and career. Cicero embodied 'the true spirit of the Academy; after examining both sides, to reject what has nothing solid in it'. Thus, while in *De legibus* Cicero recommended augury, he poked fun at it elsewhere – 'and no wonder: for though he laughed at it as a philosopher, he had a great opinion of it as a politician'. Middleton understood the double doctrine in terms of the traditional categories derived from Varro. As soon as one disentangled the distinctive approaches of the philosopher and the statesman, the seeming 'contradictions' dissolved.[67]

Middleton also went on to have a public spat with Warburton on the question of post-apostolic miracles. In *A free inquiry into the miraculous powers, which are supposed to have subsisted in the Christian church, from the earliest ages* (1749), Middleton exposed the false and fictitious pretensions to miracles in the patristic era, and questioned the authority which patristics had in a supposedly Protestant country like England. Warburton rushed into print to challenge his quondam friend. In particular, he claimed that the Emperor Julian the Apostate who re-established paganism as the religion of the Empire had planned the rebuilding of the temple of Jerusalem as a way of discrediting Christianity. Yet, Warburton argued, had not a miraculous intervention of providence – an earthquake no less – frustrated Julian's campaign?[68]

David Hume (1711–76) was another personal bugbear of the Warburtonians. He not only rejected the fundamentals of orthodox mythography; worse still he went on to reject Warburton's self-appointed role as grand panjandrum of English letters. Notwithstanding the variety of ingenious strategies in evidence within the field of Christian mythography and the debates to which those differences gave rise, there was fundamental agreement over the basic sequence of events. In the beginning, all Christian mythographers agreed, was a patriarchal monotheism. Myths and legends grew up later as the religion of Noah degenerated among his descendants into fantastical polytheisms. Hume's *Natural History of Religion* (1757) unambiguously overturned that basic scheme. Instead,

---

[67] 'Appendix: Dr Middleton's letter to Mr Warburton, Dorchester Sept. 11, 1736', in [John Towne], *The argument against the Divine legation fairly stated* (London, 1751), pp. 164–8. Cf. Middleton, *Cicero*, vol. III, pp. 344–5, 355–7.
[68] William Warburton, *Julian* (London, 1750).

Hume argued, it was the other way around; polytheism was the primeval religion of humanity and monotheism a later philosophical refinement which would have been beyond the capacities of primitive peoples. Hume argued that the 'farther we mount up into antiquity, the more do we find mankind plunged into polytheism', which, he conjectured, 'must have been, the first and most ancient religion of mankind'. Polytheism emerged 'from the incessant hopes and fears, which actuate the human mind'. Every natural boon and – more pertinently – every natural calamity suggested some intelligent being lurking behind it. Moreover, the 'universal tendency among mankind to conceive all beings like themselves' led to the personification of these imagined invisible causes of natural phenomena. Somehow a primitive 'ignorance of causes', combined with an anxiety about the future and a predisposition to 'ascribe' human characteristics to this supernatural species of being, led to the familiar polytheistic mythologies of the ancients. Theism, though admittedly ancient too, belonged nevertheless to a later stage of cultural development.[69]

Needless to say, both the double doctrine and pagano-popery were in evidence at the edges of Hume's central arguments, though no less damaging as curare-tipped darts from the wings than as the full-on blast of a philosophical cannonade. Hume recognised with approval Cicero's maintenance of a double doctrine: 'Whatever sceptical liberties that great man might take, in his writings or in philosophical conversation, yet he avoided, in the common conduct of life, the imputation of deism and profaneness', and was 'willing to appear a devout religionist'. Cicero had now been reinvented as a forerunner of Humean scepticism: polite, unobtrusive and socially conservative but at bottom a freethinker. Hume also echoed the arguments of Middleton that the prime citadel of western Christendom rested on the rock of heathendom, noting that 'the heroes in paganism correspond exactly to the saints in popery', and claimed that the 'place of Hercules, Theseus, Hector, Romulus is now supplied by Dominic, Francis, Anthony and Benedict'.[70]

Warburton and his closest ally, Richard Hurd (1720–1808), later Bishop of Worcester, together composed an anonymous reply to Hume's *Natural History*. While Warburton rejected Hume's arguments against the historical claims of the Bible – 'as if Moses had no human authority because he allows him no divine' – the authors' arguments against the 'puny dialectitian

---

[69] David Hume, *Natural history of religion* (with *Dialogues concerning natural religion*) (Oxford, 1993), pp. 135, 139, 141–2.
[70] *Ibid.*, pp. 164, 171.

from the north' were feebler than their name-calling.⁷¹ As Hume noted in a letter of 25 June 1771 to William Strahan, 'it is petulance, and insolence and abuse, that distinguish the Warburtonian school, even above all other parsons and theologians'.⁷² And that is how Warburton is remembered – if at all – today. However, the double doctrine was, of course, a very serious business for classicists and philosophers.

Indeed, a subtly framed version of the double doctrine underpinned Stona's comprehensive response to Hume's *Natural History of Religion*. Hume's fundamental assumption – that primitive peoples lacked the mental resources for the philosophical refinement associated with monotheistic beliefs, and leapt instinctively to fearful polytheistic interpretations in order to propitiate the hidden forces animating the dangerous world around them – was, Stona argued, misconceived. The human mind did not require 'the irradiation of the arts' in order to hit upon the glaringly obvious notion of a creator. The human mind – give or take a bit of refinement or polish from education, science and the arts – operated in all ages and places along the same familiar lines. Human beings were just as likely 'to discover the existence of God in the remotest ages of antiquity, as at present'. Indeed, Stona produced ethnographic evidence from the native peoples of North America, Peru and Africa for the universal primitive belief in a supreme deity or 'first cause of all things'. Polytheism, by sharp contrast, Stona argued, had been concocted, behind closed portals in the incense-filled chambers of antiquity, by designing men as an instrument of policy. Idolatry was not, as Hume proposed, the response of the primitive mind to the terrors of the environment. Far from being the natural belief of the many, it was the invention of the few, a contrivance for ease of governance in the archaic city-states of earliest antiquity, as the means to keep the many in order. As such, it was an example of the double doctrine at work, a tactic employed by the elites of the ancient world to divide and rule.⁷³

The deistic Voltaire – who singled out Warburton for his scorn in *Dieu et les hommes* (1769) – was unconvinced by the bishop's theory of the double doctrine, arguing that it had applied only to the mystery cults of Isis, Ceres and Orpheus, and had not reigned among the ancient philosophers. Voltaire could not resist drawing a dismal comparison between the noble monotheistic elite which flourished at the heart of polytheistic

---

⁷¹ [William Warburton and Richard Hurd], *Remarks on Mr David Hume's essay on the natural history of religion; addressed to the Rev. Dr. Warburton* (London, 1757), reprinted in J. Fieser (ed.), *Early responses to Hume* (10 vols., Bristol, 2001), vol. V, pp. 309–48, at pp. 310, 322.

⁷² J. Y. T. Greig (ed.), *Letters of David Hume* (2 vols., Oxford, 1932), vol. II, p. 244.

⁷³ [Stona], *Remarks*, pp. 7–11, 32–3, 42, 49–50, 84, 91, 95, 104.

antiquity and the unacknowledged polytheism of an ostensibly monotheistic Catholicism. Surely Catholic philosophers needed a special mystery-like ceremony of their own in which they might disavow the folkloric vulgarities of certain saints' rites ('allassent ensuite désavouer ces étonnantes bêtises dans une assemblée particulière')?[74]

Gibbon too was interested in the mysteries, and devoted one of his earliest works, *Critical Observations on the Sixth Book of the Aeneid* (1770), to an attack on Warburton's theories of these ancient cults. Warburton had argued that Aeneas's apparent descent into the underworld was in fact Virgil's allegory of the rite of initiation into the Eleusinian mysteries, the mystery religion which upheld the esoteric doctrine concealed from the vulgar citizenry of ancient polities. Gibbon was unconvinced. After all, Virgil's contemporary, the poet Horace, had been oblivious of any intended allegory, and Gibbon declared that he would be 'very well satisfied with understanding Virgil no better than Horace did'. Was there any evidence, indeed, that Virgil – to all intents and purposes an Epicurean, and hence assumed to be a critic of the mysteries – had ever been initiated into their secrets? Virgil, Gibbon reckoned, had simply been telling a story. The poet had narrated Aeneas's visit to the shades with no ulterior allegorical purpose in mind. The literary critic might, more reliably, treat the episode as a deferential allusion to, and borrowing from, Homer than as an allegorised system of political religion. Warburton, not Virgil, was the author fixated upon 'luxuriant systems'. Moreover, there were literary conventions and proprieties to consider; the epic was no fit genre for allegory. 'To discover … a system of politics in the Aeneid, required the critical telescope of the great Warburton', Gibbon remarked with withering irony: 'The naked eye of common sense cannot reach so far.'[75]

Long after the Warburton affair had subsided, the idea of the double doctrine continued to be a useful category of mythographical analysis. The politician and diplomat Sir William Drummond (*c*.1770–1828) extended the idea of the double doctrine to the Old Testament Hebrews in *Oedipus judaicus* (1811), a book which, despite its private circulation in a limited edition of 250 copies, proved highly controversial. Drummond argued that the Old Testament needed to be read allegorically if one were to understand

---

[74] Voltaire, 'Dieu et les hommes' (1769), in *Les œuvres completes de Voltaire* (Voltaire Foundation, Oxford, 1994), vol. LXIX, pp. 327–9.
[75] [Edward Gibbon], *Critical observations on the sixth book of the Aeneid* (London, 1770), esp. pp. 3, 16, 35, 37, 40, 48. Cf. James Beattie, 'Remarks on some passages of the sixth book of the Aeneid', *Transactions of the Royal Society of Edinburgh*, vol. 2 (1790), pp. 33–54.

The Legacies of the Ancients in Enlightenment Mythography 109

its esoteric meaning; read literally it yielded an exoteric folklore fit only for vulgar minds.[76] More common, of course, in this regard was the continuing contrast between Old Testament Israel and other ancient polities. In *An Analysis of the Egyptian Mythology* (1819) the pioneering anthropologist James Cowles Prichard traced both priestcraft and the double doctrine back to ancient Egypt, a culture characterised by its 'fondness for secrecy, and for enveloping truths or opinions in a cloak of mystery'. Yet there are echoes even here of the Warburtonian contrast between heathendom and the religion of the Hebrews. According to Prichard, what made Mosaic religion distinctive was its repudiation of imposture and 'concealment'.[77]

The rhetoric of pagano-popery also survived in nineteenth-century British culture. The evangelical lawyer John Poynder (1779–1849) published pseudonymous letters as Ignotus in *The Times* in 1817, which were republished as *Popery the religion of heathenism* (1818) and again as *Popery in alliance with heathenism* (1835). In *Vestiges of Ancient Manners and Customs, discoverable in modern Italy and Sicily* (1823), a product of his tours there in 1818–19, and again in 1820–1, John James Blunt, a Fellow of St John's College, Cambridge, rehearsed the stock elements of pagano-popish criticism, while insisting that his motives were very different from those of Middleton, the idiom's malevolent *genius loci*. Blunt equated the worship of saints with polytheism, and traced the deformities – as he saw of them – of Roman Catholicism to a 'natural disposition' which took hold both of converts from paganism who were happy to 'confound the religion they had quitted with what they had espoused' and 'sincere but ill-judging Christians' who were too ready to 'come to an accommodation with the pagans'.[78] At the height of the Tractarian crisis in the 1840s, with leading Anglicans such as Newman forsaking the Church of England for the eternal verities of Rome, the issue of pagano-popery resumed a renewed salience in Protestant apologetic. Stopford's *Pagano-Papismus* was reprinted in 1844, and the 1732 translation of Mussard, *Roma antiqua et recens*, was reissued in 1848. For some evangelicals Catholicism remained, in its fundamental elements, 'a baptized paganism'.[79]

On the other hand, critics of traditional Christianity continued to exploit the subversive potential in pagano-popery. Robert Taylor exploded the myth of an age of proto-Protestant primitive purity: 'Never was there

---

[76] William Drummond, *Oedipus judaicus* (1811), esp. pp. ii, vii, xxii, 162–4.
[77] James Cowles Prichard, *An analysis of the Egyptian mythology* (London, 1819), esp. p. 415.
[78] John James Blunt, *Vestiges of ancient manners and customs, discoverable in modern Italy and Sicily* (London, 1823), pp. vii–ix, 4, 50–1.
[79] Thomas Pearson, *Essay on infidelity* (1853: London, 1864), p. 215.

the day or the hour in which Christianity was, and its corruptions were not.'[80] Rather the Christian religion was born as an accommodation with ancient pagan forms. Christians of the second, third and fourth centuries had not only appropriated Plato, Socrates and Cicero as proto-Christian philosophers, but had 'industriously laboured to give their religion the nearest possible resemblance to the ancient paganism; and confessedly adopted the liturgies, ceremonies, and terms of heathenism; making it their boast that the pagan religion, properly explained, really was nothing else than Christianity'.[81]

Eliot, too, was keenly aware of pagano-popery. While it remains a subtly understated theme in *Middlemarch*, it had surfaced more obviously – albeit with an Ottoman twist – in *Romola* several years before. Rome was not the only city whose cityscape was redolent of mythological accretion, acculturation and hybridity. In *Romola* Eliot describes Athens under the Ottomans in a way which parodies Gibbon's portrayal of Catholic Rome:

> [T]heir matin chant is drowned by the voice of the muezzin, who, from the gallery of the high tower on the Acropolis, calls every Mussulman to his prayers. That tower springs from the Parthenon itself; and every time we paused and directed our eyes towards it, our guide set up a wail, that a temple which had once been won from the diabolical uses of the pagans to become the temple of another virgin than Pallas – the Virgin-Mother of God – was now again perverted to the accursed ends of the Moslem.[82]

Not for the first time, we see significant mythographical themes prefigured in *Romola*, which emerges here in greater clarity as a bridge between the themes of Gibbon's *Decline and Fall* and the unfinished 'Key to All Mythologies'.

---

[80] Robert Taylor, *The diegesis; being a discovery of the origin, evidences, and early history of Christianity* (London, 1829), p. 239.
[81] *Ibid.*, p. 166.
[82] George Eliot, *Romola* (1862–3: London, 1996), pp. 66–7.

CHAPTER 4

The Obsessions of Jacob Bryant: Arkite Idolatry and the Quest for Troy

> Do you not see that it is no use now to be crawling a little way after the men of the last century – men like Bryant – and correcting their mistakes? – living in a lumber room and furnishing up broken-legged theories about Chus and Mizraim? (*Middlemarch*, ch. 22)

George Eliot's Mr Casaubon was – as we have seen – a composite portrait, drawn not only from Eliot's own imagination but also from a variety of sources known to her. However, the most significant prototype for Mr Casaubon was the dominant mythographer in England during the late eighteenth century, Jacob Bryant.[1] In *A New System, or an Analysis of Ancient Mythology* (1774–6), Bryant established a persuasive way of channelling the immense variety of pagan legends into a single 'helio-arkite' scheme of interpretation. Myths were essentially compounds with two elements, one drawn from memories of the Flood, the other arising in naturalistic fashion from worship of the sun. Bryant's interpretive framework was original, yet built in plausible ways upon pre-existing traditions of mythographical investigation. Notwithstanding the cavils of its critics, orthodox as well as sceptic, Bryant's massive multi-volume work, with upwards of 500 pages in each of its three tomes, had gone into a third edition by 1807. Yet by the time of his death Bryant's *magnum opus* had also become a byword for misapplied erudition. In particular, it seemed to its critics to belong not to the cutting edge of mythological investigation, but to occupy territory that was, intellectually speaking, an arid wasteland of superficial and unsupported etymologising. If any single work provided the pattern for Casaubon's unfinished 'Key to All Mythologies', it was Bryant's *New System*.[2]

---

[1] J. C. Pratt, and V. A. Neufeldt (eds.), *George Eliot's Middlemarch notebooks* (Berkeley and Los Angeles, 1979), esp. pp. xlvii, 48, 228–9, 280.
[2] See L. Baltazar, 'The critique of Anglican biblical scholarship in George Eliot's *Middlemarch*', *Literature and Theology*, vol. 15 (2001), pp. 40–60.

Indeed, Bryant retained considerable name recognition – only in part as a figure of fun – well into the nineteenth century, and his Arkite theories enjoyed a vivid afterlife long after *A New System* had dropped out of the canon of mainstream mythography. Bryant was still a prominent target for irreligious anthropologists in the early 1870s[3], when *Middlemarch* was published.

Bryant was a kind of anti-Midas: every topic upon which he alighted inspired only error. By a further irony, the errors he coined, upheld or propagated were various. Sometimes it was Bryant's orthodoxy which underpinned his mistakes, on other occasions it was his scepticism, daring but unmoored, which allowed him to float above received wisdom into clouds of fantastical speculation. In every single one of the major antiquarian spats in which he participated, he appears to have been on the losing side. In the controversies over the disputed works of the fifteenth-century Bristolian poet, Thomas Rowley, Bryant argued that Rowley's works were authentic, rather than the masterly forgeries of the brilliant boy–poet Thomas Chatterton.[4] The diversity of the world's pagan mythologies, Bryant argued, could be reduced quite simply to distorted memories of Noah's Flood.[5] Not that Bryant adhered credulously to received orthodoxies, for he also took the view that the Trojan War had never happened – or, at least, if it had happened, it had not taken place in Asia Minor, but rather in Egypt.[6] On every count Bryant seemed magnetically attracted to error and absurdity.

One twentieth-century scholar, Edward Hungerford, reached the uncharitable verdict that Bryant 'devoted a very long life to scholarship, during the nine decades of which he came to not a single correct conclusion'.[7] Bryant's mythography – even in its own day – was the butt of scholarly jest. According to his fiercest critic, the orientalist John Richardson, Bryant's central thesis was 'a mere castle of cards, pompously reared upon a stratum of chaff'.[8] The antiquary and engraver John Landseer complained

---

[3] J. F. McLennan, 'The worship of animals and plants', *Fortnightly Review* (November 1869), pp. 564–7, (February 1870), p. 195; E. B. Tylor, *Primitive culture* (2 vols., London, 1871), vol. II, p. 217.

[4] Jacob Bryant, *Observations on the poems of Thomas Rowley, in which the authenticity of those poems is ascertained* (2 vols., London, 1781).

[5] Jacob Bryant, *A new system, or, an analysis of ancient mythology* (2nd edn, 3 vols., London, 1775–6).

[6] Jacob Bryant, *Observations upon a treatise, entitled a description of the plain of Troy* (Eton, 1795), p. 49: 'I am persuaded, that no such war, as has been represented, was carried on against Troy: nor do I believe, that the Phrygian city, so zealously sought after, ever existed.' Bryant, *A dissertation concerning the war of Troy* (n.p., 1796?); Bryant, *A dissertation concerning the war of Troy* (2nd edn corrected, London, 1799), pp. 45–50, 84; J. Wallace, 'Digging for Homer: literary authenticity and romantic archaeology', *Romanticism*, vol. 7 (2001), pp. 73–87, at pp. 73–8.

[7] E. Hungerford, *Shores of darkness* (New York, 1941), p. 20.

[8] John Richardson, *A dissertation on the languages, literature, and manners of Eastern nations* (2nd edn, Oxford, 1778), part II, p. 412.

of Bryant's reliance on spurious etymologies. Bryant, Landseer contended, 'cannot proceed through a single page – hardly through a sentence – without trusting to these slippery stepping-stones, whether his purpose be to cross a brook, or surmount a deluge ... erudition is brought to an anchor on the heights of his etymological Ararat'.[9] Bryant did not mind the opprobrium, which appears to have boosted sales. He reminisced that his publisher, Elmsly, had told him that, 'if they abuse you much longer, we must have a third edition'.[10]

For all the flaws in his unerringly misguided pseudo-scholarship, which so closely resembled Mr Casaubon's, Bryant was in other respects the antithesis of the dour, joyless pedant of *Middlemarch*. Bryant seems to have been an amiable old cove who had the gift of attracting friendship. Indeed, Bryant, who was based in the latter part of his life at Cippenham or Cypenham near Farnham Royal in Buckinghamshire, was a close and much-cherished neighbour of King George III at Windsor Castle, which was only two and a half miles away. The King's fondness for the cheerful company of the old antiquary is recorded at some length in the memoirs of the novelist Fanny Burney, who had obtained the post of second keeper of the Queen's robes. She noted that the king was 'always much entertained with Mr Bryant's conversation'; on New Year's Eve 1786, for example, George III 'stayed talking with him near an hour'. When the novelist first met Bryant in August 1786 she recorded how he 'talks a good deal, and with the utmost good-humour and ease, casting entirely aside his learning'. Unlike Eliot's mythographer, who spread scholastic gloom on every dinner table to which he was still invited, Bryant had a 'droll sort of simplicity that had a mixture of nature and of humour extremely amusing' and was 'full of anecdote and amusement'. He could be relied on for 'good-humoured chit-chat and entertaining gossiping'; moreover, 'his learning, deep as it is', Burney recounted with relief, 'taints no part of his conversation'. Bryant was capable of a 'quaint' self-mocking deprecation, and told how one of his friends described him as a scholar, who 'knows all things whatever up to Noah, but not a single thing in the world beyond the Deluge!' Burney was immensely touched when she discovered that Bryant possessed her novels *Cecilia* and *Evelina*: 'how, indeed, could I suspect such a compliment from the old Grecian? Cecilia and Evelina were not written before the Deluge!' But such badinage was typical of

---

[9] John Landseer, *Sabaean researches* (London, 1823), p. 359.
[10] Jacob Bryant, *An apology to John Richardson, Esq, of the Middle Temple, and of Wadham College, Oxford* (n.p., n.d.), p. 39.

Bryant's company, and he seems to have delighted the King and his entourage with discussion of volcanoes on the moon, his dogs (of which he was inordinately fond), his 'cudgelling' feats as a schoolboy at Eton, and the lighthearted way in which he was able to wring playful amusement out of the primeval predicament of Mr and Mrs Noah.[11]

Nor was Casaubon's prototype a scholarly irrelevance. In 1793 William Holwell (1726–98), the vicar of Thornbury in Gloucestershire and prebendary of Exeter Cathedral, who was keenly aware both of the Christian utility of Bryant's multi-volume *New System* and the fact that a work so expensive was not as widely disseminated as it might be, brought out a 'compendium' as *A mythological, etymological and historical dictionary; extracted from the Analysis of Ancient Mythology*.[12] Nor should we discount the influence of Bryant's work on the mythological imagination. As a young man, William Blake (1757–1827) was an apprentice at the studio of James Basire where he worked on engravings for Bryant's *New Analysis*.[13]

Furthermore, Bryant's followers recognised the novelty and significance of his contribution to mythography. The Reverend Philip Allwood, a Fellow of Magdalene College, Cambridge, estimated – and not without some justification – that 'more real insight into the confused and uncertain traditions of distant ages … has been obtained within the last fifty years, than ever distinguished the acquisitions of any former period'. In other words, Bryant had effected a kind of revolution in the study of this field of antiquity. Allwood set out his own mythographic scheme in *Literary Antiquities of Greece* (1799). His method of decoding mythology depended largely on 'analogy', especially the analogies detectable when various mythologies were compared with one another and with scripture. Without the analogical method, Allwood conceded, the mythologies of the ancients seemed an indecipherable jumble of local particulars. However, when, for example, a seeming miscellany of mythological details regarding fish-gods, floods and ships were 'collated', their agreement in 'general outlines' with sacred history turned out to confirm 'the universality of the deluge'.[14]

---

[11] A. Dobson (ed.), *Diary and letters of Madame D'Arblay* (6 vols., London, 1904–5), vol. III, pp. 4, 113, 115, 150, 207–10, 258, 261, 284, 287, 364–5. (After leaving the Queen's service, Burney married a French refugee, General D'Arblay.)

[12] William Holwell, *A mythological, etymological and historical dictionary; extracted from the Analysis of Ancient Mythology* (London, 1793), p. v.

[13] J. Mee, *Dangerous enthusiasm: William Blake and the culture of radicalism in the 1790s* (Oxford, 1992), p. 132; D. Weir, *Brahma in the west: William Blake and the oriental renaissance* (Albany, NY, 2003), p. 4.

[14] Philip Allwood, *Literary antiquities of Greece* (London, 1799), pp. 7, 20–1, 38.

Allwood explained the curious mechanics of the ironic processes by which true religion begat idolatry. He argued that 'a reverence for the renovators of mankind' – that is, for Noah and his sons – formed a central core of the ancient religion of mankind, but that this had soon degenerated into 'gross idolatry'. Other canonical elements of this primeval system of belief included a folk memory of the serpent in the Garden of Eden and a cult of the sun. The memories of the Fall and the Flood, together with solar worship, comprised the 'constituent parts of one grand idolatrous system; which had its commencement at Babel, and extended itself in process of time to every region of the habitable globe'. Allwood demonstrated how the initial unitary system of the post-Babelian cult had fragmented and diversified. Particular elements in this primeval legacy became detached over time from the rest of the patriarchal bequest, and were so grossly caricatured that eventually they were puffed up by later generations of uncomprehending acolytes as religions in their own right. For example, serpent-worship and 'the rites of the Ark' had been at first simply 'branches' of the same post-patriarchal 'idolatrous system'; nevertheless, 'the degree of veneration in which either of these objects was held, in preference to the other, became the means of forming different sects; which afterwards resolved themselves into others, and passed under a variety of denominations'.[15]

Eliot believed that Anglican mythographers of a Casaubonish stamp were ridiculous in large part because they were cut off from the developments in German scholarship which were transforming the fields of classical and Near Eastern antiquities. Although the milieu of Bryant slightly precedes the full blossoming of the German Higher Criticism, it overlaps with its embryonic phase, and it transpires that the Bryant circle was in touch with the latest advances in the German sciences of antiquity. Bryant's friend Samuel Henley (1740–1815) was in close communication with the German–Danish numismatist and orientalist, Professor Oluf Gerhard Tychsen (1734–1815), who taught at the University of Rostock. Henley translated Tychsen's treatises for another correspondent, Edward Moor. Henley's letters to Moor contained references to the Danish–German classicist Barthold Georg Niebuhr (1776–1831) and to Professor Günther Wahl (1760–1834), a Persianist at Halle, while Bryant himself was in touch with the Homeric scholar Professor Christian Heyne (1729–1812) of Göttingen.[16]

[15] *Ibid.*, pp. 174 fn, 308–9.
[16] Samuel Henley to Edward Moor, 16 February 1794; 20 March 1798, Boston Public Library (BPL), MS Ch.H.2.23; MS Ch.H.2.20.

There is also a case to be made that Bryant – notwithstanding his many gross mistakes and easily mocked absurdity – deserves to be counted as a far-from-insignificant luminary of the English Enlightenment. Scholarship is also about method and temperament, not simply about obtaining the right result. Bryant was, for instance, a trenchant critic of some of the wilder absurdities of Isaac Newton's theories of ancient history and chronology. Moreover, Bryant was – at least within the parameters of the moderate Christian Enlightenment – self-consciously enlightened. Although an orthodox defender of sacred history, he was no lumbering intellectual dinosaur: he devised new methods to reconcile heathen mythology with primeval Judaeo-Christian truth, and he willingly deconstructed classical legend.

For all his old-fashioned etymologising and seemingly credulous approach to mythography, Bryant was, curiously enough, a Modern. He aimed to utilise the best of contemporary scholarly methods, in particular the scepticism of the Moderns in the Battle of the Books,[17] to revolutionise the field of mythography. Unlike the Ancients, who tended to take the classics at face value,[18] Bryant was reluctant to suspend his critical faculties when faced with the supposed history of the ancient Greeks: 'on our part we have been too much accustomed to take in the gross with little or no examination, whatever they have been pleased to transmit'. However, he hoped that by 'unravelling the clue we may be at last led to see things in their original state' and to discriminate between history and mythology, between the happenings of the Greeks and elements of their purported past which they had in fact inherited from Egyptian traditions. In other words, a central component of Bryant's new science of mythology was his preparedness to recognise the errors of classical antiquity: 'It may appear strange to make use of the mistakes of any people for a foundation to build upon; yet through these failures my system will be in some degree supported.' He hoped 'to obtain much light' from 'a detection of these errors', not least as 'the Grecian writers have preserved a kind of uniformity in their mistakes'. This very 'uniformity' in the mistakes of the Greeks suggested that it might yield a single method for deconstructing their history, indeed, a key to their mythologies, as Bryant suggested in a passage phrases from which find a distinct – albeit subversive – echo in *Middlemarch*: 'If

---

[17] J. Levine, *The battle of the books* (Ithaca, NY, 1991).
[18] Cf. Bryant's critic (and a critic of Newton's revised chronology) Samuel Musgrave (1732–80), *Two dissertations. I. On the Grecian mythology II. An examination of Sir Isaac Newton's objections to the chronology of the Olympiads* (London, 1782), who, despite his scientific background, defended the veracity of the ancient Greeks.

the openings in the wood or labyrinth are only as chance allotted, we may be for ever bewildered: but if they are made with design, and some method be discernible, this circumstance, if attended to, will serve for a clue, and lead us through the maze.'[19]

Although its ultimate conclusions seemed crudely reductive, the arguments of Bryant's *New System* depended nonetheless on the cogs, wheels and pulleys of a complex hermeneutic machinery. Bryant wanted to establish the science of mythography on firmer foundations, aiming 'to divest mythology of every foreign and unmeaning ornament; and to display the truth in its native simplicity'. His quest was for what he termed 'latent truth': 'though the copy is faded, and has been abused, yet there are some traces so permanent, some of the principal outlines so distinct, that, when compared with the original, the true character cannot be mistaken'. The 'rites and mysteries of the Gentiles' were ultimately, Bryant believed, resolvable into 'so many memorials of their principal ancestors' from the patriarchal era, together with the worship of the sun.[20]

Bryant's work delighted his followers and exasperated some of the leading scholars of the time. Although several of them – including the brightest genius of the later English Enlightenment, Sir William Jones – derided it, they could not ignore it, such was its evident, if wrongheaded, sophistication. It seemed as likely to become a classic of the moderate Christian Enlightenment as the essays of Jones himself on the gods and languages of India or the historical surveys of native American, Aztec, Inca and Hindu culture by the Scottish cleric William Robertson (1721–93).[21] This is because, like their works, Bryant's *New System* seemed to chart a brilliant and ingenious route through the perilous reefs, sandbanks and silted deposits of miscellaneous heathen polytheisms to the safe haven of monotheistic Judaeo-Christian orthodoxy. Bryant's mythography offered a solution to one of the central problems of the Protestant Enlightenment: how to construct a global anthropology of pagan otherness which would bolster the unique claims of Judaeo-Christian truth set out in scripture. In this case, Bryant's solution – though no longer convincing to us – derived from the seemingly plausible contention that 'the history of the Deluge was no secret to the Gentile world'.[22]

---

[19] Bryant, *New system*, vol. I, pp. 156, 170.
[20] *Ibid.*, vol. I, pp. xi, xiii, 533.
[21] William Robertson, *History of America* (1777) and *A historical disquisition concerning the knowledge which the ancients had of India* (1791), both in Robertson, *Works* (London, 1831), pp. 816–20, 914–16, 1093–9.
[22] Bryant, *New system*, vol. II, p. 228.

As it happens, Jones's brilliant career as an orientalist[23] was intimately entwined with the follies of Bryant's demi-enlightenment.[24] Not that Bryant had any standing himself in oriental scholarship. Controversially – even to his supposed allies – Bryant placed an enormous reliance on superficial etymological similarities, a strain of philological argument which was becoming redundant with Jones's pioneering work in Indo-European linguistics. Richardson, indeed, found Bryant's use of etymological methods sorely wanting: 'Without an acquaintance with those Eastern tongues, all analysis of Eastern names must be completely fanciful.' Many Asiatic words might be 'expressed perfectly alike' in the western alphabet, Richardson noted, yet be entirely unconnected; others – confusingly – which seemed to bear no affinity whatsoever, had similar roots. Bryant lacked any solid grounding in oriental languages which might enable him to discriminate in such matters beyond the arbitrary subjectivity of his own 'fancy'. Given Bryant's limitations in oriental philology, Richardson reckoned that his bizarre etymological comparisons were 'very unfit to bear a superstructure of any magnitude', yet that, of course, was precisely what Bryant built on these tottering foundations. Linguistic 'corruptions' and subtle sound shifts did not happen in 'uniform' ways across different languages. Yet Bryant happily traced similar corruptions of the proper name Ham from China to Rome. In the lineage of the Hamites – also known as the Cuthites or Amonians – Bryant had concocted a kind of all-purpose pseudo-scholarly grouting which might fill in the dark cracks of ignorance antiquaries had inherited of the earliest periods in history: 'this learned gentleman', in Richardson's mocking words, had 'created a people to fill up every chasm of high antiquity, and to account for all the phenomena of early population, history and superstition'. Such panaceas were, of course, suspect in themselves, but doubly so in the light of Bryant's stumbling ignorance in the relevant oriental languages. However, Bryant's involvement with late Enlightenment orientalism – the relationship of his Hamite theories with Jones's work in particular – was far from straightforward, and riddled with considerably greater ambivalence than Richardson's shrill denunciations might suggest.[25]

Jones admitted that he had 'thrice perused' Bryant's *Analysis*, 'with increased attention and pleasure, though not with perfect acquiescence

---

[23] G. Cannon, *The life and mind of Oriental Jones* (Cambridge, 1990).
[24] B. W. Young, 'The lust of empire and religious hate: Christianity, history and India, 1790–1820', in S. Collini, R. Whatmore and B. W. Young (eds.), *History, religion, and culture: British intellectual history 1750–1950* (Cambridge, 2000), pp. 91–111, at p. 98.
[25] Richardson, *Dissertation*, part I, pp. 110, 116, 118, 132, 134.

in the other less important parts of his plausible system'.²⁶ After all, Bryant was, arguably, in the same line of scholarship as Jones, though his excessive etymologising and indomitable Flood-fixation seemed somewhat *de trop*. Bryant, Jones wrote – fulsomely perhaps – had within the field of primeval history 'the best claim to the praise of deep erudition ingeniously applied, and new theories happily illustrated by an assemblage of numberless converging rays from a most extensive circumference'.²⁷ Nevertheless, Bryant's scholarship fell, 'as every human work must fall, short of perfection'.²⁸ Bryant's Achilles heel was his reliance upon etymology – 'a medium of proof so very fallacious that, where it elucidates one fact, it obscures a thousand'.²⁹ Indeed, Bryant elicited from Jones an affectionate private raillery, which mixed a personal regard and admiration of Bryant's learned cleverness with a hard-headed reluctance to follow Bryant in his circuitous and unconvincing arguments. In a letter to Viscount Althorp in 1777, Jones revealed his views of the *New Analysis*:

> I hope my friend Bryant would excuse me, if he knew that I reckon his *Ancient Mythology* among my books of entertainment: I have almost finished the first two volumes of it, and have been highly pleased, though by no means perfectly satisfied with it. There is an infinite profusion of learning in his book, but I cannot help thinking his system very uncertain. I see no occasion to hunt for explanations of old fables, many of which had no foundation at all except in the poet's imagination.

Even Bryant's own destructive – and possibly counter-productive – scepticism in the face of pagan theologies elicited from Jones only a whimsical shrug: 'Bryant's ingenuity has the effect of his own Medusa, and even more; for he has converted even the gods themselves into rocks and temples.' In a later letter to Althorp, Jones confessed to being 'wonderfully diverted' with Bryant's book, but no more than that.³⁰

Yet, the situation is still more complicated; for, by a rich irony, Jones – notwithstanding all his undoubted and lasting achievements in the field of philology – was himself something of a Casaubon *avant la lettre*. Jones shared Bryant's general aim to relate gentile mythology to Judaeo-Christian

---

[26] William Jones, 'Ninth anniversary discourse', in Jones, *Eleven discourses, containing his anniversary addresses* (Calcutta, 1875 edn).
[27] Jones, 'Third anniversary discourse', p. 13.
[28] *Ibid.*
[29] *Ibid.*
[30] William Jones to Viscount Althorp, 29 August 1777, and Jones to Althorp, 8 September 1777, in G. Cannon (ed.), *The letters of Sir William Jones* (2 vols., Oxford, 1970), vol. I, pp. 239–40, 242.

truth. Bryant's fantastical 'helio-arkite' obsession[31] and Jones's scheme of Indo-European linguistics were both products of the same syncretic desire to assimilate pagan otherness to the ultimate truths of Biblical history.[32] One of the underappreciated differences between Jones and Bryant is that posterity, understandably enough in the light of the orientalist's linguistic insights, tends to overlook Jones's Casaubonish quest to reconstruct the ethnic genealogies of Noah and his sons, but not Bryant's scholarly misadventures and unredeemed quixotries.[33] Both scholars, the genius and the hobby-horsical mythographer, were, it transpires, on the trail of that same unattainable holy grail which would afford George Eliot such sport. The founder of Indo-European linguistics in his paper 'On the Gods of Greece, Italy, and India' came very close to justifying the ultimate absurdity in scholarly knight-errantry – the pursuit of a key to all mythologies no less:

> [W]hen features of resemblance, too strong to have been accidental, are observable in different systems of polytheism, without fancy or prejudice to colour them and improve the likeness, we can scarce help believing, that some connection has immemorially subsisted between the several nations, who have adopted them: it is my design to point out such a resemblance between the popular worship of the old Greeks and Italians and that of the Hindus, nor can there be room to doubt of a great similarity between their strange religions and that of Egypt, China, Persia, Phrygia, Phoenicia, Syria; to which, perhaps, we may safely add some of the southern kingdoms and even islands of America … From all this, if it be satisfactorily proved, we may infer a general union or affinity between the most distinguished inhabitants of the primitive world, and the time when they deviated, as they did too early deviate, from a rational adoration of the only true God.[34]

Jones, unlike Bryant, did not himself seek a unitary key to all mythologies. Nevertheless, Jones's project stood upon very similar theological foundations to Bryant's, namely 'in corroborating the multiplied evidences of revealed religion'.[35] For Jones Orientalism offered an additional window onto sacred truth, even if at best an awkwardly angled skylight. The Bible, after the earliest parts of Genesis, was circumscribed in its coverage, being limited to the doings of the ancient Israelites. But what of the other peoples of Asia about whom little was known after the 'short evening twilight in the venerable introduction to the first book of Moses'?[36] The Asiatic

---

[31] See also Jacob Bryant, *A vindication of the Apamean medal: and of the inscription Noe* (London, 1775).
[32] T. Trautmann, *Aryans and British India* (Berkeley and Los Angeles, 1997), pp. 28–61.
[33] However, A. David, 'Sir William Jones, Biblical orientalism and Indian scholarship', *Modern Asian Studies*, vol. 30 (1996), pp. 173–84, questions whether Jones was an uncritical scriptural literalist.
[34] Jones, 'On the gods of Greece, Italy and India', *Asiatic Researches*, vol. 1 (1789), p. 221.
[35] Jones, 'Tenth anniversary discourse', p. 111.
[36] *Ibid.*, p. 112.

hinterland beyond the narrow Middle Eastern terrain discussed in the Bible itself, so Jones surmised, was destined to provide oblique but circumstantial matter which indirectly confirmed sacred truth. Sacred concerns inflected Jones's Indian researches. For instance, Jones perceived what seemed like symbolic representations of the Flood, seeing clearly, as he supposed, the relationship between the first three avatars of Vishnu and 'an universal deluge'.[37] Jones also thought he spotted the story of the Tower of Babel lurking within two Hindu legends: 'the lion bursting from a pillar to destroy a blasphemous giant, and the dwarf, who beguiled and held in derision the magnificent Beli, are one and the same story related in a symbolical style'.[38] Nevertheless, Jones was unable to follow Bryant into the briars and thickets of his Arkite scheme. It was overly reductive to see the Flood in every myth. Jones could not, for example, 'persuade' himself that 'the beautiful allegory of Cupid and Psyche had the remotest allusion to the deluge, or that Hymen signified the veil, which covered the patriarch and his family'.[39]

If Jones did not succumb to the delusive temptations of a single key to all mythologies, he saw nevertheless a core of common factors underpinning the rise of pagan legends across various cultures. While he set out his disagreements with Newton's view that 'ancient mythology was nothing but historical truth in a poetical dress' and with Bryant's arguments that 'all the heathen divinities are only different attributes and representations of the Sun or of deceased progenitors', declaring his preference for a multifactorial explanation, he could not 'but agree, that one great spring and fountain of all idolatry in the four quarters of the globe was the veneration paid by men to the vast body of fire ... and another the immoderate respect shown to the memory of powerful and virtuous ancestors'. There was, moreover, an underlying unity to the seething proliferation of gods and goddesses across the pagan cultures of ancient Eurasia. Hindus, it transpired, were 'the adorers of those very deities, who were worshipped under different names in old Greece and Italy'.[40] The identities of particular gods and goddesses, Jones believed, could be mapped across cultures. Diana of Ephesus was 'manifestly the same goddess' as the Phoenician–Syrian goddess Astarte.[41] Although one of the greatest linguists of any age and a founding father of modern scholarship in the humanities, Jones was

---

[37] Jones, 'Third anniversary discourse', p. 21.
[38] Jones, 'Ninth anniversary discourse', p. 103.
[39] *Ibid.*, p. 105.
[40] Jones, 'Third anniversary discourse', p. 19.
[41] Jones, 'Eighth anniversary discourse', p. 96.

so nearly a Bryant, and might have been remembered, not without some justification, as yet another proto-Casaubon.

There are further ironic connections between Jones and Bryant. Indeed, Bryant's mythography provided the initial signposting on the road that led to Jones's linguistic discoveries.[42] Most particularly, Jones's scheme of ethnology drew heavily on the work of Bryant. It was a commonplace of sacred ethnology that the peoples of Europe or Eurasia were the descendants of Noah's son, Japhet.[43] Indeed, in the nineteenth century Japhetite would become a synonym of Indo-European or Aryan,[44] yet Jones, the leading pioneer of the Indo-European concept, diverged radically from this consensus. Jones took the view that the peoples who would come to be described as Indo-European were, in fact, of the lineage of one of Noah's other sons, Ham. This notion of the Hamite pedigree of the civilisations of classical antiquity Jones derived, as Thomas Trautmann has demonstrated, from Bryant's *New System*.[45] The Hamites, indeed, had played a central role in Bryant's scheme. According to Bryant the Cuthite descendants of Ham were 'the first apostates from the truth; yet great in worldly wisdom'.[46] The corruption of religious truth had moved in tandem with the rise of material civilisation. The Cuthites 'introduced, wherever they came, many useful arts'. Jones openly confessed that he had 'arrived by a different path at the same conclusion with Mr Bryant' regarding the identity and character of the descendants of Ham.[47]

Nor was Jones's career unblemished by scholarly embarrassment. In particular, Jones was taken in – via his disciple Francis Wilford[48] – by a spectacular fraud on the part of a native Indian amanuensis. Such assistants were, it seems, instructed to keep an eye open for parallels between the legends of Hindu mythology and similar episodes in the early portions of Genesis. Demand, alas, created its own supply of 'corroborative

---

[42] B. Lincoln, 'Mr Jones's myth of origins', in Lincoln, *Theorizing myth: narrative, ideology and scholarship* (Chicago, 1999), pp. 76–100, at pp. 84–7, 91, 95.
[43] C. Kidd, *British identities before nationalism* (Cambridge, 1999), pp. 9–72.
[44] T. Ballantyne, *Orientalism and race: Aryanism in the British Empire* (Houndmills, 2002), pp. 42–3; C. Kidd, *The forging of races* (Cambridge, 2006), pp. 117, 170, 175, 181, 187–9, 191–2; S. Arvidsson, *Aryan idols: Indo-European mythology as ideology and science* (transl. S. Wichmann, Chicago, 2006), pp. 42–3.
[45] Trautmann, *Aryans*, pp. 42–4; Ballantyne, *Orientalism*, pp. 28–9.
[46] Bryant, *New system*, vol. I, p. vii.
[47] Jones, 'Ninth anniversary discourse', p. 104.
[48] Cf. Francis Wilford, 'On Egypt and other countries adjacent to the Cali river, or Nile of Ethiopia, from the ancient books of the Hindus', *Asiatic Researches*, vol. 3 (1792), pp. 295–462, at pp. 312–13; William Jones, 'Remarks', *Asiatic Researches*, vol. 3 (1792), pp. 465–6; Wilford, 'An essay on the sacred isles of the west', *Asiatic Researches*, vol. 8 (1805), pp. 245–367, at pp. 250–62.

evidence' from Hindu sources for the earliest portions of sacred history.[49] Wilford – who appears to have been on his own quest for a key to reconcile Hebraic and Hindu mythologies[50] – was deceived by an over-eager pandit who *helpfully* introduced a Noah-figure with three sons into a manuscript of the *Padma Purana*. The interpolation was all too neat a fit with Christian preconceptions: 'To Satyavarman, the sovereign of the whole earth, were born three sons; the eldest Sherma, then Charma, and thirdly, Jyapeti by name.'[51] Jones's friend, Lord Teignmouth, noted how the deception had been accomplished – 'interpolated by the dextrous introduction of a forged sheet, discoloured, and prepared for the purpose of deception'.[52] Nevertheless, the news had been communicated to Jones, who had also been deceived, hence his conclusion that the deluge was 'an historical fact admitted as true by every nation … particularly by the ancient Hindus, who have allotted an entire Purana to the detail of that event'.[53] Not that there was any major disgrace in being taken in by such a deception in a faraway location and a strange language. After all, as Teignmouth noted, at home the domestic 'fabrications of a Chatterton, escaped for a season, the penetration of the learned and the acute'.[54]

Chatterton was, of course, the source of another of Bryant's blunders. Bryant stoutly defended the authenticity of the poems attributed to the fifteenth-century Bristolian, Thomas Rowley, which – it later transpired – were forgeries by the precocious Chatterton. In a letter to his friend Henley, the cleric and Shakespearean scholar, Bryant concluded that Chatterton 'cannot have been gifted with inspiration: and without that he could not have arrived at the truths, contained in these poems. They must have been by another, and far prior hand.'[55] Unfortunately, Bryant's insensitivity to the language of the poems of the supposed late medieval Bristolian was exposed by Thomas Tyrwhitt.[56] However, Bryant was not alone in ascribing the poems to a fifteenth-century original. The case for

---

[49] 'Asiatic Researches', *British Critic*, vol. 25 (April 1805), pp. 401–8, at p. 401.
[50] See esp. Francis Wilford, 'On Mount Caucasus', *Asiatic Researches*, vol. 6 (1799), pp. 455–536; N. Leask, 'Francis Wilford and the colonial construction of Hindu geography, 1799–1822', A. Gilroy (ed.), *Romantic geographies* (Manchester, 2000), pp. 204–22.
[51] Lord Teignmouth, *Memoirs of the life, writings and correspondence of Sir William Jones* (London, 1804), p. 367.
[52] *Ibid.*, p. xii.
[53] Jones, 'Ninth anniversary discourse', p. 102.
[54] Teignmouth, *Memoirs*, p. xiii.
[55] Jacob Bryant to Samuel Henley, 26 June 1781, in BPL, MS Ch.G.13.53.
[56] Thomas Tyrwhitt, *A vindication of the appendix to the poems, called Rowley's* (1782: repr. London, 1993).

the poems' authenticity was also made by another prominent antiquary, the Dean of Exeter, Jeremiah Milles (1714–84).[57]

Among the ranks of those who differed from Bryant on the Rowley question was the Reverend Alexander Catcott (1725–79), vicar of Temple parish in Bristol and a convinced Hutchinsonian like his father Alexander Catcott senior (1692–1749).[58] By a piquant irony Bryant's opponent happened to share his obsessions with the Flood. Indeed, Catcott Jr was the author of *A Treatise on the Deluge* (1761; 2nd edn, 1768), where he not only advanced a concordance between scripture and geology, but also drew upon pagan mythology as unbiased testimony from outside the Judaeo-Christian tradition to the historical fact of a universal flood. How else was one to account for the 'striking resemblances' between the scriptural version of the Deluge and 'heathen history'? Catcott pressed Ovid into the service of apologetics; did the Roman poet not describe just such a Deluge in his *Metamorphoses*? And were there not similar flood legends in Greek, Egyptian and Babylonian mythologies? There seemed to be further corroboration, Catcott reckoned, in the Hindu legend of the Flood of Sattiavarti. More uncanny still was the rainbow in the Chinese legend of the flood of Fohi – surely, Catcott thought, a 'conceit' arising from the story of Noah. Nor, Catcott noted, did the Americas lack their own versions of the Flood legend. The conclusions were obvious to draw. It seemed that 'all nations', though 'differing in opinion, customs, language, religion and even ignorant of one another's existence', had 'throughout all known ages' knowledge of a great deluge. Moreover, 'the tradition prevailing universally, it is certain that such an event did happen; – and moreover that it was universal in its effects, else it could not have been universally believed'. Catcott went even further in his edgily ecumenical embrace of heathen mythology: the very 'imperfections' – indeed sometimes 'false' elements – in the legends of the heathens bore 'witness' in themselves 'to the truth and perfection' of the Ur-version retailed by Moses.[59]

Catcott's work brings into focus the links – sometimes fortuitous (as in this case), sometimes substantive – between Bryant's mythography and his other antiquarian interests. Such connections are especially evident in Bryant's Homeric researches and his broader investigations into classical lore. Here what stands out is a vivid and somewhat peculiar contrast

---

[57] *Poems, supposed to have been written at Bristol, in the fifteenth century, by Thomas Rowley ... With a commentary, in which the antiquity of them is considered, and defended* (London, 1782).

[58] M. Neve and R. Porter, 'Alexander Catcott: glory and geology', *British Journal for the History of Science*, vol. 10 (1977), pp. 37–60.

[59] Alexander Catcott, *A treatise on the deluge* (2nd edn, London, 1768), pp. 100–28.

between Bryant's scrupulous adherence to Mosaic history as unquestionable truth and his quizzical attitude towards the profane traditions of the ancient Greeks, which he found dubious in the extreme.

In an essay 'Of the causes, whence many errors have arisen in inquiries into ancient history', Bryant sought out the origins of the 'uncertainty' and 'errors' which he detected in 'profane history'. These, he felt, had arisen from the national 'vanity', solipsism and 'false delicacy' of the ancient Greek literati: 'their ears were so unnecessarily nice, that they could not endure to represent things in their native dress, but changed the name both of men and countries', and consequently mangled the foreign traditions which they had inherited. Alas, much of the knowledge of primeval antiquity had come through these unreliable hands. Of course, Bryant conceded, due acknowledgement needed to be given to the role of the Greeks in garnering and transmitting knowledge of the most distant eras of human history, but he could not conceal his exasperation at the corruptions of data and losses of material which had accompanied their flawed salvage effort: 'when we consider how much more they might have transmitted, and how foul and turbid the streams are, that are derived to us, it takes off much from the obligation'.[60]

This scepticism lay behind Bryant's critique of Newton, whose contribution to universal chronology depended on the authenticity of the voyage of the Argonauts and the siege of Troy. Bryant conceded that the Argonautic voyage was 'always esteemed authentic, and admitted as a chronological era'. However, Bryant was sure that there were 'no such persons as the Grecian Argonauts: and that the expedition of Jason to Colchis was a fable'. Indeed, he concluded: 'It was a great misfortune to the learned world, that this excellent person [Newton] was so easily satisfied with Grecian lore; taking with too little examination, whatever was transmitted to his hands.' Bryant preferred the more sceptical astronomy of Thomas Rutherforth (1712–71), author of *A System of Natural Philosophy* (1748) to Newton's gullible acceptance of classical mythology as history.[61]

The Trojan War was another matter entirely. Here Bryant intervened in one of the major debates in late eighteenth- and early nineteenth-century classical history and topography: the quest for the location of Troy. The traditional view was that Troy had been situated on a plain in Phrygia, in the north-western portion of Asia Minor, between the Simois and the

---

[60] Jacob Bryant, 'Of the causes, whence many errors have arisen in inquiries made into ancient history', in Bryant, *Observations and inquiries relating to various parts of ancient history* (Cambridge, 1767), pp. 96–7, 99.
[61] Bryant, *New system*, vol. I, p. xi; vol. II, pp. 474, 478–80.

Scamander rivers. However, in the Enlightenment this long-established view was challenged by Jean-Baptiste Le Chevalier (1752–1836). Le Chevalier argued that Troy had been located rather on rising ground, near what was now the Turkish town of Bournabashi.[62] This gave rise to a new topographical round in the century-old battle between the Ancients and the Moderns. Writing in 1814, the geographer James Rennell (1742–1830) announced that 'the topography of the plain of Troy has become a kind of party question in literature', though he noticed that the division of opinion among modern commentators was far from even: 'by far the greater number of persons have espoused the opinion of M. de Chevalier; or what, if the reader pleases, may be termed the New Doctrine'.[63] Bryant's battles with his critics over the existence of the Trojan War and its location (if it had ever happened) constituted an important theatre of disputation in the wider pamphlet war over Troy begun by Le Chevalier.

Before examining Bryant's views it is important to note that he was not alone in his extreme scepticism about Troy. The Scottish advocate John MacLaurin (1734–96), later elevated to the judicial bench as Lord Dreghorn, had delivered a paper to the Royal Society of Edinburgh on 16 February 1784 entitled 'A dissertation to prove that Troy was not taken by the Greeks'. It was obvious, argued MacLaurin, that certain aspects of the Trojan history had no basis in historical fact, such as the story of Helen's birth, which was 'evidently an allegory, and generally thought to be an astronomical one'. But even the less flagrantly fabulous elements in the story were no more reliably grounded. The ancient Greek version of the siege itself seemed 'incredible and inconsistent with itself'. MacLaurin sounded a very sceptical note and reversed the result of the war, assuming – and he did not take it for granted – that the war had happened in the first place: '(that if ever there was at all a Trojan war), Troy was not taken by them [the Greeks], but that they were obliged, by those who defended it, to raise the siege, and retire with loss and disgrace'. What struck MacLaurin about the Homeric account of the war was its ring of utter 'falsity'.[64]

Bryant's major intervention was *A Dissertation Concerning the War of Troy* (1796?). This devastating, perverse and unexpected contribution to the debate over Le Chevalier's theories was of a piece with Bryant's earlier

---

[62] Jean-Baptiste Le Chevalier, 'Tableau de la plaine de Troye', *Transactions of the Royal Society of Edinburgh*, vol. III (1794), part ii, section ii, pp. 3–92.
[63] James Rennell, *Observations on the topography of the Plain of Troy* (London, 1814), pp. v–vi.
[64] John MacLaurin, 'A dissertation to prove that Troy was not taken by the Greeks', *Transactions of the Royal Society of Edinburgh*, vol. I (1788), part 2, section 2, pp. 43–62, at pp. 46, 50, 52.

work on mythography. Bryant believed that the only reliable history of antiquity was sacred history, and that otherwise the archaic period of classical history needed to be handled with the utmost scepticism, lest one found oneself duped by the self-regarding vanity of ancient peoples – not least the Greeks, who were renowned in Bryant's eyes for their magpie-like acquisitiveness for other nations' mythologies.[65]

The Le Chevalier debate seems to have reminded Bryant that the Trojan war constituted unfinished business left over from his *magnum opus*. Just as Bryant in his *New System* had demolished the supposedly historical foundations of the Argonautic expedition, so in his *Dissertation Concerning the War of Troy* he displayed scant regard for the conventionally accepted history – or geography – of the Trojan War. On this basis he contended that there was 'no truth in the history of the Trojan war: or if there were any original foundation for such a history, it was borrowed from another quarter, and adapted to the nation where it is now found'. The Homeric history of the Greek siege of a city in Phrygia was nothing of the sort, most likely either pure mythology or a borrowing from events far away from Asia Minor in the course of Egyptian history. The 'whole' Homeric history of the Trojan war was 'a figment', Bryant reckoned, 'and every step we take is upon fairy ground'.[66]

Bryant's views provoked outraged spluttering in many quarters. In a paper delivered at the Royal Society of Edinburgh on 4 September 1797 Andrew Dalzel (1742–1806) criticised Bryant's curious position on Troy as 'the efforts of a frigid and phlegmatic erudition'. Bryant's 'paradoxes' were 'too whimsical, too violent, and too repugnant to the best authorities of antiquity, ever to admit of anything like a proof'.[67]

Gilbert Wakefield (1756–1801), a former Fellow of Jesus College, Cambridge who had become a Unitarian dissenter, complained that Bryant's opinions on Troy reminded him of nothing so much as 'Thomas Paine's most profligate, rash, audacious and ignorant attacks on revelation', warning Bryant that the promulgation of his sceptical theory of Trojan history 'in opposition to such a concurrence of traditional evidence through all antiquity must materially impair', albeit 'unintentionally on your part, the cogency of one argument in favour of the Jewish and Christian revelations'. Although Bryant's arguments in regard to Trojan history were

---

[65] Bryant, *New system*, vol. I, p. 175.
[66] Bryant, *Dissertation concerning the war of Troy* (1st edn), pp. 9, 11.
[67] Andrew Dalzel, 'M. Chevalier's Tableau de la Plaine de Troye illustrated and confirmed, from the observations of subsequent travellers, and others', *Transactions of the Royal Society of Edinburgh*, vol. 4 (1798), pp. 29–74, at pp. 73–4.

'perfectly unexceptionable in themselves', by 'weakening the credibility of a fact so universally transmitted and believed as the siege and destruction of Troy', he called into question 'the prevalent tradition of a deluge among heathen nations'. No Trojan war, no Flood? Bryant should take especial care, for there were already in some of the sects on the fringes of Christianity notional believers who already regarded the Bible 'as a piece of parabolic scenery'.[68]

The classical scholar J. B. S. Morritt (1771–1843) was unconvinced by the benchmarks adopted by Bryant, finding that 'the scepticism which fixes a doubt upon all history prior to the Olympiads, and credits all Grecian history subsequent to that time' seemed 'to draw a line between history and fable, with a precision which can hardly be supported'. Morritt complained that Bryant's scepticism was misplaced. Why should he – of all people – be troubled by variations in the ancient tellings of the Trojan War, for Bryant had 'made use of this very mode of reasoning to prove the Mosaic account of the Deluge … through the different traditions of different nations'? 'The accounts of the Trojan War are surely not more various', reckoned Morritt, 'than the accounts of the Flood; in both cases their variety proves their generality and their generality proves their truth.'[69]

By a devious conspiracy Bryant contrived to review his own book – under the guise of an anonymous dispassionate scholar – in the *Critical Review*. In a letter of 12 September 1797 to his friend Henley, Bryant welcomed the 'hint you gave me about the *Critical Review* … as it would give me an opportunity of explaining my system further, and defending myself from some unjust insinuations'. Bryant appears to have enclosed a manuscript copy of a review, which remains in Henley's archive in the Boston Public Library, and in his letter to Henley explains the purpose of the deception which the cleric had encouraged: Bryant had tried 'to establish my arguments, and to invalidate those, which have been brought against me. And this I have done in the manner of a review, without showing any partiality, making it appear, as little as possible, the work of the author, whose treatise is described and defended'. Bryant left it to Henley – the notional source of the review for the magazine – to make 'any alteration, or amendment' he thought it required, at his 'discretion'. If long-held beliefs

---

[68] Gilbert Wakefield, *A letter to Jacob Bryant, Esq. concerning his dissertation on the war of Troy* (London, 1797), pp. 3–4, 17–19.

[69] J. B. S. Morritt, *A vindication of Homer* (York, 1798), pp. 3, 43. See also Morritt, *Additional remarks on the topography of Troy* (London, 1800). Cf. William Gell, *The topography of Troy* (London, 1804), pp. 119–24, who tries to reconcile Le Chevalier's thesis with Bryant's Arkite mythography – *contra* Bryant.

in the historicity of the Trojan War could so easily be cast adrift, Bryant's orthodox critics wondered, then how reliably anchored in history were the events of the Old Testament? Bryant confessed to his friend that 'nothing could be farther from my mind, than those imputations of raising a faction in the learned world, and of doing any injury to religion'. For Bryant's deep Christian faith supplied the obverse of a devastating ultra-enlightened scepticism on most other fronts: 'It was my wish to show', he confessed to Henley, 'that there are no histories, but the sacred, to which we can trust.'[70]

Bryant's review – as preserved in manuscript in Henley's archive and only very lightly edited in the pages of the October 1797 issue of the *Critical Review* – rehearsed the arguments of his critics in order to present Bryant as an orthodox defender of Old Testament history who merely happened to entertain doubts about the historical foundations of the so-called Trojan War. In the guise of the reviewer Bryant set out the logic of orthodox fears, with fairness and a measure of empathy, wondering 'to what can we trust, if an object of belief of so long standing, and so universally admitted, is not at last found to be a mere apologue of illusion. Religion itself is affected … For if an article, which from our childhood we have thought most certain, be proved to be groundless, upon what can we afterwards depend?' Nevertheless, such 'fears' were 'imaginary'. It was, rather, Bryant's orthodox critics who were themselves creating an unnecessary panic about the Church's wobbly historical foundations: 'there may be cause of great alarm to many well-minded believers, when they see Christianity placed on so precarious a basis. They may be led to give up a religion, which depends upon the existence or nonexistence of a city or town or rotten borough. But we hope it is better founded.' After all, the ostensibly impartial reviewer noted, Bryant's critics 'do not believe the whole' Homeric account of the Trojan War. Rather, they too, like Bryant, found some elements too grossly mythological or folkloric, and rejected them. Yet 'in doing this they act the same part, as they suppose the author to have done, and sacrifice many things, which have had the sanction of ages'. In so doing they reduced the epic deeds of archaic Asia Minor to 'a buccaneering war, and piratical transaction. But this is contrary to the whole tenor of history: and if ever faith can be by such means hurt, they contribute to its ruin'. On the other hand, Bryant – according to the fair-minded anonymous reviewer – had spent the 'greater part' of his life defending the 'authenticity' of scripture-history. In a statement which summed up

---

[70] Jacob Bryant to Samuel Henley, 12 September 1797, in BPL, MS Ch.G.13.57.

the ethos of the moderate Christian Enlightenment, the sympathetically impartial reviewer – as he seemed – insisted that there could never be any 'harm in stripping the tree of science of its spurious branches'.[71]

Notwithstanding the cavils of his many critics, Bryant remained undaunted. He also published an open defence of his Trojan thesis and its implications. Never afraid of being found in a minority of one and an outspoken pamphleteer in defence of his beloved hobby horses, he denied that his radical scepticism on the Trojan question in any way subverted his larger apologetic project: 'the alarm has been so great, that it has been said: Our holy religion is hazarded; and our faith in danger. But surely that faith must be very lukewarm, that can be affected by the talk of a wooden horse, and Phrygian borough.' The veracity of Christianity did not 'depend upon such foreign and precarious objects'. Bryant protested the absurdity of linking the fate of true religion with the robust historicity of heathen myths – ridiculing the suggestion that 'by demolishing Babel, I should injure the Holy City: or by pulling down a pagoda, ruin the church'.[72]

However, in doing so Bryant seemed oblivious of the tissue of connection which the use of collateral evidences established between the pure unadulterated truths of Christianity and the distorted truths of pagan mythology. The deployment of a mythographic scheme of apologetic made Christianity parasitic in some measure on non-Judaeo-Christian bodies of materials, whose fantastical elements had hitherto been a matter of indifference or contempt as far defenders of the Christian religion were concerned. Anglican theologians had imported their orientalist obsessions into the very bosom of the Church. The rise of the collateral evidences as a vital new branch of apologetics meant that one could indeed now ruin the church by pulling down a pagoda.

---

[71] 'A dissertation concerning the war of Troy. By Jacob Bryant', in BPL, MS Ch.G.13.62; 'Review of a dissertation concerning the war of Troy. By Jacob Bryant', *Critical Review* (October 1797), pp. 130–2. Cf. Jacob Bryant, *A treatise upon the authenticity of the scriptures and the truth of the Christian religion* (2nd edn, Cambridge, 1793).
[72] Jacob Bryant, *Some observations upon the vindication of Homer* (Eton, 1799), pp. 92–3.

CHAPTER 5

The Dispute of the Orient: Anglo-French Rivalries in an Age of Revolution

> [I]t is a pity that it [Casaubon's labour] should be thrown away, as so much English scholarship is, for want of knowing what is being done by the rest of the world. (*Middlemarch*, ch. 21)
>
> Poor Mr Casaubon himself was lost among small closets and winding stairs, and in an agitated dimness about the Cabeiri. (*Middlemarch*, ch. 20)

Anglo-German differences in the science of mythology, as we know, supply one of the crucial pivots in the plot of *Middlemarch*. Casaubon's cousin Will Ladislaw, an artist and man of the world, is aware that German philology, theology and mythography were far in advance of their English counterparts. Eliot was, of course, dramatising her own exposure to the German Higher Criticism and the effect it had on her own religious and philosophical beliefs. Nevertheless, she concealed from her readers another set of Anglo-Continental tensions which had a decisive influence on the formation of Anglican mythography between the 1790s and 1830s. Her reticence is understandable, for a triangular set of intellectual relationships is less easy to transmute into literary drama; the contrasts would be much less well-defined. On the other hand, complexity of this sort was rarely a deterrent to a novelist of Eliot's sublime gifts.

Yet behind the plot of *Middlemarch* lies an unacknowledged Anglo-French back story: a massive affair which constituted one of the dominant themes in the English response to French radicalism during the era of Revolution and Reform. As George Eliot knew, though she did not say as much in *Middlemarch*, Mr Casaubon's mythographical enterprise arose from the need to combat the spread of a subversive Gallic strain of infidel mythography associated in particular with the works of Volney and Dupuis.[1] When the cosmopolitan Ladislaw condemns English scholarship,

---
[1] N. Leask, *British romantic writers and the East* (Cambridge, 1992), pp. 104–6. Cf. M. Butler, 'Myth and mythmaking in the Shelley circle', *English Literary History*, vol. 49 (1982), pp. 50–72, which notices, at p. 56, an 'upsurge in mythological polemic' from the mid-1780s. For Eliot's knowledge of Dupuis, see J. C. Pratt, and V. A. Neufeldt (eds.), *George Eliot's Middlemarch notebooks* (Berkeley and Los Angeles, 1979), pp. 51–2.

and particularly that of his kinsman, for 'want of knowing what is being done by the rest of the world', he (or Eliot, his puppeteer) is being unfair. The deistic philosophes and demythologising ideologues of late eighteenth-century France spurred the urgency and hot polemical engagement of Anglican mythography in the generation after Bryant. As Jon Mee has argued, during the turbulent years of the French Revolution a conservative 'syncretism', grounded in the 'discourse of speculative mythography', provided a vital prop against the threat of subversion.[2] Hard as it is now to imagine, the priority of Judaeo-Christian truth over pagan mythology functioned as the intellectual keystone of the traditional Christian social order. Without it, political institutions were not built upon divine truth, but stood revealed as mere naked displays of usurped wealth and power.

It was, arguably, the very intensity of the Anglo-French wars of mythography which directed the attention of English scholars away from the German science of mythology. Indeed, the German mythological approach to biblical criticism did insinuate itself into English intellectual life,[3] but given its demanding technicality impinged less directly on the romantic era than the conflict waged on organised religion by Volney, Dupuis and their English radical followers.

Contemporaries – contemporaries, that is, of the fictional Mr Casaubon *c*.1830 – knew the anti-French rationale of the Anglican key to all mythologies. Indeed, George Cornewall Lewis (1806–63), a future Chancellor of the Exchequer and Home Secretary, in an article published in the *Foreign Quarterly Review* in January 1831 mapped the delusive quest for a 'key to all mythologies' (which, as we shall see, he all but named as such) as an Anglo-French dispute. The origins of heathen mythology, Lewis noted, were a subject of enormous controversy and the part of mythography which 'has attracted the chief notice of the writers of France and England'. The national camps were 'actuated' by sharply contrasting motives. On the one side, Volney and Dupuis were driven by a 'hatred' of Christianity, while across the Channel a mythologist like Bryant wrote out of 'love of the Christian religion'. Yet regardless of these ideological differences, Lewis perceived, both the Christian and the infidel mythographers had followed a similar approach to the matter of contention. Each had, 'by the most absurd etymologies, the most fanciful hypotheses, and the most illogical reasoning, attempted to set up a fabric which the faintest breath of criticism

---

[2] J. Mee, *Dangerous enthusiasm: William Blake and the culture of radicalism in the 1790s* (Oxford, 1992), p. 121.

[3] E. S. Shaffer, *Kubla Khan and the fall of Jerusalem: the mythological school in biblical criticism and secular literature 1770–1880* (1975: Cambridge pbk, 1980).

at once demolishes'. The French as much as the English were hostages of a delusion springing from their 'eagerness to explain upon one theory, or to refer to one origin, a mass of phenomena wholly unconnected, and springing from numberless causes'. The respective national modes of interpreting all mythologies differed drastically and prompted heated Anglo-French pamphlet wars, but were to Lewis's discriminating eyes similarly obtuse and insensitively reductive: 'Dupuis and Volney with their astronomy, and Bryant with Noah and the ark, resemble the advertising quack, whose infallible and instantaneous cure for all diseases would probably turn out not to be of use in one.'[4] For Lewis – in this instance an uncanny real-life anticipation of Eliot's creation Will Ladislaw – the German mythographical school associated with the likes of K. O. Müller, whose *Prolegomena zu einer wissenschaftlichen Mythologie* (1825) he was reviewing, provided a more sophisticated way of approaching this contentious field.

The focus of British Protestant apologetics was on the threat of French infidelity, and it is hardly surprising that the devastating assault on the historicity of the Bible associated with Volney and Dupuis should obscure for many Britons the unrelated questioning of the Bible associated with the German Higher Critics. Nevertheless, the Casaubonish milieu of early nineteenth-century mythographical apologetics was not – the plot of *Middlemarch* notwithstanding – altogether oblivious of the strange triangular relationship between French scepticism, the German Higher Criticism and the steadfast British defence of the Christian truth lurking in heathen legends. Sharon Turner, for instance, who used his *Sacred History of the World* (1832–9) to ground the historical truth of the Deluge in the rich corroborative soil of flood legends from Babylonia to the Americas, was well aware of developments in other quarters. The rise of French infidel philosophy and the French Revolution – not least Volney's deconstruction of Christ and his twelve disciples into the sun and the zodiac – had 'unreligionized' half of the French population, while a considerable 'portion of the German clergy' had begun to treat the scriptures 'as mere myths and fables'. Nevertheless, Turner had the utmost confidence in his own scheme of mythography, and ability to detect the differences between history, its distortion in legendary traditions, and unsupported mythology. The descendants of Noah had declined from patriarchal religion into pagan polytheism and idolatry in the course of five centuries after the Flood. But during this period of patriarchal religion the Noachic

---

[4] [George Cornewall Lewis], 'Mythology and religion of Ancient Greece', *Foreign Quarterly Review*, vol. 7 (1831), pp. 33–52, at p. 34.

Flood had become a central portion of the beliefs of the world's gradually dispersing peoples. Of course, the world's mythologies were of a baroque extravagance – 'wild, incongruous' with 'confusions and mistakes', as well as 'divergencies' from the Flood narrative in Genesis – yet 'quite sufficient' in several telling details 'to authenticate the fact of a general deluge'. The 'collateral corroborations' of the Flood found in every part of the world were so numerous and yet so independent of one another that they provided a compelling alternative to the deconstructive schemes of mythology advanced among French and German pseudo-mythographers.[5]

The origins of the subversive school of French orientalist mythography went back to Voltaire. In his *Dictionnaire philosophique* (1764) he drew attention to the ways in which Hindu mythology prefigured the purloined plagiarism – as he saw it – of the Hebrews whom he regarded as cultural parvenus. Was not Adimo, the first man of the Hindus, wondered Voltaire, the prototype of that Johnny-come-lately, the Old Testament Adam? Similarly, was not Brahma an obvious original model for Abraham? Voltaire not only perceived that the religions of the Orient were older and more authentic than the rites and beliefs described in the Old Testament, but observed with a particular delight that China possessed a religion of pure morality which was less riddled with metaphysical absurdities and other barbarisms than the curious Judaic cults inherited by the peoples of Europe.[6]

Voltaire made sport with the stock themes and arguments of sacred history in the extensive 'Discours preliminaire' of the revised 1769 edition of his influential *Essai sur les moeurs*, which went through many editions in French and was soon translated into English. The long introductory section on Old Testament history and the histories – tellingly – of cultures more ancient and more civilised than the Israelites, had first been published separately as *La philosophie de l'histoire* (1765). The peoples of India, China and Chaldea had not only been of greater antiquity than the wandering tribes of Jewish herdsmen described in the Bible, but the fact that these gentile peoples had lived in cities from an early stage in human history meant that they were more likely to have had annals, or to put it another way, that their histories were more reliable than those of the Pentateuch. Moreover, Voltaire could not but

---

[5] Sharon Turner, *The sacred history of the world* (3 vols., London, 1832–9), vol. II, pp. 308–45; vol. III, pp. 503–13, 531–5, esp. vol. II, pp. 309–10, 319, 338–40; vol. III, pp. 510, 533, 535.
[6] Voltaire, *Dictionnaire philosophique* (1764: Paris, 1964), esp. pp. 22–6, 76–94.

help reach the conclusion that Jewish culture – including its myths and folklore – was derivative of the sophisticated civilisations and attendant theologies of neighbouring peoples. Angels, for example, probably constituted an idea borrowed from the Chaldeans or Persians. The far-from-elusive implication was that the Old Testament was the recycled matter of more ancient, more sophisticated gentile traditions. Indeed, there were central flaws in the claim that the Old Testament offered a cogent universal history of humanity, not least as the chronology of the world set out in Genesis was insufficient to account for the inevitably gradual rise of humankind to civilisation. The narrow limits of Old Testament chronology, Voltaire insisted, proved something of an unrealistic straitjacket for the historian aiming to give a plausible account of the unfolding of civilisation. His account of pagan antiquity was also peppered with obliquely subversive references to serpents and floods. Plus there were more precise jabs at the pretensions of sacred history. Voltaire could not resist a dig at the 'faux zèle' of the first Christians who forged the Sibylline oracles of Christ's coming in order to combat the renown of the pagan oracles of heathen antiquity. Wherever one looked in the fascinating world of early antiquity presented by Voltaire it was hard to foreground a distinctive and authoritative Jewish–Christian continuum from the background influences of a more ancient and apparently more creative heathendom.[7]

In *Dieu et les hommes* (1769) Voltaire exposed the Old Testament religion of the Israelites as a motley collection of divine terminology, theological categories and rituals derived from the beliefs and practices of the surrounding cultures of the Near East.[8] Moreover, the fall of Lucifer was an oriental allegory of planetary motion – namely the movements of Venus, the morning star – all-too-vividly personified, and later transplanted into Hebraic culture. Not that the version found in the Bible was the only western version of this elaborate – and much elaborated – oriental personification of the heavenly mechanics.[9]

Chronology was essential to the process of differentiating the original from the copy in the field of comparative mythology. The history of the

---

[7] Voltaire, *Essai sur les moeurs* (1765 [1769]: 6 vols., Lausanne, 1780), vol. I, esp. pp. 41–4, 75, 84, 144, 178, 217–23, 246.
[8] Voltaire, 'Dieu et les hommes' in *The complete works of Voltaire*, (Voltaire Foundation, 1994), vol. LXIX, p. 351: 'Ils empruntent les noms de Dieu chez les Phonéciens; ils prennent les anges chez les Persans; ils ont l'arche errante des Arabes; ils adoptent le baptême des Indiens, la circoncision des prêtres d'Egypte.'
[9] *Ibid.*, p. 295: 'L'allégorie des anges révoltés contre Dieu est originairement une parabole indienne qui a eu cours longtemps après dans presque tout l'Occident sous cent déguisements différents.'

Jews – 'une nation très nouvellement établie',[10] calculated Voltaire – was not an ancient one, certainly less venerable than several oriental civilisations. It seemed obvious that the older a nation was, the more likely its religion was to be of a high antiquity ('Plus une nation est antique, plus aussi elle a une religion ancienne').[11] Tellingly, there was no evidence of the major outlines, events or personalities of Mosaic history in other oriental cultures. Thus it seemed unlikely that the stories found in Genesis did in fact constitute the ultimate Ur-history of the human race, or else some other culture would have preserved some of the debris, at the very least some remembrance of Adam or Cain or Methuselah or Noah. But the resounding and absolute silence of oriental authors and peoples in this regard was enough to convince Voltaire that the historiographical claims of the Pentateuch were unfounded.

A universal flood, Voltaire reckoned, was a scientific nonsense. To be sure, there were other great floods mentioned in the histories (or mythologies) of ancient pagan peoples – the floods of Deucalion, Ogyges and, of course, the Chaldean Xisuthrus – so it seemed reasonable to conclude that the tale of Noah was just that, a piece of folklore borrowed from the Chaldeans – 'incontestablement plus anciens que les Juifs' – and exaggerated. After all, if the story of Noah was indeed, as Christians claimed, the history of the restoration of the primeval human race after a global catastrophe, then why had this world-historical episode been 'entièrement ignoré du monde entier'? It seemed altogether plausible to Voltaire that the compilers of the Pentateuch had been 'plagiaires', latecomers into the march of civilisation who lifted extant histories or, more likely, mythologies from neighbouring cultures wholesale into their own derivative mythology.[12]

The key to Christian mythology, Voltaire calculated, lay in its chronological posteriority to other nearby cultures, whereby the obvious resemblances of Judaeo-Christian sacred history to the stories of these cultures were liable to be exposed as simulacra, at the very least of another people's history, if not as copies of astral allegories or similar fanciful concoctions. Voltaire turned upside down the arguments of Huet, who had detected remembrances of Moses in heathen mythologies, and constructed from there an apologetic defence of the ultimate underlying truth of sacred history. Instead Voltaire identified an Arab deity, Bac or Bacchus, alias Misem, as the prototype of Moses. After all, the resemblances between

---

[10] *Ibid.*, p. 335.
[11] *Ibid.*, p. 286.
[12] *Ibid.*, pp. 394–8.

The Dispute of the Orient

these two mythological personages seemed uncannily close.[13] Voltaire went on to compile a list of ancient Jewish mythological plagiarisms, noting the obvious similarities between the deeds of Hercules and Samson, the fatal feminine curiosity exhibited by both Pandora and Eve, the stories of Niobe and Edith, wife of Lot, turned respectively into a statue of marble and a pillar of salt, down to the remarkable vocal qualities of the donkey of Silenus and Balaam's ass. Voltaire made it quite apparent to his readers that in the field of ancient mythography the comparative analyses of 'Freethinkers' were much to be preferred to the unthinking orthodox Christian apologetics of the 'Non-pensants'.[14]

Sometimes Voltaire failed to apply his own distinctive scepticism to materials which seemed all-too-neatly to convict the Judaeo-Christian tradition of mythological plagiarism. Such was the *Ezourvedam* affair.[15] In 1760 Voltaire was given a French manuscript of this supposed *veda* by the Chevalier de Maudave. Voltaire was duped by the *Ezourvedam*, which he understood to be a translation by a Brahmin of an ancient Sanskrit *veda* predating and anticipating in strategic elements the Old Testament narrative, to which it constituted a standing reproach. However, Pierre Sonnerat (1748–1814) in his *Voyage aux Indes orientales* (1782) exposed the misattribution and established the true provenance – ultimately Christian and early modern – of the pseudo-*veda*. The purported *veda* turned out to be the work of early modern Jesuits in India who had attempted to present Christian traditions in terms which the indigenous peoples of India would understand. As far as Sonnerat was concerned, the supposedly subversive manuscript which Voltaire had donated to the Bibliothèque du Roi was no more than a pretended translation and certainly not one of the four *vedas*, but a piece of missionary advocacy with an ironic afterlife.[16] Notwithstanding the embarrassment attending the *Ezourvedam* affair, India in particular and the Orient in general remained potent antidotes, as far as deists and sceptics were concerned, to the delusions of Christianity.

---

[13] *Ibid.*, p. 324: 'Ce Bacchus arabe était né comme Moïse en Egypte … Il avait passé la mer rouge à pied sec avec son armée pour aller conquérir les Indes … Il fait jaillir une fontaine de vin, d'un rocher en le frappant de son thyrse. Il arrêta le cours du soleil et de la lune … Enfin on le nomma Misem qui est un des noms de Moïse.'

[14] *Ibid.*, pp. 399–401.

[15] L. Rocher 'Introduction', in Rocher (ed.), *Ezourvedam: a French veda of the eighteenth century* (Philadelphia, 1984); U. App, *The birth of orientalism* (Philadelphia, 2010), esp. pp. 45–72.

[16] Pierre Sonnerat, *Voyage aux Indes orientales* (2 vols., Paris, 1782), vol. I, p. 215: 'on voit que l'auteur a voulu tout ramener à la religion chrétienne, en y laissant cependant quelques erreurs afin qu'on ne reconnut pas le missionaire sous le manteaux du brame. C'est donc a tort que M. de Voltaire, et quelques autres, donnent à ce livre une importance qu'il ne mérite pas, et le regardent comme canonique.'

Nor was Voltaire the main bugbear of English Casaubons. The real threat to orthodoxy came from the next generation of French deconstructive mythographers – Dupuis and Volney.

Charles-François Dupuis (1742–1809) was fascinated by the early history of astronomy and its influence on ancient mythologies. He published various essays on this topic in the *Journal des Savants*, and united these in a single book as *Mémoire sur l'Origine des Constellations et sur l'explication de la fable par l'astronomie*, in 1781. Here Dupuis traced the rise of astronomy in antiquity and went on to penetrate the apparent absurdity which concealed the true meanings of ancient myths, explaining these in terms of celestial allegories ('plusieurs fables anciennes qui seroient, sans cette allégorie astronomique qui perce de toute part').[17] Logical and geometric parterres, it transpired, lay behind a tangled overgrowth of seeming nonsense. At this stage, Dupuis's reductive analysis of mythology excluded the sacred history of Judaeo-Christian tradition. The opening presented by the French Revolutionary assault on the Church provided Dupuis with an opportunity to extend his demythologising methods to the Bible.[18]

In 1794 Dupuis produced a fuller and more subversive version of his system as *Origine de tous les cultes, ou la religion universelle*, which ran to three volumes in quarto or twelve in octavo, and in 1798 he published an abridgement of his *magnum opus*, the *Abrégé*. Dupuis traced in ancient mythologies a world of borrowings, plagiarisms, extraordinary resemblances and all-too-uncanny parallels. The fictions of Judaism and Christianity wore second-hand clothes appropriated from other ancient – indeed considerably older – mythologies. But these other religions were no more authentic than Judaeo-Christianity. They might have been older, closer perhaps to being Ur-mythologies, but were ultimately no more what they pretended to be than was Christianity itself. All mythologies – according to Dupuis's key to their interpretation – were at bottom allegories of the sun, the constellations of the night sky in the northern hemisphere and the annual cycle of vegetative nature's birth, death and renewal.[19]

Dupuis was conscious that he was turning the logic of Christian mythography on its head. Whereas apologetic mythographers believed that certain primeval elements of Judaeo-Christian tradition had been vouchsafed to the first peoples of the world centuries before the coming of

---

[17] Charles-François Dupuis, *Mémoire sur l'origine des constellations, et sur l'explication de la fable, par le moyen de l'astronomie* (Paris, 1781), p. 73.
[18] J. Z. Buchwald and D. G. Josefowicz, *The zodiac of Paris* (Princeton, 2010), pp. 47–69.
[19] Dupuis, *Abrégé de l'origine de tous les cultes* (Paris, 1798), esp. ch. 9.

Christianity proper, Dupuis perceived that Christianity itself was a kind of lumber-room of much earlier philosophies of nature and the allegorised mythologies derived from them. Christianity was really no different from other ancient religions. The names and details of the allegorised mythologies might differ, but at bottom they were all forms of solar and nature worship ('Cette religion ne diffère de toutes les religions anciennes, que par des noms, des formes et des allégories différentes, et que le fond est absolument le même').[20] Nor was Christ an historical personage; rather he was a personification of the sun, and his Christian worshippers were wrong to bestow personhood upon a mere emblem ('les adorateurs du Soleil-Christ se sont trompés en donnant une existence humaine au soleil personnifié dans leur légende').[21]

Christians, argued Dupuis, were deeply ignorant about the basis of their own religion. They simply did not have the first idea about what they were really worshipping. Christianity was misunderstood plagiarism: a patchwork composed of the debris of even older religions, themselves the remains of an astral system – what eighteenth-century mythographers called Sabaism – which had long been obscured by all-too-influential allegorised versions of its long-forgotten original meanings. The Fall of Man was really the allegory of the 'serpent d'hiver'. The serpent, Python, in ancient Greek mythology, was a symbol of winter. The apples in the garden of Eden were but the symbols of the seasonal fall. Similarly, the cosmic conflict of good and evil could be traced back to the dualism of Zoroastrian mythology, to the clash of its deities of light and darkness, Ormuzd and Ahriman. Persian magi had represented the world as an egg divided into twelve parts, six belonging to the god of light, six belonging to the god of darkness. It was evident, argued Dupuis, that here the calendar and the passage of the seasons had been endowed with a moral significance that the original allegory had never possessed.[22]

Christ was known under many names in ancient and oriental religions – Hercules, Bacchus, Osiris. Ultimately, however, none of these was the Ur-Christ, for all were personifications of the sun. The 'lamb of God' turned out to be a reference to the zodiacal symbol of the lamb, or ram, of the spring equinox.[23] Egyptians – tellingly – worshipped the sun under the name of Horus, the son of the virgin Isis.[24] The Roman

---

[20] *Ibid.*, p. 411.
[21] *Ibid.*, p. 395.
[22] *Ibid.*, pp. 295, 303, 361, 385, 389.
[23] *Ibid.*, pp. 341–5.
[24] *Ibid.*, p. 360.

Christ – Bacchus – accomplished miracles, cured the sick and predicted the future.[25] The very notion of a deity who descended to earth for the good of mankind was neither peculiar to Christianity nor an idea new to it. At the controversial core of Dupuis' system of mythography was a depersonified Christianity reduced in status from sacred history to a mere allegory of nature. The supposed history of Jesus Christ was simply an allegorised fable of the passage of the seasons. It was indeed a myth with a cosmic meaning, but not in a moral sense; its significance was purely astronomical, the seeming life-cycle of the sun dramatised.[26] The alleged history of the Fall of Man in the garden of Eden turned out to be rather a tale allegorising the loss of the sun's heat and the earth's bounty with the coming of autumn, a quite different kind of fall.[27]

Of course, as the most perceptive observers noticed, the sun never quite died, nor did it need to experience complete rebirth; rather there was a gradual waxing and waning of the sun over the course of the seasons. This more subtle cycle of gradations provided the matter of many ancient mythologies, with the twelve houses of the zodiac – and the creatures which symbolised them – brought into play as elements in the legends associated with sun-deities. Dupuis believed that there were so many similarities between the legends of the sun-Christ and the corresponding myths of nearby cultures that it was hard to take the historical Christ at face value. What of the Phrygian sun-deity Atys, who was depicted – in his own version of the Passion – by a young man tied to a tree?[28]

Dupuis also believed that the Trinity was another example of the ways in which the material aspects of nature had become divinised. There were clues to this in the pantheon of the ancient polytheistic Hindus whose three main deities – the creator, the preserver and the destroyer – symbolised the personification of the powers of nature. This Ur-Trinity provided a template for the later Trinitarian godhead of the Christians. By extension, the apostle Peter was the same as the Roman god Janus, the twelve apostles being the same as the twelve deities of the ancient pantheon and ultimately resolvable into the twelve months of the solar calendar.[29]

---

[25] *Ibid.*, pp. 351–6.
[26] *Ibid.*, p. 293: 'l'histoire prétendue d'un Dieu qui est né d'une vierge au solstice d'hiver, qui ressuscite à Pâques ou à l'equinoxe du printemps'.
[27] *Ibid.*, p. 303: 'l'homme sentit le besoin de se couvrir, et qu'il fut réduit à labourer la terre, opération qui répond à l'automne'.
[28] *Ibid.*, p. 348.
[29] *Ibid.*, pp. 291, 296–7, 391–2.

The Dispute of the Orient

Almost literally, Dupuis's subject was the key to all mythologies ('la clef allégorique pour trouver le sens de ses enigmes sacrées'). A radical deconstructionist who deployed mythography to reveal the true matter of religion, Dupuis's goal was to lift the veil of allegory ('soulever le voile allégorique') which hid the real import of Christianity.[30] Christianity was but the shadow of an earlier form of religion, itself no more than an allegory of the natural world. At the end of Dupuis's journey of deconstruction lay only the allegorical capacity of the human mind and the natural world itself. Divinity was dead.

Volney advanced a similar sort of argument in his *Ruines*, but with greater imaginative flair in the setting of an oriental dream-tale.[31] Volney (1757–1820) was born Constantin-François Chasseboeuf. He adopted the name Volney in honour of Voltaire, the name combining the first syllable of his hero's name with the final syllable of Voltaire's estate, Ferney. In 1808 under the Napoleonic Empire 'Volney' was formally raised to the title comte de Volney. His first published researches examined Herodotus's system of chronology, and he won further literary renown with an account of his travels in Syria and Egypt. His interests in the Middle East and in pagan antiquity coalesced in his audacious bestseller *Les ruines ou meditations sur les revolutions des empires* (1791). This was an accomplished literary work in the form of a reverie. Volney's deployment of a dream-like fantasy provided the scantiest fig-leaf for a radical scheme of utopian politics and a comparative analysis of religions which directly challenged the supernatural authority of Christianity. Volney's *Ruines*, to be fair, punctured the supernatural pretensions of all religion, but in the course of his sinuous argument he also made it clear that Judaeo-Christianity was in several crucial respects plagiarised from other religions – themselves, of course, grounded in the human worship of nature rather than, as their clergies claimed, in divine revelation. In Volney's judgment, Christianity stood condemned twice over, being neither supernatural nor even original. By the time *Les ruines* was published Volney had been active in the early stages of the French Revolution, having been elected to the Third Estate of the States-General as a deputy for Anjou. Yet notwithstanding the radicalism of *Les ruines* – whose worryingly influential translations into English would provoke alarm among the orthodox in Britain – Volney's reformist politics seemed, in the first of several ironies which were to dog his career, suspiciously lukewarm to the Jacobins, and those ever-touchy guardians

[30] *Ibid.*, p. 310.
[31] For the Volney phenomenon in an 'orientalist' context, see App, *Birth of orientalism*, pp. 440–79.

of the pure flame of the Revolution had him imprisoned. Fortunate to survive the Reign of Terror, Volney spent a short time after his release in 1794 as a Professor at the École normale, but soon decided to leave for the safer haven of the United States. However, in the United States Volney got into a fierce debate with another émigré, the English Unitarian radical Joseph Priestley, who – though himself loathed as a subversive hothead by Church and King loyalists in England – launched a scathing attack on Volney's *Ruins*. By a further irony, British conservatives seized upon the deistic Volney's response to the Unitarian Priestley and reprinted excerpts in the *Anti-Jacobin Review*, 'not for any concurrence with the opinions which it contains, but from the consideration that a controversy between an infidel philosopher and an Unitarian philosopher, has something novel and curious in it'.[32] Priestley's hostility played a part in Volney's decision to return to France, where in yet another irony he was showered with honours by Napoleon, including his imperial title, but remained equivocal – at best – about Napoleonic absolutism. Volney returned to his antiquarian researches on the origins of religion during his later years in France, and produced a treatise, *Recherches nouvelles sur l'histoire ancienne* (1808–14; 2nd edn, 1822), which elaborated upon the critique of Christianity advanced in *Les ruines*, and was also translated into English in 1819 as *New researches into ancient history*, causing further consternation in British conservative circles.

Volney's *Ruins* was a subversive treatise on the philosophy of religion disguised as a work of fiction. It told of the narrator's visit to the Levant and his ruminations near Palmyra on the sad ruins of the past civilisations which had once dominated the region. Volney described how he had fallen into a curious reverie and was visited by an apparition – a genie of sorts – who presented to the dreaming Frenchman a vision of the world and its religions. In particular, Volney was allowed to view a mass assembly of the leaders of the world's many religions. Here, priests drawn from every sect and every corner of the globe staked and debated their rival claims to channel divine authority. The result was a heaving disputatious mass of conflicting certainties, the ironic upshot of which was, of course, to create in the reader uncertainty about any assertion of religious truth.[33]

In Volney's dream the high priest of the Zoroastrian Parsees claims that the original religion of Moses bore very little similarity to what it would

---

[32] 'The wrangling philosophers', *Anti-Jacobin Review*, vol. 2 (March 1799), pp. 331–4, at p. 331.
[33] Volney, 'Les ruines', in Volney, *Observations générales sur les Indiens ou sauvages de l'Amérique du Nord et autres textes* (Paris, 2009).

become under its later Jewish and Christian iterations. Indeed, claimed the Parsee, there were no signs in the original Mosaic form of the religion of some of the core elements of its later theology.[34] Israelite exposure in Babylonish captivity to Zoroastrian theology had transformed the simple fabric of Mosaic religion into a quasi-Persian quilt. Volney's Parsee spokesman in the dream contended that Jews and Christians in their systems of spiritual entities were but the lost children ('enfants égarés')[35] of Zoroaster.

In *Les ruines* Volney also recounted how Buddha or Fo had been born of a royal virgin and that when he had heard of this happening the king of that country had instituted a massacre of the innocents. Volney dramatised a confrontation between Buddhist lamas and Christian priests, in which the Christians claimed that the Buddhists worshipped a disfigured version of Christ, to which the lamas replied that Buddhist doctrines had spread across the Orient many centuries before the appearance of Christ. Were Christians really unacknowledged Buddhists in disguise? Or perhaps Hindus? Volney described how in Hindu mythology Krishna (tellingly 'Chrisen' in French) delivered the world from a venomous serpent. Christianity turned out to be a quilted fabric of many unwelcome surprises, exhibiting unacknowledged Zoroastrian, Hindu and Buddhist motifs.[36]

In his dream Volney was shown that enlightenment, improvement and reform could only be realised when humankind had overcome its divisions, primarily its religious differences. Yet Volney's apparition had revealed a mob-scene of squabbling priests from every religion on the planet, bickering over how to resolve the patent contradictions which beset their various incommensurate and conflicting claims to absolute truth. In the attempt by this crowd of theologians to make sense of the world's religious diversity, one and all fell into 'un labyrinthe inextricable de contradictions'.[37] In other words, religion could not explain itself, or rather no one religion could self-account for the clash of competing invocations of divine authority. Yet a future of harmonious human-centred reform was not such an impossible utopia. For, as Volney had seen in his vision, all religions sprang ultimately from the same source. Notwithstanding the incompatible beliefs which now adhered to the world's religions, in the beginning there

---

[34] *Ibid.*, p. 127: 'si vous parcourez avec attention le détail des lois, des rites, et des préceptes présumés venir directement de Moïse, vous ne trouverez en aucun article une indication, même tacite, de ce qui compose aujourd'hui la doctrine théologique des Juifs et de leurs enfants, les chrétiens. En aucun lieu vous ne verrez de trace ni de l'immortalité de l'âme, ni d'une vie ultérieure, ni de l'enfer et du paradis, ni de la révolte de l'ange'.
[35] *Ibid.*, p. 128.
[36] *Ibid.*, pp. 129–33, 160–4.
[37] *Ibid.*, p. 133.

had been a primal unity. This was because all religions were corruptions of a simple form of nature-worship. Volney set out a scheme of naturalistic explanation – a natural history of the rise and progressive complication of mythology and its religious progeny.

In *Les ruines* Volney himself came to see how the rich variation of the world's religious and mythological beliefs might be explained in a naturalistic fashion. In particular Volney perceived how the chain of ideas and associations provided mechanisms by which certain basic concepts might become figurative, then personified, elaborated and finally embellished with wholly spurious spiritual significance. The core elements of Volney's system were humankind's primeval fears and anxieties in the face of the powers of nature; the need for agrarian societies, in the Near East and especially on the banks of the Nile, to predict the seasons, not least seasonal rainfall; and the capacity of the human mind, with its linguistic resourcefulness and ingenuity, to turn concept into metaphor, perceived pattern into personification, and the material forces of nature into active, intelligent deity. Similarly, the constellations of the night sky, whether in summer or winter, became divinised and allegorised.[38]

The serpent of Eden, according to Volney, had indeed been the emblem of the Zoroastrian deity Ahrimanes. However, the Zoroastrian symbol derived – ultimately, as Dupuis too argued – from notions of winter.[39] The human mind had, by a complex process of mental associations, imbrications and connections, transformed themes associated with the death of vegetation into the religious concept of evil. Zoroastrian influences in particular were responsible for the dualistic pattern of contrast between good and evil which was interwoven into the basic forms of natural mythology. Hindu legends added a third element – that of conservation, in addition to creation and destruction – to the principal powers of divinity. Eventually this intermediate function of divine conservation provided scope for the mediatorial Christ-role in religious doctrine.[40]

Deity was a product of the interaction of the human intellect and the physical objects it contemplated. Most obviously, the stars of the firmament seemed to form various patterns in the night sky, and these accidental constellations were, in their turn, identified first with the creatures which they resembled and then turned into mythological narratives which recounted the doings of these supposed beings. Eventually, the spiral of

---

[38] *Ibid.*, pp. 136–52.
[39] *Ibid.*, p. 150: 'ce fut le serpent qui sous le nom d'Ahrimanes forma la base du système de Zoroastre; et c'est lui, o Chrétiens et Juifs, qui est devenu votre serpent d'Eve'.
[40] *Ibid.*, pp. 149–51, 159–60.

allegorising and embellishment introduced spiritual and moral elements into these fables, completing the process by which the observation of the natural world was transmuted into full-blown religion.[41]

Half a century before the insights of the philologist Max-Müller on the roots of Indo-European religion, Volney deconstructed mythology as a kind of disease of language – or 'le vice du langage', as he called it: figurative meanings, the symbols deployed to portray natural phenomena, the ambiguity and sometimes multiple signification of words, all conspired in the processes by which natural phenomena were celebrated, personified and eventually misunderstood as deities. Gods took their rise in the fog of human metaphor. Miracles too, Volney reckoned, were most improbable. They undermined the very notion of the general applicability and continuity of the physical laws of nature. Much more likely was a scenario in which miracles had arisen from the ways in which humans used figurative language to depict the world around them. Miracles as recorded in ancient religions were more plausibly a kind of outgrowth of metaphor.[42]

In *Recherches nouvelles sur l'histoire ancienne* (1814) Volney launched a more explicit attack on the first portion of the Pentateuch, arguing that the book of Genesis up to the era of Abraham was largely borrowed from the Chaldeans. Even the ancient Jewish historian Josephus, Volney pointed out, had noticed the resemblance between the first eleven chapters of Genesis and the Chaldean history of Berosus. The Flood narrative, in particular, Volney insisted, was 'une histoire purement chaldéenne'. Beyond the fact of Jewish appropriation, however, lay an original process of confabulation rather than, as had been supposed, historic fact. The Deluge in the terms set out in ancient mythologies could never, and had never, happened as described. There were too many impossibilities involved, scientific and otherwise. Rather, Volney contended, the Flood story had emerged in primeval antiquity as a compound allegorical rendering of two natural phenomena, first the passing of the old year and the coming of the new (which was akin to the creation of a new world), and second the constellations of the night sky at the time of year when the Tigris and Euphrates commonly overflowed their banks ('débordemens'). The various familiar elements in the Flood narrative, including the ark, the raven and the dove, were, it transpired, mere constellations, no more real than patterns humans had discerned in the stars. The Flood legends of antiquity, Volney argued, whether the Deluge of Noah or the similar tale

---

[41] *Ibid.*, pp. 137–41.
[42] *Ibid.*, pp. 137–8, 146, 149.

told of Xisuthrus, were only accurate in so far as these were portrayals of the calendar ('un vrai tableau de calendrier'). Noah's post-diluvian cultivation of his vineyard was, Volney went on to claim, a further aspect of the ancient calendar, which had its counterparts in the legends of Osiris and of Bacchus. Osiris, Bacchus and Noah were indeed one and the same – that is nobody, for all were resolvable into identical calendrical metaphors. The notion that the earliest descendants of Noah – weak, isolated, and with such limited resources that they would have relapsed into the savage state – could have preserved the records of sacred history in the wake of such a catastrophe seemed highly unlikely ('sa race serait retombée dans un état sauvage, qui ne permettrait ni écriture, ni conservation de souvenirs anciens'). Exegesis of this sort was necessary to explain the primeval part of Hebraic history. The story of Adam, Eve and the serpent was patently an astrological conceit ('le caractère astrologique est d'une évidence incontestable'). The original version of this myth of the autumnal equinox and the passage from the warm abundance of summer to the dark deprivations of winter lacked altogether the ethical dimension which the Fall of Man had later acquired. Even as late as the era of Abraham the supposed characters and episodes of sacred history crumbled under Volney's analysis into the dust of astrological metaphor ('Abraham n'a point été un individu historique … n'est réellement qu'un legend astrologique').[43]

Volney and Dupuis did not stand alone.[44] Behind them were the satirical sniggers of Voltaire, and their arguments were aligned with those of others. The astronomer and Revolutionary Mayor of Paris Jean-Sylvain Bailly (1736–93) – whose work Eliot read during the making of *Middlemarch*[45] – rejected the contours of sacred history, not only accepting the claim that ancient Hindu astronomy provided proof of a chronology which predated Genesis, but also locating the origins of civilisation far from the Bible lands in the fastness of northern Asia.[46] Louis Langlès (1763–1824), founding director of the École spéciale des langues orientales vivantes,[47] traced the earliest portions of the Old Testament back to pagan mythologies

---

[43] Volney, *Recherches nouvelles sur l'histoire ancienne*, (Paris, 1814), vol. I, pp. 120, 123, 132, 136, 151–3, 158, 178–9.
[44] For anticipations, see M. H. Cotoni, *L'exégèse du nouveau testament dans la philosophie française* (Voltaire Foundation, Oxford, 1984), pp. 381–7.
[45] Pratt and Neufeldt (eds.), *Middlemarch notebooks*, p. 52.
[46] Jean-Sylvain Bailly, *Lettres sur l'origine des sciences et sur celle des peuples de l'Asie* (Paris, 1777); Bailly, *Lettres sur l'Atlantide de Platon et sur l'ancienne histoire de l'Asie* (Paris, 1779); Bailly, *Traité de l'astronomie indienne et orientale* (Paris, 1787); Buchwald and Josefowicz, *Zodiac of Paris*, pp. 29–30.
[47] App, *Birth of Orientalism*, pp. 76, 473–5.

('Je regarde donc le Pentateuque comme l'abrégé des livres égyptiens dont les originaux existent encore dans l'Inde').[48] The key to all mythologies was not, it should be clear by now, a mirage visible only to Anglican apologists. Such reductive delusions also flourished in the French Revolution and at the cutting edge of freethinking. The world of Mr Casaubon was a world made by the radical French mythographers, Volney in particular.

Volney's mythographical theories constituted a central theme in British political debate between the 1790s and the 1830s.[49] According to Alexander Cook, who has worked on England's 'Volney vogue' during the age of the French Revolution, Volney was 'unquestionably the most popular revolutionary author in the anglophone world'. The republican bookseller Thomas Rickman (1761–1834) demonstrated his enthusiasm for the cause of reform by naming his children after canonical figures in the radical pantheon, including Thomas Paine, Washington, Franklin, Rousseau and Volney. Within ten years of its initial French publication there were three competing English translations of *The Ruins*.[50] Another historian of radicalism, Gwyn A. Williams, noted with some relish that it was also translated into Welsh, and that eleven English editions of Volney were published between 1793 and 1822.[51] One radical bookseller claimed in 1820 that he had sold 10,000 copies of the *Ruins*. It was not only the mere fact of Volney's 'very considerable sale' or that it had gone through 'several' English editions which worried the orthodox, but also its 'specious pretensions to candour' and the way it had been 'artfully written' to dupe 'the uneducated'.[52] According to the conservative high church magazine, the *British Critic*, 'the ignorant and unlettered' had been 'deluded' by the 'confident assertions' found in Volney's *Ruins*, while 'the impious' had been 'hardened by its blasphemies'.[53] Volney needed to be answered. Cook calculates that

---

[48] Louis Langlès, *Fables et contes indiens nouvellement traduits* (Paris, 1790), pp. xiv–xv.
[49] See e.g. E. P. Thompson, *The making of the English working class* (1963: Harmondsworth, 1968), pp. 107–8; G. A. Williams, *Artisans and sans-culottes: popular movements in France and Britain during the French Revolution* (1968: 2nd edn, London, 1989), pp. 59, 109; Mee, *Dangerous enthusiasm*, pp. 4, 7, 121, 138–40, 196–9; E. L. de Montluzin, *The Anti-Jacobins: the early contributions to the Anti-Jacobin Review* (Houndmills, 1988), pp. 155–7.
[50] A. Cook, 'Reading revolution: towards a history of the Volney vogue in England', in C. Charle, J. Vincent and J. Winter (eds.), *Anglo-French attitudes: comparisons and transfers between English and French intellectuals since the eighteenth century* (Manchester, 2007), pp. 125–46, at pp. 125, 141.
[51] G. A. Williams, 'General Editor's Preface', in E. Royle (ed.), *The infidel tradition from Paine to Bradlaugh* (London, 1976), p. x.
[52] William Cockburn, *Remarks on a publication of M. Volney, called The Ruins* (Cambridge, 1804), pp. 5, 19.
[53] *British Critic* (October 1801), pp. 337–45, at p. 337.

eleven books whose primary aim was the refutation of Volney were published in England during the first half of the nineteenth century;[54] many other works dealt glancing blows at Volney en route to other objectives.

Volney himself was a big enough problem for Anglican mythographers, but there was also the more pressing issue of a Volneyite enemy within. After all, to describe the wars of mythography as an Anglo-French dispute oversimplifies matters. National positions were complicated by internal differences. Most obviously, Tom Paine's *Age of Reason* (1794) – which championed a natural religion shorn of the folklore of the Christian tradition – offered a domestic challenge to orthodoxy which echoed that of Volney.[55]

Richard Watson (1737–1816), the Bishop of Llandaff, formerly the Regius Professor of Divinity at Cambridge and a noted scientist, took up the challenge of answering Paine's *Age of Reason* in *An apology for the Bible; in a series of letters to Tom Paine* (1796), which went through many editions and was still being reprinted in the anti-Deist pamphlet wars of the 1830s. Watson's arguments against the 'scoffs and cavils of unbelievers', such as Paine, drew in good measure upon the corroborative evidences. Indeed, Watson argued that Christians could take comfort in the fact that the Old Testament – notwithstanding, as the enlightened scientist conceded, some 'real difficulties which occur in it' – not only bore 'internal evidences of its truth' but was 'corroborated by the most ancient profane histories'. After all, most of the 'philosophers, historians and poets of antiquity' provided a supplementary reassurance for Christians, as their books 'make either the most distinct mention, or the most evident allusion to the facts related in Genesis, concerning the formation of the world from a chaotic mass, the primeval innocence, and subsequent Fall of Man, the longevity of mankind in the first ages, of the world, the depravity of the antediluvians, and the destruction of the world'. The history of Genesis was, to all intents and purposes, the same story which heathens told themselves, and where did they get it if not from the primeval traditions known by the early descendants of Noah prior to their dispersion across the globe? Nor did Watson accept the critical argument that Satan had been a Persian concept slipped into Jewish mythology at a later date during the Babylonish captivity. He asserted instead the 'universality of the doctrine concerning an evil being', found not only among the Zoroastrians but also the Egyptians, Hindus, Incas and Aztecs. Moreover, this very universality presupposed that the

---

[54] Cook, 'Reading revolution', p. 125.
[55] Thomas Paine, *The age of reason part I* (1794), in *Theological works of Thomas Paine* (London, 1819).

notion had arisen in primeval times from the pre-dispersal tradition 'concerning the fall of our first parents', albeit 'disfigured' and 'obscured, as all traditions must be, by many fabulous additions'.[56]

In turn, Samuel Francis, a medical man, produced a Volneyite response to Watson. The Old Testament, Francis contended, was not, as Christians imagined, *sui generis*, but was derived in large part from older oriental sources. Little wonder, then, that 'Abraham should resemble the Brahma of the Hindus',[57] so indebted was the Pentateuch to the mythological coinings of more ancient civilisations:

> The similarity of the mysteries of the Jews to those of the Babylonians, is too glaring not to let us see the origin of Genesis in particular. The creation in six days is a perfect copy of the Gahans, or Gahans-bars, of Zoroaster; the particulars of each day's work are literally the same. The serpent was famous among the Babylonians. The mythological deluge of Ogyges and Xisuthrus, are symbols of changes arising on earth as they imagined the revolutions of the heavenly bodies. These, a little ornamented by the historical narration of Deucalion's inundation related by Berosus, is the pattern of Noah's Flood; the ark of Osiris and emblematical dove and raven were Egyptian hieroglyphics. The man and woman in Paradise is a mere copy of Zoroaster's first pair. The original sin is Pandora's box.[58]

Francis, indeed, explicitly repudiated the contemporary Anglican search for a key to all mythologies: 'That the numerous mythological systems which have ever existed, sprang from the report of the fathers of the Jewish nation, may appear probable to a clergyman; it is but a pious whim; to me it is a proof, that all religious systems have sprung from the fancy of men.'[59] Not that the quest was a fool's errand, for all religions did have a common origin; the problem, as Francis saw it, was whether Christian mythographers could make a convincing case that 'Jehovah deserves more to be revered than the Great Whole of nature, whether called Pan, or otherwise disguised in emblems, than the harmony of the planets designed by symbols, the generative powers by Venus, or the vivifying light emanating from the bright orb of Apollo?' Metaphysical absurdities produced, in turn, distortions in the fabric of church and state. Francis realised that the 'allegorical adoration of nature could only deceive the multitude who were

---

[56] Richard Watson, *An apology for the Bible; in a series of letters addressed to Tom Paine* (1796: Glasgow, 1834), pp. 30, 53, 56.
[57] Samuel Francis, *Watson refuted: being an answer to the apology for the Bible* (1796?: London, 1819), p. 42.
[58] Ibid., pp. 28–9.
[59] Ibid., p. 69.

kept in ignorance by their priests'. But could Christians really feel superior to pagan priestcraft and fabulous exoteric doctrines framed to gull the laity? At least the polytheistic priesthoods of pagan antiquity had largely eschewed persecution for policies of religious toleration.[60]

The quest for a key to all mythologies did not lead down an obscure backwater of contemporary intellectual life. Although Mr Casaubon is presented as a quietist in retreat from the hurly-burly of the modern world, this is not how contemporary mythographers saw themselves, for the study of mythology was perceived as a potent weapon in the ideological war against radicalism, Jacobinism and atheism. Allwood, for one, thought his mythographical 'labours [might] be of some utility to my country, in this day of blasphemy and infidelity'.[61] Between the era of the French Revolution and the time of the Reform Bill in 1832 mythology assumed the significance of a gauntlet thrown down by the radical deistic Enlightenment, to which Christians of all stripes – from orthodox conservatives to those on the heterodox fringes of the Christian Enlightenment – felt compelled to respond. Priestley, indeed, was one of Volney's foremost antagonists in the anglophone world. More representative, however, of distaste for Volney's arguments were Anglican antiquarians of a more Casaubonish stamp.

The ideas of the French mythographers were so obviously devastating to Christianity that they could not simply be ignored or sidelined, but needed to be rebutted. According to Robert Adam (1770–1825), an Episcopalian clergyman in Edinburgh, Volney and Dupuis were infidels of monstrous presumption who 'have had the effrontery to tell us that Jesus Christ never existed as a man; that under his name we worship the sun; that by his twelve disciples are only meant the twelve signs of the zodiac; and that Christianity is merely a species of pagan idolatry'.[62]

Why had the 'insidious poison' of 'false philosophy' proved so deadly in France? Francis Wollaston, the rector of Chislehurst in Kent, thought that the manifest lies and absurdities (as he perceived them) of Catholic priestcraft had blinded French literati to the distinction between Christianity proper and its corrupt travesty. 'Seeing through the pageantry of popery, and observing the immoral lives of its votaries', the French had been 'too ready to suppose the whole of Christianity to be a mere fiction; and instead of rejecting the corruptions of it, rejected without sufficient examination the substance'.[63]

---

[60] *Ibid.*, p. 97.
[61] Philip Allwood, *Literary antiquities of Greece* (London, 1799), p. xvi.
[62] Robert Adam, *The religious world displayed* (3 vols., Edinburgh, 1809), vol. I, p. 152.
[63] Francis Wollaston, *A country parson's address to his flock, to caution them against being misled by the wolf in sheep's cloathing, or receiving Jacobin teachers of sedition* (London, 1799), p. 9.

William Cockburn (1773–1858), a Fellow of St John's College, Cambridge, and orthodox opponent of Volney, noted the very uncomfortable truth that while Christians 'deduce' from the similarities of the creation accounts in Genesis and in pagan mythologies 'a confirmation' of Mosaic history, Volney 'labours to draw a conclusion directly opposite'.[64] Same matter, rival conclusions? Comparative religion, it transpired, was a field whose ownership was hotly contested, yet whose yields were so often far from satisfying. The evidence of pagan mythology raised a chicken-and-egg problem. Which came first – the Book of Genesis or the ancient pagan legends which it resembled? Or, to put this another way, did pagan mythology corroborate the truths of Genesis, or was Genesis a copy of a pagan original? Thus on the one hand, Christian scholars perceived the apologetic worth of heathen mythology as a corroborative bulwark of the historical truth of the Old Testament, while on the other, Deists, sceptics and other critics of revealed Christianity seized upon mythography as a kind of siege engine with which to undermine the defences of Biblical religion.

However, Cockburn thought he had detected the weak spot in Volney's work: the claim that Jesus Christ, like Hercules and Osiris, had never existed and had been a mere personification of the sun. If Christ could be shown to have existed as an historical personage, as reliable non-Christian sources from adjacent periods such as Tacitus, Pliny and Suetonius appeared to indicate, then 'the poison tooth is drawn' and the rest of Volney's arguments became, as it were, 'mere vapour'. After all, argued Cockburn, even the pagan writer Celsus, who was keen to nail what he saw as the legend of the virgin birth, never repudiated the historical existence of Christ. Surely if there had been any doubts extant about the historical reality of Jesus Christ, Cockburn reasoned, then an accomplished anti-Christian polemicist such as Celsus would have sought to exploit that weakness in the gospel history. It seemed reasonable for Cockburn to conclude that Celsus 'no doubt adds his testimony to the evidence at least of the *existence* of that person whose *birth* he would account for by human means'. Volney, Cockburn believed, was utterly unscrupulous as a scholar, his *Ruins* a farrago of 'palpable misrepresentations, weak conclusions and absolute falsehoods'. Indeed, Volney's scholarship was no match for those 'who with honest diligence have searched among the long-buried treasures of oriental learning' (an allusion to Jones) or those who 'have penetrated, with acute fidelity, into the dark recesses of early Hellenism' (an allusion

---

[64] Cockburn, *Remarks*, p. 25.

to Bryant), and who had brought to light so many heathen 'confirmations' of scripture.[65]

Such was the immediate threat posed by Volney and Dupuis and their British disciples that in the age of Revolution the collateral evidences became perforce a crucial theatre of religious polemic. So close indeed were the parallels between Christianity and oriental mythologies that it seemed imprudent to ignore the potential of pagan mythology to confound the subversive arguments of one's deistic and atheistic enemies. For, of course, parallelism was a double-edged sword, and if religious apologists did not use the weapon themselves, then it would only be used against them, as indeed it was. Volney and Dupuis had shifted the terms of debate in the sphere of apologetics and compelled theologians to grasp a prickly problem: the shared provenance of Biblical and pagan religions. Circumspection became necessarily harder to maintain; indeed it began to smack of carelessness. Surely there had to be some sort of connexion between scripture and heathen mythologies? So uncanny were the resemblances between Judaeo-Christianity and oriental paganisms, there must, it seemed, be a close relationship. But if the key to all mythologies was not to be found in Genesis, then Genesis itself must be derivative of something else, which is why mythography constituted one of the major ideological battlegrounds of the Revolutionary and post-Revolutionary eras. The world of Mr Casaubon was a realm of reaction to the daring and subversive mythography which stood near the ideological core of the French Revolution.

Volney's *Ruins* also became entangled with domestic disputes of English Protestantism and its heterodox fringe. Here the most sophisticated theologians now became conscious of a treacherous thicket in which it was hard to discern the distinctions between Christian truth and pagan mythology. In 1792 Theophilus Lindsey (1723–1808), the leading figure in English Unitarianism, criticised Trinitarian Christianity as itself a species of 'idolatry', albeit different in kind from heathenism. If Jesus had been created by the Deity, Lindsey argued, then 'worship of him is as much and equally idolatrous, as the worship of his mother Mary'. In other words, the standard Protestant critique of Roman Catholic idolatry was equally applicable to Protestant Trinitarian worship: a manoeuvre reminiscent in technique – though not register – of Conyers Middleton. To Lindsey, a former Church of England cleric, conventional Christianity looked awfully like 'polytheism'; indeed, its corruptions had been introduced by

---

[65] *Ibid.* pp. 14–18, 20, 29.

'learned heathen converts'.[66] The spirit of Volneyism appeared to stalk the outskirts of Christianity. In 1793 the Reverend David Simpson (1745–99), a minister on the ultra-evangelical margins of the Church of England, published *An essay on the authenticity of the New Testament: designed as an answer to Evanson's Dissonance and Volney's Ruins*. Edward Evanson (1731–1805) was another former-Anglican-cleric-turned-Unitarian, who had the previous year authored a work which called into question the genuineness of the four gospels.[67] Volney's challenge to Christianity – though much more obnoxious than Evanson's – seemed to involve a related question, for Volney challenged 'the very existence of Jesus Christ'. Various *pagan* testimonies to the historicity of Christ – sometimes invoked with the authority of Bryant's *Treatise on the authenticity of the scriptures* – supplied Simpson's necessary 'antidote' to this abomination.[68]

At the centre of the storm over Volney and Dupuis was Priestley, a Unitarian divine and chemist. Priestley had left Birmingham in the wake of the loyalist church and king riots of 1791 which had damaged his house and laboratory, and made for Hackney. Eventually in 1794 he left England altogether for the republican haven of the new United States, settling in Pennsylvania. There were obvious affinities in method and content between the projects of a demythologised Unitarianism and sceptical French mythography. Priestley had no truck, after all, with the virgin birth or with what he identified as the residues of pagan polytheism which clung barnacle-like to the Christian tradition. Yet an abyss separated Priestley's attempt to rid the Christian tradition of alien accretions from the naturalistic wholesale debunking proffered by Volney and Dupuis.

Priestley's principal concern was to trace the process of corruptions by which the message of Jesus the moral teacher had degenerated into a Platonised theology upheld by priestcraft and prelacy. Oddly enough, therefore, Priestley found himself waging polemical warfare on two fronts, against entrenched Trinitarian interests within what was only a partially reformed Protestantism, and against the threat of French infidelity to undermine the authentic foundations of Christianity. There was, Priestley believed (and the French mythographers, significantly, did not), a kernel of revealed verity which lurked beneath the rotten pulp of pseudo-churchmanship. Ironically, indeed, the French infidels seemed set on reintroducing exactly the sort of pagan absurdities which Priestley

---

[66] Theophilus Lindsey, *Conversations on Christian idolatry* (London, 1792), pp. vii–viii, 77, 83.
[67] Edward Evanson, *Dissonance of the four generally received evangelists* (Ipswich, 1792).
[68] David Simpson, *An essay on the authenticity of the New Testament: designed as an answer to Evanson's Dissonance and Volney's Ruins* (Macclesfield, 1793), esp. pp. 4, 63, 71, 132.

regarded as a disastrous quasi-heathen codicil to the true inheritance of Christianity. In his *History of the Corruptions* (1782), Priestley had attributed the declension of primitive Christianity to the contaminating influence of 'the established opinions of the heathen world, and especially the philosophical part of it; so that when those heathens embraced Christianity they mixed their former tenet and prejudices with it'.[69] Now it looked as if a modern French strain of paganism was going to add an extra coating of secular mythologising to the gospel history. Priestley was committed to divine revelation. Christianity was not a mere human construct. Although Priestley insisted on the simple humanity of Christ, he did not reject his divine mission, his resurrection, or the promise of eternal life which he brought. What Priestley did was separate out the spuriously pagan from the authentically Christian elements in theology. Indeed, precisely because of his commitment to a human – and historical – Christ, Priestley was acutely irritated by attempts to reduce Christ to a non-historical symbol.

A former pupil of Priestley, John Prior Estlin (1747–1817), also entered the lists against Dupuis's mythographical system in *The Nature and Causes of Atheism* (1797). Moreover, in 1797 Priestley and Volney had a celebrated public exchange of letters, much reprinted in a variety of venues, whether as self-contained pamphlets or as magazine articles, both in the United States and in Britain. Priestley followed this with a response directed against Dupuis in *A comparison of the institutions of Moses with those of the Hindoos and other ancient nations, with remarks on Mr Dupuis's Origins of all religions*, which was published in Northumberland, Pennsylvania, in 1799. By reducing the entire Pentateuch to 'a mere Arabian tale', Dupuis's work was the 'ne plus ultra of infidelity'.[70]

Priestley was struck by the 'resemblance between the Oriental and Occidental systems' of religion. But, unlike the French infidel mythographers, he was not inclined to reduce the twelve sons of Jacob to the twelve signs of the Zodiac, or anything of that sort. Somewhat remarkably perhaps in the light of his own debunking propensities, Priestley turned out to be a champion of collateral apologetics: 'It has long appeared to me that a fair comparison of the ancient heathen religions with the system of revelation would contribute in an eminent degree to establish the evidences of the latter.'[71]

---

[69] Joseph Priestley, *An history of the corruptions of Christianity* (2 vols., Birmingham, 1782), vol. II, p. 441.
[70] Joseph Priestley, *A comparison of the Institutions of Moses* (Northumberland, PA, 1799), p. 301.
[71] *Ibid.*, pp. vii, 103.

Priestley's aim was to preserve Mosaic revelation, even at the expense of conceding an element of allegory in the antediluvian history which stood at some remove from Moses's witness to his own times. Priestley happily jettisoned the Devil and the fable of the Fall, but not 'the proper Mosaic history'.[72] Nor, of course, did Priestley reject the historic personhood of Christ which was at the core of his particular strain of Unitarianism. Christ was not part of the godhead, but nor was he a mere allegory of the sun. There was as much evidence for the existence of Christ, Priestley informed Volney, as for Pericles, Julius Caesar, Demosthenes and Cicero.[73] Yet Volney – echoing Gibbon – made sport with Priestley's seemingly capricious brand of just-so religion, whose polemical artillery was directed against traditionalists and radicals alike; by firing a 'double battery against those who believe too much, and those who believe too little', he addressed Priestley, 'you hold out your own particular sensations as the precise criterion of truth'.[74]

The Orient – or to be more precise, the ancient religious civilisations of the Near East and India – constituted the principal theatre of debate between the rival British and French schools of mythographical interpretation. However, the 'Orient' of mythographical debate in the era of the French Revolution stood at some remove from the Orientalist biases detected (properly enough), exaggerated and caricatured in the work of Edward Said.[75] In the first place, the Orient was a scene of Anglo-French rivalry, not only for the plunder of antiquities,[76] but also for their interpretation. Moreover, not all strains of eighteenth-century orientalist scholarship conjured up Orients that were antitheses of either Europe or – its close synonym – Christendom.[77] The Orient of the mythographers was not, surprisingly, the scene of un-European and non-Christian otherness; rather it provided the matter of a controversy about origins, borrowings and plagiarism. Both sides agreed that Europe and Asia, far from being discrete entities, had historically been unbounded and open to an enormous amount of cultural exchange. Eurasia, indeed, constituted a zone

---

[72] *Ibid.*, pp. 341–2.
[73] Joseph Priestley, *Letters to Mr Volney* (Philadelphia, 1797), pp. 4, 16–17.
[74] *Volney's Answer to Dr Priestley, on his pamphlet entitled, Observations upon the increase in infidelity* (Philadelphia, 1797), p. 10.
[75] E. Said, *Orientalism* (1978: Harmondsworth, 1985).
[76] M. Jasanoff, *Edge of empire: conquest and collecting in the East 1750–1850* (2005: London pbk, 2006); H. Hoock, 'The British state and the Anglo-French war over antiquities, 1798–1858', *Historical Journal*, vol. 50 (2007), pp. 49–72.
[77] Cf. R. Irwin, *For lust of knowing: the orientalists and their enemies* (London, 2007).

of shared mythological influence. Where British and French mythographers tended to disagree was over the burning question of priority. Who had influenced whom? What was the direction of imitation and borrowing? Of course, so they perceived, the various religions and mythologies of Europe, Egypt, the Near East, Persia and India – Judaeo-Christianity not excluded – derived from common origins. But were the other mythologies of ancient Eurasia derivations from the primeval Judaeo-Christian revelations set out in Genesis, as Christian mythographers believed, or were the Jews and Christians among the ranks of the plagiarists, as the sceptical French mythographers alleged?

To be sure, British and French mythographers distorted oriental religions to serve European ends, but not out of any pressing desire to denigrate the East. Rather it was the fierceness of *intra-European* – especially cross-Channel – disputes about the provenance of Christianity which fuelled debate among Orientalists and scholars in nearby disciplines. By a further irony, insofar as European mythographers betrayed the essence of Middle Eastern and Indian mythologies, they did so not from any wish to exhibit eastern religions as alien, but from the very opposite motivation; that is, with the aim of establishing just how the obviously interrelated paganisms of Eurasian antiquity related to the Judaeo-Christian tradition.

Neither camp thought of the Orient as a foil to Europe. Middle Eastern and Asian religions were not antithetical to European mythologies. Either, as one camp believed, non-Judaeo-Christian religions were at bottom derived from the primeval revelation to all humankind – as set out in Genesis – before the dispersal of peoples after Babel, or, as the other contended, Christianity was itself a copy of other Middle Eastern or Indian religions. British Protestants and French infidels uneasily concurred in the view that Greek, Roman, Egyptian, Phoenician, Babylonian, Zoroastrian and Hindu deities mapped onto one another and onto Biblical personages. They disagreed violently about which were the prototypes, though not about the common Eurasian identity of this corpus of mythology. The issues which Said has brought to the forefront of modern scholarly debate about Orientalism lurked unobtrusively in the background of late Enlightenment orientalist scholarship. The enemy for Britons was not the culture of their Empire in the east, but its radical French interpreters – or rather misinterpreters. Bias there was, in spades; however, it was grounded not in racial superiority but in religious orthodoxy. The Scots orientalist Lieutenant-Colonel Vans Kennedy (1784–1846) complained that the field of Indian mythology had been distorted by the 'usual pernicious influence' of 'that inveterate prejudice which insists on compelling the records of all

The Dispute of the Orient

nations to depose to the accuracy of the first eleven chapters of Genesis'.[78] The forlorn efforts of Francis Wilford – duped by his pandit, who supplied the desired Judaeo-Christian interpolations in the Hindu record – were a particular target of Kennedy's withering sarcasm.[79]

In his *Elements of Christian Theology* (1799), George Pretyman, the Bishop of Lincoln, stressed the importance of researches into oriental history, chronology and mythology, 'whence infidels have long derived their most formidable objections' to Mosaic truth. He rejoiced that Jones and others had brought the 'treasures of oriental learning' to public view, which demonstrated that Hindu antiquities supplied 'abundance of incontrovertible evidence for the existence of opinions in the early ages of the world, which perfectly agree with the leading articles of our faith, as well as the principal events related in the Pentateuch'. The mythologies of the east, it was obvious, consisted of 'fragments of one original truth which was broken by the dispersion of the patriarchal families, and corrupted by the length of time, allegory, and idolatry'.[80]

Thomas Maurice (1754–1824)[81] detected the 'perpetual recurrence of a sacred triad of deity in Asiatic mythology'; in other words, oriental religions, being but the 'shattered fragments' of the patriarchal religion of Genesis, were, it transpired, Trinitarian and proof of the grand unalterable truths of Christianity.[82] However, orientalist discoveries were not an unmixed blessing, for Maurice believed that Christianity was threatened from two different directions, not only directly by the infidel philosophers of France but also from the deceitful fabrications of the 'subtle sacerdotal tribe of India'.[83] Obviously, this did not constitute a concerted two-pronged attack on Christendom, yet to French Deists and sceptics the exaggerations of wily Hindu pandit-craft provided a potent arsenal of weaponry with which to attack the authority of Christian scripture. According to Maurice's pamphlet *Brahminical Fraud Detected* (1812), 'Messrs Bailly, Dupuis, Voltaire, Volney and the whole French infidel school had once

---

[78] Vans Kennedy, *Researches into the nature and affinity of ancient and Hindu mythology* (London, 1831), p. 126.
[79] Ibid., pp. 137–8; 'Appendix A', pp. 405–22.
[80] George Pretyman, *Elements of Christian theology* (1799: 3rd edn, 2 vols., London, 1800), vol. I, pp. 44–7.
[81] For Maurice's ideas and their context, see B. W. Young, 'The lust of empire and religious hate: Christianity, history and India, 1790–1820', in S. Collini, R. Whatmore and B. W. Young (eds.), *History, religion, and culture: British intellectual history 1750–1950* (Cambridge, 2000), pp. 91–111.
[82] Thomas Maurice, *Indian antiquities* (6 vols., London, 1800–1), esp. vol. I, pp. 119–21, 126; vol. IV, pp. 37, 162; vol. V, p. 12.
[83] Thomas Maurice, *Brahminical fraud detected* (London, 1812), p. 25.

hoisted their standard – the boldest standard of defiance – on the ground of the presumed unfathomable antiquity of India'.[84] Moreover, these assaults on Biblical religion – sometimes disguised by apparent indirection, sometimes veiled in superficial irrelevance – continued. The vast eons of Hindu antiquity threatened implicitly to undermine the authority of Old Testament chronology, and the existence of Hindu deities born of virgins more obviously called into question the uniqueness, historicity and divinity of Christ. As a result, an apologetic Orientalist mythography had become an essential bulwark of Christianity to ward off 'attacks, secret and avowed, from this Asiatic quarter of the world, aided by European ingenuity', which had become 'so continued, so numerous, and so artful'.[85]

Moreover, there were also plausible ways of accounting for the impostor-Christs – Krishna and Salivahana – of Hindu tradition. Maurice easily disposed of the legend of Salivahana. It dated from the time of Christ Himself and the copy-cat could easily be accounted for by the spread of the Christian message to the East. The purportedly much older account of a Christ-like Krishna Maurice undermined in two stages, first by relocating its appearance in Hindu tradition to a more recent era, and then by exposing its 'gross plagiarism' of Christ's life.[86]

Did the Oriental mythologies which bore such suspicious resemblances to Judaeo-Christianity really predate Jewish history? This raised vexing issues of chronology. Were civilisations, such as the Hindu and Chinese, which purported to be older than the Old Testament-derived system of chronology allowed, justified in their claims, or merely indulging in empty boasts of longevity which posed, therefore, no threat at all to Christian orthodoxy? As a result, chronology and the astronomical measurements which might verify or alternatively puncture such assertions of high antiquity became crucial theatres of orientalist debate.[87] The reliability of ancient Hindu astronomy – an area of study at once exotic and recondite – became an unexpected litmus test, as it were, for the standing and credibility of the Old Testament as a scheme of universal history. If modern-day British and French astronomers of the late eighteenth and early nineteenth centuries could calibrate supposedly primeval Hindu observations with their own retrospective calculations of relative positions on the night sky of ancient

---

[84] *Ibid.*, p. 6.
[85] *Ibid.*, pp. 25–6.
[86] *Ibid.*, pp. 53–5, 60–1, 65–73, 78, 81, 87–8, 110–12, 131–3.
[87] For additional layers of context and complexity, see S. Schaffer, 'The Asiatic enlightenments of British astronomy', in S. Schaffer *et al.* (eds.), *The brokered world: go-betweens and global intelligence 1770–1820* (Sagamore Beach, MA, 2009), pp. 49–104.

India, then orthodox Christian chronology was undoubtedly weakened. A great deal more was at stake than the credibility of Hindu astronomy. The quarrel over ancient Hindu astronomy was no mere antiquarian sideshow, but a vital component in a wider ideological struggle regarding the truth or falsehood of Christianity and the political system of Christian Europe which it had – until the French Revolution at least – hitherto sustained.

The French astronomer Bailly argued that the very richness of the fables told by the Hindus 'porte l'empreinte de la plus haute antiquité', for such fables were founded on a firmer platform of historic truth, and it was necessary for the orientalist to probe further 'pour séparer de ces récits les verités qui en font la base'.[88] The Hindus, Bailly believed, had an ancient past which stretched back further than that of almost any other culture, including the Hebrews.

The Scottish mathematician John Playfair (1748–1819) sided with Bailly, arguing that the observations recorded in Hindu astrological texts seemed to extend back beyond 3000 BC, possibly to 4300 BC. Playfair reckoned the locations of the sun and moon at the beginning of the Kali Yuga had been 'determined by actual observation'. Although he did judge that not all elements of the Hindu system and its various tables of astronomical calculation were 'of the same antiquity', there were too many coincidences in the astronomy of the Hindus to doubt the 'high antiquity' of its careful tradition of astronomical observation – unless, of course, 'what indeed were still more wonderful, that some ages ago, there had arisen a Newton among the Brahmins, to discover that universal principle which connects, not only the most distant regions of space, but the most remote periods of duration'.[89]

John Bentley (c.1750–1824) was the leading defender of Biblical chronology against the twin pretensions of ancient Hindu astronomy and its modern French champions.[90] Complacently irreligious philosophes were only too happy to be deceived by the absurdities of Brahmin fantasies, forgeries and interpolations. Hindu chronology was full of deliberate falsehoods, including a vast fabricated history which seemingly predated the beginnings of Mosaic history. But observers should not be duped by these

---

[88] Jean-Sylvain Bailly, *Traité de l'astronomie indienne et orientale* (Paris, 1787), pp. lxxvii–lxxviii. For a response to Bailly, see Samuel Davis, 'On the Indian cycle of sixty years', *Asiatic Researches*, vol. 3 (1792), pp. 209–27, at pp. 223–5.
[89] John Playfair, 'Remarks on the astronomy of the Brahmins', *Transactions of the Royal Society of Edinburgh*, vol. 2 (1790), part II, i, 'Papers of the Physical Class', pp. 135–92, at pp. 186–8.
[90] C. Bayly, *Empire and information: intelligence gathering and social communication in India, 1780–1870* (Cambridge, 1996), p. 255; J. Sen, *Astronomy in India 1784–1876* (London, 2014), ch. 1.

'forged epochs of antiquity'. The modern system of Hindu astronomy only dated from 538 AD, and before that its earlier system of astronomical observation could not be traced back before 1425 BC, notwithstanding its talk of huge eons of time back to the beginning of the Kali Yuga. The astronomical text, the Surya Siddhanta, which supposedly began in 3102 BC, seemed more likely in Bentley's critical reading to date from around 1000 AD.[91] Bentley also argued that the French astronomers had utterly misread the Dendera zodiacs. They had been 'deceived' into thinking of them as being around 15,000 years old, when they were, in fact, 'the Roman calendar for the year 708 of Rome, translated into hieroglyphics'.[92]

Bentley's was not the only strategy available to the orthodox in the field of oriental chronology. Maurice counter-attacked against what he believed to be the immense exaggerations of Hindu chronology. To his relief, Maurice discovered that the 'numberless yugs' of the Hindus had created merely an illusion of a vast antiquity, for the Indian astronomers had 'calculated time by the bright and dark halves of the moon; in short their boasted year was only a fortnight'.[93] The earliest periods of Hindu chronology, Maurice contended, had not been based on observation at all, but had been back-projections from a much more recent past.

The Scots Sanskritist Alexander Hamilton (1762–1824) calculated that the supposed inconsistencies between the vast aeons of Hindu antiquity and the more limited scale of Judaeo-Christian chronology were more apparent than real. Hamilton worked out, to his own satisfaction at least, that, when properly calibrated and adjusted to the chronological scheme of the Hebrew Bible (rather than the less reliable Septuagint), a smooth reconciliation was possible between the timeframes of Old Testament history and the seemingly fantastic stretches of oriental antiquity, much to the chagrin of sceptics: 'this shelter for infidelity is removed, if it can be proved to mathematical demonstration that the Hindus, Egyptians, Chaldeans, and Chinese, equally with the Hebrew, place the creation of the world at a period not exceeding 5820 years from the present time'. And so it proved. Whereas even Sir William Jones could not penetrate the 'Hindu cipher' to make plausible sense of this

---

[91] John Bentley, *A historical view of the Hindu astronomy* (London, 1825), esp. pp. vi–vii, xiv, 178, 181, 196; see also Bentley, 'Remarks on the principal aeras and dates of the ancient Hindus', *Asiatic Researches*, vol. 5 (1796), pp. 315–43; Bentley, 'On the antiquity of the Surya Siddhanta and the formation of astronomical cycles therein contained', *Asiatic Researches*, vol. 6 (1798), pp. 537–88; Bentley, 'On the Hindu systems of astronomy and their connection with history in ancient and modern times', *Asiatic Researches*, vol. 8 (1805), pp. 193–244; Francis Wilford, 'On the chronology of the Hindus', *Asiatic Researches*, vol. 5 (1799), pp. 241–95.

[92] Bentley, *Hindu astronomy*, p. 251.

[93] Maurice, *Brahminical fraud*, p. 7.

secret chronological scheme, Hamilton's intricate – and arbitrary – systems of calendrical calculations contrived to make 'Hindu dates correspond with the Hebrew text of our scripture'. Had he devised a key to all chronologies? Hamilton believed furthermore that Hinduism, like Christianity a fellow offshoot from the patriarchal religion of Noah, was itself founded on sacred truth, something which unsympathetic Christian critics had hitherto failed to notice. If only, as Christian orientalists, Hamilton repined, we would 'divest ourselves of that intolerant spirit with which sarcasms have been thrown against [the] religion … [and] chronology' of the Hindus, then his fellow scholars would not only discover a powerful arsenal to deploy against the deists, but also find a more propitious means of winning Hindu converts. By this Hamilton did not mean converting benighted idolatrous Hindus from outright error to an altogether unfamiliar truth, but demonstrating an updated Christian truth to the Indian followers of the patriarchal religion of antediluvian times, a religion admittedly which had seen some corruptions in the long course of human history and was 'now' partially 'clouded by fable'. But otherwise, to all intents and purposes, Hindus were for Hamilton an archaic branch of proto-Christians manqués. 'Why', he asked, 'should we suppose [Hindus] ignorant of those sacred truths taught by the Deity in the earliest periods of the world?' After all, in its 'pristine' state, Hinduism was quite simply the religion of Noah. Inspired by this insight, Hamilton's orientalism was extraordinarily sympathetic to non-European cultures. The first ages of Hindus, Egyptians and Chaldeans were 'not mythological' or based, as the overly Eurocentric Maurice supposed, on 'oriental vanity and fiction', but the unprejudiced orientalist could 'recognize' in the primeval dynasties of each civilisation 'the antediluvian patriarchs'. Hamilton challenged canonical mythographic identifications such as the equation of Buddha with the legendary Chinese founder Fohi, and ultimately with Noah. Rather Hamilton, seemingly influenced in this matter by the Jesuit Figurist Father Prémare, identified Buddha as the antediluvian patriarch Enoch.[94]

One of the peculiarly intractable difficulties of historical interpretation – not least as it invites ridicule from those unwilling to exercise the historical imagination – is the suspension of disbelief in the unlikely controversies which once exercised our forebears. Surprising as it sounds, the Cabeiri, or Cabiri, a mysterious and relatively minor group of ancient pagan deities, played a now forgotten role in the ideological repulse of Jacobin doctrine

---

[94] [Alexander Hamilton], *A key to the chronology of the Hindus* (2 vols., Cambridge, 1820), vol. I, pp. x–xiii, xvii–xix, 3–4, 6, 15, 25, 41–2, 93; vol. II, pp. 103, 130, 191, 195, 267–71.

during the age of the French Revolution, and also featured in contemporary orientalist discussion.[95] The ethnic provenance of the Cabiri was mysterious, though they were probably Samothracian in origin. Nevertheless, the father of the Cabiri, according to fragments of the Phoenician writer Philo of Byblos preserved in Eusebius, was the god Sydyk,[96] whose associations seem to have resided further to the east. Why did these obscure divinities exercise such a fascination upon late eighteenth- and early nineteenth-century mythographers, as George Eliot hinted, if only to poke fun at this curious phenomenon? If Christianity were true, and Deism an abominable abuse of God-given reason, then what better foundation for the establishment and propagation of the truth than independent, non-Judaeo-Christian corroboration of Noah and the Flood? This is exactly what the cults of Sydyk and the Cabiri seemed to offer. In the first place, Sydyk and the Cabiri were associated with the construction of ships and the protection of sailors. In addition, it was argued that there were seven Cabiri, who taken together with their father Sydyk amounted to eight deities — surely, not coincidentally, the number of humans who survived in the Ark and went on to repeople the world? The Cabiri seemed to offer a vindication of the historicity of the Flood, and, by extension, the authority of the Bible, so sorely mocked by the Enlightenment and its monstrous Jacobin progeny.[97]

It seems likely that when George Eliot mentioned the myth of the Cabiri she was alluding to the work of Faber, a prolific high church moderate evangelical[98] and mythographer who had argued that the seven Cabiri were the same deities that the Greeks knew as the seven Titans. As one of the Titans was named Iapetus, Faber was delighted to find confirmation of his thesis from the 'scriptural name of Japhet being accurately preserved in the list of the Titans'.[99] Indeed, the associations of the Cabiri with fertility might also mean that Eliot was having yet another sly dig at Mr Casaubon's virility. However, there is a further wrinkle. The German scholar Creuzer — a

---

[95] Francis Wilford, 'Remarks on the name of the Cabirian deities', *Asiatic Researches*, vol. 5 (1799), pp. 297–301.
[96] H. W. Attridge and R. A. Oden (eds.), *Philo of Byblos: the Phoenician history* (Washington, DC, 1981), pp. 46–7, 58–9.
[97] The Cabiri — who are now reckoned to be four deities — had long interested English mythographers, though there was no consensus about the identity of Sydyk and the Cabiri. Richard Cumberland, the Bishop of Peterborough, had identified Sydyk with one of the sons of Noah, possibly Ham, rather than with Noah himself.
[98] P. Nockles, *The Oxford movement in context: Anglican high churchmanship 1760–1837* (Cambridge, 1994), esp. pp. 32, 34, 42, 106, 284.
[99] George Stanley Faber, *A dissertation on the mysteries of the Cabiri* (2 vols., Oxford, 1803), vol. I, p. 130.

central figure in the new mythography to which Ladislaw alluded – had also been obsessed by the Samothracian Cabiri.[100]

Faber rejected the idea that pagan mythology was – appearances notwithstanding – 'a thing altogether capricious'. Rather he regarded the world's various heathen legends 'as jointly forming a single well-compacted and regular system'. At the base of this system was a universal tradition – the early history of Genesis, up to the Tower of Babel, before the ancestors of humankind had dispersed to the corners of the earth. What the world's myths shared was a unity in utterly 'arbitrary circumstantials', which could not be explained away in a naturalistic fashion. There was 'such a singular and minute and regular accordance' among the mythologies of the world's far-flung pagan cultures, not least in 'fanciful speculations, and in artificial observances', that only a 'common origin' could plausibly explain this implausibly coincidental phenomenon.[101]

Faber claimed that 'if we examine the legendary histories of the chief deities worshipped by the gentiles, we shall almost invariably find them replete with allusions to the creation and Paradise on the one hand and to the deluge and the Ark on the other'. What struck Faber with especial force was that so many pagan mythologies seemed to acknowledge two golden ages in the past, one following the Creation, and the second following a great deluge. In gentile mythology 'the antediluvian world itself was the successor of a yet prior mundane system'. Moreover, the experiences of Adam and Noah seemed remarkably similar. Both had experienced the trauma of loss and destruction, and each had fathered three sons – respectively Cain, Abel and Seth, and Ham, Shem and Japhet. Such similarities in the sacred histories of Adam and Noah accounted for the two distinct characters known as Menu in Hindu mythology, and the twin Buddhas of the East. Indeed, from the parallel histories of the father of mankind at the Fall and the Flood, it seemed, there 'originated the oriental doctrine of avatars or various successive incarnations of the same demon-god'.[102]

Eight was not the only number of significance in pagan mythology; Faber also uncovered patterns of three. In part, this was because Noah was 'revered in the triple character of the destroyer, the creator, and the preserver', but emblems of three also referred to the three sons of Noah. What triadic symbols did not refer to – and here Faber was most insistent – was the doctrine of the Trinity. Such a tradition was an impossibility, for, he argued, 'though paganism may have superadded many inventions

[100] G. S. Williamson, *The longing for myth in Germany* (Chicago, 2004), pp. 127, 131–3.
[101] George Stanley Faber, *The origin of pagan idolatry* (3 vols., London, 1816), vol. I, pp. 57–9.
[102] *Ibid.*, vol. I, pp. 10–11, 14–16.

of its own, it certainly can borrow nothing from patriarchism except what patriarchism itself already possessed'. But the Trinity had not yet been revealed to man by the time of the dispersal of nations at Babel, despite the misguided views of the Hutchinsonians in this regard. Faber – though otherwise credulous – was robust on this point, and concluded, sensibly enough, that 'if neither Adam nor Noah possessed it, the apostates of Babel could not have borrowed their doctrine of a triad in the great father from the doctrine of the Holy Trinity'.[103]

Indeed, Faber's theology differed subtly but significantly from that of the Hutchinsonians. Whereas the Hutchinsonians tended to favour the identity of the three great revelations to humankind, Faber, though recognising the 'close connection' which subsisted between what he termed the patriarchal, Levitical and Christian dispensations, nevertheless parsed these as 'three progressive forms or modifications'.[104]

Faber contended that mythographers faced an unexpected puzzle. Such was the ingenuity of humans that one might expect that pagan peoples as they grew more remote from their Noachic origins would develop a tremendous variety of idolatrous and superstitious rites: 'Of superstition the vagaries are so endless and so extraordinary ... the obvious tendency of this inventive humour the production of variety'. Instead what the evidence of mythography and orientalist studies of pagan rites revealed, at least so it struck Faber, was a remarkable 'uniformity' in a field where variation was to be expected. The corroborative evidences provided an answer to 'the riddle of pagan uniformity'.[105]

Faber lamented that Christian apologists so often tended to find themselves on the defensive against the aggressive arguments of the deists. In a change of strategy he decided to launch 'offensive operations' against the Volney school in *The Difficulties of Infidelity* (1824). Here Faber exposed as he saw it the far-fetched leap of doubt involved in rejecting Christianity, asking whether 'the disbelief of Christianity does not involve a higher degree of credulity than the belief of it'. The collateral evidences from heathendom played a central role in this campaign. How were deists to explain away 'the universal attestation of mankind' to an ancient worldwide Deluge? Flood stories which followed a set pattern of angry deity, mass annihilation in a deluge, the saving of a chosen family, and so forth were part of 'the general tradition of all nations in every quarter of the globe' – Europe, Africa, Asia, the Americas – and

[103] *Ibid.*, vol. I, pp. 107, 109.
[104] Faber, *A treatise on the origin of expiatory sacrifice* (London, 1827), p. 10.
[105] *Ibid.*, pp. 49, 51.

'embodied in the national mythology and religion of every people'. This presented mythographers with their heroic task, to unlock the secrets of the world's pagan mythologies, to reveal to sceptics and scoffers the Flood history 'systematically embodied in the popular mythology of every pagan nation'. Moreover, in this particular regard the geology of earth's ragged, pockmarked surface provided physical confirmation of the grand sacred truths vouchsafed to mythography. Surely, wondered Faber, 'to adopt the infidel system evinces more credulity than to adopt the Christian system'?[106]

Anglican mythography – though ideologically charged and unyielding in the face of deism and scepticism – was far from monolithic, and other apologists took a very different line from Faber on the Trinity. Robert Gray, for example, the future Bishop of Bristol, contended that there had been intimations of the Trinity in the Old Testament, and that this doctrine had persisted in the heathen world 'corrupted and disfigured under an endless variety of forms', most obviously in the triad of the Brahmins.[107]

There were other major disagreements *within* the world of orthodoxy. Faber took the line that animal sacrifice was part of the patriarchal revelation to humankind, and as such had been received by the Noachids and their descendants throughout the pagan world.[108] In this he contradicted John Davison (1777–1834), a former Fellow of Oriel College, Oxford, who published *An inquiry into the origin and intent of primitive sacrifice* (1825), in which Davison argued that sacrifice was a human creation rather than a divine ordinance.[109] Given Davison's concession that sacrifice did not derive straightforwardly from the 'light of nature', it was most puzzling that this somewhat 'arbitrary' practice should be so universal. 'Universal accordance in matters purely arbitrary evinces, of necessity, that those matters had a common origin',[110] Faber reckoned, and rejected Davison's argument, as he did the influential position of the seventeenth-century French Catholic mythographer Huet, that the rites of the gentiles derived from a Mosaic source.[111] Not so, contended Faber, for the practice of sacrifice was to be found among heathen communities 'anterior' to the era of Moses. The universality of expiatory sacrifice among heathen peoples was part of

---

[106] Faber, *The difficulties of infidelity* (London, 1824), pp. ix, 1, 49–54, 272.
[107] Robert Gray, *The connection between the sacred writings and the literature of Jewish and heathen authors, particularly that of the classical ages, illustrated, principally with a view to evidence in confirmation of the truth of revealed religion* (2nd edn, 2 vols., London, 1819), vol. I, pp. 138–47.
[108] Faber, *Expiatory sacrifice*.
[109] John Davison, *An inquiry into the origin and intent of primitive sacrifice* (London, 1825).
[110] Faber, *Expiatory sacrifice*, p. 50.
[111] Huet, *Demonstratio evangelica* (Paris, 1679).

Faber's suite of collateral evidences, an integral component in 'the whole manifestly connected theology of the gentiles'.[112]

The Reverend John Carwithen (1781–1832) in the Bampton Lectures of 1809 claimed that it was precisely because Deists and sceptics had invested so much ideological capital in Hindu mythology that its surprising vindication of the Old Testament was so devastating to the enemies of Christianity, for in this case 'coincidence and corroborative testimony are also perfectly undesigned', not least in those places 'where infidelity had expected to gain a signal triumph by wounding Christianity through the sides of Judaism'. Thus, while the 'partisans of infidelity' had expressed the 'sanguine hope' that sacred history 'would be weakened by the discovery of this unexpected mine of ancient literature' in India, they had instead found 'to their mortification and regret, that it forms a part of that impenetrable rock on which the fabric of Christianity is raised'.[113]

John Overton (1763–1835) decided that the most appropriate theatre on which to counter-attack against Volney was sacred chronology. Astutely, Overton decided that certain elements of sacred history were indefensible, but that if these outworks were abandoned then the citadel of sacred history was sounder as a result, if not impregnable. On the other hand, Volney's insights when analysed properly turned out to rest upon 'a miserable sandy foundation'. Indeed, Volney's boast that the 12,000 years of Zoroastrian chronology undermined the authority of Moses might be transformed into a bulwark of sacred history. Overton saw that the notion that the Flood had been global was a weak point in Christian apologetic; but if it were abandoned and much of the primeval history told in Genesis interpreted properly as a regional history, then sacred history as a whole emerged all the stronger, not least if the Septuagint chronology were rejected and preference given to the Hebrew Bible, for now the chronologies of other civilisations, such as the Chinese and the Zoroastrian, provided unbiased pagan support for the truth of Christianity: 'If there is no occasion to suppose the flood not over the whole globe, to the destruction of every son of Adam, then numerous difficulties which infidels exult in, will at once be removed. The chronology from the sons of Noah ... will be the Hebrew chronology with the addition of 8,000 years before the Fall. And all other chronologies that rest upon the indisputable astronomical epochs will agree with Moses in his Hebrew.' Overton's point was that, read aright and with suitable allowances for traditional errors which needed quite properly to

---

[112] Faber, *Expiatory sacrifice*, pp. 50–1.
[113] John Carwithen, *A view of the Brahminical religion* (London, 1810), pp. 27, 77.

be rejected, sacred and profane chronology were connected and mutually corroborative. Overton also set out a full repudiation of Volney's dismissive interpretation of Christ as an emblem of the natural world. Instead Overton spelled out in detail Christ's genealogy from the earliest periods of sacred history. Unlike Volney's Christ, Overton's was tangibly historical. Indeed, Overton was sufficiently satisfied with his own ingenious labours to imagine that over time his work in chronology would turn the tables on the current Volneyite attack on scripture truth: 'while our present thoughtless youth are reading Volney's *Ruins*, their posterity will in their turn read the ruins of Volney, or Volney's cause ruined'.[114]

The Reverend J. B. Emmett thought that Volneyan scepticism could only be taken so far, until, in the case of the Flood for example, it ran into the obstacle of the curious fossil record, 'skeletons of fishes ... found at great elevations above the level of the sea'. The theories of Christian mythography interlocked neatly with such evidence, but not Volney's irreligious speculations that the Flood was a mere allegory of cyclical phenomena couched in a language derived from astrological imagery: 'if we suppose the Chaldean Deluge to be the termination of the solar circle; if we suppose the Egyptian to be no more than the overflowing of the Nile; neither of these can so disturb the element of the fishes in England, Russia, America etc. as to make them take refuge upon the tops of mountains'.[115]

Some apologists made apparent concessions to the claims of the radical enlightenment. Thomas Broughton, in *The Age of Christian Reason*, a riposte both to Tom Paine's *Age of Reason* – obviously – and to Volney, deployed the mythographical strategies (though not the subversive intent) of Conyers Middleton as a means of defending Christianity from the infidel mythographers. Up to a point, Volney was right. Elements of Christianity had indeed been derived from pagan sources. It was the 'abominable union of paganism and Christianity' found in Roman Catholicism which had dangerously exposed true Christianity to the attacks of deists and sceptics. But it was a serious mistake to confound the essence of Christianity, Broughton argued, with the corruptions of Rome.[116]

Nor did everyone within the ranks of orthodoxy agree with the bizarre strategic reliance upon the corroborative power of pagan mythology.

---

[114] John Overton, *The genealogy of Christ, elucidated by sacred history ... with a new system of sacred chronology* (2 vols., London, 1817), vol. I, pp. xiv–xv, 62, 107, 113, 122, 134–6; Overton, *The books of Genesis and Daniel (in connection with modern astronomy) defended against Count Volney and Dr Francis* (London, 1820), pp. 35, 54.

[115] J. B. Emmett, *Remarks on the late Count Volney's New Researches on Ancient History; to which are added general remarks on infidelity* (London, 1823), pp. 46, 48.

[116] Thomas Broughton, *The age of Christian reason* (London, 1820), pp. 10, 179.

Charles Blomfield (1786–1857), later Bishop of London, gave a series of sermons at Cambridge in January 1818 in which he argued – against the distinct and far-from-coordinated assaults of sceptics and unitarians – that the tradition of a promised redeemer had been present throughout the Old Testament. However, notwithstanding his apologetic commitment to the historicity of the Old Testament, Blomfield was reluctant to tie his scheme to the corroborative evidences. Indeed, he lamented the 'fanciful' defences advanced by 'some over-zealous advocates' of Christian orthodoxy, who 'have forced into the service of truth proofs of such a dubious nature, as to weaken the cause which they were intended to support. Great ingenuity and learning have been employed, in vain attempts to persuade the world, that a knowledge of the triune God was disseminated by the patriarchs in Chaldea and Egypt; that it was preserved in Samothrace by the votaries of the Cabiri; and taught by Plato in the groves of Academus.' Yet, notwithstanding this outburst against dubious collateral apologetics, even Blomfield acknowledged in one specific case that 'the mythological history of the Titanomachia' (the war of the Titans) was a 'corruption' of the Genesis account of the Luciferian revolt of the angels.[117]

Pagan–Christian parallels could be dangerous, for it was all too easy to confound chicken and egg. Godfrey Higgins (1772–1833) the squire of Skellow Grange, near Doncaster, deployed mythological resemblances between the ancient religions of Asia and the west as a means of subverting traditional orthodoxies.[118] Indeed, the phenomenon of aristocratic irreligion – of the sort espoused by Higgins, who was under the influence of the French astronomer Bailly[119] – further complicated the battle lines in early nineteenth-century Britain's wars of mythography. Take, for example, Sir Willliam Drummond's *Oedipus Judaicus* (1811), which he had privately printed in a deliberately limited run of 250 copies, in large part because it contained opinions which Drummond had 'no wish of promulgating to the mob'. Drummond's main point was that the Old Testament needed to be read allegorically rather than literally. Drummond argued that ancient nations – the Hebrews included – had organised their religions on the basis of a two-fold doctrine, an inner doctrine known to the initiated and an outer doctrine where philosophical truths were concealed under the form of symbols. A literal Old Testament was, Drummond contended, indefensible. Why did Christian literalists fail to see the allegory in the Old

---

[117] Charles Blomfield, *A dissertation upon the traditional knowledge of a promised Redeemer which subsisted before the advent of Our Saviour* (Cambridge, 1819), pp. viii, 135.
[118] Godfrey Higgins, *Anacalypsis* (1836: London, 1878).
[119] Godfrey Higgins, *The Celtic druids* (London, 1827), pp. 45–52.

Testament? He was perplexed that readers of Genesis were untroubled 'that far the greater portion of the human race is doomed to suffer eternal torments, because our first parents ate an apple, after having been tempted by a talking serpent. They find it quite simple, that the triune Jehovah should dine on veal cutlets at Abraham's table'. This sort of flat-footed exegesis was to misunderstand 'the character and genius of the ancient Oriental writings'. Indeed, Moses emerges from Drummond's analysis as little more than a calendrical reformer.[120]

Notwithstanding the limited circulation of Drummond's work it provoked a vigorous response.[121] In particular, George Townsend parodied Drummond's methods in the mythographical spoof, the *Oedipus Romanus* (1819), in which he reduced the twelve Caesars of ancient history to the twelve signs of the zodiac. However, beyond his cod-allegorising Townsend had a serious message. He saw that if Drummond's zodiacal theories were correct, 'the Deity has, in that case, communicated either no revelation to man, or a revelation which discusses the squabbling of some unknown people, at some remote age, about the reform of an almanac, and the alteration of a calendar – Inspiration become the dream of folly, superstition and ignorance – The divine legation of Moses is levelled to that of Numa, Lycurgus or Solon – The prophets are converted into enthusiasts or impostors – Christ himself ... is an astronomical emblem, the child in the arms of Virgo'. If in lieu of the laws of God found in authoritative scriptures 'we are presented with broken zodiacs, and all the lumber of eastern vanity', then morality, obligation and social cohesion were threatened.[122]

The battle over Volney's *Ruins* was not concluded by the end of the Napoleonic Wars. Cook counts eight English editions of Volney between 1819 and 1835, which excludes reprints, excerpts and serialisations.[123] The stock means of answering Volney was to advance the Anglican interpretation of the origins of myth; which means that a Casaubonish strategy was – however out of step with early nineteenth-century advances in Biblical scholarship – still an *ideological* necessity into the 1830s.

If Casaubon was – as Eliot indicated – using yesterday's weapons, so too was a whole battalion of mythographers, and he was certainly not fighting yesterday's battles. A reviewer in the *Christian Remembrancer* celebrated the fact that by 1830 – at the very period when the action of *Middlemarch*

---

[120] William Drummond, *Oedipus judaicus* (1811), pp. ii, iv, vii, xii, xix, 162–4, 179, 183.
[121] J. Godwin, *The theosophical enlightenment* (Albany, NY, 1994), p. 43.
[122] G. Townsend, *The Oedipus Romanus* (London, 1819), pp. 138–43.
[123] Cook, 'Reading revolution', p. 141 fn.

commences – the 'ribald revilings of the infidel Paine' had 'long since sunk into merited insignificance'. However, the reviewer warned, other debunkers tended to crop up from time to time, 'who affect to underrate the writings of Moses', and to 'involve his plainest statements in the mists of allegorical interpretation'. In response to these impertinent cavillers, he invoked 'the concurrent testimony of pagan history' – in other words, what we might call the key to all mythologies – to 'substantiate their truth': 'The striking marks of similarity between the Hindu, the Phoenician, the Egyptian and the Grecian cosmogonies, and the Mosaic account of creation ... sufficiently show that they must have originated in one common source.' Nor was there 'a nation, whether in the eastern or the western hemisphere, which has not its tradition of a *universal* deluge'.[124]

The radical threat of heterodoxy, freethinking and blasphemy had remained serious during the decades following the conclusion of the Napoleonic Wars,[125] not least as it became hard to draw the line between ultra-Protestant purity of doctrine – true Christianity indeed – and outright irreligion. Sampson Mackey, a Norwich shoemaker, attempted to separate Jesus the moral teacher – 'the Christian moralist', 'the great promulgator of Christian morality' – from the myths and allegories which had grown up around his name. Much of scripture, as well as mythology, was figurative; indeed the history of Jesus needed to be divested of its allegorical 'pagan vestments' borrowed from Egypt and the east. Mackey's naturalistic key to all mythologies was geographical, agrarian and astronomical. Ancient mythologies derived originally from attempts to make sense of the passing of the seasons, fluctuations in the level of great rivers, the Nile especially, and changes in the constellations of the night sky. Mackey traced the sphinxes of Egypt – mere 'chimerical monsters' – back to zodiacal references to the sun being in Leo; thus, these 'compound monsters were not gods ... but registers of time which were preserved with veneration'. Similarly, the myth of Leda and the swan Mackey read as an allusion 'to those times when snow descended in the last month of the year, and when the sun was in Gemini'. The literal truths of Christianity were rendered precarious by Mackey's deconstructive project, for all ancient religions were contaminated with these kinds of zodiacal allegory and became a nonsense if their message were not filtered through the demystifying lens of the astronomer.[126]

[124] *Christian Remembrancer* (June 1830), vol. 12, pp. 335–42, at pp. 335–6.
[125] Godwin, *Theosophical enlightenment*, p. 52.
[126] Sampson Arnold Mackey, *The mythological astronomy of the ancients* (2 vols., Norwich, 1822–3), vol. I, pp. 31–2, 34, 97; vol. II, pp. xi, xxii, 123–7, 160, 177.

The anxious 'Tory' campaign in the press against the corrosive effects of France's infidel enlightenment did not fade away in the aftermath of Waterloo, but ran on vigorously into the 1830s.[127] So too did blasphemy prosecutions of the propagandists of Volneyesque irreligion. After all, Anglican defenders of the established order in church and state perceived an intimate connection between blasphemy and political sedition.[128]

Richard Carlile (1790–1843), a controversial critic of traditional religion and the publisher of Paine's works, was imprisoned in 1817, 1819–25, 1832–3 and again in 1834, the year in which he converted from materialistic atheism to a more nuanced allegorical appreciation of Christianity. By the same token, the 'Reverend' Robert Taylor, a Volneyesque critic of the foundations of Christianity who served as chaplain and secretary to the radically revisionist and deistic Christian Evidence Society, was imprisoned for blasphemy in 1828–9 and 1831–3. Indeed, both of Taylor's principal works, the *Syntagma* (1828) and the *Diegesis* (1829), which reduced the Christian religion to a solar myth, described the author as a prisoner in Oakham Gaol.

Taylor had earned notoriety as 'the Devil's chaplain'. He had taken holy orders in the Church of England upon his graduation from Cambridge, and served as a clergyman in Sussex and the Midlands. However, his unorthodox blend of deism and astronomical allegorising had necessitated his departure from clerical office. After a period in Dublin, where he set up a Society of Universal Benevolence and its mouthpiece, the *Clerical Review*, he came to London and resumed clerical office – of sorts – in the Christian Evidence Society. There was nothing sheepish, however, about this nonbeliever's performance of his clerical duties. Taylor wore extravagant clerical attire, took the performance of the liturgy, or his own variant of it, seriously, and attempted to recreate the full drama and sense of occasion of Anglican worship (albeit semi-parodically) within his own properly interpreted brand of Christianity.[129] According to Taylor, Christ was, in the first place, derived from the Indian deity 'Chrishna' (a spelling he insisted upon in preference to Krishna),[130] though all the Christ-like deities as well as Christ himself were ultimately personifications of the sun. This, Taylor contended, was the simple key to all mythologies, though the confusions

---

[127] P. Harling, 'The perils of "French philosophy": Enlightenment and revolution in Tory journalism, 1800–1832', in H.-J. Lusebrink and J. Popkin (eds.), *Enlightenment, revolution and the periodical press, Studies on Voltaire and the Eighteenth Century* (2004) 6, pp. 199–220.
[128] See e.g. J. C. D. Clark, *English society 1688–1832* (Cambridge, 1985), pp. 381–2; R. Hole, *Pulpits, politics and public order in England 1760–1832* (Cambridge, 1989), ch. 14.
[129] J. Wiener, *Radicalism and freethought in nineteenth-century Britain: the life of Richard Carlile* (Westport, CT, 1983), pp. 130–1.
[130] Robert Taylor, *Syntagma of the evidences of the Christian religion* (London, 1828), p. 87.

of scholars and theologians on this topic were easily explained. The various changing 'epithets and names' for the sun in different mythologies had led to the understandable 'difficulty … in tracing the identity of the parent figments through the multifarious forms of the ancient idolatry'. Yet in fact he concluded 'it is but one and the same deity and demi-god who is meant under a hundred designations'. Moreover, many of the stories associated with these personifications of the sun – and Christ in particular – were attributable to astronomical observations as they related to the calendrical symbols of the zodiac: 'as various are the allegories and fictions of his passing through the zodiacal sign of the virgin, which, of course, would remain a virgin still; his descending into the lower parts of the earth; his rising again from the dead; his ascending into heaven … By all which metaphorical personifications were typified the natural history or circumstances observable in the sun's progress through the twelve months which constitute the natural year.'[131] Taylor also explained the crucifixion as a distorted tradition of the Egyptian worship of the Nile: 'the religious honours paid to the Nile … were necessarily addressed to the upright post with a transverse beam, indicating the height to which its waters would reach, and the extent to which they would carry the benefits of fertilization. The demon of famine was happily expressed by the naked and emaciated being nailed upon it.'[132]

Carlile's position as a demystifier of Christianity who tried both to prick its pretensions and to read it aright was as ambiguous as Taylor's. Indeed, Carlile eventually described himself – disconcertingly – as a 'christian atheist'.[133] Indeed, Carlile's defection from '"orthodox" atheism', as Joel Wiener has described it, led to a flurry of letters from disgruntled freethinkers to his magazine the *Republican*.[134] Carlile contended that ancient history was a compound of literal historical truth and various allegories, and that the proper understanding of 'Christianity' required that one jettison faux-historicity in order to interpret the deeper symbolic truths which lay behind the bogus pseudo-historical fantasy.[135] Jesus was not a person, but an allegory, moreover a dual allegory, representing both nature – as in other Volneyesque decodings – and science. Indeed, contended Carlile, the persecution of Christ represented the persecution of the scientific

---

[131] Robert Taylor, *The diegesis; being a discovery of the origin, evidences, and early history of Christianity* (London, 1829), p. 160.
[132] Taylor, *Syntagma*, p. 96.
[133] Wiener, *Radicalism and freethought*, p. 135.
[134] *Ibid.*
[135] Richard Carlile, *An abstract, embodying the evidences, of the lectures, delivered by Mr Carlile, at Brighton and elsewhere, in the year 1836, to prove that the Bible is not a book of historical record, but an important mythological volume* (London, 1837), pp. 3–5, 9.

worldview ever since the fall, the fall itself being the fall of mankind from a proper scientific outlook into superstition.[136] The plight of Jesus, indeed, was analogous to the legend of Prometheus.[137] Whatever the Bible was it did not tell the proper history of the Jews, for Carlile could find no authenticating body of evidence for their history prior to about 250 BC.[138] The names of supposed ancient Israelite personages in the Old Testament were rather terms for attributes, qualities, and philosophical concepts and duties, for which he helpfully provided a glossary in his *Dictionary of some of the names in the sacred scriptures* (1839). The Bible did not relate history, but an allegory of philosophical 'principles, mythologically dramatized'.[139] The virgin birth, which corresponded to the birth of Minerva from Jupiter, was the birth of science; Christ's turning of water into wine was the seasonal transformation from the wetness of winter to the fruits of summer; and the crucifixion signified a protest, according to Carlile, against priestcraft and persecution.[140] Christianity, it transpired, was but a version of the truths allegorised in the legends of pagan mythology. But realising this was the first step on the road not to a denial of Christianity, but to a proper appreciation of what it really meant, an allegory both of the natural world and of the human mind's capacity to understand it.

Another radical, R. J. Rowe, in *A Dissertation on the Ruins* (1832), invoked Volney to challenge not only the originality but also the authenticity of the Pentateuch. The Pentateuch had been copied from other older mythologies; moreover, Moses himself had not been the plagiarist. Rather, according to Rowe, Hilkiah, the high priest of the Israelites, had composed the Pentateuch 800 years after the time of Moses. Hilkiah had, moreover, used Chaldean, not Hebrew, sources in constructing his supposedly sacred history. Not that the Chaldean story was itself divinely inspired; for instance, Rowe debunked the Chaldean account of the Flood as a mere 'astrological fiction'.[141]

The subversive tenets of the radicals inevitably prompted a flurry of rebuttals from figures such as J. R. Beard (1800–76) and John Pye Smith (1774–1851).[142] Beard interrogated the assumption that Christ was

---

[136] *Ibid.*, pp. 6, 11.
[137] Hole, *Pulpits*, p. 212.
[138] Richard Carlile, *A dictionary of some of the names in the sacred scriptures* (Manchester, 1839), p. iii.
[139] Carlile, *Abstract*, p. 24.
[140] *Ibid.*, pp. 6, 9–11.
[141] R. J. Rowe, *A dissertation on the ruins* (London, 1832), esp. pp. 45, 65, 209.
[142] J. R. Beard, *The historical evidences of Christianity unassailable, proved in four lectures, addressed to the Reverend Robert Taylor and Mr Richard Carlile* (London, 1826); [John Pye Smith], *An answer to a printed paper entitled Manifesto of the Christian Evidence Society* (London, 1827).

somehow derived from the Hindu prototype of Krishna (or Chrishna). The superficial and misleading similarity in the names was no more profound or instructive than the assumption that a 'Jacobite' and a 'Jacobin' might hold common political views. Indeed, Beard went on to argue, there were many more 'instances of dissimilarity' in the stories of Christ and Krishna than the very small number of apparent parallels between them.[143] Nor was Christ a pale derivative simulacrum of the Prometheus symbol, but someone whose historical existence was well attested.[144] Another anonymous orthodox critic, writing in 1830, complained that the 'resemblances' which Taylor had 'endeavoured to vamp up between the history of the Christian religion and the pagan mythology' merely rebounded against the case he was trying to make, for similarities were to be 'discovered in the mythological tales of all the nations of the earth; some being the corrupted relics of the tradition' carried away by the divergent lines of Noah's progeny at the dispersion. Moreover, the sheer 'extent of the revelation made to the antediluvian world', particularly with reference to the promise of a Redeemer, was not to be discounted or underestimated. Therefore, seeming anticipations of Christ-like figures and elements in heathen mythologies of the pre-Christian era should not be used to condemn Christ as a piece of plagiarised paganism, but rather the reverse, as an ironic confirmation of primeval revelation. From his researches in gentile mythology Taylor had managed only 'to contrive a story sufficiently plausible to deceive those who seek to be deceived'.[145]

The mythographical conflict begun in the Revolutionary era between radicals and conservatives continued into the 1840s. During the summer of 1843, for example, Edinburgh witnessed a crackdown on the blasphemous book trade.[146] Moreover, authoritarian measures to stamp out radical irreligion were still accompanied by a vigorous literature of mythographical apologetic. In *The connexion between revelation and mythology* (1845) the Egyptologist Anne Flinders (1812–92) rejoiced in 'an end to the vain attempts of scepticism to play off heathen legends against the truth of scripture'. Mythology furnished decisive evidence 'to the contradiction of the sceptic and the unbeliever', and Trinitarian patterns in ancient legends also provided a firm rebuttal even to the 'denials of Socinianism'.

[143] Beard, *Historical evidences*, pp. 84–7.
[144] *Ibid.*, p. 26.
[145] *Remarks on the work of the Reverend Robert Taylor, styled the Diegesis* (London, 1830), pp. 29–30.
[146] E. Royle, *Victorian infidels: the origins of the British secularist movement 1791–1866* (Manchester, 1974), pp. 83–5, 308.

Christianity was established on the sturdiest and most impregnable of rocks; evidence which derived not from its own believers and friends, but from 'enemies and idolaters'. The blasphemies aired by radical critics of Christianity evaporated, when 'even the absurd and polluted mythology of paganism is constrained to bear its share of the universal testimony to the truth of the scripture record'.[147]

---

[147] [Anne Flinders], *The connexion between revelation and mythology* (London, 1845), pp. 18, 79–80.

CHAPTER 6

Fish-gods, Floods and Serpent-worship: From Apologetics to Anthropology

[S]he had listened with fervid patience to a recitation of possible arguments to be brought against Mr Casaubon's entirely new view of the Philistine god Dagon and other fish-deities. (*Middlemarch*, ch. 20)

George Eliot's Mr Casaubon, with his key to all mythologies, would have been, surely *was*, a member of the Ethnological Society; he would have been badly out of place among the fiercer spirits of the Anthropological Society. (John Burrow, *Evolution and Society*)

A handful of imaginary mythographers are interspersed among the genuine scholars who surface in *Middlemarch*. In particular Eliot invents a shoal of bogus dons who debated matters mythographical with Causaubon, namely Messrs Pike, Tench and Carp. Is there some deeper layer of allusion in this superficial jest about fish? Eliot also refers in *Middlemarch* to 'fish-deities', among whom she includes the Philistine god Dagon. Are the fish-deities connected in some way to the joke about the scholars with fishy names? This chapter will explore the nineteenth-century debate about fish deities as distorted remembrances of the Flood. It will also explore another similar theme associated with the animal world which attracted considerable attention from mythographers in the early and mid-nineteenth century, the issue of whether forms of serpent-worship in the ancient pagan world and in contemporary 'primitive' societies referred back to the Fall of Man in the Garden of Eden. In the early nineteenth century the apologetic school of collateral evidences used the evidence of such cults to reinforce its arguments about the original unity of all mythologies; later, however, anthropologists appropriated the matter of serpent-worship and put it to other ends.

Nevertheless, the division between the apologetic and the anthropological deployment of serpent-worship was, as we shall see, far from clear cut. There was also a strain of ethnology – alluded to by John Burrow in his classic work *Evolution and Society*[1]– which constituted an

[1] J. W. Burrow, *Evolution and society* (Cambridge, 1966), p. 123.

intermediate genre between older forms of religious apologetic and a fully secularised, or indeed decidedly anti-religious, anthropology. By the time of *Middlemarch*'s publication, the debate over serpent-worship took place on a strange terrain fought over by several scholarly armies, not simply by defenders of orthodoxy and by those anthropologists who would reduce fish-gods and serpent-gods to mere tribal totems. A range of other battalions swarmed over this battleground, including solarists, whose methods were rooted in the insights of Max-Müller's philology (the disciplinary rival to anthropology), and a low-minded kind of scholar, indebted both to the satirical scoffing of eighteenth-century deism and to another strain of modern anthropological investigation, which saw resemblances between the serpent and the phallus.

Christian champions of collateral apologetics saw Noah everywhere, hiding undecoded behind numerous pagan myths, if not, for some quixotic mythographers, behind *all* of them. When water, boats, fish, or – best of all – mermen appeared in heathen mythologies, then mythographers knew how to unpack and demystify these emblems and allegories. Vernon Harcourt – one of the templates for Casaubonish mythography known to Eliot[2] – was obsessed by arks and fish and all things aquatic. Even the siege of Troy failed to escape Harcourt's penchant for converting mythological fodder into flood stories. Was not Helen of Troy, he asked rhetorically – and as he did so, stretching to ludicrous lengths the legend of Leda and the swan – the offspring of aquatic parents? In confirmation of his Procrustean thesis, Harcourt conjured up supporting evidence of a still more dubious kind, to the effect that Helen was a priestess of the Arkites and associated with the dove.[3] Small wonder that John Landseer despaired of the 'learned gentlemen who have *literally deluged* philosophy and free enquiry, with their incessant references to Noah's flood and his miraculous preservation'.[4]

Mythographic attention focused on the Near Eastern mermen-deities, the Assyrian Oannes and the Phoenician god Dagon. These were creatures with human heads and voices, and fish tails, though in the case of Oannes feet which emerged at the tail. Both Dagon and Oannes were identified as founders of the arts and sciences. Oannes, as described by Berosus, had emerged from the sea each morning to instruct the Babylonians in the arts, and had retired to the sea in the evening. Oannes and Dagon were

---

[2] A. Fleishman, *George Eliot's intellectual life* (Cambridge, 2010), p. 21.
[3] Vernon Harcourt, *The doctrine of the deluge* (2 vols., London, 1838), vol. I, pp. 340, 389.
[4] John Landser, *Sabaean researches* (London, 1823), p. 112.

essentially one and the same, that is deifications of Noah, the figure who had emerged from the sea – or deluge – to re-establish civilisation.

Faber noted that the knowledge the ancient Chaldeans had of the Creation of the world derived from 'the teaching of an amphibious creature denominated Oannes. His form consisted of the body of a man terminating in the tail of a fish.' Oannes had taught a cosmogony similar to the Mosaic version found in Genesis, but mingled, so Faber perceived, 'with perpetual allusions to the deluge'. This helped to clarify the real identity of the fish-god: 'The genuine prototype of the Babylonian man of the sea, the teacher of all the useful arts, and the revealer of the process of creation, is clearly the patriarch Noah.' Similarly, Noah could be detected in the Philistine fish-god Dagon, as Po or Buddha – 'the sovereign prince in the belly of a fish' – and 'Vishnu in the fish avatar'.[5] Indeed, this 'emblematical deity' – the half-man, half-fish emblem of Noah – was 'common throughout Asia'.[6] Faber contended that in many ancient mythologies the presiding male deity – typically, of course, a fish-god – was a remembrance of Noah. However, his partner, the leading female deity, was not Noah's wife, but rather an allegory of the Ark, for had not that vessel been a kind of 'universal mother to the renovated human species'?[7] For example, Astarte, 'the mythological consort of Cronus, or Noah' was the same goddess as Venus, 'who was usually represented by the poets rising in youthful beauty from the waves of the troubled ocean, and surrounded by fishes and other aquatic animals'; yet both symbolised 'the Noetic Ark, which by the allegorizing spirit of antiquity was personified in the character of a graceful female'.[8]

Cory noted that when Berosus described the semi-piscine Oannes as spending his nights in the sea, this should not be read in terms of actual nights, but as a distorted memory of the traumatic darkness of the Flood. 'Unconscious that Noah is represented under the character of Oannes', Cory noted, 'Berosus describes him, from the hieroglyphical delineation, as a being literally compounded of a fish and a man, and as passing the natural, instead of the diluvian, night in the sea'.[9]

Did it matter which half of the deity was fish-like and which was human? The archaeologist Austen Henry Layard (1817–94) noted that in

---

[5] George Faber, *The origin of pagan idolatry* (3 vols., London, 1816), vol. I, pp. 206–8.
[6] George Faber, *Horae Mosaicae* (2 vols., Oxford, 1801), vol. I, p. 31.
[7] Faber, *A dissertation on the mysteries of the Cabiri* (2 vols., Oxford, 1803), vol. II, pp. 88, 92.
[8] Faber, *Cabiri*, vol. I, p. 81.
[9] Isaac Preston Cory, *The ancient fragments; containing what remains of the writings of Sanchoniatho, Berossus, Abydenus, Megasthenes and Manetho* (London, 1828), p. ix.

depictions of Dagon on cylinders and on gateways the 'head of the fish formed a mitre above that of the man, whilst its scaly back and fanlike tail fell as a cloak behind, leaving the human feet and limbs exposed'.[10] The mitre was a bizarre remembrance of Noah, a fishhead-shaped ecclesiastical accoutrement. On the other hand, might the mitre provide evidence of a very different sort, a sinister clue to the pagan origins of the papacy, if not episcopal Christianity more generally? Thus mused Alexander Hislop (1807–65), a Scottish Free Church minister, according to whose pamphlet, *The Two Babylons*, (first published in 1853 and on its third edition within a decade), Popery was 'baptized paganism', but of a very specific sort; for the Pope wears the mitre of Dagon, the fish-god of the Philistines and Babylonians. Catholicism, with its emphasis on the emblematic representation of Christ as a fish, was, it transpired, an all-too-obvious front for a Babylonian fish-cult.[11]

By the early nineteenth century, apologetic mythography had acquired a more cosmopolitan tinge, informed in particular by a range of evidence from India. Mythographers noted that the Hindu deity Vishnu also had a celebrated fish avatar, and seemed to provide further confirmation of the widespread remembrance of Noah. Vishnu was a further variant of Oannes and Dagon, that is, a misremembered pagan deification of Noah, the figure who had emerged from the sea – or deluge – to re-establish civilisation. The Reverend Peter Roberts, a critic of Volney, stressed the associations in Hindu mythology of Vishnu with fish, with water and with preservation: 'The emblem is as clearly that of the preservation of the family of Noah at the Deluge, and as strong a proof of the truth of the Mosaic history of it, as it is possible for an emblem to be.'[12]

Exploration, missionary work and ethnography were further broadening the range of the corroborative evidences available to apologists. New materials from Polynesia appeared to provide yet further corroboration for the Old Testament. William Ellis (1794–1872) of the London Missionary Society was able to trace a memory of the Deluge in the legends of Polynesia. 'The canoe of the Polynesian Noah' was part of a global ensemble of Flood myths which testified to the truth of the Pentateuch:

> The brief yet satisfactory testimony to this event, preserved in the oral traditions of a people secluded for ages from intercourse with other parts of

---

[10] Austen H. Layard, *Discoveries in the ruins of Nineveh and Babylon* (London, 1853), p. 343.
[11] Alexander Hislop, *The two Babylons; or the papal worship proved to be the worship of Nimrod and his wife* (1853: 3rd edn, Edinburgh, 1862), pp. 3, 314.
[12] Peter Roberts, *Christianity vindicated, in a series of letters, addressed to Mr Volney* (London, 1800), pp. 174–6.

the world, furnishes strong additional evidence that the scripture record is irrefragable. In several respects, the Polynesian account resembles not only the Mosaic, but those preserved by the earliest families of the postdiluvian world, and supports the presumption that their religious system has descended from the Arkite idolatry, the basis of the mythology of the gentile nations.[13]

By the same token, indigenous knowledge of the Fall seemed also to be universal. John Liddiard Nicholas described a Maori belief

that the first woman was made of one of the man's ribs; and to add still more to this strange coincidence, their general term for bone is Hevee, which, for aught we know, may be a corruption of the name of our first parent, communicated to them perhaps, originally, by some means or other, and preserved without being much disfigured, among the records of ignorance.[14]

Reverend George Turner (1817/18–91) noticed something remarkably similar among the people of Fakaafo of the Tokelau group:

The first man, who had previously been a stone, thought one day he would make a woman. He collected the light earth on the surface of the ground, in the form of a human body, with head, arms, and legs. He then plucked out one of his left ribs, and thrust it into the breast of his earth model. Instantly the earth came alive, and up starts a woman. He called her Ivi (according to English orthography it would be Eevee), which is their word for rib. How like to our Eve![15]

'Distance' in Protestant ethnology was not a function of geography or of racial difference from white Europeans, but resided in large part in the 'distance to which those under its [paganism's] influence departed from the knowledge and service of the true God'.[16] The Polynesian Ivi – though geographically remote – offered evidence, so it seemed, of a traditional memory not so distant from primeval truth.

Serpent-worship provided an apologetic outwork for Christianity of still greater impregnability than flood legends. After all, snakes were far from appealing creatures, and, if anything, a nuisance and danger to humans, but hardly an edible boon to be celebrated, unlike fish. Hence it seemed

---

[13] William Ellis, *Polynesian researches, during a residence of nearly eighty years in the Society and Sandwich Islands* (2nd edn, London, 1831), vol. I, pp. 393–4.
[14] John Liddiard Nicholas, *Narrative of a voyage to New Zealand, performed in the years 1814 and 1815, in company with the Rev. Samuel Marsden, Principal Chaplain of New South Wales* (2 vols., London, 1817), vol. I, p. 59.
[15] George Turner, *Nineteen years in Polynesia: missionary life, travels and researches in the islands of the Pacific* (London, 1861), p. 323.
[16] Ellis, *Polynesian researches*, vol. I, p. 381.

difficult to construct a naturalistic explanation for the presence of serpents in so many of the world's mythologies. There must, in other words, be some particular (rather than general) reason for the widespread – but altogether unnatural – worship of snakes or similar reptiles and dragons in most, if not all, of the world's heathen religions and mythologies. A universal remembrance, however distorted, of the Fall seemed the most likely and persuasive explanation for a counter-intuitive phenomenon which ran so decidedly against the grain of human experience. Moreover, why, some wondered, were trees so often worshipped in conjunction with serpents? Mythological evidence of such fine-grained particularity – and peculiarity – seemed unanswerable.

According to *A Summary of Christian Instruction* (1826), which provided a handy compendium of apologetic arguments and sources, the 'remarkable coincidence between sacred and profane history' showed 'the genuineness of the former'. The seeming fact that pagan fables were – all-too-obviously – 'drawn from imperfect accounts of sacred history, plainly discover the scriptures to have been the original, of which the other is an imperfect copy'. There appeared to be widespread acknowledgement in heathen cultures of the Fall of Man: 'The Egyptian writers, Plato, Strabo, Ovid, Virgil and others mention the state of innocence and the fall.' Moreover, 'many particulars relating to Adam and Eve, the forbidden tree, and the serpent, are to be found among the natives of Peru and the Philippine islands'.[17]

James Christie (1730–1803), the antiquary and auctioneer, traced the process by which early humankind's unwished-for estrangement from God, first by way of the Fall and then the Flood, was marked by ceremonies of propitiation, which, in time, became corrupted – only gradually and far from intentionally – by the addition of new features. In their turn these gave rise to paganism, creeds of accidental alienation, though not in their very essence alien:

> When that bond of duty which originally connected man with his Creator was broken, and man became obnoxious to sin, expiatory sacrifices were instituted by divine command, prefigurative of a more complete atonement. They were afterwards disfigured by many human additions, which, however, gross and vain, must nevertheless be considered as attempts, on the part of man, to approach to God, expressing a sense of alienation, the deterioration of man's nature, and a hope of restitution. To this sense of exclusion from the presence and favour of the Deity, was added the fear of excision as due to sin, and as was actually experienced in the Flood, with a partial

---

[17] *A summary of Christian instruction* (London, 1826), pp. 149–50.

exception. This fallen state and merited punishment have been implied, if not directly acknowledged, in every sacred rite of the Gentile world, in their sacrifices and ceremonies, in the fables of their poets, and the devices of their sculptors.

Numerology and iconology lay at the heart of Christie's enterprise. Throughout the mythologies of the world, he detected references to the number eight, an allusion to the eight human survivors of the Flood, and to the number three, signifying the three male branches of Noah's progeny. A common pattern could be detected in the myths and imagery of global heathendom. From a Carthaginian terracotta depicting a 'cluster of three pomegranates bound together by a serpent' to the ongoing nurturing of serpents in 'the pagodas of Hindustan', from the story of Hercules and the apples of the Hesperides to the tale of Atalanta, 'who stopping to pick up the three golden apples, was thrown out of the chase, and accordingly resigned her virgin state', Christie perceived references to the Fall. Indeed, the Christian idea of redemption was at the heart of paganism: 'The hope of regaining this state of bliss, and the divine promise that man should be eventually reinstated, were fondly cherished by the pagans, and recorded though misrepresented by numerous fables and devices.' Heathen religion, in the eyes of Christie, was not a gross idolatry, but a genuine if 'imperfect' attempt to resume contact with the true God: 'All these memorials of the regret and hope of the early pagans, show a deep sense of their loss of communion with the Deity, as enjoyed in Paradise, and of the bodily decay and debasement that resulted from the Fall.'[18]

During the late eighteenth and early nineteenth century the quest for serpent myths became just as prominent in collateral apologetics as the search for fish-deities. Nevertheless, this reptilian obsession did not lack critics. Did the book of Genesis unambiguously mention a 'serpent'? Might the creature who tempted Eve have been a rather different animal? If so, then the very universality of serpent-worship was irrelevant and proved nothing. Sometimes the critics were radical freethinkers. Samuel Francis contended that the serpent was 'an emblem ... copied from the Egyptians, but by the Jews considered a real snake, which talked and walked upright. It was but a poor imitation of the Ahrimanes of Zoroaster.'[19] According to Francis, 'Mr Serpent would make a fine figure in Aesop's fables.'[20] However,

---

[18] James Christie, *An essay on that earliest species of idolatry, the worship of the elements* (Norwich, 1814), pp. 1, 4–5, 12, 15, 21–5.
[19] Samuel Francis, *Watson refuted: being an answer to the Apology for the Bible* (1796?: London, 1819), p. 69.
[20] *Ibid.*, p. 99.

old-fashioned orthodox writers had other qualms about the serpent. The Bishop of London thought it symptomatic of the utter degradation of ancient heathenism that its depraved idolaters had worshipped 'birds and beasts, insects and reptiles (especially that most odious and disgusting reptile the serpent)'.[21]

More devastating still, the early nineteenth-century debate over *nachash* – the Hebrew term used in Genesis for the supposed serpent – challenged the utility, indeed the very significance, of apologetic arguments drawn from serpent-worship. The Methodist biblical scholar Adam Clarke questioned whether serpent – as opposed to ape – was an appropriate rendering of *nachash*.[22] Clarke, moreover, was an open opponent of the collateral evidences, an apologetic strategy which threatened to render the Bible seemingly as irrational as the heathen mythologies to which it was assimilated. According to the tidily rational Methodist, much of the supposed corroboration of scripture from heathen mythology was 'so precarious, uncertain, and dubious, as rather to disserve the cause of divine revelation, than to promote it'. Clarke worried about 'the propensity among many learned and pious men, to grasp at shades of similitude in the mythology of the Asiatic nations'. He rehearsed the sad tale of the way Wilford and Jones had been deceived by 'artful brahmins' who hoped 'to ingratiate themselves' with their Christian rulers by forging documentary evidence which, 'with a little wire-drawing, could be brought to countenance our scripture facts'. Thus myths, such as that of Satyavarman and his three sons, Sherma, Charma and Jyapeti, had been 'eagerly embraced, printed and widely circulated as wonderful confirmations of divine verities'.[23]

Although the idea of collateral evidences was 'well intended', it had, Clarke believed, exposed Christian orthodoxy to great dangers, playing indeed into the hands of the infidel disciples of Volney: 'while I have the blasphemies of Volney before me, who wished to make it appear that the whole history of our most blessed Lord and Saviour Jesus Christ, was no other than a marred copy of the history of the Indian Krishna, I judge it highly imprudent and dangerous, to admit of such vouchers for the authenticity of the sacred records'. Moreover, Voltaire, in his short tale *Le taureau blanc*, had made use of the serpent, along with Balaam's ass and the witch of Endor, to poke fun at the apparent absurdity of sacred

---

[21] Beilby Porteous, *A summary of the evidences for the truth and divine origin of the Christian revelation* (9th edn, London, 1805), p. 7.

[22] Adam Clarke, *The holy bible ... with commentary and critical notes* (6 vols., London, 1836 edn), vol. I, pp. 50–3.

[23] [Adam Clarke], 'Reply to various critiques on the first part of Dr A. Clarke's Hebrew Bible', *Classical Journal*, vol. 3 (June 1811), pp. 423–44, at pp. 431–2, 436–7.

history.[24] The Bible needed to be read aright, precisely in order to fox those deists and sceptics who would use irrational misunderstanding, mistranslation and misinterpretation to subvert the entirety of scripture. Christians needed to be on their guard, lest in devising apologetic arguments that were too clever by half, they unintentionally weakened their own cause.[25]

Clarke was especially anxious about the way in which legends of serpents and rites of worship were being made to fit the Procrustean bed of Old Testament scholarship. For if the supposed serpent was, in fact, an ape, then of what significance was the legend of Krishna bruising the serpent's head? 'I heartily regret', bemoaned Clarke, 'that such an evidence was ever introduced in favour of the Mosaic account of the fall of man'. Clarke showed how his interpretation of *nachash* fitted into his overall principles of scriptural interpretation. 'I look', he said, 'for reason in divine revelation; and I am never disappointed. When I meet an interpretation of any passage that is irrational, I consider it at once to be erroneous, and endeavour to find out that meaning which is consistent with the dignity of revelation'.[26]

Clarke's interpretation of *nachash* provoked protest from several quarters. Indeed, the debate serves to demonstrate the influence of collateral evidences in Anglican apologetics. John Bellamy in his pamphlet *The Ophion* (1811) took Clarke to task for his presumption in claiming to know better than the collective wisdom of the learned Septuagint the meaning of *nachash*. What, Bellamy wondered, was 'more calculated to bring pure religion into disgrace, or to assist the Deist in defaming the scriptures, than supposing that a monkey was the agent employed in the Fall of man?' In a wonderful irony of circuitous reasoning, Bellamy turned to the collateral evidences of pagan legend for corroboration of his own traditional reading of Genesis: 'In the heathen mythology, which was founded on the scriptures, we have a description of the garden of Jupiter, ie Joa-pater; and the golden apples of the Hesperides, kept by a sleepless dragon, which was evidently taken from the serpent, and the forbidden fruit in paradise.' How would Clarke account for the widespread worship of the serpent 'in all the nations of the East'? For Bellamy this historical and ethnographic fact constituted 'a convincing proof' that a widely diffused serpent-worship 'took its rise from the serpent in paradise'. 'The monkey had nothing to do in this business', insisted Bellamy, who regretted the way hermeneutic fickleness and fashion were in danger of bringing the scriptures into

---

[24] Cf. Voltaire, 'Le taureau blanc', in Voltaire, *Candide et autres contes* (Paris, 1992), pp. 235–72.
[25] [Clarke], 'Reply', pp. 436–7, 439–40.
[26] *Ibid.*, pp. 430–1, 436, 439–40, 443.

'ridicule': 'Yesterday we understood that a serpent tempted Eve; today we are told it was a monkey; and tomorrow perhaps the leviathan' (by which Bellamy meant a crocodile).[27]

Daniel Guildford Wait of St John's College, Cambridge, writing under a Hebrew pseudonym which translated as 'The Investigator',[28] criticised Clarke's interpretation of *nachash* in the pages of the *Classical Journal*. Wait found Clarke's identification to be over-hasty, not least as it seemed like the airiest speculation when set against the compelling weight of collateral evidence culled from heathen mythography. 'Some tradition of a serpent has been current through all nations', he noted, and the more recently obtained evidence drawn from Hindu legend of Krishna crushing the head of the serpent appeared to offer strong confirmation for the lessons drawn from the serpent myths of Greco-Roman culture.[29]

In a subsequent pamphlet, *A Defence of a critique of the Hebrew word Nachash* (1811), Wait laid down a more forceful challenge to Clarke's misguided rejection of the serpent as the tempter of Eve. Not that Wait was willing to be boxed into a corner regarding exactly which type of reptile Eve had encountered in the Garden, for, of course, 'there existed no Linnaean distinction between serpents and reptiles in the days when the Bible was written'. Wait was unconvinced by Clarke's attempts to explain away the frequent recurrence of serpent tales in ancient mythology, for example as zodiacal allegories: 'As to the Doctor's evading Apollo killing the python ... by referring them to astronomy ... these would never have formed part of astronomy, had they not been intended to commemorate signal events.' Surely there was an underlying tradition from which legends of serpents and dragons ultimately derived? 'From time immemorial, suggestions, partly true, partly false' had 'existed concerning the serpent', which were found 'among all nations of all faiths'. These, Wait reckoned 'must have originated from some source', of the highest antiquity, and could not 'but tend to corroborate the received opinion'. However, the problem was not simply one of Clarke's cavalier approach to scriptural interpretation, but the damage which an inter-denominational wrangle about the zoological identity of Eve's tempter would do to the wider cause of the Christian faith, now assaulted by critics who rejected the divine inspiration of scripture altogether. Wait feared that Clarke's 'objections will have opened a wider door to infidelity and error, than all his powers,

---

[27] John Bellamy, *The Ophion* (London, 1811), pp. 4, 6, 9, 21, 27, 84.
[28] J. W. Etheridge, *The life of the Rev. Adam Clarke D.D.* (London, 1859), p. 326; Daniel Guildford Wait, *A defence of a critique of the Hebrew word Nachash* (London, 1811), p. v.
[29] [Daniel Guildford Wait], 'On the word Nachash', *Classical Journal* (March 1811), pp. 70–6.

efforts or ingenuity can avail to close'. Indeed, his speculations regarding a simian *nachash* seemed to provide apt material for raillery. 'Were Voltaire alive', Wait speculated, 'I am persuaded that the Doctor's ape would form a rare subject for a satire.'[30] While a degree of hermeneutic ingenuity was just about acceptable in the normal run of Biblical scholarship when dealing with decidedly knotty passages, increased caution was vital in 'times of enthusiasm and infidelity', for then it was crucially important to avoid any situation whereby the core articles of the Christian faith were unnecessarily 'undermined by fanciful interpretations of the scriptures'.[31]

Curiously, Clarke's arguments also provoked opposition from sceptical critics of divine revelation. Godfrey Higgins thought the serpent an allegory, and claimed he was as justified in thinking this as Clarke had been in identifying the serpent as 'an ape'. Indeed, Higgins found the whole of Genesis to be allegorical.[32]

Notwithstanding Clarke's eccentric Methodist scruples, the anthropology of serpent-worship became an important sub-genre of early nineteenth-century Anglican apologetic. The Reverend Samuel Burder (1773–1836) contended that it was from the history of the Fall that 'the heathen appear to have derived those distorted traditionary stories of Hercules carrying off the golden apples of the Hesperides, though guarded by a tremendous serpent or dragon, whom he vanquished'.[33] The Reverend Henry Dimock ascribed a central role to the misremembered memory of the serpent in the rise of idolatry.[34] The traveller and antiquary Lieutenant Colonel William Francklin (1763–1839) emphasised the striking universality of serpent-worship, as far apart as the religions of Egypt, Persia, Greece, Mexico and Peru, which seemed to quell any doubt about its 'antediluvian extraction'.[35]

The Reverend George Holden, in *A Dissertation on the Fall of Man* (1823), rejected figurative interpretations of the Fall, as well as Clarke's interpretation that an ape-like creature had tempted Eve. Countries far removed from one another appeared to agree on core elements of the history of the

---

[30] Wait, *Defence of a critique*, pp. x, 35, 67–8. See also Wait, *An inquiry into the religious knowledge which the heathen philosophers derived from the Jewish scriptures* (Cambridge, 1813), esp. pp. 69–70.

[31] Daniel Guidford Wait, *A critical examination of some scriptural texts which maintain the doctrine of a trinity in unity* (London, 1819), p. iii.

[32] Godfrey Higgins, *Anacalypsis* (1836: London, 1878), pp. 113, 182.

[33] Samuel Burder, *Oriental literature, applied to the illustration of the sacred scriptures* (2 vols., Londson, 1822), vol. I, p. 3.

[34] Henry Dimock, 'Miscellaneous observations on the serpent', in *Critical and explanatory notes on Genesis etc.* (London, 1804), pp. 306–13.

[35] William Francklin, *Researches on the tenets and doctrines of the Jeynes and Boodhists ... in which is introduced a discussion on the worship of the serpent in various countries of the world* (London, 1827), pp. 15–16.

Fall. These stories were too fanciful, too detailed, too peculiar indeed, to be independent inventions. How might one account for similarities between Ahriman in the Zend Avesta, the Caliya of Hindu theology, the Typhon of the Egyptians and the Python of the Greeks? Holden was particularly intrigued by the existence of so many tales in which intermediate deities bruised the heads of serpents. The pattern was too oddly distinctive to have arisen in so many different places from the natural operations of the human mind; only a diffusionist explanation compelled Holden's assent. Moreover, there was the further problem that humans tended to recoil from the sight of these reptiles. Why should they be so universally venerated when they produced so much fear and loathing? 'It cannot be conceived', he pondered, 'how mankind can be brought to pay divine adoration to an animal so loathsome and disgusting, and to which there seems a natural antipathy in the human species, except from some traditional record of its instrumentality in the Fall; yet the fact is certain of its being regarded with religious veneration all over the world.' There was no other avenue of explanation along which a mythographer might travel: all these legends 'appear to have similarly originated ... from some remembrance of the form which Satan assumed in Paradise'. According to Holden, such pagan traditions of the Fall supplied a 'two-fold testimony' for the literal truth of the Bible, as they not only established the general 'credibility' of the Old Testament but also confirmed a 'literal' reading of the scriptures, 'since they correspond with that interpretation and no other'.[36]

In *The testimony of profane antiquity to the account given by Moses of Paradise and the Fall of Man* (1825), Matthew Bridges (1800–94), the Anglo-Catholic hymnist and Hutchinsonian, who would eventually go over to Rome, focused not on serpent-worship but on the centrality of trees in primeval paganism and on elements of propitiatory sacrifice in the heathen world. Most obviously, pagan worship in 'groves, gardens or sacred enclosures' was a vestigial memory – and thus 'collateral proof' – of Eden. What else was the sacred oak grove of the Druids but an oblivious heathen quasi-remembrance of Eden and the Fall of Man? The 'earliest species of idolatry' was tree-worship, the 'consecration of memorials of that paradise which man had lost, through the suggestions of the tempter'. Shadows of the Fall were detectable in the legends of Pandora and of Orpheus. The myth of Atlantis was a distorted memory of Eden. Cerberus, who defended the entrance to Hades, was a pagan corruption of the Cherubim who guarded the way to the Tree of Life in Genesis. In addition, some sort of idea of

[36] George Holden, *A dissertation on the fall of man* (London, 1823), pp. 160, 275–6, 280, 402–5.

deliverance, or, by extension, atonement was universal, and had 'found its way … to every part of the habitable globe'. 'However obscurely', man's apostasy and the need to reconcile heaven and earth could be found in many ancient tales. Hercules was a heathen version of the promised deliverer, and the story of his exploits in the Garden of the Hesperides was a garbled sense of the promised deliverance. In Hindu legend Krishna had struggled with a serpent. Amid 'the darkness of the night of heathenism', Bridges noticed the tacit recognition of 'the necessity of an atonement for man's sin by the voluntary blood-shedding of some pure and propitiatory victim'. Bridges perceived that 'an idea of lost integrity seems to have pervaded the whole pagan world'. Golden ages – that is, 'vestiges of paradise' – were found in the myths of the Goths, Romans, Greeks, Druids, Egyptians and Hindus. Nevertheless, the relationship between scriptural history and heathen legend was much more complicated than a straightforward one-to-one correspondence. This was because, Bridges reckoned, the distinct histories of the Fall and the Flood had become confused and entangled within pagan mythologies. It was the role of the mythographer to disentangle, as far as was possible, the separate strands of biblical history which had become so promiscuously intertwined in the distorted traditions of heathendom. In many mythical episodes there was some kind of 'allusion … to both these traditions blended together'. The story of Jason and the Argonauts, for example, provided 'an instance of the admixture of diluvian with paradisiac memorials'. The Argonautic voyage was a memory of the Flood, while the golden 'fleece suspended on an oak in the midst of a grove' recalled the Fall and the promise of future propitiatory atonement. However, the confounding of histories and their symbolic remembrance was itself a token of the cunning of divine providence, for such instances exhibited 'just that kind of variation from the original and true history, which proves that there was no collusion between the borrowed tradition, and the inspired account'. Bridges reckoned it 'absurd to look for entire consistency' in pagano-patriarchal legend; the 'very inconsistencies' in heathen tales bore 'an unwilling' – hence all the more credible and robust – 'witness to the truth'.[37]

The Reverend John Bathurst Deane (1797–1887) in *The worship of the serpent traced throughout the world* (1830) found stories of triumphant gods and vanquished serpents in the mythologies of Egypt, India, Greece, Persia, Scandinavia and Mexico. Deane contended that there was 'nothing in the

---

[37] Matthew Bridges, *The testimony of profane antiquity to the account given by Moses of Paradise and the Fall of Man* (London, 1825), pp. 6–7, 20–1, 42, 67, 72, 82–5, 93, 111–12, 117, 140–1, 144–6, 157, 160, 171, 183–5, 210, 217, 230.

belief which would *naturally* suggest itself to the imaginations of people so remote and so unconnected'. He was forced to conclude, therefore, that 'where so many independent traditions coincide, the most ancient must be the one from which all the rest were originally derived'. All other traditions were dimly remembered versions of the Hebrew story of the Fall. Deane aimed to 'establish, by the testimony of heathen authorities, the credibility of the temptation and fall of man in Paradise, by the agency of Satan in a serpent's form'. While he noted that 'accidental circumstances' undoubtedly affected heathen religions, leading to a proliferation of 'gods and altars, worship and sacrifices', he also perceived within the rich diversity of paganism the uncanny spread of 'the sacred serpent from Paradise to Peru'. Indeed, the serpent was, he reasoned, 'the most ancient of the heathen gods', the common underpinning of all pagan systems. Not only had accidental accretions produced a diversity of religions out of a single aboriginal serpent idolatry, but the different characteristics of the serpent-god had themselves been personified into a plurality of deities. Deane concluded that 'no nations were so geographically remote, or so religiously discordant, but that one – and only one – superstitious characteristic was common to all', namely 'the same sacred serpent'. The heathen corroboration of Genesis was, however, even more striking in its correspondence with a Christian original. The world's pagan religions not only 'preserved' in their mythologies a memory of the Fall, but also exhibited 'a strong vestige of the promise of redemption'. Deane noted that 'the bruising of the serpent' was found in the legends of Egypt, India, Greece, Persia, Scandinavia and Mexico. Everywhere he perceived both 'a triumphant god, and a vanquished serpent'. Apollo, Hercules, Krishna and Thor had all slayed dragons or serpents. Surely, Deane reckoned, this was unlikely to be a 'casual coincidence', but provided overwhelming evidence of the universal incorporation of central Christian truths within the core of what seemed – superficially at least – to be the sprawling polytheistic mess of supposed heathen un-truth.[38]

Alexander Lindsay, the 25th Earl of Crawford, contended that 'corroborative proofs of the Fall' were 'almost universal over the globe', and could be traced in 'traditions of a golden age, and of the degeneracy of man' as well as 'in the Ophite worship, or adoration of malignant deities incarnate in the serpent form'. There was, moreover, an 'obscure expectation' found in Hindu, Greek and Norse mythologies of 'a divine avenger, destined to deliver man by slaying the serpent'.[39]

---

[38] John Bathurst Deane, *The worship of the serpent traced throughout the world* (London, 1830), esp. pp. vii–viii, 40, 359, 367–70.
[39] Alexander Lindsay, *A letter to a friend on the evidences and theory of Christianity* (London, 1841), p. 31.

So great indeed was the quantity of scholarly, or pseudo-scholarly, literature on the subject of ophiolatry by the middle of the nineteenth century that the classical antiquary and historian John Kenrick (1788–1877) gave vent to the complaint that 'the beguiling of Eve was the first, but by no means the last, piece of mischief which the serpent has inflicted on mankind. We reckon among the evils clearly traceable to his spite against the human race, the many unprofitable volumes which he has caused to be written respecting himself and his operations.'[40] Still the problem persisted.

According to Farrar, an Anglican ethnologist sceptical of the apologetic value placed on mythographical evidence, legends of evil serpents could be quite simply explained in naturalistic terms: 'why have we been so often told that the story of the Fall explains the enmity of mankind to the serpent, when such detestation arises at once from its deadly venom, small dull eye, and hideous aspect?' Serpent legends were rather part of a whole class of myths, Farrar contended, which were 'wholly unconnected with revelation, though constantly referred to it', that is 'independent natural beliefs', arising from humankind's relationship with the natural world. Did it really take exposure to the story of the Fall of Man for the peoples of pagan cultures to devise stories of evil serpents?[41]

Moreover, in one of the foundational texts of the new science of anthropology, E. B. Tylor (1832–1917) let forth an exasperated riff on the same theme. In *Primitive Culture* (1871) Tylor lamented the way in which the subject of serpent-worship had been appropriated by 'speculative' mythographers, 'who mixed it up with occult philosophies, Druidical mysteries, and that portentous nonsense called the "Arkite symbolism"', for it was 'in itself a rational and instructive subject of inquiry'.[42] Purged of theological excrescence, Tylor argued, the subject of serpent-worship was grist to the new science.[43] Yet Tylor's forerunners within the embryonic study of primitive cultures were less fastidious about the distinction between the disinterested description of social phenomena and the apologetic significance of social facts.

There is much in the chequered lineage of early anthropology from which today's anthropologists – a predominantly secular profession – might

---

[40] John Kenrick, 'Serpent worship and the age of Stonehenge', *Prospective Review*, vol. 27 (July 1851), pp. 299–307, at p. 299.
[41] F. W. Farrar, 'Traditions, real and fictitious', *Transactions of the Ethnological Society of London*, vol. 3 (1865), pp. 298–307, at p. 300.
[42] E. B. Tylor, *Primitive culture* (2 vols., London, 1871), vol. II, p. 217.
[43] *Ibid.*, vol. II, pp. 215–20.

wish to avert their gaze. Although by the late nineteenth century anthropologists lurked – at best – on the heretical margins of Christianity, like William Robertson Smith (1846–94),[44] or, more commonly, engaged in *deliberately* subversive debunking of Christian assumptions, the deeper origins of the discipline in the first half of the nineteenth century found it implicated in the globalising strategies of Christian apologetics. Although the Enlightenment featured among the subject's multiple lines of ancestry, so too did a theologically driven approach to anthropological questions.

What form did these glimpses of the unmentionable take? The early nineteenth-century prehistory of the discipline was dominated by the search for unity – for an Adamic, Edenic, patriarchal, Noachic and pre-Babelian unity – which underlay, it was assumed, the world's languages, races, cultures, religions and mythologies. In the beginning was the primeval unity described in the first ten chapters of the book of Genesis. The cultural, ethnic, religious and linguistic diversity of the world needed to be explained in terms which conserved the core truths and intellectual authority of Genesis.

This proto-anthropology was predicated not on difference, but on the ways in which anthropological, biological, medical, philological and mythological researches were capable of transforming apparent, but merely superficial, differences into basic resemblance and indeed commonality. Apologetic anthropology investigated difference, variety and otherness in order to reconstruct a primeval unity from which the world's seemingly – but only seemingly – distinct races and cultures ultimately derived. Did not all humankind descend from Adam and Eve? Was not original sin a universal condition which sprang biologically from the loins of the first pair of humans? Were not Noah and his family – with their shared language, race and religion – the only survivors of the universal flood? Skin-deep racial diversity needed to be explained in such a way as conserved the sacred truth of aboriginal monogenesis. All races sprang from a common origin, and physical anthropology had to account for that fact. A primeval language accessible to all humanity preceded the confounding of languages at Babel. By the nineteenth century, philologists and lexicographers had begun to identify clusters of languages kin to one another, but between the clusters lay problematic and seemingly impassable deserts of incomprehensibility. The world's rich linguistic variety needed to be sifted to find common elements – of grammar, diction and so forth – which might be deployed to build bridges across the apparent gulfs which separated one

---

[44] W. Johnstone (ed.), *William Robertson Smith: essays in reassessment* (Sheffield, 1995).

language group from another. Similarly, the world's religions, deities, rites and legends might well yield a unitary 'key to all mythologies'. Polytheistic diversity, therefore, might be plausibly shoehorned into a single patriarchal Ur-religion and common history.

The subject areas which eventually became full-fledged academic disciplines, such as comparative religion, linguistics and anthropology, owed a debt – however indirect – to the globalising imperatives of Christian apologetic. Several of the most characteristic features of nineteenth-century anthropology were prefigured in the Christian search for collateral evidences. Social facts of the sort which became the objects of anthropological research had for previous enquirers possessed a theological meaning.

There were different ways for mythographers to reconcile serpent-worship with the defence of Christian orthodoxy. For James Cowles Prichard – a pioneer in the fields of anthropology and linguistics, fields which he attempted to align with a Christian monogenist position regarding the origin of all races from a single source[45] – serpent-worship was not a relic of the Fall. Rather, in his *Analysis of the Egyptian Mythology* (1819), the question of ophiolatry was subordinated to a sophisticated argument – independent of scripture – proving that the origins of religion lay in divine revelation. Prichard argued that if religion had arisen originally from nature (rather than revelation), as the deists claimed, then its trajectory of development would have shadowed the progress of the human mind, moving from a crude and sensual polytheism towards a purer and more philosophical monotheistic belief. However, the facts of ancient religion generally ran in the opposite direction, with pagan religions undergoing a process of corruption from primitive simplicity to debased polytheism. According to Prichard, what had happened was obvious: the original truth of a revealed monotheism had been gradually lost as the various emanations and attributes of the single deity had become personified into a multiplicity of individual gods. In Egypt religion had become utterly debased, with the people worshipping various animals as gods. Yet, Prichard argued, the original truth had not been entirely lost, at least to an elite within Egypt. While a hereditary caste of priests gulled the people with the worship of animals, including serpents, the priests had preserved elements of the primitive revelation within their own esoteric cult.

From apologetics of the Prichardian sort, anthropology acquired its ambitious global perspective. Not only did British anthropology develop – as

---

[45] For the place of mythography in Prichard's ethnology, see H. F. Augstein, *James Cowles Prichard's anthropology* (Amsterdam, 1999), pp. 183–219.

Fish-gods, Floods and Serpent-worship 193

some commentators have argued – as a simple offshoot of power relations within a global empire, it also emerged as an ironic by-product of a theological project to make sense of the world's teeming diversity.[46] Of course, historians of anthropology have addressed the role of Christian missionaries as pioneers of ethnographic fieldwork, but the connection with Christianity went deeper than mere methods of approach deriving from the acculturation which was a necessary prelude to the process of conversion; it was also a matter – at least initially – of a shared intellectual vision.

As early as the 1840s – and in defence of scriptural truth – Anne Flinders had noted that the 'chief feature of every pagan mythology is a slain god'. Now this, she calculated, was a most curious phenomenon, for 'the very essence of deity is immortality, and if a god dies, in his own nature, he becomes a mere mortal, and consequently ceases to be a god altogether'. If logic dictated that gods could not die, and the very idea of a slain god was 'a thing repugnant to the natural reason and imagination of man', then naturalistic explanations would not suffice to explain such legends. Therefore, she argued, such stories could only arise from patriarchal 'tradition', notably 'a corrupted remembrance of original truth'.[47] Needless to say, half a century later, the anthropologist James Frazer – turning Flinders's position on its head – would in *The Golden Bough* (1890) derive a very different conclusion from this strange phenomenon of the slain god.

If Frazer was the ironic culminating reversal of the 'key to all mythologies', there were other traces of a curious descent. Anthropology in the decades preceding *The Golden Bough*, though detached from Christian objectives and sometimes daringly irreligious in its implications, bore traces of the collateral apologetics from which it indirectly descended. Methods of cross-cultural comparison, the interest in survivals, questions of descent and diffusion, the decoding of symbolism, were all – if only in part – anthropology's bequest from Christian ethnology. Of course, there were other – less obtrusively religious – wells from which anthropologists drew, most obviously the Scottish Enlightenment and utilitarianism; nevertheless, the theology of evidences went some way towards supplying the shape and strategies – if not the substance – of late nineteenth- and early twentieth-century anthropology.

The tensions between the unavowed pedigree of anthropology in apologetics and the discipline's emergence as an irreligious social science came into focus in the late 1860s and early 1870s in debates over the question of

---

[46] G. Stocking, *Victorian anthropology* (New York, 1987), pp. 48–53.
[47] Anne Flinders, *The connexion between revelation and mythology* (London, 1845), pp. 78–9.

how to interpret serpent-worship. *Middlemarch* was conceived and published during a period of intense and sometimes disquieting controversy about the provenance of a phenomenon which had once seemed to provide cast-iron justification for the historicity of Genesis.

The Scots-born historian of ancient Indian art and architecture, James Fergusson (1808–86), provoked considerable discussion with *Tree and Serpent Worship* (1868; 2nd edn, 1873) which relocated the problem in the field of race science. Serpent-worship, he argued, was a kind of racial 'fossil', a remnant of an ancient and unsophisticated primeval people who had preceded the Aryans and the Semites. 'Animal worship', declared Fergusson, was 'perfectly consistent with the lower intellectual status of the Turanian races' and it was 'essentially among them only' that it was found to prevail. No Semitic or Aryan people – being 'higher' races – had ever consciously 'adopted' serpent-worship as a 'form of faith'. Nevertheless, serpent-worship could sometimes be found in Aryan and Semitic cultures, and as such constituted 'a valuable ethnographic test of the presence of Turanian blood in the veins of any people among whom it is found to prevail'. The role of the serpent in the Old Testament Fergusson regarded as 'an outcrop from the older underlying strata of the population'. Fergusson traced the beginnings of Judaism proper from the time of Abraham, but the people of Israel had been prone to 'backsliding', and had occasionally succumbed to revivals of the serpent-worship championed by 'the pre-existing races among whom they were located'. Similarly, Fergusson likened ophiolatry in parts of the Aryan world to 'the tares of a previous crop springing up among the stems of a badly-cultivated field of wheat'. Fergusson interpreted Hercules's slaying of a serpent as a myth which represented the conquest by an Aryan people of an earlier body of Turanian settlers in ancient Greece.[48] In response, the archaeologist and art historian John Burley Waring (1823–75), who had scant regard for 'the almost boundless sea of fable and fabulous ideas connected with the serpent' – in which he included the 'childlike naïveté' of the 'Jewish fable of the Fall of mankind' – also rejected the argument that cults of tree- and serpent-worship were celebrated in tandem; they were 'as a rule … distinct forms of worship, and only occasionally found in combination'.[49]

Fergusson's was not the only major point of reference in the debate over serpent-worship. So too was the series of lengthy articles in the *Fortnightly Review* in 1869–70 by the Scots lawyer and pioneering social anthropologist

[48] James Fergusson, *Tree and serpent worship* (2nd edn, London, 1873), pp. 3, 7, 13–14, 35, 42.
[49] J. B. Waring, *Ceramic art in remote ages* (London, 1874), pp. 17, 21.

John F. McLennan (1827–81) on the subject of 'The worship of plants and animals'.[50] McLennan's articles startle the reader familiar with *Middlemarch* and its targets, for McLennan's own principal target appears to be Bryant, supposedly a long-discredited mythographer. Furthermore, McLennan proposes his own key to all mythologies, almost in those very words. Fetishism – the notion that spirits resided in animals and plants – was 'at the root of all mythologies'. McLennan's real subject, one of his signal contributions to anthropology, was totemism, a version of fetishism 'plus certain peculiarities'. These comprised the association of a special fetish for each tribe, its hereditary transmission through the maternal line and the role of totemism in exogamous marriage practices. Indeed, McLennan had arrived at the study of totemism from an original point of departure in the anthropology of marriage. In an earlier work, *Primitive Marriage* (1865), McLennan showed how the social practices of marriage had evolved from a primeval promiscuity co-existing with female infanticide, which had led to the phenomenon first of aggressive bride capture from other tribes and eventually to the custom of exogamy. In these early stages, polyandry predominated along with a recognition only of uterine kinship through the mother. Patriarchal monandry – marriage involving a single male, whether monogamous or polygamous – developed later. McLennan's work on totemism was a natural outgrowth of his work on primeval marriage and kinship systems. Totems had descended through the prevailing maternal system of kinship that had operated in the early stages of tribal exogamy. The term totem, McLennan noted, derived from 'the name given by certain tribes of American Indians to the animal or plant which, from time immemorial, each of the tribe has had as its sacred or consecrated animal or plant'. However, totemism itself was a universal phenomenon. The aboriginal Australian term for the tribal symbol was, for example, the 'kobong'. Tribal lineages believed themselves 'descended from the totem, and, in every case, to be, nominally at least, of its breed or species'. This had a central function in the operation of kinship and marriage systems. Animal worship was not what it had seemed to previous generations of scholars. McLennan – who had read Fergusson's recent work on *Tree and Serpent Worship* – singled out apologetic interpretations of serpent-worship for deconstruction: 'We take the case of the serpent first, because for several reasons it has been more studied than any other. The serpent faith was very widespread, and it has attracted special notice from the part assigned to the

---

[50] Eliot read McLennan during the gestation of *Middlemarch*, see J. C. Pratt and V. A. Neufeldt (eds.), *George Eliot's Middlemarch notebooks* (Berkeley and Los Angeles, 1979), Appendix, p. 284.

serpent in Genesis, in connection with the fall of man. Faber and Bryant have both pretty fully investigated this subject.'

McLennan challenged neither the ubiquity nor great antiquity of serpent-worship. But it was emblematic of something other than Genesis. Sometimes, indeed, Bryant was closer than he knew to the nature of serpent totemism, but was blinded by his convictions: 'Whole peoples, says Bryant, had the serpent-name, and counted themselves as being of the serpent-breed.' Exactly so, contended McLennan; serpent totemism rested on the notion of descent from a serpent ancestor. The insights of totemism also offered McLennan the opportunity once and for all to expunge Bryant's Arkite theories from serious discourse. Fish-gods and half-fish mermen and mermaid deities were exposed as the tribal totems of fish-tribes: 'We have seen fishes giving stock names to tribes of men now existing, and can understand how, having been totems, they should have become gods to the tribes that had them in that character.' Another 'arkite symbol' of Bryant's, the dove, met the same fate. Bryant's 'Arkite system', McLennan concluded, was 'worth nothing, either as an explanation of animal worship, or as evidence of the Deluge having occurred'.[51]

A decade later, Robertson Smith, a believing anthropologist and biblical critic, Arabist and embattled professor within the Free Church of Scotland, would confirm the applicability of McLennan's insights to the chosen people of the Old Testament. In his essay 'Animal worship and animal tribes among the Arabs and in the Old Testament', Smith revealed in some detail the presence of archaic totemism in the beliefs and social system of the Hebrews. David, indeed, seemed 'to have belonged to the serpent stock'. No longer did serpent-worship proffer the promise of corroboration; rather, in a signal reversal of the old tropes of pagano-popery, the Hebrews themselves were now revealed as having harboured heathen superstitions 'not one whit less degrading than those of the most savage nations'.[52]

However, back in the late 1860s and early 1870s totemism was not the only potent threat to the decaying authority of Casaubonish mythographers. In his two-volume work, *Ancient Faiths Embodied in Ancient Names* (1st edn, 1868–9; 2nd edn 1872–3) Thomas Inman (1820–76) reversed the direction of mythographical speculation about the serpent. Rather than

---

[51] J. F. McLennan, 'The worship of animals and plants', *Fortnightly Review* (October 1869), pp. 407–27, at pp. 408–9, 413, 422, 427; (November 1869), pp. 562–82, at pp. 563–9; (February 1870), pp. 194–216, at pp. 195, 201, 209; McLennan, *Primitive marriage* (Edinburgh, 1865).

[52] William Robertson Smith, 'Animal worship and animal tribes among the Arabs and in the Old Testament', *Journal of Philology*, vol. 9 (1880), pp. 75–100, at pp. 99–100.

interpreting pagan myths as corrupted versions of Judaeo-Christian truth, Inman contended that all religions – Christian and pagan alike – developed out of a basic urge to celebrate human sexuality and procreation. Sex was the link which explained the similarities between Hebrew and Hindu religions. Inman noted that 'the cobra in India and the asp in Egypt' were 'able to raise and distend themselves, thus becoming erect'. Hence, snakes in ancient cultures had become 'emblematic of male activity, and covertly represented the phallus'. No wonder serpent-worship was universal. The meeting of Eve – representative of 'the female fissure' – and the serpent was an easily decoded allegory of the encounter of human reproductive organs. However, Inman dared to go further. Trinitarian deities – whether of the Father, Son and Holy Spirit type, or like Brahma–Vishnu–Shiva – derived from 'the phallus and its two appendages'. Latin provided the wispiest of veils for spelling out in graphic detail the implications of his researches: the 'triple idea of the Creator', he argued, 'is to be found in fascinum cum testibus duobus' (the phallus with two testes). The Christian Trinity, it transpired, was 'a modest adaptation of an ancient and indecent myth'. By extension, the pattern of 'four great gods' found in so many religions – as in, say, the Trinity plus the Virgin Mary – were representative of the 'threefold lingam and the single yoni'.[53]

The anthropologist Charles Staniland Wake (1835–1910) proceeded on a similar track, though significant detours brought him to a different destination. In a paper read before the Anthropological Society in 1870, entitled 'The influence of the phallic idea in the religions of antiquity', Wake traced the phallic origin of many central elements in ancient mythology and folklore from the Mosaic account of the Fall to such practices as circumcision and the use of wedding rings (an obvious symbol of coitus). 'The fundamental basis of Christianity', he argued, was 'more purely "phallic" than that of any other religion now existing.' However, Wake – who was alert to the emergent idea of totemism – eschewed bluntly reductive conclusions, and remained intrigued by the elision in ancient religions of the phallic idea and ancestor-worship – a connected but rather different concept. Moreover, fecundity and father-worship – themselves hard to disentangle – had also been associated, in turn, with the sun, another life-giving body and source of fruitfulness. Wake detected a complex set of linkages among ancestral father-gods, phallic worship and solar deities.[54]

[53] Thomas Inman, *Ancient faiths embodied in ancient names* (1868–9: 2nd edn, 2 vols., 1872–3), vol. I, pp. 89, 496, 498, 532; vol. II, p. 359.
[54] C. S. Wake, 'Influence of the phallic idea in the religions of antiquity', in Horder Westrupp and C. S. Wake (eds.), *Ancient symbol worship* (1875: repr. London and New York, 1972), pp. 36, 61, 69, 77–8.

In a further essay, devoted specifically to 'The origin of serpent-worship', Wake placed emphasis on the notion that ancestor-worship was the moving force behind the cult of snake gods, and explained how the spirit of a tribal ancestor was in due course translated into the ether and transformed into a sky god. Hence, the curious connexions Wake noted between solar and serpent deities.[55]

All was not lost, however, for vicarage Casaubons. Some apologetic mythographers cleverly appropriated anthropological and archaeological findings and methods for their own ends. Indeed, in response to the recent subversions of serpent-based apologetics, there appeared a sudden rash of Casaubonish readings of ancient ophiolatry. In 'The serpent myths of ancient Egypt' (1873), W. R. Cooper, secretary of the Society for Biblical Archaeology, contended that it was impossible to account for the strange particularities of pagan serpent mythology – as in Egypt – except as repositories of Judaeo-Christian dogma.[56] John Phené, a member of the Anthropological Institute of Great Britain and Ireland and of the British Archaeological Association who was also involved in the Palestine Exploration Fund and the Society for Biblical Archaeology, was obsessed with serpent symbolism, and pressed both archaeological and anthropological evidence into the service of apologetics. Modern ethnographic findings from the Americas reinforced a Christian interpretation of serpent-worship. Consider, Phené urged, 'the points of agreement at the greatest geographical distances'. The conjunction with tree-worship was, moreover, 'strongly corroborative' of 'a common tradition' ultimately derived from a memory of Genesis. Similarly, a further connection between solar- and serpent-worship suggested an ethical dimension – a battle of good and evil at the heart of pagan mythologies. One fact was so strikingly distinctive and peculiar that it defied any other explanation than that of collateral apologetics: how could one explain, Phené asked, the tradition that celebrants of the ancient mysteries called out 'eve' or 'eva' when they held living snakes in their hands? Anthropological insight could, nevertheless, produce a better – and more sceptical – understanding of Christian folklore. Phené reinterpreted the hagiographical legend of St Patrick driving the snakes out of Ireland as an allegory of ethnic displacement: 'it is clear that men addicted to serpent worship, and not serpents themselves were the fugitives'.[57]

---

[55] C. S. Wake, 'The origin of serpent worship', *Journal of the Anthropological Institute of Great Britain and Ireland*, vol. 2 (1873), pp. 373–86.
[56] W. R. Cooper, *The serpent myths of ancient Egypt* (Victoria Institute, London, 1873).
[57] John Phené, *On prehistoric traditions and customs in connection with the sun and serpent worship* (2nd edn, repr. from *Journal of the Victoria Institute*, London, 1875), pp. 25–7, 36, 38.

Fish-gods, Floods and Serpent-worship

Eliot was well-versed in this debate. She had read much of the oeuvre of Max-Müller,[58] but was also acquainted with the anthropological work of McLennan on totemism.[59] *Middlemarch* appeared in the midst of a vigorous set of controversies among anthropologists, archaeologists, race-scientists, philologists and apologetic mythographers, which revolved around the controverted significance of serpent-worship. Eliot does not deal with the debate directly, but it provides the backdrop to contemporary understandings of mythography in the years when she alighted on the character of Mr Casaubon. The transition from apologetics to anthropology is part of the unacknowledged iceberg of intellectual history which lurks below the surface of *Middlemarch*. However, in the early 1870s it remained an open question – though not, of course, to Eliot – whether collateral proofs of fish-gods and serpent cults were something of an absurdity, or did indeed vindicate scripture.

---

[58] Fleishman, *Intellectual life*, pp. 7. 47, 178.
[59] A. Fleishman, *George Eliot's reading: a chronological list*, supplement to no. 54–5, *George Eliot–George Henry Lewes Studies* (2008), pp. 46, 52–3, 55.

CHAPTER 7

Epilogue: The Keys to All Mythology in 1872

> But it was clear enough to her that he would expect her to devote herself to sifting those mixed heaps of material, which were to be the doubtful illustration of principles still more doubtful ... And now she pictured to herself the days, and months, and years which she must spend in sorting what might be called shattered mummies, and fragments of a tradition which was itself a mosaic wrought from crushed ruins – sorting them as food for a theory which was already withered in the birth like an elfin child. (*Middlemarch*, ch. 48)
>
> With his taper stuck before him he forgot the absence of windows, and in bitter manuscript remarks on other men's notions about the solar deities, he had become indifferent to the sunlight. (*Middlemarch*, ch. 20)
>
> The subject Mr Casaubon has chosen is as changing as chemistry: new discoveries are constantly making new points of view. (*Middlemarch*, ch. 22)

The death of Mr Casaubon part way through the narrative of *Middlemarch* – at a point where even his wife, who had married him as an aspirant amanuensis, has come to recognise the futility of his project – is also meant to signal the extinction of Christian mythography as a viable form of intellectual life in the England of the 1830s. Already overtaken by pioneering developments in the German science of mythology, it was discredited and lacked any intellectual cachet, or so Eliot would have us believe. No longer could myth be used to support biblical truth; rather, the Bible had itself been exposed as a kind of mythology. A relic of a misguided, bygone antiquarianism, mythographical apologetics had no place in the reformed – and demythologised – world of social improvement and science.

However, as we have seen, the British wars of mythography did not come to an end in the 1830s. Across the four decades between the setting in which the action of *Middlemarch* takes place and the era of the book's publication, mythographers went on acquiring new forms of apologetic weaponry. Mere pea-shooters these might prove, as Eliot rightly perceived and as we know in hindsight, but at the time developments in mythography and in related bodies of scholarship such as Assyriology, Egyptology and Middle Eastern archaeology seemed to many commentators like the

Epilogue: The Keys to All Mythology in 1872

heavy artillery of a new military counter-revolution.[1] Indeed, by a delicious irony, 1872 – the very year *Middlemarch* was published – witnessed a major leap forward in corroborative apologetics.

An uncritical Casaubonish quest for a key to all mythologies might well be regarded by the first readers of *Middlemarch* as a quixotic tour down a cul-de-sac of irrelevance; but, in fact, by 1872, recent discoveries in the archaeology of the Middle East allied to the decipherment of long-lost scripts from the region held out some prospect that scholars might be able to rescue a core of historical truth from the ancient legends of the countries adjacent to the lands of the ancient Hebrews.

Ironically, the beginnings of the counter-insurgency can be traced back to the era of Mr Casaubon's demise. As early as the 1830s the Congregationalist theologian George Redford expressed optimism that 'our advanced position in science proves a vantage ground for the further corroboration of scripture'. New discoveries, he claimed, were 'at the present time, supplying numerous verifications, which could not have been anticipated by any projected calculation of probabilities'. Whereas in the era of Volney the study of pagan civilisations had constituted 'one of the main supports of infidelity', the onward march of scholarship seemed – somewhat unexpectedly to the scoffers – to have reinforced rather than overwhelmed the besieged citadel of Old Testament chronology. At last, 'the day', once so confidently awaited by 'these vain boasters' – Bailly, Voltaire and Volney – 'is arrived ... The hieroglyphics are read'. Notwithstanding the eager anticipation of sceptics and infidels that sacred history would be wrecked on the evidence of ancient Egypt, recent decipherments in Egyptology 'all testify that their discoveries tend uniformly to support the accuracy of the Mosaic records'. The 'zodiacs of Dendera and Esneh, the Rosetta stone, and the tombs of the Egyptian kings, have refused to supply any contradiction of the sacred record'. Of course, continued Redford, the enemies of Christianity turned to other heathen sources in the un-pious hope that these would prove the wreck of orthodoxy: 'At one time it was thought that Assyria and Chaldea must be rich in materials for the confutation of the brief chronology of scripture', and on fuller investigation 'would supply ample proof of an origin incomparably older than Moses assigns to them.' Again, however, 'all the monuments were mute, or the few that

---

[1] D. Gange, *Dialogues of the dead: Egyptology in British culture and religion, 1822–1922* (Oxford, 2013), see esp. pp. 3, 7, 25, 77, 124, 126, 138, 157; T. Larsen, 'Nineveh' and M. Seymour, 'Babylon', in D. Gange and M. Ledger-Lomas (eds.), *Cities of God: the Bible and archaeology in nineteenth-century Britain* (Cambridge, 2013), pp. 111–35, 164–96.

spoke disappointed the gainsayer, and corroborated Moses'. Nor did the evidence of India or China provide the unholy grail after which 'learned unbelievers' quested. The stupendously long chronologies of the ancient Asian civilisations turned out themselves to be fantastical, argued Redford. The supposed gigantic timescales of Asian chronology which seemed likely to obliterate the contours of sacred history had 'dwindled into dwarves'.[2]

Cory contended similarly that it was only in the nineteenth century that a proper mythographical 'connexion' between heathen legends and scripture had at last become possible. Hitherto the remains of heathen mythology had been 'too much broken' to present to the mythographer 'the entire system of heathen mythology'. Although the science of mythography had suffered from a 'want of sufficient data', two recent discoveries – the newly acquired knowledge of Hindu legends and the decipherment of Egyptian hieroglyphics – had made a kind of key to all mythologies a more viable project: 'it is only by the enlarged view of the fragments of all the different nations compared with one another, and indeed, by the light afforded us within the last few years, that we have been enabled to connect them, and obtain the complete system'.[3]

Indeed, when Cory's *Ancient Fragments* was – tellingly – republished in a new and updated edition in 1876, the editor E. Richmond Hodges celebrated the progress which had been made since Cory's day: 'During the past quarter of a century a new and unexpected revelation has come to us from the plains of Mesopotamia and the banks of the Tigris.' Once upon a time, 'Nineveh was but a name, and Babylon an abstraction', but no longer. Hodges thought that orthodox scholarship stood 'upon the threshold of the temple of truth'. Indeed, 'amidst all this ruin and obscurity' it was now clear that there 'existed a *key* to unlock the treasures of the past' – the providential bequest of cuneiform, found in 'cylinders of baked clay and burnt bricks'.[4]

In the interim there had been considerable acquisitions in the materials available to collateral apologists. During the 1840s the Scots Presbyterian astronomer, Thomas Dick (1774–1857), was celebrating the turning of the tide against the specious claims of deists and infidels. Dick noted that the ancient astronomical tables of the Hindus and the

---

[2] George Redford, *Holy scripture verified* (London, 1837), pp. 14, 18–19, 176–8, 180.
[3] Isaac Preston Cory, *Mythological inquiry into the recondite theology of the heathens* (London, 1837), pp. 3–4, 87–8.
[4] E. Richmond Hodges, 'On the origin, progress and results of hieroglyphic and cuneiform decipherment', in Hodges (ed.), *Cory's ancient fragments* (new and enlarged edn, London, 1876), pp. xvi–xvii, xxx.

Egyptian zodiac at Dendera, then thought to be about 15,000 years old, had been 'triumphantly exhibited by certain sceptical philosophers about thirty or forty years ago, as insuperable arguments against the truth of the Mosaic chronology'. But now, Dick smugly reported, the Indian tables had been exposed as more recent compilations and the zodiacs at Dendera – once 'confidently expected to revolutionize the whole Christian world' – had been shown to belong to Roman Egypt of the first few centuries AD.[5]

In the same decade, William Osburn contended that the decipherment of hieroglyphics, far from subverting the Pentateuch (as the deists had assumed it would), had rather 'subserved the cause of scriptural truth'. Whereas Dupuis had purportedly 'demonstrated' that the circular zodiac of Dendera was four thousand years older than the Christian era, and other sceptics had claimed a highly subversive antiquity of 17,000 years for the temple at Esneh, a reading of the hieroglyphics had punctured these ill-founded assaults on sacred chronology. The discovery that the name of Augustus featured on the zodiac at Dendera and Antoninus on the temple of Esneh revealed these instead to belong to the era of the early Roman Empire. The new science of Egyptology raised upon the painstaking code-breaking of Jean-François Champollion (1790–1832) and Thomas Young (1773–1829) had, contrary to the vain expectations of the Volney school, 'exercised much influence in exposing the pretensions of a class of arrogant writers upon antiquity, who had assumed a tone of all but infallibility in perverting every thing ... to support their opposition to the Bible'. By a happy irony, no longer were the 'time-worn monuments' of ancient Egypt 'the favourite resort of modern infidelity'.[6]

The monuments of ancient Egypt might well yield up the key to all mythologies, but it was not clear whether these insights would serve to vindicate Christian orthodoxy, or instead open the way for further attacks on the historicity of the Bible. In *Horae Aegyptiacae* (1851), Reginald Poole (1832–95) recalibrated the chronology of ancient Egypt so that it might 'confirm' rather than 'contradict' sacred history. In particular, Poole used archaeological evidence to show the 'contemporaneousness' (rather than chronological succession) of 'certain of the first seventeen dynasties' in

---

[5] Thomas Dick, *Discoveries of modern geology not inconsistent with revelation* (Edinburgh, 1842), p. 10.
[6] [William Osburn], *The antiquities of Egypt; with a particular notice of those that illustrate the sacred scriptures* (London, 1841), pp. 79–80, 235. See also Osburn, *Ancient Egypt, her testimony to the truth of the Bible* (London, 1846). For the achievements of Young and Champollion, see J. Ray, *The Rosetta Stone and the rebirth of ancient Egypt* (Cambridge, MA, 2007).

Manetho's list of pharaohs. The history of Egypt was more abbreviated, it transpired, than it seemed at first sight.[7]

Undeniably, there were setbacks. William Brown Galloway, the vicar of St Mark's in Regent's Park, lamented that the 'deadliest form of infidel attack' on Christian truth so far had been 'the union of German rationalistic criticism with Egyptological studies'. The principal villain was the Prussian Egyptologist Lepsius whose researches exploded the traditional parameters of Biblical chronology. Yet even Galloway perceived a glimmer of light in the field of Egyptology, not least from the more sober investigations of Sir Gardener Wilkinson (1797–1875).[8]

Emerging disciplines offered opportunities as well as threats. In his 1859 Bampton Lectures, George Rawlinson (1812–1902) warned that the world's mythologies could not be plundered willy-nilly by uncritical apologists hoping thereby to ground scripture on an independent and unbiased historical foundation. While heathen legends did contain some 'dim knowledge' of primeval history, Rawlinson argued, the 'historical element' was 'so small', 'so overlaid with fable' and combined with ingredients which were 'palpably imaginative', that 'no manner of reliance' could be placed on these 'pretended histories', which had not the 'slightest title to be used as tests whereby to try the authenticity of any other narrative'. However, Rawlinson was not about to surrender the historical claims of the Old Testament in the face of the demythologising critics of 'German neology'. Recent developments in the study of hieroglyphics and cuneiform held out the prospect that a more sophisticated, selective and critical theology of collateral evidences might be raised on the robust foundations of the new sciences of Egyptology and Assyriology. Rawlinson rejoiced, with good reason he believed, in the cumulative effect of careful piecemeal discoveries, noting 'the multiplication of minute parts of agreement between the sacred and the profane, which resulted from the advances made in deciphering the Assyrian, Babylonian, Persian and Egyptian records'. Assyriology, in particular, seemed to offer a copious 'supply of fresh illustrations of the Mosaic narrative'. Rawlinson noted, with some optimism, that the findings of 'modern research' were 'perpetually adding fresh weight' to the profane collateral evidences to the truth of the Pentateuch.[9]

James Reddie, the Secretary of the Victoria Institute, a learned society established in 1865 with the object of defending the truths of scripture

---

[7] Reginald Stuart Poole, *Horae Aegyptiacae* (London, 1851), esp. pp. 79–80, 210.
[8] William Brown Galloway, *Egypt's record of time* (London, 1869), pp. 2–3, 11.
[9] George Rawlinson, *The historical evidences of the truth of the scripture records stated anew, with special reference to the doubts and discoveries of modern times* (London, 1859), pp. v–vii, 54–5, 75, 77.

against 'the oppositions of science, falsely so called',[10] detected 'converging proofs' of the Old Testament's historicity. What particularly arrested his attention was the surprising unity which underlay the otherwise 'apparently arbitrary character' of mythological figures found by archaeologists working on *different* ancient civilisations: 'Similar figures are found upon the Dendera plansiphere and zodiac of Esneh, and upon sarcophagi from Egypt, and landmark-stones from Assyria'. There was 'nothing in nature to suggest them', he contended, yet they were 'found nearly identical among the ancient nations of the old world, and sufficiently similar even in America, to indicate the same common origin'.[11] Had archaeology confirmed the key to all mythologies?

A confident expectation that a series of advances in Egyptology, linguistics, anthropology, cuneiform decipherment and archaeology would result in an enhanced new science of collateral evidences also surfaced in the work of the Scots Presbyterian minister the Reverend Joseph Goodsir (1815–93), who delivered a series of sermons in the spring of 1869 on the pagan corroboration of Christianity. Four of these were published at first in the *North British Advertiser* and then in an extended version as a book in 1871, *Seven Homilies on Ethnic Inspiration*. Goodsir was abreast of the latest developments in the human sciences, and in related – but as yet unpunctured – pseudo-sciences, such as the pyramidology of the Scottish astronomer Charles Piazzi Smyth (1819–1900). The evidences, according to Goodsir, were getting stronger, not weaker, and pagan mythologies – in the new light cast by the various emergent branches of comparative philology and Near Eastern archaeology – were indeed 'found to illustrate and confirm, in the manner and spirit of quite unbiased witnesses' the truths of scripture. Intellectual ingenuity had proved not to undermine scripture but to validate it. Goodsir was delighted by the irony that 'guesses made at the end of the last, or beginning of this century on the strength of Biblical history, have been proved correct in unexpected and remarkable modes'. Indeed, Goodsir firmly believed that the science of collateral evidences progressed like any other, and he ranked the major figures in the scientific search for the key to all mythologies in teleological terms. Bryant, for example, deserved the honour owing to a pioneer in the discipline, but he had lacked 'that wider knowledge of mythology, ethnography, and language gained since his day', and had lapsed – inevitably enough – into 'erroneous explanations of ethnographic and linguistic facts' and some 'hasty and untenable results'.

[10] 'Objects', *Journal of the Transactions of the Victoria Institute*, vol. 1 (1867), p. vi.
[11] James Reddie, 'On the various theories of man's past and present condition', *Journal of the Transactions of the Victoria Institute*, vol. 1 (1867), pp. 174–98, at p. 194.

Faber marked an improvement on the mythography of Bryant, not least in his access to the insights of Sanskrit scholarship. However, there had been a series of 'rapid advances' in the years after Faber's works. Rich insights had been derived from the study of language groups, which corresponded significantly with the divisions of the three lineages of the Noachids, namely the descendants of Ham, Shem and Japhet. The resulting science of comparative philology, as well as major achievements in Egyptology and Middle Eastern archaeology, had revolutionised the science of evidences. In particular, Sir Henry Rawlinson's work on the 'Chaldean Bible' appeared to depict 'primeval events ... written by the Chaldeans themselves on bricks in post-diluvian times'. The cuneiform bricks were the most 'marvellous corroboration' of scripture. Far from Christian mythography being a discredited field, the amazing concordance of corroborative discoveries across the Middle East allowed scholars to 'discern certain identical fundamental facts shining through them all, and indicating unmistakably their earliest origin in a common groundwork of fact'. Moreover, ethnographic work in lands outside Europe and the Near East, particularly Polynesia and the Americas, had provided additional 'world-wide testimony' to the truths of primeval sacred history. Indeed, the discovery of a 'key' to all mythologies seemed imminent. Advances in Sanskrit and Persian, Goodsir noted, had introduced 'the use of a key to unlock the meaning of the traditions and myths of the entire Indo-Germanic races ... illustrating and confirming not only Chaldean and Egyptian traditions and myths, but, above all, the statements of the Bible'. At the very moment when *Middlemarch* and the ill-starred futility of Casaubon's 'Key to All Mythologies' were about to be launched on the world, Goodsir, who was very well-informed about the current state of play across a range of relevant disciplines, continued to perceive 'the sun of the Bible-truth ... irradiating, however dimly ... [the] highest mythologic cloud-land'.[12]

In a speech of 31 May 1869 to the Royal Asiatic Society, its incoming president Sir Henry Rawlinson (1810–95) gave 'a sketch of the progress which was being made in oriental studies, referring particularly to the labours of Mr George Smith in collecting and arranging the fragments of the Nineveh library, and expressing his conviction of the connection subsisting the Babylonish documents in our possession and the earliest Biblical notices. He had no doubt that they would be able to derive the whole of

---

[12] Joseph Goodsir, *Seven homilies on ethnic inspiration; or the evidence supplied by the pagan religions of both primaeval and later guidance and inspiration from heaven* (London and Edinburgh, 1871), pp. vii, x, 9, 13, 28, 36, 226, 234–7, 248.

Epilogue: The Keys to All Mythology in 1872

the history given in the book of Genesis from the time of Abraham from the original documents, and it was not too much to expect that almost the same facts and the same descriptions would be found in the Babylonish documents as in the Bible.'[13]

Mid-nineteenth-century mythography was not simply a subject under assault from new scientific insights such as Indo-European linguistics or the anthropology of totems; it was also a science self-consciously emerging from the doldrums. Its practitioners had long been conscious of missing links, especially a lack of first-hand knowledge of the nearby civilisations which lay largely offstage the main drama of biblical history. But now it seemed as if providence were filling in these crucial gaps.

Had apologetic mythography withered? It is hard to disentangle Eliot's wishful thinking both from our retrospective knowledge and from the messy realities of contemporary intellectual debate. Disciplines were shifting, new discoveries were being made, and (though in retrospect things became much clearer) at the time these developments did not all point in the same confident direction. In the years around 1872 the disciplinary grounds nearest to mythography were decidedly marshy, and undisputed terra firma hard to locate.

In some ways the cutting edge of intellectual life in 1872 was more hesitant, if not ambivalent, on the subject of Christianity's relationship with mythology than the world of 1830 in which Eliot had situated the unfortunate Mr Casaubon. New evidence from cuneiform discoveries had the potential not only to confirm mythographical debunkings of Christian truth, but also to reaffirm the historicity of the Pentateuch. It was not so much a question of what the archaeological evidence said, as how its significance was parsed. If the Flood was aligned with the Gilgamesh epic (discovered, as we shall see, in 1872), did this undermine the uniqueness and veracity of the Noachic Deluge or did it provide reliably unbiased external corroboration from an adjacent pagan culture of the fact of a great flood? Indeed, one of the most curious phenomena of the mid-nineteenth century was the reconversion of several important secularist leaders back to the Christian faith. The crisis of faith, which captures Eliot's own circumstances and world view, was paralleled by a 'crisis of doubt'.[14]

More than thirty years after the supposed death of mythography the Bryant school tottered on. Farrar, a fierce critic of heathen evidences, complained as late as 1864 that the mythography of Bryant was still part of the

[13] *Pall Mall Gazette* (1 June 1869), p. 7.
[14] T. Larsen, *Crisis of doubt: honest faith in nineteenth-century England* (Oxford, 2006).

intellectual currency of British life: 'It is perhaps a proof that these absurdities are not exploded, that we find Bryant's crude vagaries quoted with approbation, and at full length, in the very last edition of the *Encyclopaedia Britannica*, finished only last year.'[15]

In the early 1870s purveyors of a modified Casaubonism still abounded. The Reverend Sabine Baring-Gould (1834–1924), while conceding the 'exaggeration of Oriental imagery', contended that a 'residuum, small, no doubt, of genuine tradition' might be quarried from pagan mythologies. Much as Bryant and his contemporaries had done a century before, Baring-Gould found that the histories of the Fall and the Deluge had survived, semi-salvaged as it were, in the legends of heathen cultures.[16] The 1870 edition of Eadie's *Biblical Cyclopaedia* persisted with mythological evidences. Noah, according to the *Biblical Cyclopaedia*, was to be 'found under a great variety of names ... in Eastern mythology', stories which, however fanciful, were recognised to be 'corroborative of the ancient scriptural narrative'. Similarly, tales of mythical creatures, such as 'the dragons of Colchis and the Hesperides' and 'the hydra of Lerna', it identified as 'traditionary symbols of the early connection of Satan with man's innocence and fall'.[17]

In 1870 a group of Anglicans and Nonconformists founded the Christian Evidence Society, which, through its pamphlets and then from 1874 its short-lived *Christian Evidence Journal*, kept up a barrage of apologetic in defence of the historicity of the Bible.[18] In 1871 the Society published George Rawlinson's explication of *The Alleged Historical Difficulties of the Old and New Testaments*, the Reverend Charles Row's evaluation of *Mythical Theories of Christianity* and the Reverend F. C. Cook's *Completeness and Adequacy of the Evidences of Christianity*.

Recent developments seemed to offer further corroboration of scripture. In 1871 the Reverend Bourchier Wrey Savile (1817–88) included a chapter entitled 'Egyptology in confirmation of scripture' in *The Truth of the Bible*, a work of apologetic which drew upon archaeological evidence.[19] In a paper delivered on 6 February 1871 Savile remarked that both

---

[15] F. W. Farrar, 'Traditions, real and fictitious', *Transactions of the Ethnological Society of London*, vol. 3 (1865), pp. 298–307, at p. 299.
[16] Sabine Baring-Gould, *Legends of Old Testament characters* (2 vols., London, 1871), vol. I, pp. vi, 26–40, 116–33.
[17] John Eadie, *A Biblical Cyclopaedia* (1848: 12th edn, London, 1870), pp. 479, 591.
[18] G. Huelin, 'The Christian Evidence Society from 1870 to 1983', in J. W. Gann (ed.), *A history of the Christian Evidence Society* (Christian Evidence Society, 2005), pp. 34, 36; D. A. Johnson, 'Popular apologetics in late Victorian England: the work of the Christian Evidence Society', *Journal of Religious History*, vol. 11 (1981), pp. 558–77.
[19] Bourchier Wrey Savile, *The truth of the Bible* (London, 1871), ch. xi.

Egyptological and cuneiform studies had provided welcome 'confirmation' of the 'truth and integrity' of scripture.[20]

Some apologists attempted a reconciliation between Casaubonish mythography and the new sciences of the nineteenth century. Might the latter, some wondered, provide unexpected confirmation of the truths of sacred history? On 1 May 1871 the Reverend J. H. (Jonathan) Titcomb (1819–87) delivered to the Victoria Institute a paper entitled 'Ethnic Testimonies to the Pentateuch'. Titcomb wove the insights of the new taxonomy of language groups – Turanian, Hamitic, Semitic, Aryan – into a conjectured history of the dispersal of the descendants of Noah after Babel and – crucially – the gradual corruption of their rites and legends. The Turanian peoples of east Asia, Polynesia and the Americas yielded telling evidence of the truth of Genesis. For example, the Aztec goddess Cioactl was unmistakably the 'Mosaic Eve', the Polynesians commemorated eight survivors of the Flood, and the Chinese had a 'traditionary remembrance of the time of Noah'. Similar traces of the earliest books of Genesis could be found, Titcomb argued, within the mythologies of the Hamitic, Semitic and Aryan peoples. The Fall of Man, indeed, seemed 'universally stamped upon the human mind'. But was all this mere airy and vapid apologetics? Might these ethnic testimonies crumble to dust at the first sneer of a Ladislaw? Was it really possible to take a bit of myth from here, a bit of myth from there, and, on that slender basis, which lacked grounding in a single defined context, attempt to reconstitute an Ur-history behind a variety of tales and legends? Titcomb's 'ethnic testimonies', he contended, were 'like the fossil bones of some old ichthyosaurus' – 'broken and disjointed, part being found in one spot and part in another', but susceptible to comparison, classification and possible reconstruction, indeed 'quite sufficient to convince the skilful palaeontologist that they are fragments of one great original'.[21]

Titcomb was also aware of the potential of a budding science of biblical archaeology, which was ripening not, as might be expected, in Palestine, but in the corroborative lumber-rooms of the nearby pagan civilisations of the Middle East: 'Discoveries recently being made among slabs, bricks, cylinders, and clay tablets belonging to the ruined cities of Upper and Lower Mesopotamia, have had the effect of so strongly confirming scripture as almost to create a new science, viz. biblical archaeology.' Amazingly,

---

[20] Bourchier Wrey Savile, 'On the evidence of the Egyptian monuments to the sojourn of Israel in Egypt', *Journal of the Transactions of the Victoria Institute*, vol. 6 (1873), pp. 93–107, at p. 93.

[21] J. H. Titcomb, 'Ethnic testimonies to the Pentateuch', *Journal of the Transactions of the Victoria Institute*, vol. 6 (1873), pp. 234–58, at pp. 235, 238–9, 257.

some of these heathen remains seemed 'to bear upon facts so early as those contained in the Pentateuch'; and he cited a Babylonian cylinder depicting a man and a woman picking fruit from a tree, under the gaze of a nearby serpent.[22]

As late as 1869, the search for the key to all mythologies remained the public pursuit of the Prime Minister.[23] William Gladstone's *Juventus Mundi* (1869) viewed Homeric Greece through the lens of old-style Christian mythography. Gladstone was drawing on a respectable and well-established tradition of Homeric scholarship. Most notably, John Williams, the Archdeacon of Cardigan, had argued in the 1840s that the 'patriarchal tradition' of the Noachids survived into the Homeric age. According to Williams, Homeric literature appeared to 'prove that the light originally derived from Heaven was never ... thoroughly extinguished' among the pagan Greeks.[24] Williams's *Homerus* (1842) conceded that the Homeric epics seemed – superficially at least – to be very unpromising ground for the Christian apologist. After all, by the era of Homer the patriarchal religion of the Noachids had been substantially transformed by generations of gentile descendants, resulting in a 'corruption so complete' that the original truth was largely concealed from view. Nevertheless, there were unexpected rewards for those who tried to make sense of the Homeric system. In particular, the concept of 'atè', or fate, provided the grand cipher by which the Homeric theology might be reconciled with the patriarchal Ur-tradition of Judaeo-Christianity. Atè was – anticipating a phrase – the 'key' to Homeric mythology:

> This doctrine, when applied to the whole action and details of the Iliad, will furnish us with the key, which rightly used, will open to us new apartments in the magnificent structure of that great poem, and enable us to recognise it exoterically as a splendid and harmonious whole, constructed for the express purpose of vindicating the justice of the Deity, and of displaying the inseparable connection between sins and eventual punishment.[25]

Gladstone accepted the variegated nature of Homeric paganism, which he attempted to taxonomise. Some of its divinities, he conceded, were mere deified men, and others personations of either natural phenomena or human characteristics, but certain Homeric gods, he argued, were 'copies, distorted and depraved, of a primitive system of religion given by God to man'. Although there was no simple one-to-one correspondence between

---

[22] *Ibid.*, p. 247.
[23] D. Bebbington, *The mind of Gladstone: religion, Homer and politics* (Oxford, 2004), esp. pp. 178–215.
[24] John Williams, *Primitive tradition* (Edinburgh, 1843), pp. 36, 39.
[25] John Williams, *Homerus* (London, 1842), p. 109.

events in the early chapters of Genesis and the figures of the Homeric pantheon, gods such as Zeus, Apollo, Athene, Leto, Iris and Kronos attracted Gladstone's attention as partial and corrupted derivations of Hebrew scripture. In addition to Trinitarian elements, the notion of a deliverer at once human and divine, and the conceit of a rainbow as the symbol of communication between God and man, Gladstone also perceived within Homeric theology a 'kernel' of 'deontology', a moral framework of ethical duties. In particular, he noted 'the idea of sin, considered as an offence against the divine order' seemed 'strongly implied' in the Homeric term 'atasthalie', a term for 'deep, deliberate wickedness'. Yet, his Casaubonish tendencies notwithstanding, Gladstone also considered himself a man of science keenly in touch with the latest developments in Homeric scholarship and with the new discipline of Aryan philology. There was 'a very strong presumption', he concluded, 'that the Hellenic portion of the Aryan family had for a time preserved to itself, in broad outline, no small share of those treasures, of which the Semitic family of Abraham were to be the appointed guardians'.[26] Gladstone would come to welcome the pathbreaking discoveries of Assyriologists as a further confirmation of his apologetic interpretation of Homer.[27]

Today we endorse Eliot's assumption that the 'key to all mythologies' was a delusion, but in the early 1870s the evidence did not all point in a single direction. Indeed, it was possible to argue that the eighteenth- and nineteenth-century enemies of Christianity were themselves victims of a delusion. Thomas Cooper (1805–92), an erstwhile freethinker who had converted back to Christianity, published in 1871 a work entitled *The Bridge of History Over the Gulf of Time*, which was a defiantly assertive defence of the historicity of Christ against both the Straussian school and those who would reduce the story of Christ to a solar allegory. The Higher Critics seemed to have no trouble, for example, with Caesar's *Gallic War*, a work which Cooper contended was of no greater historicity than the gospels. There was just as much 'circumstantial evidence' for the authenticity of the gospels, which led Cooper to conclude that 'Strauss has not an inch of ground to stand upon, when he denies that we know who wrote the gospels, when they were written, and where they were written. His "mythical

---

[26] William Gladstone, *Juventus mundi* (London, 1869), esp. pp. 204–9, 214–15, 219, 288, 330–1, 387; D. M. Schreuder, 'History and the utility of myth: Homer's Greece in Gladstonian Liberalism', in F. West (ed.), *Myth and mythology* (Canberra, 1989), pp. 51–84, esp. pp. 51, 64, 72.
[27] William Gladstone, 'An essay on the points of contact between the Assyrian tablets and the Homeric text', in Gladstone, *Landmarks of Homeric study* (London, 1890), pp. 127–60.

system", which held me in bondage for twelve years, I feel has utterly lost its hold upon me.' At least Strauss and Ernest Renan agreed that Jesus – however much reduced in stature – had actually existed, which was more than could be said for the solarists, for whom Christ was merely an astronomical allegory. The solarist line of interpretation had been initiated, as Cooper noted, by the French sceptics Volney and Dupuis; however, his main targets were the homegrown examples of this debunking tendency, in the works of Drummond, Higgins and Taylor. As a former deist himself, Cooper had a sure – and once-sympathetic – grasp of the solarists' account of Christianity. Their theory was that 'no real human person called Jesus of Nazareth ever existed; that Christ only represents the Sun, like the Krishna of the Hindoos, the Osiris of the Egyptians, the Mithras of the Persians, the Phoebus Apollo of the Greeks' and that Christianity amounts to no more, historically speaking, than 'the old fable of the sun in a new form: the story so often repeated in the mythologies of the ancient nations … slightly altered'. But on what foundation of evidence did these speculations rest? None whatsoever, claimed Cooper. The solarist interpretation of Christ and his twelve apostles was itself a mythological fantasy, contradicted by the gospel narrative and the external sources which corroborated it. To this zealous ex-Deist in the early 1870s, Christian apologetics seemed more historically reliable than the just-so stories of modern infidelity.[28]

On the other side of the fence, of course, the key to all mythologies remained a potent *secular* idea: a method for deconstructing all religions, Christianity included. The anti-vivisectionist and women's suffrage campaigner Frances Power Cobbe (1822–1904) took the view in 1869 that developments in mythography during the previous 'twenty years' held out the prospect of a 'not wholly incomplete "Philosophy of All Religions"'. As far as Cobbe was concerned, the orthodox interpretation of the world's pagan myths – 'the short and easy method of our fathers which derived them all out of that very capacious receptacle, Noah's Ark' – was as redundant as pre-Darwinian biology. Instead the persistence of irrational myths – 'heirlooms of fancy', or 'wild-flower myths' – provided an evidential mainstay for social 'psychology' and an ethnological science of ancient races and their migrations. 'Fables and forms of worship' afforded 'hints of incalculable value in aiding the philologist and the ethnologist in tracking out the various branches of the human family in their wanderings over the globe.'[29] In a similar vein the African explorer William Winwood Reade (1838–75)

---

[28] Thomas Cooper, *The bridge of history over the gulf of time* (London, 1871), pp. 2–5, 135–6.
[29] Frances Power Cobbe, 'Fergusson's Tree and serpent worship', *Fraser's Magazine*, vol. 79 (April 1869), pp. 417–30, at pp. 417–18.

Epilogue: *The Keys to All Mythology in 1872* 213

bracketed Christianity with ancient mythologies in his freethinking classic, *The Martyrdom of Man* (1872). While Old Testament Judaism was a blatant copy from Zoroastrianism, all religions were reducible, ultimately, to the mental confusions of humankind in the savage state. 'A day will come', Reade predicted, 'when the European God of the nineteenth century will be classed with the gods of Olympus and the Nile.'[30]

Indo-European philology also provided apparent sustenance for occult variations on an older strain of Volneyesque deconstruction which sought its own key to all mythologies outside the pale of Judaeo-Christian tradition. In 1869 the anticlerical French spiritualist Louis Jacolliot (1837–90) published *La Bible dans l'Inde*, in which he traced ancient mythologies – Egyptian, Greek, Roman and biblical – as well as their attendant priesthoods back to a Sanskrit cradle ('berceau'). It was not only European languages which had their roots in Sanskrit India; Moses – like the Egyptian Menes and the Cretan Minos – was a derivation of the Hindu Manu, and Jesus Christ turned out to be an emanation of the Indian figure Iezeus Christna.[31] Jacolliot's work very quickly appeared in English translation as *The Bible in India* (1870).

In an uncanny conjunction of ironies, Max-Müller, an émigré German philologist much admired by Eliot,[32] a pioneer in the field of comparative religion and in some ways the very embodiment of the world of learning championed by Ladislaw of which Casaubon was oblivious, published a rebuttal to critics of the 'keys to all mythology' in the December 1871 issue of the *Contemporary Review*, at the very moment when *Middlemarch* began to appear. The ancient Greeks themselves, Max-Müller reminded scholars, had subscribed to the idea of a kind of key to all mythology: 'many of the most distinguished minds of ancient Greece agreed in demanding an interpretation, whether physical or metaphysical, of Greek mythology, partly in order to satisfy those classical scholars, who, forgetful of their own classics, forgetful of their own Plato and Aristotle, seem to imagine that the idea of seeing in the gods and heroes of Greece anything beyond what they appear to be in the songs of Homer, was a mere fancy and invention of the students of comparative mythology'. In other words, the key to all mythologies was not a chimera. Both Socrates and Plato had 'pointed frequently to what they called the *hyponoia*, the under-current, if I may say so, or the under-meaning of ancient mythology'. Of course, for Max-Müller the key

---

[30] William Winwood Reade, *The martyrdom of man* (1872: London, 1968), pp. 141–2, 162–8, 432.
[31] Louis Jacolliot, *La Bible dans l'Inde* (Paris, 1869), esp. pp. 4, 18, 63–4.
[32] For the importance of Max-Müller to Eliot's view of mythology, see J. C. Pratt and V. A. Neufeldt (eds.), *George Eliot's Middlemarch notebooks* (Berkeley and Los Angeles, 1979), esp. pp. xlviii–lii, 285.

to all mythology was not the simple assimilation of myth to its Biblical Ur-foundations sought by Mr Casaubon. Rather, Max-Müller believed that mythology was an 'inevitable' and 'inherent necessity of language', being 'the dark shadow which language throws on thought'. Language was open to corruption and proliferation in various ways, not least personification in languages where nouns, for example, were gendered. The divine personages of polytheistic religion developed from 'ancient language going beyond its first intention'. Max-Müller's insight was profound: mythology was 'an inevitable catastrophe in the life of language'. Nevertheless, he downplayed his own originality. He pointed to a long lineage of earlier thinkers who recognised something of this degenerative process at work in language. The whole history of philosophy 'from Thales down to Hegel' was 'an uninterrupted battle against mythology, a constant protest of thought against language'. In this sense, philosophy was indeed a set of footnotes to Plato, the western tradition of philosophical inquiry sensing something of a double doctrine in mythology, whether an intentional veiling or, as Max-Müller himself believed, a natural and invisible organic process by which meaning became distorted. Whatever their conflicting perspectives on other questions, philosophers had consistently looked upon mythology 'as something which, whatever it may mean, does certainly not mean what it seems to mean'. Mythology, Max-Müller concluded, was a 'refraction of the rays of language', indicating how Sanskrit, the ancient language of India which bore marked affinities in language, culture and mythology to the kindred Indo-European languages of Greece and Rome, might prove 'the master-key to many a lock which no Greek key will open'.[33]

However, the early 1870s witnessed the emergence of a major struggle in British intellectual life between the solarist-philologists, led by Max-Müller, for whom the polytheistic pantheons of Indo-European peoples were but muddled representations of the dawn sun, and evolutionary anthropologists who found glaring flaws in the solarist thesis.[34] The solarist *Mythology of the Aryan Nations* by the Reverend George Cox (1827–1902) appeared in 1870, while the primary point of reference for evolutionary anthropologists was E. B. Tylor's *Primitive Culture*, published in 1871.[35] However, the direct attack on the solarists began in earnest in 1873 with Andrew Lang's essay

---

[33] Friedrich Max-Müller, 'On the philosophy of mythology', *Contemporary Review*, vol. 19 (1871), pp. 97–119, at pp. 98–9, 104–6, 111–14.

[34] There is a lucid discussion of the rival positions of Max-Müller's solarism and Tylor's evolutionist anthropology in M. Wheeler-Barclay, *The science of religion in Britain 1860–1915* (Charlottesville, VA and London, 2010), pp. 37–103.

[35] R. M. Dorson, *The British folklorists* (London, 1968), p. 210.

'Mythology and fairy tales' in the *Fortnightly Review*. Here Lang rejected the notion that Mährchen (folk-tales) were 'the detritus of the higher mythology' studied by Max-Müller and his school, but derived from an earlier evolutionary stage of animal-worship and totemism. Indeed, how could the Indo-Europeanists explain the existence of similar folk-tales among non-Indo-European peoples? Common features in the folklore of Indo-Europeans, Finns, Siberians and Zulus suggested to Lang that 'the myths of the dawn and of the sun, can no longer be considered primary'. Folktales belonged rather to a stage of cultural development which preceded the separation into Aryan, Semitic and other basic language groups. Lang was incensed by Cox's feeble resort to starkly different explanations for the emergence of serpent-worship among Indo-European and non-Indo-European peoples, and withering in his criticism of the Aryan solarists and their failure properly to address ethnographic evidence from the non-Indo-European world: 'There can be no miracle so great as what we are asked to believe – that the force of the changed meanings of words compelled the Greeks to construct fictitious traditions exactly tallying with the actual practices of living savages.'[36]

Notwithstanding his long, outspoken campaign against the solarists, Lang's commitment to evolutionary anthropology would later give way to something which verged – no more than that, perhaps[37] – on the semi-Casaubonish. Lang was a founding member of the Society for Psychical Research, founded in 1882, and retained a belief in the existence of supernatural phenomena; no arid materialist he. Moreover, in his anthropological work, Lang came to the view that some of the most primitive peoples had held beliefs in a supreme, ethical deity. In particular, ethnographic information about Australian Aborigines seemed to indicate that this primitive people – an uncontaminated control-group, remote and far-removed from the familiar monotheistic religions – had worshipped a high father-god.[38]

A further scholarly feud divided the domain of Aryan linguistics and mythography: the vexed question of the relationship between the Aryan and Semitic cultures. The mythographer and philologist Robert Brown (1844–1912),[39] the author of *Poseidon: A Link Between Semite, Hamite and*

---

[36] Andrew Lang, 'Mythology and fairy tales', *Fortnightly Review* (May 1873), pp. 618–31, esp. pp. 620, 628.
[37] See the nuanced discussion of Lang in Wheeler-Barclay, *Science of religion in Britain*, pp. 104–39.
[38] Dorson, *British folklorists* (London, 1968), pp. 212–16, 245–6; G. Stocking, *After Tylor: British social anthropology 1888–1951* (London, 1995), pp. 55–60; R. Ackerman, *J. G. Frazer: his life and work* (1987: Cambridge pbk, 1990), pp. 150–1.
[39] For Brown, see Dorson, *British folklorists*, pp. 177–81.

Aryan (1872), noted that 'although so much has been written respecting the belief and religious systems of the Ancients, yet modern discovery is ever supplying fresh material for investigation, and frequently disproving long-cherished theories and ideas'. Indeed, Brown engaged directly with the fallacy – only now being exposed to wider ridicule in *Middlemarch* – of the 'key to all mythologies'. According to Brown, 'The great mistake generally committed in attempts to interpret mythology is the natural error of stretching a particular theory or system beyond its proper limits, as if one key were sufficient to open all locks.' However, his objection was to a monocular mythography, not to the attempt to reduce the diversity of ancient mythology to a set of common forms: 'The natural phenomena theory and the Euhemeristic theory are both admirably useful; but, to ignore the merits of either, and, consequently, to depend wholly on the other, must necessarily be productive of serious error in many instances.' His concern was that each of these basic lines of interpretation was 'being stretched beyond its proper limits'. Indeed, notwithstanding Brown's pointed rejection of the single key to all mythologies, he openly championed the idea that the deities of antiquity could be reduced to some kind of scheme, so long as it incorporated both allegories of nature and Euhemerised personages. Deities had multiplied because, as he observed, 'the symbol is constantly confounded with the thing signified'. Similarly, he held fast to the core truth – though not, of course, the exclusive insight – of Euhemerism, 'despite the sneers which have been bestowed in some quarters on the system of Euemeros'. Ultimately, for all Brown's scepticism, he believed that the many gods of pagan polytheisms were 'capable of being resolved into a few'. Although, he conceded, 'the principle of identity' of the gods 'may easily be incorrectly extended, yet in many instances one personage becomes manifold and multiform, as witness Hoa-Ana, Oannes, Onnes, Oan, Oe, Dagon, Sidon, and Poseidon'.[40] Indeed, Brown believed that apologetic mythography had nothing to fear from the new classifications of language groups, as the discovery of 'the primitive unity of the Aryan family' was a philological fact in 'perfect harmony with Biblical statement'.[41]

It was not only the 'key' of apologetic Anglican mythography which attracted criticism. The notion advanced by Aryan philologists that behind every deity, behind every legend, there loomed the sun and the dawn

---

[40] Robert Brown, *Poseidon: a link between Semite, Hamite and Aryan* (London, 1872), pp. 1, 79, 108–9, 114–15, 124–5.

[41] Robert Brown, *The religion of Zoroaster considered in connection with archaic monotheism* (London, [1879]), p. 17.

attracted critics for its apparent crude insensitivity to the rich diversity of mythological stories which it purported to explain. The historian Edward Freeman (1823–92) found himself 'a little suspicious of a theory which so perfectly and consistently explains everything'. Freeman was, of course, 'quite ready to admit' the sky 'as one source of legend among others', but not to 'admit it as an universal solvent'. It was 'the very completeness of the new theory, its claim to be of universal application, its assertion of a power to open every lock and to untie every knot' which made him 'shrink from fully accepting it'. Not that Freeman rejected the insights of the new comparative philology, merely that some of its devotees had 'sometimes ridden' this hobby horse 'a little too hard'.[42]

Strange and counter-intuitive as it might seem, during the 1870s a dawning awareness of the surprising robustness of other supposed 'myths' reinforced the authority of sacred history. Developments in archaeology, not least Schliemann's controversial discoveries at Hissarlik in 1873,[43] meant that in the adjacent field of classical studies there was a retreat in the late nineteenth century from what Frank M. Turner has called the 'historical agnosticism' about myth associated with the radical utilitarian-inspired historiography of George Grote (1794–1871).[44] Troy was no longer myth but archaeological fact, and this particular refurbishing of legend as historical truth inspired and delighted defenders of sacred history.[45]

Such was the pace of discovery that some improbably tall tales in ancient texts began to seem less questionable. Was the Pentateuch, for example, any less reliable than Herodotus, the so-called 'father of lies', with his accounts of pygmies, monsters and other bizarre forms of quasi-humanity? 1872 – the year in which *Middlemarch* appeared – also saw the publication of *The Country of the Dwarfs* by the explorer Paul du Chaillu (1835–1903), who had discovered the pygmies of central Africa in the course of a long expedition in the mid-1860s. At first du Chaillu, who saw the tiny dwellings of the pygmies before he saw the pygmies themselves, thought that these had been built to house idols or fetishes, not human beings

---

[42] Edward Freeman, 'Stray thoughts on comparative mythology', *Fortnightly Review* (November 1870), pp. 536–48, at pp. 543–4, 548. Cf. [Henry Hewlett], 'The rationale of mythology', *Cornhill Magazine* (April 1877), pp. 407–23, at p. 412.
[43] See Philip Smith, 'Preface', Heinrich Schliemann, *Troy and its remains* (ed. Smith, London, 1875) for the significance of the discovery.
[44] F. M. Turner, 'The triumph of idealism in Victorian classical studies', in Turner, *Contesting cultural authority* (Cambridge, 1993), p. 348.
[45] D. Gange and R. Bryant Davies, 'Troy', in Gange and Ledger-Lomas (eds.), *Cities of God*, pp. 39–70; Bebbington, *Mind of Gladstone*, pp. 202–4.

on an unimaginably miniature scale. When du Chaillu first encountered the Obongos, the pygmy people, he related his discovery to the presumed unreliabilities and absurdities of ancient geography:

> It was true the great historian Herodotus had described a nation of dwarfs as living in the head-waters of the Nile; Homer had spoken of the cranes and of the land of the pygmies; and Strabo thought that certain little men of Ethiopia were the original dwarfs, while Pomponius Mela had placed them far south, and, like Homer, spoke of their fighting with cranes; but then nobody had believed these stories. Could it be possible that I had discovered these people, spoken of thousands of years before?

Du Chaillu was particularly fascinated by the supposed legend in Homer that once upon a time great birds had attacked the pygmy race of men. It turned out from Du Chaillu's investigations that the Obongos travelled long distances to hunt cranes. Thus, it seemed, the fabulous Homeric tale of cranes attacking pygmies turned out rather to be an ethnographic fact turned upside down in oral transmission, but grounded nonetheless in truth.[46] The implications of such discoveries, which turned the categories of history and mythology inside out, were momentous. If miniature humans, once supposed fanciful, turned out to be real, then the sacred history set out in Genesis no longer seemed so implausible.

More spectacular still was the paper, 'The Chaldean account of the deluge', presented by George Smith (1840–76), a curator at the British Museum, on 3 December 1872 to the Biblical Archaeology Society.[47] To an audience which included the Prime Minister, Gladstone, Smith revealed the discovery and decipherment of part of what is now known as the epic of Gilgamesh. Serendipitously, amidst the heaps of cuneiform tablets acquired by the Museum from the Assyrian researches of Layard, Smith had come across compelling *archaeological* evidence for a flood-story uncannily similar to that found in Genesis. The cuneiform fragments which included the flood legend came from the library of the palace of Ashurbanipal at Nineveh. The library had been discovered in the early 1850s by Layard's collaborator, Hormuzd Rassam (1826–1910), a Chaldean Christian from Mosul, who had excavated in Iraq on his own under the auspices of the British Museum after Layard moved on from archaeological researches to begin a political career.[48] Smith's discovery was a media sensation, and the

---

[46] Paul du Chaillu, *The country of the dwarfs* (London, 1872), pp. 153–5, 171–2, 176, 186–7.
[47] George Smith, 'The Chaldean account of the Deluge', *Transactions of the Society of Biblical Archaeology*, vol. 2 (1873), pp. 213–34.
[48] D. Damrosch, *The buried book: the loss and rediscovery of the great epic of Gilgamesh* (New York, 2006), pp. 99, 112–13.

Daily Telegraph provided funds for Smith to carry out his own archaeological researches in Ottoman Iraq. On his first trip in 1873 Smith discovered further material on the Flood, which did not relate, as he surmised, to the Gilgamesh story, but to a separate Akkadian flood myth, the epic of Atra-Hasis. On a subsequent field trip in 1874 Smith made further stunning discoveries – including tablets which contained versions of the creation, Fall and Babel – which he collated with the flood story, as *The Chaldean Account of Genesis* (1876). However, on a further trip to the Middle East in 1876, he succumbed to dysentery and died in Aleppo.

Somewhat confusingly today, at least for readers who consult Smith's version of the flood legend and who search in vain for the name Gilgamesh, the reconstructed story as it appeared in the 1870s narrated rather the doings of one 'Izdubar'. Smith made a few minor mistakes in the rendering of proper names, which was understandable, for Assyrian names sometimes contained Sumerian signs as well as more predictably Akkadian characters; in particular, Smith rendered the proper name of Gilgamesh, which he failed to realise incorporated Sumerian elements, as Izdubar. What Smith misread as two Akkadian characters signifying, as he thought, 'iz' and 'du', were Sumerian signs indicating a sound either like 'gis-ga' or 'gil-ga'. In addition, the final syllable, which was Akkadian, had alternative sounds of 'bar' or 'mesh'. Smith guessed wrongly.[49] However, the central character of Izdubar/Gilgamesh was not the figure within the deciphered cuneiform fragments who most intrigued readers. Rather what excited most interest was the tale within the tale, for the legend of Izdubar (or Gilgamesh) contains the story of Uta-napishtim, a Noah-like figure who survived a great deluge, and whose experience of this flood precisely mirrored Noah's.

The discovery was clearly momentous, but Smith hesitated to pronounce prematurely about the significance of the Izdubar/Gilgamesh story. His findings were, he admitted, 'provisional' and he thought it vital to 'obtain the recognition of the evidence' in the first place 'without prejudice' as to its theological (or secular) meaning. Of course, the 'inscriptions describing the Flood' provided 'an independent testimony in favour of the Biblical narrative at a much earlier date than any other evidence', but Smith argued that it was 'in vain' to ask, 'Did either of these two races, Jews or Babylonians, borrow from the other the traditions of these early times, and, if so, when?' Indeed, Smith confessed that in deciphering the fragments and making wider sense of them, 'I have changed my own opinions many times, and I have no doubt that any accession of new

[49] *Ibid.*, pp. 28–9.

material would change again my views'. Nor was intellectual progress in Assyriology a straightforward matter of lineal progression towards a better understanding of antiquity: rather, 'in cuneiform matters we have often had to advance through error to truth'.[50]

As Robert Ackerman notes, the Assyrian and Babylonian discoveries forced Protestants 'to see that the people and events of the Bible had a new, denser kind of historical reality and did not exist in some special never-never world'.[51] However, the implications were tantalisingly ambiguous. If the milieu of the Old Testament now seemed less exceptional than before, it also seemed more tangible and real. The modern chronicler of Smith's achievement, David Damrosch, remarks that the discovery of the Gilgamesh flood story ignited a wide-ranging and heated controversy, though one which was carried out in a fog of ambiguity: 'What did the Babylonian version prove, the truth of biblical history or its falsity?'[52] The Babylonian flood story might offer a corroboration of Genesis, but equally it might well provide evidence that there had been a series of ancient Middle Eastern flood legends, with none – including the biblical one – any more historically grounded than the others.

Of course, some experts immediately perceived the critical import of Smith's discovery. The Assyriologist Archibald Sayce (1845–1933) saw that the Izdubar legend was the 'key' to these strange, heathen mythologies found in the early portions of the Pentateuch: 'the monuments of Babylonia alone will give us the key to the meaning of those old tales which form the background of Jewish history and the hallowed horizon of our own religious thought'. Sayce believed that Smith's discovery brought into focus 'the untenability of the traditional view of the Old Testament' and served 'to confirm the conclusions of scientific criticism'. No longer was it possible to argue – what was in essence the Casaubonish line – that 'the Chaldeans preserved a heathenized recollection of an event, the true history of which is recorded in Genesis'. Rather Genesis, it was now obvious to the unbiased, was derived from Mesopotamian myths of the calendar. ' "Orthodoxy," so called', announced Sayce, a believing critic, had been 'deprived of its last resource'.[53] Sayce's view was, however, starker than the general run of excited ambiguity which greeted Smith's decipherment.

---

[50] George Smith, *The Chaldean account of Genesis* (London, 1876 edn), pp. vii, 286, 291, 301.
[51] R. Ackerman, *The myth and ritual school* (1991: New York and London, 2002), p. 40.
[52] Damrosch, *Buried book*, p. 5.
[53] A. H. Sayce, 'The Chaldean account of the Deluge and its relation to the Old Testament', *Theological Review* (July 1873), pp. 364–77, at pp. 371–2, 377.

If Smith's decipherment of the Gilgamesh epic did not settle matters decisively one way or the other, it nonetheless left open the possibility – no more than that, perhaps, but it was enough – that the earliest parts of the Old Testament constituted genuine matter of history. Sir George Denys thought it likely that the Hebrew Flood derived from earlier pagan legends; nevertheless, he conceded that this was not the view of *The Times*, which celebrated Smith's findings as a 'confirmation' of scripture, and acknowledged wryly that 'Mr Smith was not sent out to Assyria by the *Daily Telegraph* for the purpose of upsetting the Mosaic cosmogony'.[54]

Indeed, developments in Assyriology provided an ironic boost to sacred history. Daniel Smith – who interpreted the myth of Cadmus, the bringer of the alphabet to ancient Greece, as evidence for the origin of letters in the Middle East – found in the cuneiform discoveries a key to the language and alphabet of the ancients, alluded to in the title of his posthumous work, *Cuneorum clavis* (1875): 'Who can say what treasures of knowledge may not yet lie buried in Nineveh's ancient ruins, and in the mounds around? ... Who can tell what memorials of the antediluvian world, preserved from the Deluge ... and handed down in the family of Shem to the first rulers of this ancient empire, may not still be discoverable?' Cuneiform survivals, he contended, served 'as a connecting link between the antediluvian world and the present day'.[55] The sacred events of Genesis – along with the associated key to mythologies – seemed, at least in some micawberish quarters of intellectual life, less remote and more attainable in the wake of the cuneiform breakthroughs than earlier in the century.

The brilliant French Assyriologist François Lenormant (1837–83) was careful to avoid the exaggerations which he felt had attended the anglophone reception of Smith's discovery. The Babylonian story of the Deluge recounted on the fragments of cuneiform brick did not settle the authority of Genesis one way or the other ('elle apporte aucune preuve ou aucun argument nouveau pour ou contre l'authenticité de la tradition biblique'). After all, that the Babylonians had possessed a Flood legend had been known since the fragments of the history of Berosus which Eusebius, presented by Lenormant as a patristic champion of the collateral evidences *avant la lettre*, had preserved as a way of corroborating Christian 'truth' ('dans l'intention de corroborer les récits de livres saints par le témoignage de la tradition orientale païenne'). But question marks, inevitably, remained over the purported antiquity and uncorrupted authenticity of the materials

---

[54] George Denys, *The Chaldean account of Genesis* (London, [1877]), pp. 4–6, 13, 18.
[55] Daniel Smith, *Cuneorum clavis: the primitive alphabet and language of the ancient ones of the earth* (ed. H. W. Hemsworth, London, 1875), pp. 14–15.

upon which Eusebius drew, which were themselves drawn from the 'redactions' of Abydenus and Alexander Polyhistor ('Sur les seuls fragments de Bérose, on pouvait se demander si la tradition diluvienne était vraiment très-antique et indigène à Babylone, ou si elle n'était pas d'introduction assez récente et due à une influence des idées juives'). The real significance of Smith's discovery, Lenormant argued, was that it provided independent corroboration for the Babylonian story of the Flood found in Berosus and proved that the provenance of the Flood story was local to Babylon and of the very highest antiquity ('remontait à une extrême antiquité').[56]

Even in the German world, whose advanced critical scholarship notoriously escaped the notice of Mr Casaubon, arguments of a Casaubonish kind were not yet extinct. In 1872–3 the professor of theology at Erlangen, Johannes Heinrich August Ebrard (1818–88), delivered lectures which recapitulated some of the old-style collaborative evidences. The lectures were published in two volumes as *Apologetik* (1874–5) and translated into English by two Scots Presbyterian clerics, the Reverends William Stuart and John Macpherson, in 1886. Ebrard's work purported to be a scientific vindication of Christianity and he utilised ethnographic materials from across the globe to make the case for the 'unity' of humankind's primitive beliefs. The anthropology of religion and mythology told a story of declension from an original monotheism into fantastical corruptions, yet underneath which elements of the early portion of Genesis happened to peek through, such as the near-ubiquity of serpent myths. Ebrard rejected the notion that because biblical and heathen traditions were similar, this meant – as infidel philosophers claimed – Biblical religion rested on no surer a foundation than did heathenism. Quite the opposite, argued Ebrard. Paganism unexpectedly buttressed the claims of Christian truth. Just as 'a lie is the ape of truth', so paganism was 'the ape of the revelation of God' ('Die Lüge ist der Affe der Wahrheit, das Heidenthum der Affe der Offenbarung Gottes').[57]

From its inception, the key to all mythologies had been a genre rich in ironies and ambiguities. In the same way that Christian identifications of pagan mythologies as distorted versions of Genesis lay open to the counter-charge that Genesis itself was mere plagiarised paganism, so too the rise of Egyptology, Assyriology and other branches of Middle Eastern archaeology yielded new versions of an old dilemma. Who was copying whom? The coy presentation of parallels oozed ambiguity. Could one ever

---

[56] François Lenormant, *Le Déluge et l'épopée babylonienne* (Paris, 1873), pp. 6–8, 24.
[57] J. H. A. Ebrard, *Apologetics; or the scientific vindication of Christianity* (3 vols., Edinburgh, 1886), vol. III, pp. 320–2, translating Ebrard, *Apologetik: wissenschaftliche Rechtfertigung des Christenthums* (2 vols., Gütersloh, 1874), vol. II, p. 503.

be certain which episode constituted the Ur-history and which its mythical distortion, or indeed whether all such recountings were mere legends? The English intelligentsia of the 1870s knew much more about ancient Middle Eastern history than its forebears of the 1830s, but it was no more decided in its verdict.

Ambiguities abounded in the field of cuneiform discovery. Even where critics rejected outworn Biblical orthodoxies, the terms of rejection – however optimistically misunderstood – remained suggestive of new possibilities. Although the French–German Assyriologist and chronologist Jules Oppert (1825–1905) regarded the traditional chronology of Genesis as untenable and thought the authentic chronologies of Middle Eastern civilisations extended further back to 'un âge extrêmement reculé', he also perceived that current research in the field indicated a common origin for the most primeval of myths ('il tend à réduire les légendes primordiales de l'humanité à une seule origine').[58] Of course, there was no suggestion here that this insight in any way vindicated Biblical truth, but it did point to a tantalising possibility. Was there a unified history – a key to all mythologies, after all, perhaps – which underpinned the various ancient 'mythological' literatures of the Middle East, the Bible included? And might this lead in turn to a recognition – even from the most hard-headed of Biblical critics – that the Old Testament preserved, albeit indirectly and as part of a portfolio of ancient traditions from the region, a body of authentic history? Would the newly discovered commonalities in the region's 'Genesis' stories usher in a new and providentially informed awareness that the Bible was, notwithstanding the cavils of the critics, a matter of historic truth?

New cuneiform discoveries led to a renewed questing for mythological keys, though these were serious professional ventures much better equipped academically than the forlorn wanderings of a Casaubon. Sayce, the Oxford Assyriologist and orientalist, detected solar, zodiacal and astronomical myths lurking under the legendary histories revealed by cuneiform, and also engaged in other forms of mythographical unmasking, noticing how 'we often find the same deity appearing under several forms' and tracing the 'mythological tendency to evolve many new forms and persons out of one original'.[59] Sayce also recognised archaeology as an answer to the cavils of Biblical critics. While the text of the Old Testament had become riddled with errors of transcription at the hands of centuries

---

[58] Jules Oppert, *La chronologie de la Genèse* (Paris, 1878), pp. 5, 20.
[59] Archibald Sayce, 'Assyrian discoveries: a lecture delivered at the London Institution, January 28, 1874', *Fraser's Magazine* (June 1874), pp. 702–11, at p. 707.

of copyists, the ongoing jigsaw of cuneiform reassembly provided, perhaps with 'greater certainty' than the scriptures themselves, a picture of the primeval Middle East. Hitherto all the extra-scriptural evidence that scholars could find for the patriarchal world beyond the Old Testament itself were the narratives of Manetho, Berosus and Philo Byblius: unreliable corroboration at best. But suddenly all had changed, and for the better: 'The marvellous discoveries of the last half-century have thrown a flood of light on the ancient oriental world, and some of this light has necessarily been reflected on the Book of Genesis ... A dead world has been called again to life by the spade of the excavator and the patient labour of the decipherer.'[60]

It was tempting for some to conclude that the hard, material facts of archaeology trumped the airy speculations of the Higher Critics.[61] As late as the 1880s Claude Reignier Conder (1848–1910) boasted that 'huge libraries of controversy have been swept away when the spade of the excavator has dug up the truth'. Archaeological finds, Conder anticipated, would make an enduring contribution to the field, surviving 'as permanent knowledge when the most advanced criticism has become old-fashioned theory'.[62]

The jurist and theologian Samuel Richard Bosanquet (1800–82) rejoiced that 'modern science' was 'joining hands with antiquity'. In particular, developments in Sanskrit scholarship promised to revolutionise the study of sacred history. According to Bosanquet, 'the doubting and confirmation of Bible history and truth, is one of the great topics and businesses of the day'. Of course, he acknowledged, 'the Bible is upon its trial', but he anticipated only 'the elucidation and confirmation' of Old Testament history 'by additional testimonies from parallel histories'. Not only did the double doctrine – the idea of sacred 'truth enfolded in learned and abstruse enigmas' – remain alive in intellectually respectable quarters as late as 1880, so too did the Casaubonish dream of collateral proofs.[63]

The Scottish judge and prolific jurist Hugh Barclay (1799–1884) incorporated the latest insights of Smith's cuneiform researches into what was otherwise a conventional system of collateral apologetics. The significance of Gilgamesh was providential, the opening of 'a rich and almost inexhaustible storehouse of corroborative evidence of pre-historic facts'; evidence,

---

[60] Archibald Sayce, *Fresh light from the ancient monuments* (1884: Religious Tract Society, London, n.d.), pp. 18–19, 22.
[61] B. MacHaffie, 'Monument facts and Higher Critical fancies: archaeology and the popularization of Old Testament criticism in nineteenth-century Britain', *Church History*, vol. 50 (1981), pp. 316–28.
[62] C. R. Conder, 'Ancient Palestine and modern exploration', *Contemporary Review*, vol. 46 (December 1884), pp. 856–69, at pp. 859, 869.
[63] S. R. Bosanquet, *Hindu chronology and antediluvian history* (London, 1880), pp. 56–9.

moreover, which punctured the secularising pretensions of Biblical criticism. It was a matter of relief that 'Nineveh and other ancient cities have been disentombed from their slumber of ages, and disclose new and irresistible proofs of the facts briefly recorded in the divine page.'[64] By the same token, a decade after the publication of *Middlemarch* and fifty years after the era when the fictional Mr Casaubon was already presumed to be a ridiculous anachronism, the Dundee physician William Galloway felt confident enough to publish his own 'key to all mythologies'. Galloway's *Dissertations on the Philosophy of Creation and the first ten chapters of Genesis allegorized in mythology* (1885) was a reconciliation of heathen creation myths with the truths set out in scripture. Galloway took a straightforwardly reductive view of heathen mythology as 'a system of idolatrous religion, founded upon the mythologization of the first ten chapters of Genesis'. Pagan legends were not to be read as fables, but as the historic 'facts of sacred history allegorized'. In answer to those subversive critics who contended that the Pentateuch had not been composed until after the time of Solomon, and probably not until after Malachi, Galloway counterposed the 'testimony of all heathen nations in their cosmogonies and theogonies' to the primeval composition of the initial chapters of Genesis.[65]

These were, nevertheless, the final spasms of a genre whose death was slow, protracted and punctuated by moments of unexpected vitality and influence. The general public was well enough aware of developments in Assyriology to appreciate Gilbert and Sullivan's characterisation in *The Pirates of Penzance* (1879–80) of a 'modern Major-General' who could write his 'washing bills in Babylonic cuneiform'.[66] Yet in the end the freethinkers, as Eliot firmly believed, seemed to have all the best tunes.

Late in his career the poet, radical and one-time Christian Socialist Gerald Massey (1828–1907), who had, by a neat intertextual irony, been the model for the eponymous central character in George Eliot's *Felix Holt, the Radical* (1866), turned to comparative mythography, and in particular to Egyptology. However, his key to all mythologies proved to be subversively anti-Casaubonish, for Massey (whose reading as a young man had, significantly, included the work of Volney) identified the origins of Christianity in astronomical allegory. What Massey referred

---

[64] Hugh Barclay, *Heathen mythology corroborative or illustrative of holy scripture* (Glasgow, 1884), pp. 78–9.
[65] William Galloway, MD, *Dissertations on the philosophy of the Creation and the first ten chapters of Genesis allegorized in mythology* (Edinburgh, 1885), pp. vi, ix, 43–4, 47, 55, 222.
[66] W. S. Gilbert, *The Savoy Operas* (2 vols., London, 1957), vol. II, p. 128.

to as 'equinoctial Christianity' was derived ultimately from the ancient 'zootypes' of a primeval 'pre-anthropomorphic mode of representation': the pedigree of the Christ-myth was originally 'the ram and afterwards the fish', later the Egyptian deities Horus and Osiris, whose careers had included a virgin birth, crucifixion and resurrection. Although tales of Jehoshua ben Pandira, an Egyptian-trained thaumaturge of the late second century BC, provided additional matter, Massey insisted that Christ had never lived. Judaeo-Christianity, whether the supposed fall, flood-myth or 'Jesus-legend', derived from a legacy of transformations and misinterpretations. According to Massey, the 'primordial matter' of zodiacal animals had become allegorised into 'spiritual typology', and eventually reduced by crude 'literalizers' and 'carnalizers' to episodes in the purported history recounted in the Bible.[67]

The immediate future of the key to all mythologies lay with Frazer and his debunking finale to the genre, *The Golden Bough* (1890). Here Frazer lassoed a stray assortment of miscellaneous evidence into a unitary interpretation of all mythologies, within which Christianity stood revealed as a derivative fertility cult. Frazer never resorted to overt 'parallelism' of a demonstrative sort, yet the subversive implications of his work were obvious. Indeed, the prolixity and snowballing encyclopaedic ambitions of Frazer's work, as it grew between the two-volume first edition of 1890 and the twelve-volume third edition of 1906–15, merely reinforced the notion that this massive deconstruction of religion marked the ironic fulfilment of the fictional Casaubon's delusive project: an uncanny example of life imitating art, albeit with a cruel twist. An 'armchair' scholar with a totalising vision and a grand insensitivity to context and provenance, Frazer turned out to be the unwitting continuator of the unfinished 'Key to All Mythologies'. The world of Mr Casaubon endured – if only through the looking glass.[68]

---

[67] Gerald Massey, *A book of the beginnings* (2 vols., London, 1881), vol. I, p. 9; Massey, *The natural Genesis* (2 vols., London, 1883), vol. II, pp. 160–1, 187, 479–80, 482, 489–92, 503; Massey, *Ancient Egypt the light of the world* (2 vols., London, 1907), vol. I, pp. 2, 9, 544; vol. II, pp. 727–8, 743–8, 905; D. Gange, 'Religion and science in late nineteenth-century British Egyptology', *Historical Journal*, vol. 49 (2006), pp. 1083–103, at pp. 1096–8.

[68] Ackerman, *Frazer*; S. Connor, 'The birth of humility: Frazer and Victorian mythography', in R. Fraser (ed.), *Sir James Frazer and the literary imagination* (Houndmills, 1990), pp. 61–80.

Index

Abydenus, 45, 222
Adam, Robert, 150
Adams, William, 42
Allwood, Philip, 114–15, 150
Ancients and Moderns, 116
Anthropological Institute of Great Britain and Ireland, 198
Anthropological Society, 197
anthropology, 8, 176–7, 190–6, 197–8, 199, 226
archaeology, Near Eastern, 201–7, 209–10, 218–23, 224, 225
Argonauts, 15, 81–2, 188
Aristotle, 9, 213
Assyriology, 204, 205, 206–7, 209–10, 211, 218–25
astronomy, 43, 48, 76–7, 78, 82, 83, 125, 138, 146, 158–60, 168
Augustine, St, 58, 86, 88

Babel, Tower of, 44, 71, 73, 115, 121, 130, 156, 163, 164, 191, 209, 219
Bailly, Jean-Sylvain, 146, 157, 159, 168, 201
Bampton Lectures, 40, 64, 66, 166, 204
Bancroft, Richard, Archbishop of Canterbury, 9
Barclay, Hugh, 224–5
Baring-Gould, Sabine, 208
Baronius, Cesare, Cardinal, 9–10, 54
Basire, James, 114
Bate, Julius, 103
Bayle, Pierre, 85
Beard, J.R., 173–4
Bellamy, John, 184–5
Bentley, John, 159–60
Bentley, Richard, 88
Berington, Simon, 95
Berosus, 45, 46, 145, 149, 177, 178, 221, 222, 224
Biblical Archaeology Society, 218

Bichat, Marie-François Xavier, 29
Blackwell, Thomas, 76, 81, 82–3
Blake, William, 114
Blomfield, Charles, Bishop of London, 168
Blondel, David, 52
Blunt, John James, 109
Bochart, Samuel, 37
Bogan, Zachary, 36
Bosanquet, Samuel Richard, 224
Bouvet, Joachim, 37
Brabant, R.H., 16
Bray, Cara, 20
Bray, Charles, 13
Bridges, Matthew, 61, 187–8
British Archaeological Association, 198
Broughton, Rhoda, 18, 19
Broughton, Thomas, 167
Brown, Robert, 215–16
Bryant, Jacob, 5, 6, 35, 39, 75, 111–30, 132, 133, 152, 153, 195, 196, 205, 206, 207–8
Burder, Samuel, 186
Burney, Fanny, 113–14
Burton, Robert, 57

Cabiri, 6, 7, 23, 161–3, 168
Carlile, Richard, 77, 171, 172–3
Carwithen, John, 40, 166
Casaubon, Isaac, 8–10, 16, 17–18, 51–2, 92
Casaubon, Meric, 8, 10
Catcott, Alexander, 124
Catcott, Alexander, Snr, 124
Cato the Elder, 87, 88
Celsus, 151
Chaillu, Paul du, 217–18
Chalmers, Thomas, 64–5
Champollion, Jean-Francois, 203
Chandler, Edward, Bishop of Durham, 54

Chatterton, Thomas, 112, 123–4
Choul, Guillaume du, 91
Christian Enlightenment, 116, 117, 130
Christian Evidence Society, 70, 171, 208
Christie, James, 181–2
chronology, 48, 81–2, 116, 125, 141, 158–61, 166–7, 201–2
Cicero, 36, 85, 86–8, 90, 91, 105, 106, 110
Clarke, Adam, 64, 183–6
Clemens of Alexandria, 52
Cobbe, Frances Power, 212
Cockburn, William, 151–2
Collins, Anthony, 87–8
Colotes, 88
Conder, Claude Reignier, 224
connection, 43–4
Constantine, Emperor, 50–1
Conybeare, John, Bishop of Bristol, 62
Cook, F.C., 208
Cooper, Thomas, 211–12
Cooper, W.R., 198
Cory, Isaac Preston, 46, 75–6, 178, 202
Costard, George, 43, 76–7, 80, 83–4
Cox, George, 214, 215
Creuzer, Georg Friedrich, 23–6, 162
Croese, Gerard, 36
Cudworth, Ralph, 52–3, 68–9
Cumberland, Richard, Bishop of Peterborough, 43, 46, 47, 94
cuneiform, 202, 205, 206, 207, 209, 218–22, 223–5

Dagon, 7, 176, 177–9, 216
Dalzel, Andrew, 127
Davidson, David, 44
Davison, John, 165
Dawson, Thomas, 40–1
Deane, John Bathurst, 188–9
Delany, Patrick, 32
Dendera, 160, 201, 203, 205
Denys, Sir George, 221
Dewar, Daniel, 48
Dick, Thomas, 202–3
diffusionism, 33
Dilke, Sir Charles, 16
Dimock, Henry, 186
disease of language, 33–4, 84, 144, 145, 213–14
Doddridge, Philip, 59
double doctrine, 36, 76, 81, 83, 84–5, 87–91, 102–9, 149–50, 168, 214, 224

Druids, 89, 187, 188
Drummond, Sir William, 108–9, 168–9, 212
Duport, James, 36
Dupre, James, 93
Dupuis, Charles-François, 70, 78, 131, 132–3, 138–41, 144, 146, 150, 152, 153, 154, 157, 203, 212

Eadie, John, 208
Ebrard, J.H.A., 222
Echard, Laurence, 53
Eco, Umberto, 4
Egyptology, 77, 200–5, 209, 222–3, 225–6
Eliot, George, life, 2, 5, 18, 20–1, 30
Eliot, George, works, *see individual titles*
Ellis, William, 179–80
Emmett, J.B., 167
Estlin, John Prior, 154
Ethnological Society of London, 67
Euhemerism, 32–3, 37, 99, 103, 216
Eusebius, 45, 162, 221, 222
Evanson, Edward, 153
evidences, theology of, 38–43, 46–9, 54, 62–72, 130, 148, 157, 166, 167–8, 192, 204, 207, 224–5

Faber, George Stanley, 5, 7, 37, 40, 63, 77, 162–6, 178, 196, 206
Farmer, Hugh, 98, 99–100
Farrar, F.W., 67–8, 190, 207
Felix Holt, the Radical, 225
Fell, John, 98, 100
Fergusson, James, 194, 195
Feuerbach, Ludwig, 22, 23
Figurism, 37, 161
fish-gods, 6, 7, 114, 176–9
Flinders, Anne, 174–5, 193
Floyer, Sir John, 53
Forbes, Duncan, of Culloden, 71, 72, 73, 74
Foucquet, Jean-Francois, 37
Francis, Samuel, 149–50, 182
Francklin, William, 186
Frazer, James, 19, 26, 193, 226
Freeman, Edward, 217
French critical mythography, 8, 131–47

Gale, Theophilus, 61, 93
Galloway, William, 225
Galloway, William Brown, 77, 204
Geddes, Michael, 93, 94
geology, 4, 15, 42

Index

George III, 113, 114
German mythography, 3, 13, 14, 16, 22–6, 115, 131, 132–3, 162, 200, 222
Gibbon, Edward, 55, 79, 80, 98, 101–2, 108, 110
Gilbert, W.S., 225
Gilgamesh, 218–22
Gladstone, William, 8, 36, 49, 210–11, 218
Goldsmith, Oliver, 45
Goodsir, Joseph, 205–6
Gordon, George Hamilton-, fourth earl of Aberdeen, 8
Gorres, Joseph, 24
Gray, Robert, Bishop of Bristol, 43–4, 165
Gregory, Olinthus, 62–3
Grey, Richard, 104
Grote, George, 217
Guigniat, Joseph-Daniel, 23

Halyburton, Thomas, 59
Hamilton, Alexander, 160–1
Hamilton, Sir William, 100–1
Harcourt, Leveson Vernon, 14–15, 42, 177
Hare, Augustus William, 12–13
Hare, Julius Charles, 12
helio-arkite mythography, 35, 37, 111, 120
Henley, Samuel, 115, 123, 128–9
Hennell, Charles, 20–2
Hennell, Sara, 20
Henri IV, king of France, 9
Henry, Matthew, 54
Hermes Trismegistus, 9–10, 37, 50, 51
Herodotus, 141, 217, 218
Heylin, Peter, 52
Heyne, Christian, 115
Higgins, Godfrey, 168, 186, 212
Higher Criticism, 3, 21–3, 131, 133, 204, 211, 224, 225
Hislop, Alexander, 179
Hodges, E. Richmond, 202
Holden, George, 187
Holwell, William, 114
Homer, 13, 16, 25, 36, 51, 77, 82, 89, 108, 115, 124, 127, 129, 210–11, 213, 218
Horace, 108
Horsley, Samuel, Bishop of St Asaph, 55–6, 60–1
Huet, Pierre Daniel, Bishop of Avranches, 17, 37, 136
Hulse, John, 40
Hume, David, 39, 80, 81, 105–7
Hurd, Richard, Bishop of Worcester, 106

Hutchinson, John, 71, 72, 74
Hutchinsonianism, 71–6, 97, 103, 124, 164, 187
Hystapes, 56

idolatry, attitudes to, 56–62
Impressions of Theophrastus Such, 11–12
Indo-European philology, 33, 118–23, 207, 211, 213–17
Inman, Thomas, 196–7

Jackson, John, 43
Jacolliot, Louis, 213
James VI and I, King of Scotland and England, 9
Jehoshua ben Pandira, 226
Jenyns, Soame, 39, 62
Jesus, historical reality of, 22, 40–1, 49, 140, 143, 151, 155, 158, 167, 171–4, 211–12, 226
Jones, Sir William, 40, 68, 117, 118–23, 151, 160, 183
Jones, William, of Nayland, 74–5
Jortin, John, 54
Joseph of Arimathea, 21
Josephus, 45, 145
Julian the Apostate, Emperor, 105
Justin, 50

Kedington, Roger, 62
Kennedy, Vans, 156–7
Kennett, Basil, 85–6
Kenrick, John, 190
Kneale, Matthew, 4
Knight, Richard Payne, 37
Knox, William, 60

Lactantius, 50–1, 52
Landseer, John, 112–13, 177
Lang, Andrew, 18–19, 214–15
Langlès, Louis, 146
Lardner, Nathaniel, 41
Layard, 218
Layard, Austen Henry, 178, 218
Le Chevalier, Jean-Baptiste, 126–7
Lenormant, Francois, 221–2
Lepsius, Karl Richard, 77, 204
Lewis, George Cornewall, 132–3
Lewis, Maria, 14
Lindsay, Alexander, 25th Earl of Crawford, 42, 189
Lindsey, Theophilus, 152–3

Livingstone, David, 68
Lobeck, Christian August, 25
London Missionary Society, 66, 179
Lowick, 3, 74–5
Lowth, Robert, Bishop of London, 5, 7, 55
Lowth, William, 6–7

Mackay, Robert, 16, 25–7
Mackey, Sampson Arnold, 77, 170
MacLaurin, John, Lord Dreghorn, 126
Macpherson, John, 222
Manetho, 45, 46, 204, 224
de Marolles, Michel, 91
Martyr, Justin, 52
Massey, Gerald, 225–6
Maurice, Thomas, 157–8, 160, 161
Max-Müller, Friedrich, 33, 145, 177, 199, 213–14, 215
McLennan, John F., 194–6, 199
Meagher, Andrew, 97
Michell, Richard, 66
Middlemarch, Dorothea Casaubon, 3, 4, 11, 16
Middlemarch, Edward Casaubon, 1–5, 11, 15–16
Middlemarch, fish-scholars, 11, 176
Middlemarch, Tertius Lydgate, 29–30
Middlemarch, Will Ladislaw, 3, 6, 20–1, 22
Middleton, Conyers, 5, 6, 79, 80, 84, 90, 94–6, 97–8, 101, 104–5, 106, 109, 152, 167
Milles, Jeremiah, 124
Millington, Thomas, 70–1
Moffat, Robert, 68
Moor, Edward, 63–4, 115
Morritt, J.B.S., 128
Mount, Ferdinand, 4
Müller, Karl Otfried, 24, 133
Mushet, Robert, 68–9
Mussard, Pierre, 92–3, 109

nachash, 183, 184–6
Napoleon, 142
Nares, Edward, 64
Newman, John Henry, Cardinal, 109
Newton, Isaac, 43, 80, 81–2, 116, 121, 125, 159
Nicholas, John Liddiard, 180
Niebuhr, Barthold Georg, 115

Oannes, 45, 69, 177–9, 216
Oppert, Jules, 223
Opsopoeus, Johannes, 51

Orientalism, 63–4, 68, 76, 118–23, 130, 149, 151, 155–61
Origen, 50
Ormerod, Oliver, 92
Osburn, William, 203
Overton, John, 166–7
Ovid, 75, 124, 181

pagano-popery, 6, 35, 37, 57, 79–80, 84–5, 91–8, 101–2, 106, 109–10, 167
Paine, Thomas, 101, 127, 148, 167, 170, 171
Palestine Exploration Fund, 198
Paley, William, 64
Parkhurst, John, 74
Pattison, Mark, 15–20
Payne, Squier, 46
Peacock, Thomas Love, 12
Peters, Charles, 104
Phené, John, 198
Philo of Byblos, 45, 162, 224
Phlegon of Trallis, 40
Plato, 21, 22, 36, 50, 51, 68–9, 89, 93, 96, 110, 153, 168, 181, 213, 214
Playfair, John, 159
Pliny, 151
Plutarch, 85, 86, 87, 88
Polyhistor, Alexander, 222
Pomponius Mela, 218
Poole, Reginald Stuart, 203–4
Porteous, Beilby, Bishop of London, 65, 183
Poynder, John, 109
Prémare, Joseph Henri Marie de, 37, 161
Pretyman, George, Bishop of Lincoln, 42–3, 157
Prichard, James Cowles, 109, 192
Prideaux, Humphrey, 43, 58–9
Priestley, Joseph, 97–8, 142, 150, 153–5

radicalism, English, 7, 8, 101, 141, 147–50, 169–73
Rassam, Hormuzd, 218
Rawlinson, George, 40, 204, 208
Rawlinson, Sir Henry, 206–7
Ray, John Mead, 47
Reade, William Winwood, 212–13
Reddie, James, 204–5
Redford, George, 47–8, 201–2
Renan, Ernest, 212
Rennell, James, 126
Richardson, John, 63, 112, 118
Rickman, Thomas, 147
Roberts, Peter, 179

Robertson, William, 117
Romola, 14, 110
Row, Charles, 208
Rowe, R.J., 173
Royal Asiatic Society, 206
Russell, Michael, Bishop of Glasgow and Galloway, 44
Rutherforth, Thomas, 125

Sabaism, 139
Sanchoniathon, 45, 46, 94
Savile, Bourchier Wrey, 208–9
Sayce, Archibald, 220, 223–4
Scaliger, Joseph Justus, 8
Scenes of Clerical Life, 13
Schleiden, Matthias, 30
Schliemann, Heinrich, 217
Schwann, Theodor, 30
Scott, Sir Walter, 12, 22
serpent-worship, 59, 182–99
Seward, Anna, 96
Seward, Thomas, 96
sexual allegories, 35, 37, 100–1, 196–7
Sharpe, Gregory, 41
Sherlock, Thomas, 104
Shore, John, Lord Teignmouth, 123
Shuckford, Samuel, 43
Sibyls, 50–1, 52–6, 58, 135
Simpson, David, 153
Smith, Daniel, 221
Smith, George, 206, 218–21
Smith, John Pye, 173
Smith, William Robertson, 191, 196
Smyth, Charles Piazzi, 205
Society for Biblical Archaeology, 198
Society for Psychical Research, 215
Socrates, 110, 213
solar allegories, 35, 133, 138–9, 150, 155, 171, 172, 198, 211–12, 214–17, 223
Sonnerat, Pierre, 137
Spearman, Robert, 73–4, 77, 97
Spencer, John, 75
St John, Henry, Viscount Bolingbroke, 45–6, 90–1, 96–7
Stillingfleet, Edward, Bishop of Worcester, 32
Stona, Thomas, 91, 107
Stopford, Joshua, 92, 109
Strabo, 9, 181, 218
Strahan, William, 107
Strauss, D.F., 22, 23, 211, 212

Strong, Emily Frances, 15–16
Stuart, William, 222
Suetonius, 9, 41, 151
syncretism, 50

Tacitus, 41, 151
Taylor, Robert, 34, 69–70, 109–10, 171–2, 174, 212
Tenison, Thomas, Archbishop of Canterbury, 58
Thales, 214
Theophrastus, 9, 11
Tillard, John, 104
Titcomb, J.H., 209–10
Toland, John, 76, 88–9
totemism, 195–6
Townsend, George, 169
Townsend, Joseph, 42
Tractarians, 109
Trinity, 64, 66, 68–9, 71, 73–6, 96, 97, 101, 103, 140, 152–5, 157, 163–4, 165, 174, 197
Troy, 15, 112, 125–30, 217
Turner, George, 66, 180
Turner, Robert, 53
Turner, Sharon, 46, 133–4
Twysden, John, 52
Tychsen, Oluf Gerhard, 115
Tylor, E.B., 190, 214
Tyrwhitt, Thomas, 123

Varro, Marcus Terentius, 86, 88, 90, 105
Vergil Polydore, 91
Victoria Institute, 204, 209
Virgil, 50, 51, 52, 55, 108, 181
Virgil, fourth Eclogue, 10, 51, 53, 55
Volney, Constantin, 78, 131, 132–3, 141–6, 148, 149, 150–3, 154, 155, 157, 164, 166–7, 169, 171, 172, 173, 179, 183, 201, 203, 212, 213, 225
Voltaire, 107–8, 134–8, 141, 146, 157, 183, 186, 201
Voss, J.H., 13

Wahl, Gunther, 115
Wait, Daniel Guildford, 65–6, 185–6
Wake, Charles Staniland, 197–8
Wakefield, Gilbert, 127–8
Walker, Thomas, 97
Warburton, William, 5, 6, 7, 81, 84, 87, 102–5, 106–8, 109
Ward, Mrs Humphry, 20, 48–9
Wardlaw, Gilbert, 66–7

Waring, John Burley, 194
Watson, Richard, 148–9
Wellwood, Henry Moncrieff, 56
Whiston, William, 53
Wilford, Francis, 68, 122–3, 157, 183
Wilkinson, Sir Gardener, 204
Williams, John, 77, 210
Wise, Francis, 33
Wolf, Friedrich August, 16, 25
Wollaston, Francis, 150

Xisuthrus, 45, 136, 146, 149

Young, Arthur, 37
Young, Thomas, 203

zodiacal allegories, 12, 35, 133, 138, 139–40, 144, 146, 150, 154, 169, 170, 172, 173, 223, 225–6
Zoroastrianism, 37, 96, 139, 142–4, 148–9, 156, 166, 182, 213

IDEAS IN CONTEXT

Edited by David Armitage, Richard Bourke, Jennifer Pitts and John Robertson

1. RICHARD RORTY, J. B. SCHNEEWIND AND QUENTIN SKINNER (EDS.)
   Philosophy in History
   Essays in the historiography of philosophy
   PB 978 0 521 27330 5

2. J. G. A. POCOCK
   Virtue, Commerce and History
   Essays on political thought and history, chiefly in the eighteenth century
   PB 978 0 521 27660 3

3. M. M. GOLDSMITH
   Private Vices, Public Benefits
   Bernard Mandeville's social and political thought
   HB 978 0 521 30036 0

4. ANTHONY PAGDEN (ED.)
   The Languages of Political Theory in Early Modern Europe
   PB 978 0 521 38666 1

5. DAVID SUMMERS
   The Judgment of Sense
   Renaissance naturalism and the rise of aesthetics
   PB 978 0 521 38631 9

6. LAURENCE DICKEY
   Hegel: Religion, Economics and the Politics of Spirit, 1770–1807
   PB 978 0 521 38912 9

7. MARGO TODD
   Christian Humanism and the Puritan Social Order
   PB 978 0 521 89228 5

8. LYNN SUMIDA JOY
   Gassendi the Atomist
   Advocate of history in an age of science
   PB 978 0 521 52239 7

9. EDMUND LEITES (ED.)
   Conscience and Casuistry in Early Modern Europe
   PB 978 0 521 52020 1

10. WOLF LEPENIES
    Between Literature and Science: The Rise of Sociology
    PB 978 0 521 33810 3

11. TERENCE BALL, JAMES FARR AND RUSSELL L. HANSON (EDS.)
    Political Innovation and Conceptual Change
    PB 978 0 521 35978 8

12. GERD GIGERENZER *et al.*
    The Empire of Chance
    How probability changed science and everyday life
    PB 978 0 521 39838 1

13. PETER NOVICK
    That Noble Dream
    The 'objectivity question' and the American historical profession
    HB 978 0 521 34328 2
    PB 978 0 521 35745 6

14. DAVID LIEBERMAN
    The Province of Legislation Determined
    Legal theory in eighteenth-century Britain
    PB 978 0 521 52854 2

15. DANIEL PICK
    Faces of Degeneration
    A European disorder, c.1848–c.1918
    PB 978 0 521 45753 8

16. KEITH BAKER
    Inventing the French Revolution
    Essays on French political culture in the eighteenth century
    PB 978 0 521 38578 7

17. IAN HACKING
    The Taming of Chance
    HB 978 0 521 38014 0
    PB 978 0 521 38884 9

18. GISELA BOCK, QUENTIN SKINNER AND MAURIZIO VIROLI (EDS.)
    Machiavelli and Republicanism
    PB 978 0 521 43589 5

19. DOROTHY ROSS
    The Origins of American Social Science
    PB 978 0 521 42836 1

20. KLAUS CHRISTIAN KOHNKE
    The Rise of Neo-Kantianism
    German academic philosophy between idealism and positivism
    HB 978 0 521 37336 4

21. IAN MACLEAN
    Interpretation and Meaning in the Renaissance
    The case of law
    HB 978 0 521 41546 0
    PB 978 0 521 02027 5

22. MAURIZIO VIROLI
    From Politics to Reason of State
    The acquisition and transformation of the language of politics 1250–1600
    HB 978 0 521 41493 7
    PB 978 0 521 67343 3

23. MARTIN VAN GELDEREN
    The Political Thought of the Dutch Revolt 1555–1590
    HB 978 0 521 39204 4
    PB 978 0 521 89163 9

24. NICHOLAS PHILLIPSON AND QUENTIN SKINNER (EDS.)
    Political Discourse in Early Modern Britain
    HB 978 0 521 39242 6

25. JAMES TULLY
    An Approach to Political Philosophy: Locke in Contexts
    HB 978 0 521 43060 9
    PB 978 0 521 43638 0

26. RICHARD TUCK
    Philosophy and Government 1572–1651
    PB 978 0 521 43885 8

27. RICHARD YEO
    Defining Science
    William Whewell, natural knowledge and public debate in early Victorian Britain
    HB 978 0 521 43182 8
    PB 978 0 521 54116 9

28. MARTIN WARNKE
    The Court Artist
    On the ancestry of the modern artist
    HB 978 0 521 36375 4

29. PETER N. MILLER
    Defining the Common Good
    Empire, religion and philosophy in eighteenth-century Britain
    HB 978 0 521 44259 6
    PB 978 0 521 61712 3

30. CHRISTOPHER J. BERRY
   The Idea of Luxury
   A conceptual and historical investigation
   PB 978 0 521 46691 2

31. E. J. HUNDERT
   The Enlightenment's 'Fable'
   Bernard Mandeville and the discovery of society
   HB 978 0 521 46082 8
   PB 978 0 521 61942 4

32. JULIA STAPLETON
   Englishness and the Study of Politics
   The social and political thought of Ernest Barker
   HB 978 0 521 46125 2
   PB 978 0 521 02444 0

33. KEITH TRIBE
   Strategies of Economic Order
   German economic discourse, 1750–1950
   HB 978 0 521 46291 4
   PB 978 0 521 61943 1

34. SACHIKO KUSUKAWA
   The Transformation of Natural Philosophy
   The case of Philip Melanchthon
   HB 978 0 521 47347 7
   PB 978 0 521 03046 5

35. DAVID ARMITAGE, ARMAND HIMY AND QUENTIN SKINNER (EDS.)
   Milton and Republicanism
   HB 978 521 55178 6
   PB 978 0 521 64648 2

36. MARKKU PELTONEN
   Classical Humanism and Republicanism in English Political Thought 1570–1640
   HB 978 0 521 49695 7
   PB 978 0 521 61716 1

37. PHILIP IRONSIDE
   The Social and Political Thought of Bertrand Russell
   The development of an aristocratic liberalism
   HB 978 0 521 47383 5
   PB 978 0 521 02476 1

38. NANCY CARTWRIGHT, JORDI CAT, LOLA FLECK AND THOMAS E. UEBEL
   Otto Neurath: Philosophy between Science and Politics
   HB 978 0 521 45174 1

39. DONALD WINCH
Riches and Poverty
An intellectual history of political economy in Britain, 1750–1834
PB 978 0 521 55920 1

40. JENNIFER PLATT
A History of Sociological Research Methods in America
HB 978 0 521 44173 5
PB 978 0 521 64649 9

41. KNUD HAAKONSSEN (ED.)
Enlightenment and Religion
Rational dissent in eighteenth-century Britain
HB 978 0 521 56060 3
PB 978 0 521 02987 2

42. G. E. R. LLOYD
Adversaries and Authorities
Investigations into Ancient Greek and Chinese science
HB 978 0 521 55331 5
PB 978 0 521 55695 8

43. ROLF LINDNER
The Reportage of Urban Culture
Robert Park and the Chicago School
HB 978 0 521 44052 3
PB 978 0 521 02653 6

44. ANNABEL BRETT
Liberty, Right and Nature
Individual rights in later scholastic thought
HB 978 0 521 56239 3
PB 978 0 521 54340 8

45. STEWART J. BROWN (ED.)
William Robertson and the Expansion of Empire
HB 78 0 521 57083 1

46. HELENA ROSENBLATT
Rousseau and Geneva
From the first discourse to the social contract, 1749–1762
HB 978 0 521 57004 6
PB 978 0 521 03395 4

47. DAVID RUNCIMAN
Pluralism and the Personality of the State
HB 978 0 521 55191 5
PB 978 0 521 02263 7

48. ANNABEL PATTERSON
   Early Modern Liberalism
   HB 978 0 521 59260 4
   PB 978 0 521 02631 4

49. DAVID WEINSTEIN
   Equal Freedom and Utility
   Herbert Spencer's liberal utilitarianism
   HB 978 0 521 62264 6
   PB 978 0 521 02686 4

50. YUN LEE TOO AND NIALL LIVINGSTONE (EDS.)
   Pedagogy and Power
   Rhetorics of classical learning
   HB 978 0 521 59435 6
   PB 978 0 521 03801 0

51. REVIEL NETZ
   The Shaping of Deduction in Greek Mathematics
   A study in cognitive history
   HB 978 0 521 62279 0
   PB b 978 0 521 54120 6

52. MARY S. MORGAN AND MARGARET MORRISON (EDS.)
   Models as Mediators
   Perspectives in natural and social science
   HB 978 0 521 65097 7
   PB 978 0 521 65571 2

53. JOEL MICHELL
   Measurement in Psychology
   A critical history of a methodological concept
   HB 978 0 521 62120 5
   PB 978 0 521 02151 7

54. RICHARD A. PRIMUS
   The American Language of Rights
   HB 978 0 521 65250 6
   PB 978 0 521 61621 8

55. ROBERT ALUN JONES
   The development of Durkheim's Social Realism
   HB 978 0 521 65045 8
   PB 978 0 521 02210 1

56. ANNE MCLAREN
   Political Culture in the Reign of Elizabeth I
   Queen and Commonwealth 1558–1585
   HB 978 0 521 65144 8
   PB 978 0 521 02483 9

57. JAMES HANKINS (ED.)
   Renaissance Civic Humanism
   Reappraisals and reflections
   HB 978 0 521 78090 2
   PB 978 0 521 54807 6

58. T. J. HOCHSTRASSER
   Natural Law Theories in the Early Enlightenment
   HB 978 0 521 66193 5
   PB 978 0 521 02787 8

59. DAVID ARMITAGE
   The Ideological Origins of the British Empire
   HB 978 0 521 59081 5
   PB 978 0 521 78978 3

60. IAN HUNTER
   Rival Enlightenments
   Civil and metaphysical philosophy in early modern Germany
   HB 978 0 521 79265 3
   PB 978 0 521 02549 2

61. DARIO CASTIGLIONE AND IAIN HAMPSHER-MONK (EDS.)
   The history of political thought in national context
   HB 978 0 521 78234 0

62. IAN MACLEAN
   Logic, Signs and Nature in the Renaissance
   The case of learned medicine
   HB 978 0 521 80648 0

63. PETER MACK
   Elizabethan Rhetoric
   Theory and practice
   HB 978 0 521 812924
   PB 978 0 521 02099 2

64. GEOFFREY LLOYD
   The Ambitions of Curiosity
   Understanding the world in Ancient Greece and China
   HB 978 0 521 81542 0
   PB 978 0 521 89461 6

65. MARKKU PELTONEN
   The Duel in Early Modern England
   Civility, politeness and honour
   HB 978 0 521 82062 2
   PB 978 0 521 02520 1

66. ADAM SUTCLIFFE
    Judaism and Enlightenment
    HB 978 0 521 82015 8
    PB 978 0 521 67232 0

67. ANDREW FITZMAURICE
    Humanism and America
    An intellectual history of english colonisation, 1500–1625
    HB 978 0 521 82225 1

68. PIERRE FORCE
    Self-Interest before Adam Smith
    A genealogy of economic science
    HB 978 0 521 83060 7
    PB 978 0 521 03619 1

69. ERIC NELSON
    The Greek Tradition in Republican Thought
    HB 978 0 521 83545 9
    PB 978 0 521 02428 0

70. HARRO HOPFL
    Jesuit Political Thought
    The society of jesus and the state, c.1540–1640
    HB 978 0 521 83779 8

71. MIKAEL HORNQVIST
    Machiavelli and Empire
    HB 978 0 521 83945 7

72. DAVID COLCLOUGH
    Freedom of Speech in Early Stuart England
    HB 978 0 521 84748 3

73. JOHN ROBERTSON
    The Case for the Enlightenment
    Scotland and Naples 1680–1760
    HB 978 0 521 84787 2
    PB 978 0 521 03572 9

74. DANIEL CAREY
    Locke, Shaftesbury, and Hutcheson
    Contesting diversity in the Enlightenment and beyond
    HB 978 0 521 84502 1

75. ALAN CROMARTIE
    The Constitutionalist Revolution
    An essay on the history of England, 1450–1642
    HB 978 0 521 78269 2

76. HANNAH DAWSON
    Locke, Language and Early-Modern Philosophy
    HB 978 0 521 85271 5

77. CONAL CONDREN, STEPHEN GAUKROGER AND IAN HUNTER (EDS.)
    The Philosopher in Early Modern Europe
    The nature of a contested identity
    HB 978 0 521 86646 0

78. ANGUS GOWLAND
    The Worlds of Renaissance Melancholy
    Robert Burton in context
    HB 978 0 521 86768 9

79. PETER STACEY
    Roman Monarchy and the Renaissance Prince
    HB 978 0 521 86989 8

80. RHODRI LEWIS
    Language, Mind and Nature
    Artificial languages in England from Bacon to Locke
    HB 978 0 521 874750

81. DAVID LEOPOLD
    The Young Karl Marx
    German philosophy, modern politics, and human flourishing
    HB 978 0 521 87477 9

82. JON PARKIN
    Taming the Leviathan
    The reception of the political and religious ideas of Thomas Hobbes in England 1640–1700
    HB 978 0 521 87735 0

83. D. WEINSTEIN
    Utilitarianism and the New Liberalism
    HB 978 0 521 87528 8

84. LUCY DELAP
    The Feminist Avant-Garde
    Transatlantic encounters of the early twentieth century
    HB 978 0 521 87651 3

85. BORIS WISEMAN
    Lévi-Strauss, Anthropology and Aesthetics
    HB 978 0 521 87529 5

86. DUNCAN BELL (ED.)
    Victorian Visions of Global Order
    Empire and international relations in nineteenth-century political thought
    HB 978 0 521 88292 7

87. IAN HUNTER
   The Secularisation of the Confessional State
   The political thought of Christian Thomasius
   HB 978 0 521 88055 8

88. CHRISTIAN J. EMDEN
   Friedrich Nietzsche and the Politics of History
   HB 978 0 521 88056 5

89. ANNELIEN DE DIJN
   French Political Thought from Montesquieu to Tocqueville
   Liberty in a levelled society?
   HB 978 0 521 87788 6

90. PETER GARNSEY
   Thinking About Property
   From antiquity to the age of revolution
   HB 978 0 521 87677 3
   PB 978 0 521 70023 8

91. PENELOPE DEUTSCHER
   The Philosophy of Simone de Beauvoir
   Ambiguity, conversion, resistance
   HB 978 0 521 88520 1

92. HELENA ROSENBLATT
   Liberal Values
   Benjamin Constant and the politics of religion
   HB 978 0 521 89825 6

93. JAMES TULLY
   Public Philosophy in a New Key
   Volume 1: democracy and civic freedom
   HB 978 0 521 44961 8
   PB 978 0 521 72879 9

94. JAMES TULLY
   Public Philosophy in a New Key
   Volume 2: imperialism and civic freedom
   HB 978 0 521 44966 3
   PB 978 0 521 72880 5

95. DONALD WINCH
   Wealth and Life
   Essays on the intellectual history of political economy in Britain, 1848–1914
   HB 978 0 521 88753 3
   PB 978 0 521 71539 3

96. FONNA FORMAN-BARZILAI
    Adam Smith and the Circles of Sympathy
    Cosmopolitanism and moral theory
    HB 978 0 521 76112 3

97. GREGORY CLAEYS
    Imperial Sceptics
    British critics of empire 1850–1920
    HB 978 0 521 19954 4

98. EDWARD BARING
    The Young Derrida and French Philosophy, 1945–1968
    HB 978 1 107 00967 7

99. CAROL PAL
    Republic of Women
    Rethinking the republic of letters in the seventeenth century
    HB 978 1 107 01821 1

100. C. A. BAYLY
     Recovering Liberties
     Indian thought in the age of liberalism and empire
     HB 978 1 107 01383 4
     PB 978 1 107 60147 5

101. FELICITY GREEN
     Montaigne and the Life of Freedom
     HB 978 1 107 02439 7

102. JOSHUA DERMAN
     Max Weber in Politics and Social Thought
     From charisma to canonization
     HB 978 1 107 02588 2

103. RAINER FORST
     (translated by Ciaran Cronin)
     Toleration in Conflict
     Past and present
     HB 978 0 521 88577 5

104. SOPHIE READ
     Eucharist and the Poetic Imagination in Early Modern England
     HB 978 1 107 03273 6

105. MARTIN RUEHL
     The Italian Renaissance in the German Historical Imagination
     1860–1930
     HB 978 1 107 03699 4

106. GEORGIOS VAROUXAKIS
    Liberty Abroad
    J. S. Mill on international relations
    HB 978 1 107 03914 8

107. ANDREW FITZMAURICE
    Sovereignty, Property and Empire, 1500–2000
    HB 978 1 107 07649 5

108. BENJAMIN STRAUMANN
    Roman Law in the State of Nature
    The classical foundations of Hugo Grotius' Natural Law
    HB 978 1 107 09290 7

109. LIISI KEEDUS
    The Crisis of German Historicism
    The early political thought of Hannah Arendt and Leo Strauss
    HB 978 1 107 09303 4

110. EMMANUELLE DE CHAMPS
    Enlightenment and Utility
    Bentham in French, Bentham in France
    HB 978 1 107 09867 1

111. ANNA PLASSART
    The Scottish Enlightenment and the French Revolution
    HB 978 1 107 09176 4

112. DAVID TODD
    Free Trade and its Enemies in France, 1814–1851
    HB 978 1 107 03693 2

113. DMITRI LEVITIN
    Ancient Wisdom in the Age of the New Science
    HB 978 1 107 10588 1

114. PATRICK BAKER
    Italian Renaissance Humanism in the Mirror
    HB 978 1 107 11186 8

115. COLIN KIDD
    The World of Mr Casaubon
    Britain's Wars of Mythography, 1700–1870
    HB 978 1 107 02771 8